WASTELANDS AND PLANNING FOR DEVELOPMENT

About the Authour

S.C. Kalwar, Professor and Head, Department of Geography, Member, Board of Studies in Geography, Member of Academic Council and Senate, University of Rajasthan, Jaipur, is a specialist in Agricultural Geography, Rural Development, Land Use Planning, Economic Geography Wasteland Development Studies, Environment and Surveying. He has written/edited 16 books related to resources, wasteland, ecology, environment, poverty and socio-economic development and has participated in about 36 conferences/seminars/symposia of national and international level. He has contributed 66 research papers in various journals of repute. He is a member of Editorial Board of 'Studies in Geography' and member of an Advisory Committee of "Charamavati", a research journal.

Prof. Kalwar was President of the All Rajasthan Geographers Association (RGA) in 2005-06 and is a life member of National Association of Geographers of India, Rajasthan Geographers Association, Asian Environment Council and Indian Institute of Geomorphology. He was also a member of National Committee, Government of India for evaluating Hindi books on environment for giving prize to the authors at national level, Ministry of Home Affairs, Government of India, New Delhi (2002). He was selected for a Research Award (Career Award) in 2002 by the University Grants Commission, New Delhi.

WASTELANDS AND PLANNING FOR DEVELOPMENT

Prof. S.C. Kalwar
Department of Geography
University of Rajasthan
Jaipur

CONCEPT PUBLISHING COMPANY, NEW DELHI-110059

Cataloging in Publication Data—DK
Courtesy: D.K. Agencies (P) Ltd. <docinfo@dkagencies.com>

Kalwar, S. C. (Sugan Chand), 1947-
Wastelands and planning for development / S.C. Kalwar.
p. cm.
Study conducted at Jaipur District of Rajasthan, India.
Includes bibliographical references (p.)
Includes index.
ISBN 13: 9788180694660
ISBN 10: 8180694666

1. Waste lands—India—Jaipur (District). 2. Reclamation of land—India—Jaipur (District). 3. Land use—India—Jaipur (District)—Planning. I. Title.

DDC 333.731 370 954 4 22

ISBN-13: 978-81-8069-466-0
ISBN-10: 81-8069-466-6

First Published 2008

Published and Printed by
Ashok Kumar Mittal
Concept Publishing Company
A/15-16, Commercial Block, Mohan Garden
NEW DELHI-110059 (India)
Phones: 25351460, 25351794
Fax: 091-11-25357103
E-mail : publishing@conceptpub.com

Prof. Mohammad Shafi
Professor Emeritus —Ex-Pro-Chancellor
President of India conferred 'PADAM SHREE',
UGC- Award of SARASWATI SAMMAN - BHOOGOL RATNA
Highest Award of the Russian Academy of Sciences,
ACADEMICIAN, POORVANCHAL RATNA,
Laureat d'Honneur by IGU in Glasgow (U.K.)

DEPARTMENT OF GEOGRAPHY
ALIGARH MUSLIM UNIVERSITY
ALIGARH - 202 002, INDIA

FOREWORD

Land is a non-renewable resource. Over the years, the country's land use has suffered from different types of degradation, caused by biotic and abiotic pressures. Increasing population puts heavy demands on land resources. India has only 2.4 per cent of the world's geographical area, but supports over 16 per cent of the world's population. The grazing area is limited. It is 0.5 per cent of the world's grazing area, but has over 18 per cent of the world's cattle population.

National Remote Sensing Agency (NRSA) carried out a districtwise mapping of wasteland on 50,000 scale using satellite data. The wastelands in the country have been placed at 63.80 million hectares. Ways and means should be thought out for the utilization of these lands.

S.C. Kalwar has produced a highly meticulous work in respect of the wastelands of Jaipur District (Rajasthan) taking the help of NRSA and choosing village as the unit of study and has shown the exact location of the wasteland and the type of the wasteland. With this study, the reclamation of the wastelands becomes scientific and easy. This is the first work of its kind and needs to be carried out in other states of India. The maps are highly attractive with scientific basis. The book is a milestone in land use planning and provides incentives to students and planners to carry out such type of study. One would like to have a copy of this book on one's shelf.

Prof. (Emeritus) Mohammad Shafi

Department of Geography
Aligarh Muslim University
Aligarh

PREFACE

The present work is the outcome of a research project entitle "Identification, Spatial Distribution and Planning for Reclamation/Development of Wasteland in Jaipur District" sponsored by the University Grants Commission, New Delhi under the scheme of UGC Research Award under IX Plan. I am grateful to the University Grants Commission, New Delhi for this Research Award.

Wasteland is described as "degraded land which can be brought under vegetative cover with reasonable effort, and which is currently under-utilized and land which is deteriorating for lack of appropriate water and soil management or on account of natural causes. Wastelands can result from inherent/imposed disabilities such as by location, environment, chemical and physical properties of the soil or financial or management constraints."

Land is a non-renewable resource. Due to increasing pressure of population, there is an excessive demand of land for food, fodder, fuel and fiber has necessitated adoption of scientific measures for increasing land productivity and bringing more areas under cultivation/forest. At the same time land degradation due to desertification, soil salinity, waterlogging, excessive soil erosion due to deforestation, unscientific agricultural practices etc., has resulted in the creation of vast stretches of wastelands and a decrease in per capita cultivable land besides ecological balance.

Keeping in view degradation and ecological balance, the then Prime Minister of India had observed "Continuing deforestation has brought us face to face with a major ecological and socio-economic crisis. The trend must be halted. He proposed immediately to set up a National Wastelands Development Board (NWDB) with the object of bringing five million hectares of land every year under fuelwood and fodder plantations".

Conventionally, the information on different categories of wasteland is arrived at by compilation from village records, which is primarily statistical in nature. With the advent of remote sensing from space, a major technological break through has happened in the method of acquiring information on natural resources.

Wasteland maps for the entire country on 1:1 million scale, prepared for the first time using 1980-82 satellite data sets available in the archives of NRSA Data Centre (From the American Landsat satellite) in 1985 by National Remote Sensing Agency of Department of Space, proved the utility of satellite data in identification and assessment of the type and areal extent of wastelands. Further, this exercise lead to embarking upon a major national mission, at the behest of Ministry of Rural Development, towards a systematic, districtwise wastelands mapping effort on 1:50000 scale using satellite data. Micro watershed and village boundaries have also been incorporated in the maps.

In the present study village/town has been taken as a study unit and wasteland data of each category of every village/town of Jaipur district (Total villages/towns 2203) have been computed with Digital Planimeter from the wasteland maps obtained from NRSA, Hyderabad, Andhra Pradesh. For detailed sample study LISS III satellite image of February 28, 2003 has been processed and interpreted of fifty sample villages, 4-8 villages in cluster from each category. Planning for reclamation/development has also been recommended on the basis of spatial distribution of wastelands in sample villages and economic aspects of wastelands have also been discussed.

The entire study is divided into eight chapters including introduction. The first two chapters are devoted to introdution, physical and cultural environs. The remaining six chapters deal with various aspects of identification, spatial distribution and planning for reclamation/ development of wastelands in the study area. Chapter third describes identification of wastelands by Directorate of Economics and Statistics, Soil Survey, Directorate of Agriculture, All India Soil Survey. NATMO, CAD (Wasteland Development Unit), Bhumbla and Khare, SOI, IGFRI Jhansi, NRSA, Forest Department, CAZRI, S.S. Yadav, B.S.N.L. Lucknow, I.C.A.R. New Delhi, Technical Task Force Group, NWUM-NRSA etc.

Spatial distribution of wastelands especially area under wastelands in the district, wasteland pattern in the country, state and study area, spatial distribution of gullied/ravinous land, degraded forest, sands-desertic land, scrub, saline/alkaline land, degraded pasture, barren hill, mining-industrial wasteland and total wasteland have been discussed in chapter fourth. In this chapter each category of wasteland has been discussed according to tehsilwise area, percentage to total geographical area, percentage to tehsil wasteland, percentagewise distribution of wasteland villages/towns, tehsilwise total wasteland villages. Next chapter deals with correlation between determinants (slope, ruggedness number, dissection index, drainage density, rural population, literacy, S.T. S.C., agricultural population, size of holding, irrigated land) was wasteland in fifty sample villages selected from different categories of wasteland.

Intensive study of sample study areas/sample villages has been discussed in chapter sixth. These sample areas/villages have been selected from the nine different areas having various types of wastelands in the study area. In this chapter location, relief, drainage, soil, population, general land use, identification of wastelands, spatial distribution of wastelands (with the help of LISS III satellite image and classified image), ownership pattern, characteristics of wastelands, reclamation of wastelands by the farmers themselves and planning for reclamation/development of wastelands have been discussed of each sample study area/sample village.

Chapter seventh is devoted to planning for reclamation/development of wastelands. In this chapter planning for reclamation/development of wastelands in all the sample villages selected from different categories of wasteland considering location of occurrence wasteland, land capability class, water potentiality, soil depth, slope, association, process of degradation, degree of severity and land use/land cover have been recommended. Model cost estimation per hectare for reclamation/development and financial requirement for the development of wasteland has been calculated for all the categories of wasteland at tehsil level in the district. Besides this total expenditure, income, cost-benefit ratio from development of wastelands in Jaipur district and wasteland reclamation/development regions have been discussed in this chapter. Last chapter is devoted to summary and conclusion.

It is hoped that this work would be useful for State Forest, Agriculture and Horticulture Department, Soil Scientist, Planners, Non-Government Organizations, Research Scholars of Geography, Economics, Botany and researchers of other allied disciplines.

I am also grateful to Dr. N.C. Gautam, Retd. Group Director, Land Use and Cartographic Division, NRSA, Hyderabad, Andhra Pradesh; Prof. H.S. Sharma, Retd. Dean, Faculty of

Science, University of Rajasthan, Jaipur; Prof. N.L. Gupta, Retd. Professor and Head, Department of Geography, M.L. Sukhadia University, Udaipur; Prof. Noor Mohammed, Professor and Head, Department of Geography, School of Economics, Delhi University, Delhi; Prof. R.K. Rai, Retd. Dean, Environmental Sciences, NEHU Shilong (Meghalaya); Dr. J.R. Sharma, Director, Regional Remote Sensing Service Centre, Jodhpur; Dr. M.P. Poonia (Incharge), Dr. K.R. Khincher, Dr. B.K. Singh, Scentists, Remote Sensing Division, B.M. Birla Science and Technology, Centre, Jaipur; Prof. M.H. Qureshi, CRDS, JNU, New Delhi and Shri R.C. Chaturvedi, S.S. Jain Subodh College, Jaipur and Shri Raj Bihari, RFO Bundi.

I am also thankful to my colleagues Dr. M.K. Khandelwal, Head of the Department, Dr. R.D.Gupta, Dr. R.D. Gurjar, Dr. R.N. Mishra, Dr. R.D. Doi, Dr. T.S. Chauhan, Dr. B.L. Gupta, Dr. R.K. Gurjar, Dr. P.R. Binda, Dr. K.M. Sharma and Shri D.L. Mali, Department of Geography, University of Rajasthan, Jaipur for their help and co-operation.

Last but not the least, I shall failing in my duty if I do not mention the name of my wife Mrs. Santosh Kalwar for keeping me free from all the responsibilities of domestic work during the entire period of this project. Shri T.C. Jeckwal, Personnel Officer, JVVN, Kota Circle, Kota, Dr. (Mrs.) Vidya Kalwar, Dr. (Miss) Seema Kalwar (Daughters) Lecturer in Geography, Amber Maharani College, Amber (Jaipur) and Dr. Avinash Kalwar (Son) Leturer, Shri Bhawani Niken Post Graduate College, Jaipur also deserve thanks for their co-operation and help.

Shri Jai Singh, Shri Tapesh Kashyap and Shri Vinod Khandelwal deserve special thanks for their help in computer typing and other computer related work.

I am grateful to Prof. Mohammad Shafi, Professor Emeritus - Ex Pro-Chancellor, Padam Shree, U.G.C. Award of Saraswati Samman - Bhoogol Ratna, ACADEMICIAN (Highest Award of Russian Academy of Sciences), Pooravanchal Ratna, Laureat, Honneur by IGU in Glasgow (U.K.) for guidance and suggestions at every stage of this work and writing the foreword of this book.

The publisher, M/s. Concept Publishing Company, New Delhi not only undertaking the task of publication but doing fairly good job in stipulated time. I am grateful to Shri Ashok Kumar Mittal of Concept Publishing Company for meticulous execution of this publication.

March 22, 2007 **Prof. S.C. Kalwar**
Vinayak Chaturthi (Chaitra Shukl)
Vikram Samvat 2064

CONTENTS

LIST OF FIGURES

LIST OF TABLES

LIST OF PLATES

1

INTRODUCTION

The Problem to be Investigated

Wasteland is briefly defined as that land, which is degraded and is presently lying unutilized except current fallow due to different constraints. Land degradation due to increasing biotic interference has resulted in salinity and alkalinity, water logging, gully and ravinous erosion, deforestation, encroachment of deserts, etc. converting productive lands into wasteland. This has resulted in dependence on the improved yield from the limited land rather than expanding the area for agriculture production. This requires methods for collection up to date and accurate information on the spatial and area extent of all such degraded lands or wasted lands for their better utilization and management.

Increasing demand for food, fodder, fuel and fibre has necessitated adoption of scientific measures for increasing land productivity and bringing more areas under cultivation /forest. At the same time land degradation due to desertification, soil salinity, waterlogging, excessive soil erosion due to deforestation, unscientific agricultural practices etc., has resulted in the creation of vast stretches of wastelands and a decrease in per capita cultivable land besides ecological imbalance. To increase productivity through irrigation is at the saturation stage and there is a very limited scope for extension of net sown area without reclamation of wastelands. For the ecological balance one-third geographical area is desired under forest, which may be achieved by reclaiming wastelands.

The spatial study of wastelands is essentially a geographical problem, which involves the role of such factors as relief, geology, soil, drainage and climate etc. All these aspects are directly related to the wasteland problems.

As per the wastelands statistics generated by the maps prepared by NRSA, 20.17 per cent of the country's geographical area is under wastelands. In Rajasthan State it is 30.87 per cent while in Jaipur district, wasteland occupies 17.34 per cent of the total geographical area.

To bring all the wastelands under productive use is very necessary through a programme of afforesation, pasture development, cropping and other economic uses. This calls for the development of appropriate technology for wasteland development and management. For development planning reliable database on the type, extent, location and ownership of wastelands are required.

Keeping in view degradation and ecological imbalance, the Prime Minister of India late Shri Rajiv Gandhi had observed "Continuing deforestation has brought us face to face with a major ecological and socio-economic crisis. The trend must be halted. He proposed immediately to set up a National Wastelands Development Board (NWDB) with the object of brining five million hectares of land every year under fuel wood and fodder plantations". On the recommendations of the NWDB a detailed project proposal was prepared for identification and mapping of wastelands.

In India where pressure on agricultural land is enormous any conversion of agriculturally productive land into wastelands has to be avoided and areas which have already turned into wasteland must be reclaimed. The expansion of limited physical land through wasteland reclamation for profitable purpose and increase of agricultural/forest productivity is the fundamental premise of this work. The present project will identify map, interpret wastelands of different categories and suggest planning for reclamation/development of wastelands.

Fifty villages have been selected for the detailed study by using satellite images and fields work. Thus there is neither overlapping nor repetition of any work. When one looks for cultivation, and presupposes the hazard that can be caused by the wastelands to the neighbouring non-wastelands, it becomes essential to find the development indicators in this aspect. In order to identify the development trends, it is indispensable to monitor the transmutations. The maps prepared under the present project will be useful to monitor certain developments of deterioration or improvement and all this can be easily checked.

Review of Literature

Important researches were done by Dudley Stamp and Miss Alice Coleman in Great Britain. Similar investigations were done in other countries like Russia, China, Australia, Europe etc. on the lines proposed by Dudley Stamp. Relevant contributions made so far by Dac Gregar and Datta in their "The Utilisation of Wastelands" (1947) and Kennedy K. in his "Australia's Wasteland" are now bountiful (1962). These researchers have analyzed and classified the wastelands, their distribution and their reclamation measures. Ministry of Food and Agriculture carried out Land use survey in Delhi state in 1959 to locate wastelands and to suggest measures for their reclamation.

Majority of such works dealt with the problems and possible reclamation of saline-alkali soils and waterlogged lands. USA Salinity Laboratory and Academy of the Sciences of the Russia also carried out detailed studies on their distribution and reclamation progress in their respective countries. Among other related studies, attempts by Leather (1893), Hill (1903) Barnes and Barkat Ali (1930), Taylor (1940), Aggarwal (1954 and 1957), Uppal (1961), Bhattacharya (1964), Pilai and Panikar (1965), Prasad R. (1969), Singh (1972), Gedroiz (1977), Ray Chaudhary (1977) are significant.

The problem of saline and alkaline lands received scientific consideration in India in 1886 when J.W. Wilson (An Indian Scientist) discussed the whole problem with E.W. Hilgard in 1906 one of the pioneer soil scientist of America in relation to Indian agriculture.

J.W. Leather 'the renowned agricultural chemist was the first scientist to make systematic study of the problem of salt affected lands in the country by suggesting a few methods for reclamation of usar land in relation to the salt tolerance of crop plants.

Qzanne, the Director of Agriculture, Bombay (1886) made a survey of the problems of saline and alkaline lands and reported that these lands were deteriorating due to the seepage and percolation from canals. In 1903 Government of Bombay appointed a committee to consider measures for checking damage of lands under salinity and alklinity. In 1912 Gedroiz explained the genesis of saline lands and the process of alkalinization. Kelley (1928) and McGeorge (1944) successfully applied the theory of Gedroiz to American soils to understand the genetic relationships of white and black alkali lands and the basic principles involved in their reclamation. Puri (1933) studied the problem of alkali lands, their characterization, diagnosis and reclamation which, was completely based upon the theory of Gedroiz.

In 1930, Uttar Pradesh Government constituted a committee for usar land reclamation. The purpose of this committee was to give advice on all the aspects of saline and alkali lands such as their characteristics, reclamation and the measures for prevention of the spread of usar. The committee studied the problem in detail and suggested setting up of a waste land reclamation board to deal with all the problems of waste lands.

U.S. salinity laboratory 1954 did a pioneer work in this direction which was critically examined by Agrawal and Yadav and other research associates. In Uttar Pradesh in the diagnosis and characterization of saline and alkaline lands of the Indo Gangetic alluvium. Academy of the sciences of Russia did a remarkable work by analysing the problem of saline land distribution and its reclamation. The work done by Uppal, Kanwar and Nigam provides the measure to reclaim saline and alkali lands along with the assessment of their potential. Barnes, Dhar and Singh worked on the reclamation of alkali wastelands through biochemical factors while Prasad and Yadav studies indicate towards the water quality, drainage measures, cultivation, sowing time, nutrient requirements, control of pests and diseases, economics of reclamation, facilities for reclamation and required educational training for the reclamation by the farmers.

Reh Committee and the Usar Land Reclamation Committee have discussed usar land identification, their diagnosis and investigation into the causes of deteriorating soils fertility by 'Reh' in different areas. They have also analysed reclamation of usar areas with suitable measures through irrigation, drainage, gypsum and pyrites and other scientific methods.

The study of Raheja on saline and alkaline lands provides many valuable suggestions for their reclamation and recommends planting of trees, growing grasses and crops and the other scientific methods. The work done by Auden, Milne and Hills is also on the same pattern and stresses saline and alkali lands, water logged lands and their distribution and characteristics, reclamation measures through proper scientific management in accordance with their problems.

The Indian Council of Agricultural Research (ICAR) and States Soil Conservation Research also carried out a survey of soils of India and have suggested soil conservation measures through a scientific reclamation of wastelands. The committee on natural resources planning commission studied in detail the wastelands along with their distribution and reclamation measures in different parts of the country. Central Soil Salinity Research Institute (CSSRI) Karnal 1969 has been consistently doing a remarkable work on all the problems of saline and alkaline lands spreading throughout the country. Scientists of Central Aid Zone Research Institute (CAZRI) Jodhpur e.g. Singh (1982), Sen (1972, 1989), Aggarwal (1981), Costin., E (1974), Dhar (1985), Gupta (1976, 1986), Kaul (1985) have done work on sand dunes formation, distribution, sand dune stabilization, moisture varation, crop production in desert, desert soil characteristics and shelter belt etc. Similarly Punjab Singh (1990), Deb Roy (1980), Patil (1977), Rrojosts (1979) have discussed the various aspects of silvipastoral system of management and production of biomass.

Some of the important studies on the location and extent of wastelands in India have been carried out by the Ministry of Food and Agriculture (1961), Planning Commission (1963), Ministry of Home Affairs (1972), National Remote Sensing Agency (1980-2000), and by a few individuals like Vohra (1980), Bhumbla and Khare (1984), etc. Sharma (1968), Ahmad (1970), Bali (1972), and the Natural Resources Committee, Planning Commission (1965) analyzed the ravine distribution in India along with their reclamation measures.

However, works by few geographers on wastelands make important contributions through Shafi (1968), Dixit (1969), Singh (1969), Vohra (1972), Roy (1973), Singh (1974), Bhardwaj (1979), Sethi (1981), Jain (1982), Yadav (1985) and Gupta (1997).

Shafi (1968) attempted an analysis, distribution pinpointing the problems of wasteland in India with special reference to other uncultivated lands and fallows other than current fallows, waterlogged, ravine land and saline-alkali soil. He critically examined the reclamation measures suggested by the Wastelands Survey and Reclamation Committee and additionally their cost-benefit analysis. Singh's work on Koil Tehsil of Aligarh district is a good attempt towards the utilization of wasteland studies. Her study of the uncultivated lands refers to block wise wasteland locations and their reclamation and resettlement suggesting also the required remedial measures, etc.

Anita Jain (1982) taking Udaipur district as a case study has examined the varied characteristics of wastelands and has identified factors responsible for land lying waste within operational holdings. The cost of reclamation and utilization of the various type and size of wastelands reclaimed by the cultivators during the last two decades have also been studied. Similarly, Yadav's work on Sultanpur district refers to the typology and distribution of wastelands in their spatial and temporal contexts. Various environmental and anthropogenic factors responsible for their formation have been identified. The genesis and capability classification suggesting the various measures along with the economics of each type of wasteland reclamation has also been attempted through input-output balance analysis.

Kalwar, Khandelwal and Agarwal (1996) also have made attempt for spatial distribution of wastelands in Rajasthan state and Bassi tehsil of Jaipur district. Kalwar and Agrawal (1999) suggested various measures for development of wastelands in Rajasthan, Kalwar (1998) discussed identified and spatial distribution of wastelands in semi Arid areas of Rajasthan and Chouhan T. S. (1986) discussed about wastelands in Rajasthan in "Agriculture Geography : A Case Study of Rajasthan State". Gupta and Maroo (1991) have discussed wastelands at various levels i.e. tehsil, patwar mandal, village and households to understand the problem from different angles and aspects. Hills, barren uncultivable lands, old fallow and cultivable wasteland have been considered for the wasteland analysis in the Chittaurgarh district.

Rachana (2002) has analysed spatial distribution, ownership pattern and reclamation of wastelands in Jhunjhunu district (Rajasthan). Her study is based on wasteland maps 1997 selecting whole district as a unit of study and has discussed spatial distribution of wastelands in detail with the help of maps.

Padmini and Mahapatra (2001) delineated gullied and ravinous lands in a part (692 km^2) of lower Chambal valley using remote sensing and GIS during 1984-98. Doi (2005) has also discussed the microwastershed wise ravines in Morel river basin using R.S. and GIS.

This brief overview reveals that majority of these works mainly deal with the problems and reclamation of saline-alkail soils and waterlogged lands and their emphasis is on the related pedogenic factors for wasteland formation. So far, cultivable wastelands have attracted greater attention but little effort has been done towards the study of uncultivable wastelands from different dimensions. The emphasis on their problems, suitability for producing fuel, fodder and for environmental betterment, etc. as a potential resource is still lacking. Efforts to examine the real causes of land lying as waste within operational holdings have still to be taken seriously. Ownership pattern of wastelands and their capability for agricultural and non-agricultural pursuits have also not been adequately studied or even touched.

Thus, a study dealing with wastelands should be topical to meet the objectives of self-sufficiency in food, fodder, fuel, timber and ecological balance, being the vital needs of present time. The present study is an attempt in this direction dealing with this potential resource. Wastelands need to be evaluated accurately for the future land use planning in the area, which has substantial percentage of such lands. Various type of wastelands need different reclamation measures depending on the type, degree of degradation, ownership of land, available resources, suitability class, size of wasteland etc.

In the present study village/town has been taken as a study unit and wasteland data of each category of every village/town of Jaipur district have been computed from the wasteland maps obtained from National Remote Sensing Agency (NRSA), Hyderabad (AP). For detailed sample study LISS III satellite image of February 28, 2003 has been processed and interpreted of 50 sample villages, 4-8 villages in cluster from each category. Planning for reclamation/development has also been recommended on the basis of spatial distribution of wastelands in sample villages and economic aspects of wastelands have also been discussed.

Objectives

(i) To identify and assess the typology and extension of wastelands in Jaipur district.

(ii) To identify various environmental and anthropogenic factors which may be responsible for the formation of different type of wastelands.

(iii) To suggest suitable remedies for the reclamation of each type of wasteland along with socially and economically appropriate technology for the wasteland development and to suggest measures for their reclamation into cropland, pastures, silvi pastures, energy plantation etc.

(iv) To assess the economics of wasteland reclamation/ development through an input-output balance analysis.

Indicators

To explain the factors influencing wastelands, a cluster of 4-8 villages from the each category of wastelands have been selected from the different parts of the study area. The indicators chosen for the present study are broadly grouped into two categories i.e. dependent and independent variables. The independent variables have been chosen from natural, cultural, economic and technological areas. Informations and data about the independent variables have been obtained from the related office/agencies and the topographical sheets. The factors like slope, ruggedness number, dissection index and drainage density etc. have been computed with appropriate formula.

Dependent variables

(i) Gullied and/or ravinous land
(ii) Degraded notified forest land
(iii) Sands-desertic land
(iv) Land affected by salinity
(v) Land affected by alkalinity
(vi) Degraded pasture/grazing land
(vii) Land with or without scrub
(viii) Barren hills/rocky
(ix) Mining/industrial wasteland

Independent variables

Environmental Determinants

(a) Morphometric.
X_1 Slope
X_2 Ruggedness number
X_3 Dissection index
(b) Hydrological Factor :
X_4 Drainage density
(c) Social Factors :
X_5 Rural population density per km^2
X_6 Percentage of literacy
X_7 Percentage of Scheduled Tribe Population
X_8 Percentage of Scheduled Caste Population
X_9 Percentage of population engaged in agriculture
(d) Economic Factors :
X_{10} Average size of holding in hectare
X_{11} Percentage of irrigated land to total cultivated land
(e) Economic and Technological Factors :
X_{12} Number of livestock population per 100 hectare land
X_{13} Number of pump sets and diesel engines per 100 hectares of NSA
X_{14} Number of tractors per 100 hectares of NSA

Hypotheses

The following hypotheses have been tested in this study:

(i) It is assumed that more is the level of technology, the lesser would be the amount of wastelands.
(ii) With the increase in ruggedness number and dissection index, the area under barren hills/rocky has also increased.

(iii) There is a more wastelands in those areas where percentage of irrigated land is low and very low.

(iv) Population engaged in agriculture is less in the areas of having more land under wastelands.

(v) It is assumed that areas of more land under degraded forest and gullied and/or ravinous land also have high percentages of scheduled tribe population.

(vi) Large size holdings have high percentage of wastelands.

Source of Database

S. No.	Database Theme	Source
1.	Administrative Units of the district	Collectorate, Jaipur
2.	Map of the district having village boundaries	Directorate of Census Operations, Jaipur and Collectorate, Jaipur
3.	Geology	Geological Survey of India, Western Circle, Jaipur
4.	Minerals	Directorate, Mines and Geology, Government of Rajasthan, Jaipur
5.	Topographical Features	Topographical Maps, Survey of India, Dehradun (U.A.)
6.	Slope Map	NATMO, Kolkata and Topographical sheets 45M, 45N, 54A and 54B
7.	Drainage Map	Topographical Maps, Survey of India, Dehradun (U.A.)
8.	Soils	Soil Survey, Government of Rajasthan, Durgapura, Jaipur
9.	Climatic data	IMD, Regional Centre Jaipur and Hydrology, Irrigation Deptt. Govt. of Rajasthan, Jaipur
10.	Hydrology Map, Groundwater Potential Zones and Salinity Map	Groundwater Board, Govt. of Rajasthan, Jaipur
11.	Population data	Directroate, Census Operations, Jaipur
12.	Livestock resources	Collectorate, Jaipur and Tehsil Headquarters, district Jaipur
13.	Village wise wasteland data	Wasteland Maps (Watershed wise) obtained from NRSA, Hyderabad (A.P.)
14.	Sample study of various categories of wastelands	IRS-IC/ID LISS-III Precision geocoded scene (1:50,000)
15.	Land use data	Collectorate, Jaipur and Patwar circles of sample study areas
16.	Pumpsets and diesel engines	Collectorate, Jaipur
17.	Number of Tractors	Collectorate, Jaipur

Wasteland Data from Wasteland Maps of Jaipur District

On comparing pervious wasteland maps and maps of sample study areas prepared by B.M. Birla Science and Technology Center, Jaipur in 2003, it is observed that minor or no changes have been occurred in wastelands in the study area. Village wise wasteland data have been computed with Digital Planimeter from the following wasteland maps (watershed wise on 1.50,000) prepared by National Remote Sensing Agency, Hyderabad.

Table 1.1 : List of Wasteland Maps of Jaipur district

1.	45 J/13	13.	45 N/3	24.	54 A/2
2.	45 J/14	14.	45 N/5	25.	54 A/3
3.	45 M/4	15.	45 N/6	26.	54 A/4
4.	45 M/7	16.	45 N/7	27.	54 A/5
5.	45 M/8	17.	45 N/9	28.	54 A/6
6.	45 M/11	18.	45 N/10	29.	54 A/6
7.	45 M/12	19.	45 N/11	30.	54 A/8
8.	45 M/14	20.	45 N/13	31.	54 B/1
9.	45 M/15	21.	45 N/14	32.	54 B/2
10.	45 M/16	22.	45 N/15	33.	54 B/3
11.	45 N/1	23.	54 A/1	34.	54 B/5
12.	45 N/2				

Source : National Remong Sensing Agency, Hyderabad (A.P.)

Villagewise Wasteland Data Computed with Digital Planimeter of Jaipur District

Area under different categories of wasteland of each village/town of the study area has been calculated with Digital Planimeter. Total number of villages and towns in the district are 2203. Table 1.2 shows tehsilwise number of villages/towns.

Table 1.2 : Tehsilwise Number of Villages/Towns in Jaipur district

S. No.	Tehsil	Number of Villages	Towns	Total
1.	Amber	196	1	197
2.	Chomu	95	1	96
3.	Jamwa Ramgarh	241	—	241
4.	Phulera	215	4	219
5.	Dudu	147	1	148
6.	Phagi	170	1	171
7.	Jaipur	102	1	103
8.	Sanganer	209	2	211
9.	Bassi	214	1	215
10.	Chaksu	279	1	280
11.	Kotputli	137	1	138
12.	Viratnagar	93	1	94
13.	Shahapura	89	1	90
	Total	2187	16	2203

Source : Directorate, Census Operation, Jaipur and Collectorate, Jaipur.

Wasteland Data Used for Identification and Spatial Distribution of Wastelands in the Study Area

Villagewise wasteland data of different categories computed by the author himself with Digital Planimeter have been utilized for the identification and spatial distribution of wastelands in the study area while satellite images February 28, 2003 have been utilized for the sample villages.

Satellite Images Utilized for the Study of Sample Villages

For detailed study, 50 sample villages have been selected from the different categories of wastelands. The following satellite images of February 28, 2003 have been utilized for the detailed study.

(i) IRS- IC/ID PAN
(ii) IRS - IC/ ID LISS III
(iii) Precision geocoded scene (1:50,000)

Methodology

The present study is concentrated on identification of wasteland categories and spatial distribution of wastelands in Jaipur District. Distribution patterns of wasteland categories have been shown on maps based upon the wasteland maps on 1:50,000 obtained from National Remote Sensing Agency (NRSA), Govt. of India. Distribution of wastelands have been analysed upto villages level and selected group of 4-8 villages which have concentration of particular wasteland category, as representative area. One group of villages for each wasteland category has been taken into consideration for detailed analysis by remote sensing technology using IRS LISS-III images of year 2003. The categories for which representative areas have been selected are as under:

(1) Degraded notified forest land,
(2) Gullied and or Ravinous lands,
(3) Sands - desertic land,
(4) Land with or without scrub,
(5) Land affected by salinity,
(6) Land affected by alkalinity,
(7) Degraded pasture/grazing lands,
(8) Barren hill/Rocky/Stony wasteland,
(9) Mining/industrial wasteland.

Base maps of the selected areas have been prepared from topographical sheet on 1:50,000 scale taking roads, forest boundaries, location of settlements etc. Village boundaries are taken from district census hand book and super imposed on base maps. All base maps and village boundaries have been scanned and digitized in arc/info software. All these maps are projected in polyconic projection on 1:50,000 scale.

Satellite images of IRS-LISS III have been loaded on computer in Geomatica software for geometic rectification and further land use analysis. These images have been rectified with the base maps in such a way that all the features of maps are registered on the images of the same features. Mask of each representative areas, as mentioned above have been prepared to demarcate the area of interest. By using these masks 3 bands of satellite images have been extracted which are used for creating false colour composits on Geomatica software and created files for each representative area for further analysis.

Satellite images have been processed using supervised classification method on the geomatica software. First various land use categories were identified as per spectra characteristic of different land use categories and various associated elements like tone, texture, colour, association etc. Homogeneous areas of each class have been used as training sites for supervised classification. Supervised classification results have been stored on one blank channel which was showing various land use categories. Small scattered pixels/ group of pixels (upto 3 pixels) have been merged into nearby bigger classes through "seave" programme. All land use classes are separated in the form of Bit Maps. The Bit Maps of various wasteland categories have been again mapped on a single channel to get a composite wasteland map of the each representative area. Appropriate map composition have been prepared for FCC images and wasteland classified images in Geomedia software. Masks have been prepared for each village in each of the representative area for calculating automatic area under the village and each category of wastelands. Areas of wasteland categories were calculated for each village and tables prepared to show areas of different categories in each village. Appropriate map compositions have been prepared for creating output images of row satellite image (FCC) and classified wasteland categories image. Prints of these outputs have been prepared on 1:50,000 scale on A/4 size photographic high quality paper.

Cartographic techniques including maps and diagrams as the fundamental tools for explaining geographic phenomena in a region, have been used for the present study to depict the spatial, temporal and structural variations of wasteland. Similarly, the choropleth techniques along with one and two dimensional diagrams have also been used to explain identification, spatial distribution of wastelands and planning for reclamation/development of wastelands.

The following formula have been used for morphometric analysis:

Slope

The average slope is calculated using the C.K. Wentworth's method:

$$\tan \theta = \frac{N \times V.I}{636.6}$$

Where N = Number of contour crossings per kilometre
V.I = Vertical Interval (Contour interval)

Ruggedness Number

Drainage lines are drawn on the actual map of the village from the topogrophical sheet. Besides this cadostral map also has been consulted to know the actual length of the drainage and the total length as such is divided by the area to calculate the drainage density of the village and relative relief has been calculated subtracting the minimum height from the maximum height of the village. Lastly ruggedness number is computed:

$$\text{Ruggedness Number} = \frac{\text{Drainage Density x Relative Relief}}{5280}$$

Drainage Density

As discussed earlier drainage lines are drawn for the selected villages and the length of the drainage lines per unit area are measured and lastly, drainage density is computed as below:

$$\text{Drainage Density} = \frac{\text{Total Drainage Length}}{\text{Total Area}}$$

To know relationship between dependent variables and independent variables is an essential in a scientific investigation. For quantitative measurement of the degree and direction of correlation is worked out as suggested and defined by Karl Pearson's coefficient of correlation and the correlation matrix is prepared to see the correlation of independent variables with the various types of waste lands.

Formula for the correlation

$$r = \frac{\sum xy - \frac{\sum x \sum y}{n}}{n \sqrt{(\sum x)^2 \frac{\sum x^2}{n}}} \quad \sqrt{\sum \gamma^2 - \frac{(\sum \gamma)^2}{n}}$$

The form of linear regression analysis between dependent variable Y and an independent variable X is given as

$Y = \alpha + 2 (+ U)$

Where the constants are the intercept and the slope of the straight line and U is the error term.

The basic objective of a regression analysis is to estimate the values of α and β. The estimated least square form of the relationship is given by Johnston*

$Y = a + b X$

Where

$$b = \frac{\sum xy - \frac{\sum x \sum y}{n}}{\sum x^2 - \frac{(\sum n)^2}{n}} \text{ is an estimate of } \beta$$

and $a = \bar{y} - b\bar{x}$ is and estimate of ℓ

Test of the significance used is given below:

$$t = \frac{b - o}{-SE(b)}$$

with (n-2) degree of freedom.

$$\text{Where} \quad -SE(b) = \frac{\sigma u}{\sqrt{\sum X^2 - \frac{(\sum X)^2}{n}}}$$

$$\text{and } \sigma u^2 = \frac{\sum X^2 \frac{(\sum Y)^2}{n} - b\left\{\sum XY - \frac{\sum X \sum Y}{n}\right\}}{n - 2}$$

Regression Equation of Y on X

The regression equation of Y on X is expressed as follows:
$Y = a + b\,x$

It may be noted that in this equation 'Y' is a dependent variable, i.e., its value depend on X. 'X' is independent variable, i.e., we can take a given value of X and compute the value of Y.

Regression Equation of X on Y

The regression equation of X on Y is expressed as follows:

$Xc = a + by$

To determine the value of a and b, the following two normal equations are solved simultaneously:

% X = Na + b %y
% XY = a %y + b %y2

Regression Coefficient

X on Y	Y on X
%dxdy = [(%dx)(%dy)]/N	%dxdy = [(%dx) (%dy)]/N
Bxy = %dzy = [(%dy)^2]/N	byx = %d^{2}x - [(%dx)^2]/N

Analysis of Time Series

1. % (y-y) = 0 i.e. the sum deviations of the actual values of y and the computed values of y is zero.

2. $\%(y\text{-}y)^2$ is least i.e. the sum of the squares of the deviations of the actual and computed values is least from this line and hence the name method of least squares.

The method of least squares may by used either to fit a straight line trend or a parabolic trend. The straight line trend is represented by the equation –

$$Yc = a + bx$$

Where Yc is used to designate the trend values to distinguish them from the actual Y values, a is the Y intercept or the computed trend figure of the Y variable when X = 0. b represents the slope of the trend line or the amount of change in Y variable that is associated with a change of one unit in X variable. The X variable in time series analysis represents time.

$$Y = a + bx$$
$$\%y = Na + b\%x \qquad (1)$$
$$\%xy = \%ax + b\%x^2 \qquad (2)$$

Brief Description of the Study Area

Jaipur District is situated between 26°23′ and 27°51′ north latitude and 75°55′ and 76°10′ east longitude in the eastern part of Rajasthan state. It touches in the west by Sikar and Nagaur districts of Rajasthan in the north Mahendragarh District of Haryana State, in the south by Tonk, in the east by Alwar and Dausa districts and in the south west by Ajmer district (Fig. 1.1). It occupies an area of 10876.78 km^2 which is 3.17 per cent to the total area of the state. This district has 4 sub-divisions, 13 tehsils, 16 towns, 2187 villages. The following table shows name of sub-division, tehsil, number of villages and name of towns.

Table 1.3 : Administrative Units in Jaipur District

Sub Division	Tehsil	Number of villages	Town
	1. Amber	196	Amber
1. Amber	2. Chomu	95	Chomu
	3. Jamwa Ramgarh	241	
2. Sambhar	4. Phulera	215	Phulera, Sambhar, Jobner, Naraina
	5. Dudu	147	Dudu
	6. Phagi	170	Phagi
	7. Jaipur	102	Jaipur
3. Jaipur	8. Sanganer	209	Sanganer, Bagru
	9. Bassi	214	Bassi
	10. Chaksu	279	Chaksu
	11. Kotputli	137	Kotputli
4. Kotputli	12. Viratnagar	93	Viratnagar
	13. Shahapura	89	Shahapura
Total	13	2187	16

Source : Collectorate Jaipur and Census Operations, Rajasthan, Jaipur.

Tehsilwise village maps have been obtained from the Directorate, Census Operations, Rajasthan, Jaipur and the same have been enlarged on tracing paper and finally superimposed

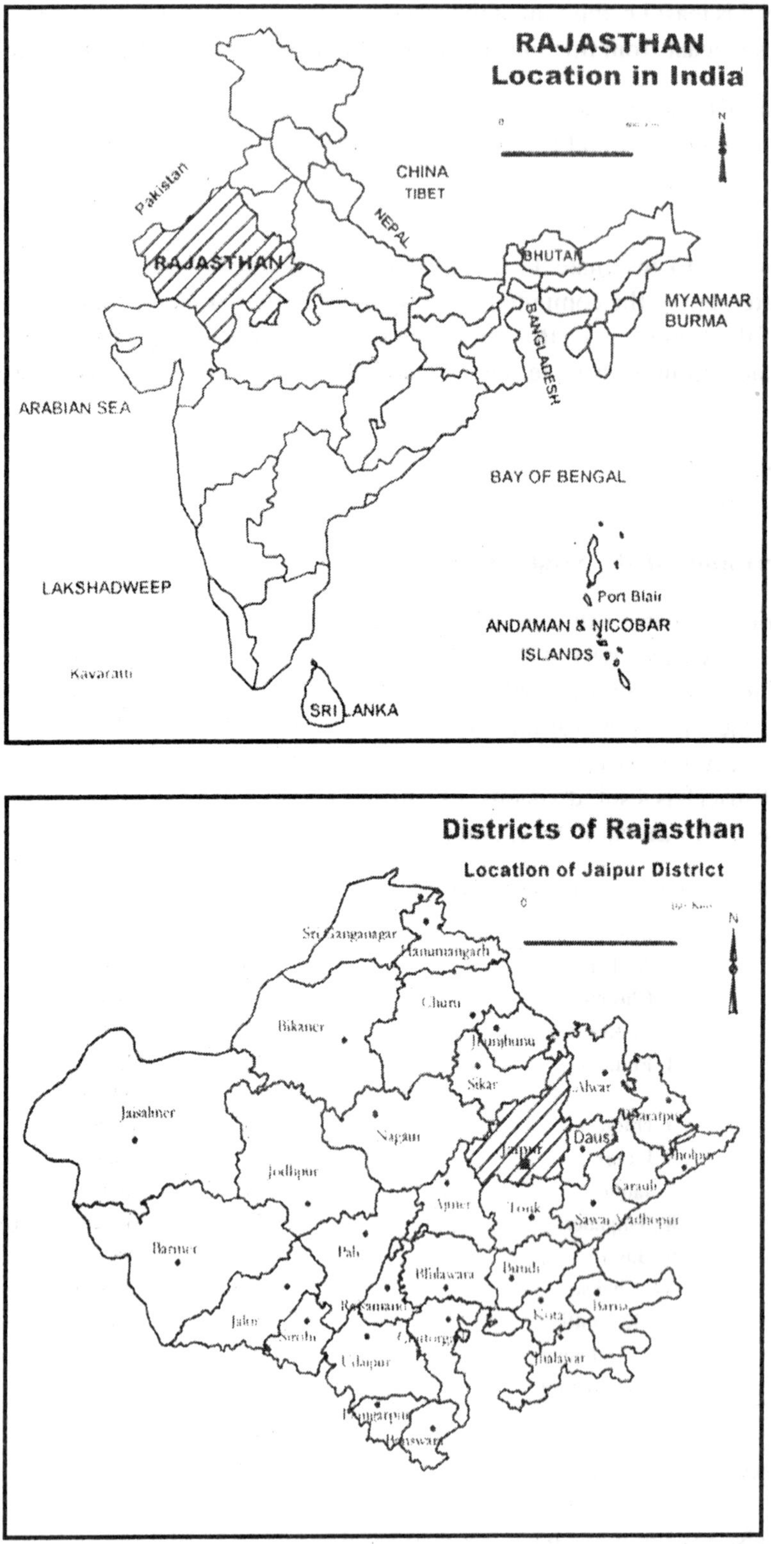

Fig. 1.1 : Location Map

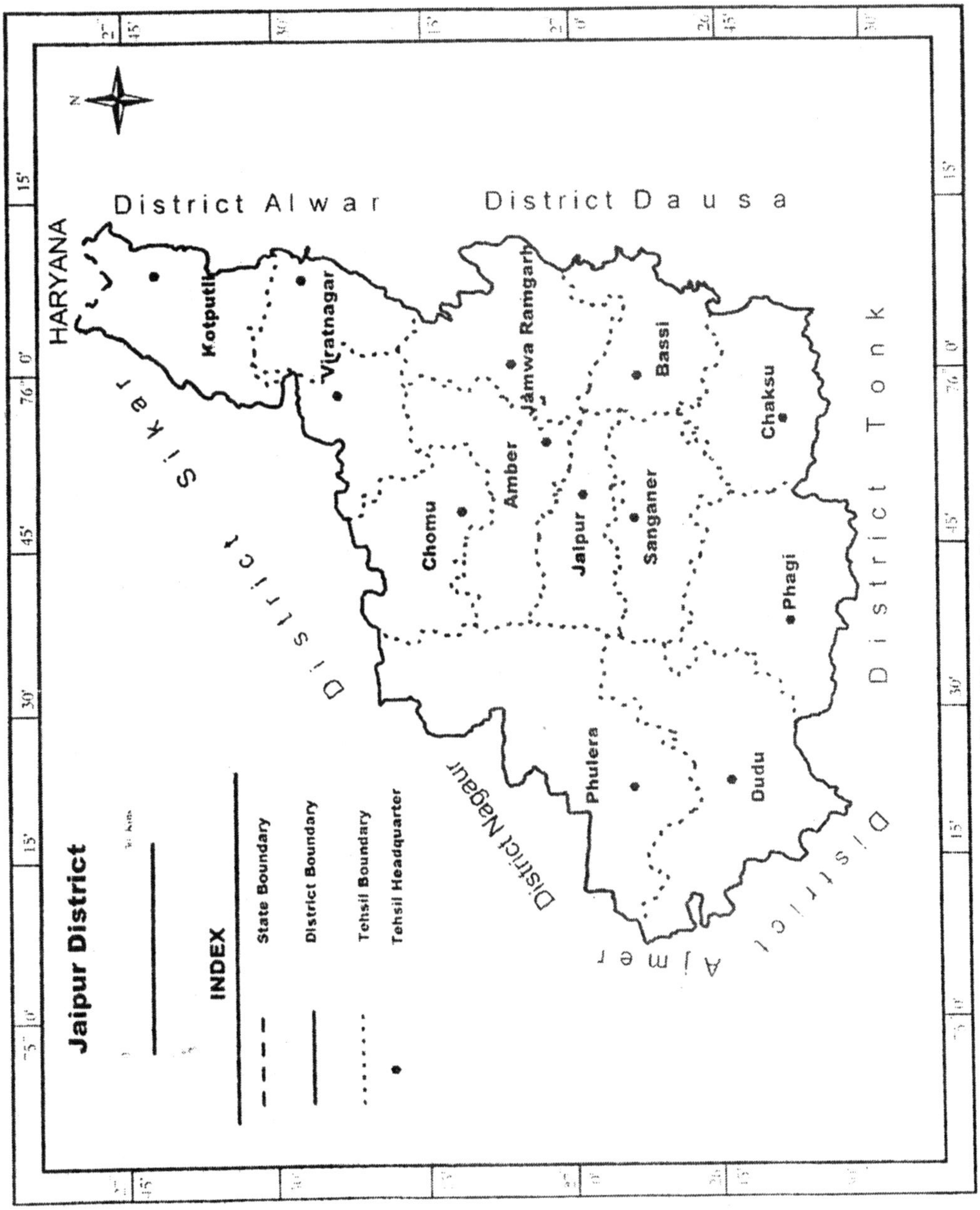

Fig. 1.1 : Location Map

on the topographical sheet keeping in mind the permanent features of the village for getting morphometric information i.e. slope, ruggedness number, drainage density and dissection index etc. of the village.

Table 1.4 shows tehsilwise name of village/town with code number in Jaipur district. These code numbers have been shown in Fig. 1.2.

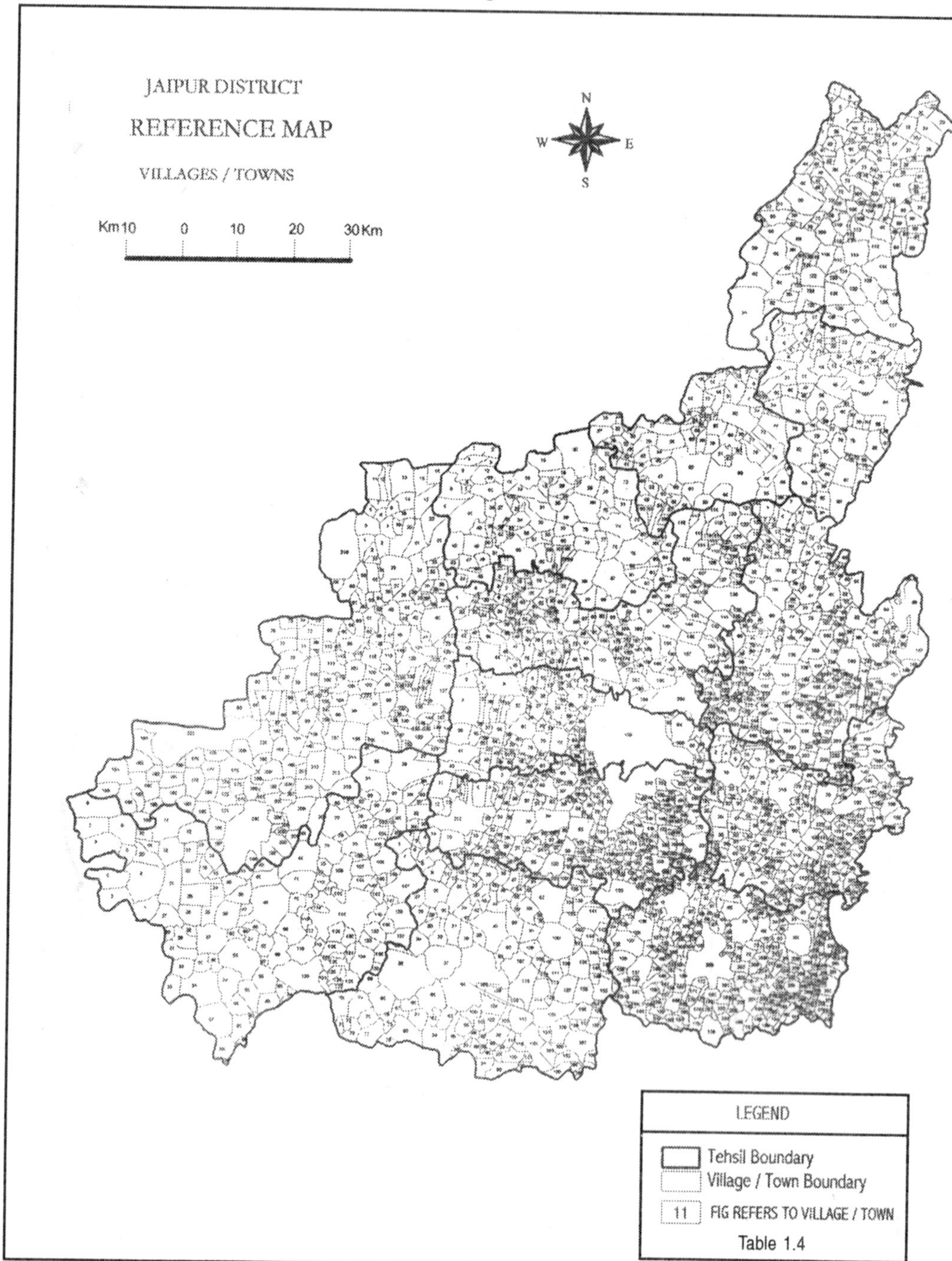

Fig. 1.2 : Viliage / Town Reference Map of Jaipur District

Table 1.4 : Tehsilwise Name of Villages with Code Number in Jaipur District

Village Code	Village Name
Tehsil Kotputli	
1.	Deota
2.	Banar
3.	Chhardara
4.	Ramgarh
5.	Panera
6.	Ramnagar
7.	Baneti
8.	Dhawali
9.	Hasanpura
10.	Raikaranpura
11.	Bakhrana
12.	Amarpura
13.	Nangal Checheeka
14.	Jaisinghpura
15.	Gopalpura
16.	Karwas
17.	Banka
18.	Kaloohera
19.	Gonera
20.	Keshwana Gujar
21.	Keshwana Rajput
22.	Malpura
23.	Mordha
24.	Paniyala
25.	Kherki Mukkar
26.	Been Jahera
27.	Sangtera
28.	Shekhupur
29.	Molahera
30.	Kherki Veerbhan
31.	Kharkhari
32.	Ramsinghpura
33.	Ajeetpura Khurd
34.	Poorannagar
35.	Nareda
36.	Chimpanpura
37.	Narsinghpura
38.	Kayampurawas
39.	Bhopatpura
40.	Churi
41.	Pawala Rajput
42.	Nawalkushalpura
43.	Padam Ki Dhani
44.	Kuhara
45.	Kalyanpura Kalan
46.	Kharab
47.	Pichani
48.	Shuklawas
49.	Purushottampura
50.	Beri
51.	Sudarpura
52.	Dhadha
53.	Gulabgarh
54.	Talwa
55.	Dantil
56.	Meerapur
57.	Dwarikapura
58.	Jeengor
59.	Chandoli
60.	Dudawas
61.	Buchara
62.	Rooppura
63.	Fathepura Khurd
64.	Bhonawas
65.	Torda Kalan
66.	Taskola
67.	Panditpura
68.	Rampura
69.	Bharaj Bhuree
70.	Sujatnagar
71.	Beethloda
72.	Pawana Aheer
73.	Fathepura Kalan
74.	Saroond
75.	Bhojawas
76.	Jagdishpura
77.	Khera Nihalpura
78.	Nurangpura
79.	Chanchaki
80.	Shyamnagar
81.	Tapri
82.	Barabas (Rural)
83.	Basri (Rural)
84.	Chaturbhuj
85.	Balawas (Rural)
86.	Buchahera (Rural)
87.	Bamanwas
88.	Gopipura
89.	Nangal Panditpura
90.	Hansiyawas
91.	Tamoriwas
92.	Nagriwas
93.	Jahidpura
94.	Pejooka
95.	Basai
96.	Bhaloji
97.	Khurdi
98.	Amai
99.	Pootli
100.	Sundarpura
101.	Kiratpura

(Table 1.4 Contd.)

Table 1.4 (Contd.)

Village Code	Village Name
102.	Kansli
103.	Rahera
104.	Kalayanpura Khurd
105.	Kanwarpura
106.	Mohanpura
107.	Mahrampur Rajput
108.	Ajeetpura Kalan
109.	Bhainslana
110.	Koojota
111.	Mahrampur Nawab
112.	Gordhanpura
113.	Duduka
114.	Pathreri
115.	Rughnathpura
116.	Aspura
117.	Kirarod
118.	Pragpura
119.	Lanana
120.	Manjukot
121.	Kakrana
122.	Paota
123.	Kooner
124.	Khelna
125.	Ladaka Was
126.	Theekariya
127.	Torda Brahmanan
128.	Tulsipura
129.	Barnagar
130.	Kalyanpura
131.	Jodhpura
132.	Bhankhari
133.	Mandha
134.	Panch Pahari
135.	Pachhodala
Tehsil Viratnagar	
1.	Neemli
2.	Bahrangpura
3.	Rampura Khurd
4.	Kairli
5.	Hanumannagar
6.	Antela
7.	Bahdoda
8.	Leelka
9.	Dhani Gaiskan
10.	Bhabroo
11.	Sitapura
12.	Luhakana Kalan
13.	Luhakana Khurd
14.	Dhoolkot
15.	Kishanpura
16.	Banipark
17.	Bagawas Ahiran
18.	Taliyara
19.	Bhagatpura
20.	Jaisinghpura
21.	Surajpura
22.	Bahadurpura
23.	Dheetoli
24.	Devipura@ Batiya Ka Bas
25.	Bahrampur
26.	Jadoo Ka Bas
27.	Bhojpura @ Lakhawala
28.	Rughnathpura @ Talooka
29.	Deoli
30.	Badshahpur
31.	Sothana
32.	Kankrana Chhota
33.	Kankrana
34.	Papra
35.	Chak Kharda
36.	Kuhada
37.	Bandh Muzaffarpur
38.	Chak Muzaffarpur
39.	Chak Gorawari
40.	Isamailpur
41.	Mahasingh Ka Bas
42.	Sujapur
43.	Chak Chamroli
44.	Gopipur
45.	Papri
46.	Biyawas
47.	Dhobiyawala
48.	Chattarpura
49.	Jawanpura
50.	Khatolai
51.	Aspura
52.	Leelon Ka Bas
53.	Surpura
54.	Jogiyon Ki Dhani
55.	Bagawas Chaurasi
56.	Beelwari
57.	Bas Udaisingh
58.	Kukdela
59.	Khera
60.	Norangpura
61.	Bhairunpura
62.	Sewara
63.	Teori
64.	Gyanpura
65.	Daulaj
66.	Chak Bai Ka Bas
67.	Bhojera
68.	Satana
69.	Jodhoola
70.	Jodhoola Upla

(Table 1.4 Contd.)

Table 1.4 (Contd.)

Village Code	Village Name
71.	Galawas
72.	Chheed
73.	Maliwara
74.	Poorawala
75.	Med
76.	Shyampura
77.	Bhamod
78.	Pando
79.	Barwara
80.	Palri
81.	Ramsinghpura
82.	Badodiya
83.	Amloda
84.	Kalyanpura
85.	Harikishanpura
86.	Gheota
87.	Bihajar
88.	Bhindor
89.	Sundarpura
90.	Badshahpur
91.	Gudha Baijnathpura
92.	Berki
93.	Talba
Tehsil Shahapura	
1.	Chhapra Khurd
2.	Chhapra Kalan
3.	Basri Ganeshpura
4.	Neejhar
5.	Govindpura Dhabai
6.	Satwas
7.	Jaje Kalan
8.	Rampura
9.	Gautamnagar
10.	Girdharpura
11.	Sanga Ka Bas
12.	Ramchandrapura
13.	Bari Jori
14.	Jaswantpura
15.	Chak Sanga Ka Bas
16.	Karnisagar
17.	Chimanpura
18.	Rughnathpura
19.	Saiwar
20.	Nathawala
21.	Amarpura
22.	Swamipura
23.	Bhanipura
24.	Bichpuri
25.	Devipura
26.	Pathano Ka Bas
27.	Amarsar
28.	Nayan

Village Code	Village Name
29.	Kalwaniyaon Ka Bas
30.	Trilokpura
31.	Goplpura
32.	Ranipura
33.	Jodhpura
34.	Hanutpura
35.	Chak Hanutpura
36.	Kareeri
37.	Vilandarpur
38.	Chak Dhanota
39.	Govindpura Basri
40.	Raopura
41.	Dhanota
42.	Murlipura
43.	Kalyanpura
44.	Markhi
45.	Hanutiya
46.	Tejpura
47.	Radawas
48.	Jagatpura
49.	Mahar Khurd
50.	Parmanpura
51.	Gulab Bari
52.	Majeepura
53.	Shyosinghpura
54.	Amloda
55.	Dhaoli
56.	Sepatpura
57.	Nayabas
58.	Gona Ka Sar
59.	Gaila Dahra
60.	Gonpur @ Dangawali
61.	Mamtori Kalan
62.	Vishangarh
63.	Peeplod Nathu
64.	Peeplod Narain
65.	Dhelawas
66.	Chatarpura
67.	Khori
68.	Sherpura
69.	Vidara
70.	Rajpura
71.	Let Ka Bas
72.	Lakhni
73.	Kant
74.	Naje Khurd @ Vishanpura
75.	Madho Ka Bas
76.	Lobrawas
77.	Devan
78.	Kumbhawas
79.	Nithara
80.	Baori Ki Dhani
81.	Ghasipura

(Table 1.4 Contd.)

Table 1.4 (Contd.)

Village Code	Village Name
82.	Khojawala
83.	Mamtori Khurd
84.	Nawalpura
85.	Chharsa
86.	Surana
87.	Shakatpura
88.	Khora Larkhani
89.	Hanutpura
Tehsil Chomu	
1.	Bagri
2.	Sirsa
3.	Ranjeetpura
4.	Nangal Govind
5.	Kishanpura
6.	Haboo Ka Bas
7.	Bagron Ka Bas
8.	Asti Kalan
9.	Asti Khurd
10.	Bhutera
11.	Madho Ka Bas
12.	Udgwar @ Gudalya
13.	Choota Gudha
14.	Nangal Kalan
15.	Raisingh Ka Bas
16.	Dhodhsar
17.	Nadyan
18.	Singod Khurd
19.	Singod Kalan
20.	Khejroli
21.	Chak Dalelpura
22.	Nangal Koju
23.	Kanwarpura
24.	Chak Laddu
25.	Niwana
26.	Deothala
27.	Barh Deothala
28.	Dhobolai
29.	Chak Charanwas
30.	Syaoo
31.	Govindgarh
32.	Malikpur
33.	Charanwas
34.	Sandarsar
35.	Kumbha Ka Bas
36.	Barh Abhaykaranpura
37.	Aleesar
38.	Baga Ka Bas
39.	Damba Ka Bas
40.	Nopura
41.	Hasteda
42.	Baori Gopinath
43.	Gori Ka Bas

Village Code	Village Name
44.	Sabal Pura
45.	Ghinoi
46.	Dhani Nijharna
47.	Dola Ka Bas
48.	Bai Ka Bas
49.	Mandha Bhinda
50.	Dolatpura
51.	Kanarpura
52.	Bimalpura
53.	Jalimsingh Ka Bas
54.	Dhana Ka Bas
55.	Kaladera
56.	Khannipura
57.	Narsinghura
58.	Ugriyawas
59.	Jaisinghpura Nathawatan
60.	Guwardi
61.	Chak Tankarda
62.	Deopura
63.	Dhara Tankarda
64.	Jodhpura
65.	Tankarda
66.	Loharwara
67.	Balekhan
68.	Anatpura Chimanpura
69.	Itawa Bhopji
70.	Bishanpura @ Charanwas
71.	Amarpura
72.	Tigriya
73.	Barwara
74.	Nangal Bharda
75.	Udaipura
76.	Harota
77.	Bhopawas
78.	Hathnoda
79.	Samod
80.	Malera
81.	Jatanwali
82.	Dahra
83.	Mahar Kalan
84.	Sambhoopura
85.	Vijaisinghpura
86.	Kushalpura
87.	Morija
88.	Jetpura
89.	Anatpura
90.	Cheethwari
91.	Fatehpura
92.	Sultanpura
93.	Jheera
94.	Kanpura
95.	Samarpura

(Table 1.4 Contd.)

Table 1.4 (Contd.)

Village Code	Village Name
Tehsil Phulera	
1.	Kishanpura @ Nathi Ka Bas
2.	Sanwat Ka Bas
3.	Basri Khurd
4.	Ralawata
5.	Malikpura
6.	Rampura
7.	Surpura
8.	Bajiyon Ka Bas
9.	Charanwas
10.	Turkyawas
11.	Looniyawas
12.	Gadri
13.	Badhal
14.	Kabron
15.	Itawa
16.	Kanwarpura
17.	Junsya Kalan and Khurd
18.	Deva Ka Bas
19.	Deesa
20.	Dholya ka bas
21.	Bagawas
22.	Lalasar
23.	Doongri Khurd
24.	Doongri Kalan
25.	Harsoli
26.	Charanwas
27.	Devalya
28.	Doongarsi Ka Bas
29.	Kesa ka bas
30.	Charanwas
31.	Ramsinghpura @Sanga ka bas
32.	Mohanpura
33.	Jalra
34.	Abhaipura
35.	Rampura
36.	Gumanpura
37.	Basri Kalan
38.	Khijooriya
39.	Harnthpura
40.	Bhainsawa
41.	Beniya Ka Bas
42.	Mohan Ka Bas
43.	Dhana Ka Bas
44.	Karansar
45.	Kheri Milak
46.	Loharwara
47.	Laxmipura
48.	Vijai Govindpura
49.	Kheerwa
50.	Raghunandanpura
51.	Pachkodiya
52.	Salagrampura
53.	Ramjipura
54.	Ramjipura Kalan
55.	Sundarpura
56.	Mudiyagarh
57.	Samdari
58.	Pratappura
59.	Meendi
60.	Nandri
61.	Salhadipura
62.	Shyosinghpura @ Gujaron
63.	Sukhalpura
64.	Moondoti
65.	Pratappura
66.	Bhojpura Khurd
67.	Anatpura
68.	Mandha Bheemsingh
69.	Paharpura
70.	Prempura
71.	Bijarniyaon Ka Bas
72.	Bhainslana
73.	Bhookhron Ki Dhani
74.	Sundon Ka Bas
75.	Janiyon Ka Bas
76.	Bhadwa
77.	Dogiwalon Ka Bas
78.	Sinodiya
79.	Shyampura
80.	Khatwari Khurd
81.	Khatwari Kalan
82.	Tyoda
83.	Bag Ki Dhani
84.	Tyod
85.	Kazipura
86.	Rasolpura
87.	Kanwarasa
88.	Ameepura
89.	Khandel
90.	Prithvipura
91.	Jaisinghpura
92.	Jetpura
93.	Jagmalpura
94.	Gumanpura
95.	Machar khani
96.	Dehra
97.	Agarpura
99.	Dhani Nayan
100.	Saunda Ki Dhani
101.	Bansipura
102.	Babrewalan Ki Dhani
103.	Jorpura Jobner
104.	Pratppura
105.	Manoharpura
106.	Saipura
107.	Singuri
108.	Moondwara
109.	Kori

(Table 1.4 Contd.)

Table 1.4 (Contd.)

Village Code	Village Name	Village Code	Village Name
110.	Shambhoopura	164.	Itawa
111.	Dyodhi	165.	Kanchroda
112.	Gedha Ka Bas	166.	Samalpura
113.	Aidan Ka Bas	167.	Haripura
114.	Charanwas	168.	Baghpura
115.	Turkyawas	169.	Matarda
116.	Bhojpura Kalan	170.	Mandpi
117.	Chirnotiya	171.	Shrirampura
118.	Murlipura	172.	Morooda
119.	Thakursi Ka Bas	173.	Midkya
120.	Doongri	174.	Panwa
121.	Hingoniya	175.	Shyama Ki Dhani
122.	Gudha Mansingh	176.	Kochya Ki Dhani
123.	Kudiyaon Ka Bas	177.	Gopalpura
124.	Sundariyabas	178.	Habaspura
125.	Jorpura	179.	Bhirawata
126.	Tibariya	180.	Ringi
127.	Bassi Naga	181.	Korseena
128.	Kuchyawas	182.	Dodwara
129.	Joshiwas	183.	Sarthala
130.	Khejrawas	184.	Chhapri
131.	Bhikhawas	185.	Govindpura
132.	Roopsi Ka Bas	186.	Jawli
133.	Sankhla Ka Bas	187.	Sitarampura
134.	Ramsinghpura	188.	Mordi Khurd
135.	Kalakh	189.	Shekhpura
136.	Bagron Ka Bas	190.	Nangal
137.	Haripura	191.	Kalyan
138.	Dakaniyawas	192.	Dobri
139.	Baminiyawas	193.	Singla
140.	Chak Budhji Ka Bas	194.	Hachookra
141.	Chandpura	195.	Sholawata
142.	Budhji Ka Bas	196.	Sirohi Khurd
143.	Gokulpura	197.	Kotheda
144.	Dhani Chandpura	198.	Naradpura
145.	Bassi Jhajhra	199.	Peethyawas
146.	Kheri Aloopha	200.	Chainpura
147.	Aidan Ka Bas	201.	Morsar
148.	Gurha Kumawatan	202.	Charanwas
149.	Rampura	203.	Ramnagar
150.	Sardarpura @ Dhakawala	204.	Bhawasa
152.	Bobas	205.	Kandeoli
153.	Kanwarpura	206.	Shardulpura
154.	Asalpur	207.	Shyosinghpura
155.	Badh Mathuradas	208.	Akoda
156.	Dhani Boraj	209.	Palbas
157.	Bhagwatpura	210.	Kheriram
158.	Majipura	211.	Samota Ka Bas
159.	Ursinghpura	212.	Rojri
160.	Malyawas	213.	Hirnoda
161.	Peepli Ka Bas	214.	Dhinda
162.	Norangpura	215.	Maheshwas
163.	Tejya Ka Bas		

(Table 1.4 Contd.)

Table 1.4 (Contd.)

Village Code	Village Name
Tehsil Dudu	
1.	Sirohi Kalan
2.	Gahlota
3.	Chhirr
4.	Sali
5.	Surree
6.	Panwa Kalan
7.	Marwa
8.	Adarwa
9.	Morda
10.	Mordi Kalan
11.	Mamana
12.	Neemli
13.	Dantra
14.	Jhakolar
15.	Anwaliya
16.	Beegolao
17.	Bokarawas
18.	Jarawata
19.	Peegoon
20.	Khajpura
21.	Deopura
22.	Hatoopura
23.	Sakhoon
24.	Shyopura
25.	Jaspura
26.	Nayagaon
27.	Ladera
28.	Patoori
29.	Dantri
30.	Kila
31.	Mahatgaon
32.	Benee Khera
33.	Rahlana
34.	Koriya Bujurg
35.	Gaiga
36.	Parasoli
37.	Gainji
38.	Udaipuriya
40.	Nanan
41.	Jekampura
42.	Malera
43.	Kachnar
44.	Sawarda
45.	Beejolao
46.	Dudu
47.	Jolya
48.	Bhojpur
49.	Shriramnagar
50.	Gopipura
51.	Charasada
52.	Chhapya
53.	Harsouli
54.	Gagardoo
55.	Laporiya
56.	Sanodiya
57.	Dhadhonli
58.	Itakhoi
59.	Gothra
60.	Nagri
61.	Kachnariya
62.	Kairiya Khurd
63.	Ursewa
64.	Kheri Charnan
65.	Norangpura
66.	Sunadiya
67.	Tan Chhaparwara
68.	Chhaparwara
69.	Khuriyal
70.	Bagait
71.	Gidani
72.	Chak Maheshpura
73.	Paloo Khurd
74.	Paloo Kalan
75.	Mokhampura
76.	Keriya
77.	Bichoon
78.	Jewlyan Ka Bas
79.	Basra
80.	Sorthan Ka Bas
81.	Bhairana
82.	Nayabas
83.	Gopalpura
84.	Ugariyawas
85.	Rampura@Bariyan
86.	Gurha Barsal
87.	Boraj
88.	Dewala
89.	Keshrisinghpura
91.	Chan Chukiya
92.	Mahlan
93.	Kalyansar
94.	Girdharipura
95.	Nasnota
96.	Jharna
97.	Kotjewar
98.	Kapriyawas Khurd
99.	Kapriyawas Kalan
100.	Shyosinghpura Basri
101.	Chak Nasnota
102.	Garoti
103.	Sitarampura
104.	Garota
105.	Karwo Ka Bas
106.	Khatwar
107.	Gangati Kalan

(Table 1.4 Contd.)

Table 1.4 (Contd.)

Village Code	Village Name
108.	Anantpura
109.	Akhepura
110.	Manpura
111.	Maheshpura
112.	Chandarmool
113.	Gurha Saipura
114.	Shtyosinghpura@Basra
115.	Mauzamabad
116.	Kakrala
117.	Barh Kakrala
118.	Baneshpura
119.	Mangal Wara
120.	Sewa
121.	Kalyanpura
122.	Roshanpura @ Baneriya
123.	Raseeli
124.	Reta
125.	Reti
126.	Fariyadpura
127.	Shrirampura
128.	Dogra
129.	Kheri Suwa
130.	Meeraura
131.	Dogri
132.	Dhamana
133.	Chak Meerapura
134.	Lordi
135.	Sawai Mansinghpura
136.	Sawai Madhosinghpura
137.	Biharipura
138.	Sanwali
139.	Dedoo
140.	Rampura Bhoortiya
141.	Chak Jhag
142.	Kishanpura
144	Gangati Khurd
145	Tan Jhag
146	Shriniwaspura
147	Jhag
Tehsil Phagi	
1.	Bookni
2.	Hingoniya
3.	Nandlalpura
4.	Sherpura
5.	Sawai Jaisinghura
6.	Chhardara
7.	Govindpura @ Basra
8.	Rata Khera
9.	Kansel
10.	Jagat Shriomanipura
11.	Sanwal
12.	Kunj Biharipura
13.	Rotwara
14.	Koonchyawas
15.	Bheempura
16.	Madanpura@Katariya Ka Bas
17.	Gulabpura
18.	Rampura Chokhawala
19.	Jabar
20.	Raithal
21.	Harbanshpura
22.	Keeratpura
23.	Amarpura
24.	Sawa Ka Bas
25.	Mandor
26.	Teekel Narukan
27.	Salarsoo
28.	Pinach
29.	Rewantpura
30.	Teelel Purohitan
31.	Awandiya
32.	Pachala
33.	Jhodinda Bhojpura
34.	Shankarpura
35.	Chainpura @ Bharatpura
36.	Chauru
37.	Chakwara
38.	Sultaniya
39.	Deonagar
40.	Ladana
41.	Rampura
42.	Balapura
43.	Nawalkishorpura
44.	Gohandi
45.	Chak Gulabpura
46.	Jankinathpura
47.	Heerapura
48.	Nihalpura @ Miyan Ki Barh
49.	Karwa
50.	Hari Rampura
51.	Beer Ramchandrapura
52.	Renwal Manji
53.	Daloowala
54.	Kishanpura
55.	Raipura
56.	Gopalnagar
57.	Khejra Ka Bas
58.	Harsooliya
59.	Mohanpura Prithvisingh
60.	Jaichand Ka Bas
61.	Thala
62.	Bhojpura
63.	Barh Bishanpura @ Kagya
64.	Phagi
65.	Lasariya
66.	Palri

(Table 1.4 Contd.)

Table 1.4 (Contd.)

Village Code	Village Name
67.	Nari Khera
68.	Nareda
69.	Chhapri
70.	Mandawari
71.	Ganeshpura Faujiyan
72.	Gulabpura @ Gopalpura
73.	Ghatiyali
74.	Mandawara
75.	Hachookara
76.	Dalniya
77.	Kudli
78.	Dhwaliya
79.	Kansya
80.	Mendwas
81.	Sirsya
82.	Maharajpura @ Nainasya
83.	Jaisinghpura@Gadoonda
84.	Nimera
85.	Shri Ramganj
86.	Jagannathpura
87.	Bimalpura
88.	Ramchandrapura
89.	Barh Ramchandrapura
90.	Kishorpura
91.	Mohanpura Rajastan
92.	Sameliya
93.	Mordi
94.	Barh Mordi
95.	Lakhawas
96.	Parwan
97.	Gokulpura
98.	Khadooj
99.	Dwarkanathpura @ Keriya
100	Madanpura
101	Kanwarpura
102	Ratanpura
103	Nathmalpura
104	Mandi
105	Rampura Railway
106	Mohanpura Ranwa
108	Jhadla
109	Kantoli
110	Mandaliya Joga
111	Khijooriya
112	Jharana Khurd
113	Jhonpariya
114	Jharana
115	Madhorajpura
116	Khera Hanumanji
117	Harsundarpura @ Hatheli
118	Pawasoo Khera
119	Ajnota
120	Dhunwaliya

Village Code	Village Name
121	Mandap
122	Chandama Khurd
123	Chandama Kalan
124	Unt Ka Khera
125	Beechi
126	Jugal Kishorpura
127	Bhankrota
128	Peepla
129	Veerampura
130	Chittora
131	Pratappura
132	Shrirajpura
133	Manpur Gate
134	Chandawas
135	Ganeshpura
136	Dabla Khurd
137	Dabla Bujurg
138	Basri Jogiyan
139	Mohabbatpura
140	Kundanpura
141	Pahariya
142	Narayanpura
143	Sitarampura
144	Shri Jaipalpura Goojronwa
145	Barhali
146	Bokrawas
147	Mustafabad @ Masta
148	Deomand
149	Dabich Maliyan
150	Dabich Goojaran
151	Fatehrampura
152	Dabich
153.	Shri Ramjipura
154.	Ramsinghura
155.	Gopalpura
156.	Dosra
157.	Dosra Khurd
158.	Prempura
159.	Sehdariya
160.	Muratpura
161.	Bhanpura
162.	Sangrampura
163.	Hanootiya
164.	Hanootiya Kalan
165.	Mukandpura
166.	Didwata
167.	Govindpura @ Mandaliya
168.	Nondpura
169.	Sarswatipura
Tehsil Sanganer	
1.	Sitapura
2.	Sanjariya
3.	Hardhyanpura

(Table 1.4 Contd.)

Table 1.4 (Contd.)

Village Code	Village Name	Village Code	Village Name
4.	Dahmi Khurd	57.	Jaishinghpura
5.	Dahmi Kalan	58.	Srirampurabas Bhankrota
6.	Ghegha	59.	Chimanpura
7.	Chimanpura	60.	Hasmpura Bas Bhankrota
8.	Bhosinghpura	61.	Sriramgopal Pura @ Bhojy
9.	Barha Waniya	62.	Keshopura
10.	Awaniya	63.	Bhankrota Kalan
11.	Kodar	64.	Asarpura
12.	Bagru Rawan	65.	Ganpatpura Chak No. 2
13.	Chhitroli	66.	Nandkishorpura @ Manyaw
14.	Shyosinghpura	67.	Mangyawas
15.	Rampura Unti	68.	Singhrpura
16.	Jhund	69.	Narottampura
17.	Anoppura	70.	Ramsinghpura @ Rampura
18.	Laxminarayanpura	71.	Ganpatpura
19.	Narwariya	72.	Ganpatpura Chak No. 1
20.	Bhankrota	73.	Golyawas
21.	Ramdattpura	74.	Ramsinghpura @ Dhaulai
22.	Hariharpura	75.	Balrampura @ Khejra Ka Bag
23.	Barh Hariharpura	76.	Kalyanpura
24.	Barh Ajairajpura	77.	Hajyawala
25.	Jagannathpura	78.	Barh Mohanpura
26.	Devisinghpura	79.	Sukhiya
27.	Sirani	80.	Mohanpura
28.	Suratpura	81.	Jagatshiromanipura
29.	Ajairajpura	82.	Chak No. 12
30.	Lahhawas	83.	Muhana
31.	Jaijaspura	84.	Neota
32.	Hasampura	85.	Hasampura Bas Neota
33.	Chirota	86.	Chak Basri
34.	Palri Parsa	87.	Shri Ramjipura
35.	Narsinghpura @ Dadiya	88.	Chak No. 7
36.	Kalwara	89.	Chak No. 6
37.	Bhambhoriya	90.	Sawai Jaisinghpura
38.	Bagru Khurd	91.	Prempura
39.	Teelawas	92.	Daulatpura
40.	Harchandpura	93.	Bhapura
41.	Rampurawas Deoliya	94.	Chatarpura
42.	Balmukundpura @ Nada	95.	Chak No. 1 2 3 4 5 14
43.	Prithvisinghpura @ Naiwal	96.	Chak Sherwali
44.	Nangal Barh Gujran	97.	Kishnpura @ Khatipura
45.	Thikariya	98.	Kapoorawala
46.	Sarangpura	99.	Kishorpura
47.	Ramchandpura	100.	Pawaliya
48.	Narsinghpura	101.	Jaisinghpura @ Roopwas
49.	Mahapura	102.	Manpura Teelawala
50.	Chatarpura @ Lalya Ka Bas	103.	Hargun Ki Nanagal @ Charam
51.	Jhani (Jhanyee)	104.	Balawala
52.	Khatwara	105.	Jaisinghpura @ Tejawala
53.	Peepla Bharatsingh	106.	Acharawala
54.	Mandau	107.	Aghaipura
55.	Chak Harbanshpura	108.	Mahasinghpura @ Keshyawa
56.	Harbanshpura	109.	Jagnathpura

(Table 1.4 Contd.)

Table 1.4 (Contd.)

Village Code	Village Name
110.	Madrampura
111.	Saipura
112.	Ratalya
113.	Shrirampura
114.	Lakhana
115.	Jatawala
116.	Bhater
117.	Sitarampura
118.	Manyoriyawala
119.	Kokawas
120.	Badanpura
121.	Purshottampura @ Dadiya
122.	Ganwar Jatan
123.	Watika
124.	Ramsinghpura
125.	Chak Watika Wali
126.	Chak Amjhar
127.	Dayalpura
128.	Manpura @ Bhatawala
129.	Surajpura
130.	Kheri Gokulpura
131.	Ganwar Brahman
132.	Baksawala
133.	Govindpura
134.	Shikarpura
135.	Jotrawala
136.	Ramsinghpura Bas Sangane
137.	Bambala
138.	Shyopur
139.	Dehlawas
140.	Nagariyawala
141.	Chak Getor
142.	Manoharpura
143.	Jagatpura
144.	Barh Teelawala
145.	Teelawala
146.	Mahal
147.	Ramnagariya
148.	Barh Karol
149.	Bhairoon Karol
150.	Shri Govindpura
151.	Udaipur Gilhariya
152.	Kho Rebariyan
153.	Bhaogarh Bandha
154.	Looniyawas
155.	Hirapura
156.	Khori
157.	Lakhesara
158.	Chak Mata Shoola
159.	Govindpura @ Rohpara
160.	Kalyanpura @ Khatipura
161.	Jaipura
162.	Chak Karol
163.	Jhujharpura @ Mendla
164.	Chainpura
165.	Barh Chela
166.	Narsinghpura @ Raksa
167.	Seesyawas
168.	Dantli
169.	Siroli
170.	Murlipura
171.	Shri Kishanpura
172.	Khosar
173.	Chatarawala
174.	Barh Shyopur
175.	Sukhdeopura @ Nohara
176.	Indrapuri
177.	Sitapura
178.	Mishra Ka Bas
179.	Laxmipura@Nataniwala
180.	Sukhdeopura @ Nataniwal
181.	Aswala
182.	Shyosinghpura@ Kallawal
183.	Sukhpura
184.	Jaisinghpura@Buhariya
185.	Shyampura Buhariya
186.	Sanwat Ka Bas
187.	Mohanpura
188.	Khetaura
189.	Laxmipura
190.	Barika Bas
191.	Shriram Ki Nangal
192.	Sawai Jaisinghpura @ Bas
193.	Rampura@Kanwarpura
194.	Ramchandpura
195.	Vidhani
196.	Jeerota
197	Sawai Jaisinghpura
198.	Vimalpura
199.	Saligrampura
200.	Goner
201.	Chak Saligrampura
202.	Jaichandpur
203.	Mathurawala
204.	Beelwa Kalan
205.	Manpur Nagalya
206.	Jairajpura
207.	Nangapura
208.	Prahladpura
Tehsil Jaipur	
1.	Manda Bhopawas
2.	Charanwas
3.	Lalpura
4.	Pachar
5.	Ramla Ka Bas
6.	Kalwar
7.	Gajadharpura

(Table 1.4 Contd.)

Table 1.4 (Contd.)

Village Code	Village Name
8.	Sanchoti
9.	Chak Barh
10.	Sarna Chaur
11.	Chak Toytawala
12.	Bhoodarpura
13.	Basri
14.	Chak Basri
15.	Chak Sarna Doongar
16.	Baori
17.	Sarna Doongar
18.	Goytawala
19.	Charan Nadi
20.	Nangal Jaisa Bohra
21.	Niwaroo
22.	Mansa Rampura
23.	Peethawas
24.	Lalchandpura
25.	Chak Baori
26.	Nari Ka Bas
27.	Manchwa
28.	Pindolai
29.	Sabrampura
30.	Champapura
31.	Dharampura
32.	Bhambori
33.	Sundariyawas
34.	Durjaniyawas
35.	Sarang Ka Bas
36.	Kanwar Ka Bas
37.	Kapariyawas
38.	Gurliya
39.	Baseri
40.	Shyosinghpura @ Shyopur
41.	Begas
42.	Chak Begas
43.	Ramsinghpura
44.	Achanchukya
45.	Mansinghpura
46.	Fatehpura
47.	Barh Fatehpura
48.	Himmatpura
49.	Sitapura @ Ramolai
50.	Jaisinghpura Kankroda
51.	Kishorpura @ Kankroda
52.	Laxmipura @ Chak Mauja
53.	Mundiya Purohitan
54.	Chak Ramsar
55.	Kanarpura @ Khanga-Ki Dhani
56.	Keshyawala
57.	Srirampura @ Tewariwala
58.	Dhankya
59	Nandgaon Barsana
60.	Mundiya Ramsar
61.	Sinwar

Village Code	Village Name
62.	Vijaypura
63.	Kishorpura
64.	Hathod
65.	Beer Hathod
66.	Govindpura
67.	Chak Peethawas @ Bararam
68.	Harnathpura
69.	Gokulpura
70.	Bishnawala
71.	Meenawala
72.	Sirsi
73.	Jaipuriyon Ka Bas
74.	Nansoosar
75.	Bindayaka
76.	Neemera
77.	Natlalpura
78.	Bichpari
79.	Jai Bhawanipura
80.	Govindpura @ Jaichandpur
81.	Mukandpura
82.	Maharajpura
83.	Srirampura
84.	Kanakpura
85.	Panchyawala
86.	Lalarpura
87.	Girdharipura
88.	Dhauwas
89.	Gajsinghpura
90.	Badarwas
91.	Heerapura
92.	Manpura Sarwa
93.	Kilangarh
94.	Jaisinghpura Khor
95.	Roopaki Nangal
96.	Malpura Doongar
97.	Beer Malpura @ Mukandpur
98.	Malpura Chaur
99.	Sumel
100.	Balloopura
101.	Vijaypura
102.	Bagrana
Tehsil Amber	
1.	Raithal
2.	Ballupura
3.	Chak Jaisinghpura
4.	Tadawas
5.	Pratappura Kalan
6.	Pratappura Khurd
7.	Khapariya
8.	Durga Ka Bas
9.	Mundiya
10.	Chak Mundiya
11.	Disan

(Table 1.4 Contd.)

Table 1.4 (Contd.)

Village Code	Village Name
12.	Sahab Rampura
13.	Kalyanpura
14.	Patti Sitarampura
15.	Anoppura
16.	Dola Ka Bas
17.	Khatiyon Ka Bas
18.	Pragpura
19.	Bheelpura
20.	Radhakishanpura @ Pokhar
21.	Harbanshpura @ Ramgatta
22.	Nara
23.	Biharipura
24.	Sirsali
25.	Gudha Surjan
26.	Mohanpura
27.	Mukandpura
28.	Raghunathpura
29.	Barna
30.	Jaisinghpura Shekhawatan
31.	Barsinghpura
32.	Vijaipura
33.	Punana
34.	Bishanpura
35.	Radhapura
36.	Sirsi
37.	Radhakishanpura
38.	Yadav Khera
39.	Nangal Ladi
40.	Bichpari
41.	Chandrapura Jatan
42.	Bugalya
43.	Sherawatpura
44.	Mundota
45.	Jiloi
46.	Maheshwas Khurd
47.	Maheshwas Kalan
48.	Jaitpura
49.	Chak Rojda
50.	Chak Jaitpura
51.	Naradpura
52.	Dadar Baoribas
53.	Bas Baori
54.	Sudarshanpura
55.	Yadav Khera
56.	Khannipura
57.	Shripura
58.	Lalpura
59.	Lalgarh
60.	Jalsoo
61.	Deogudha
62.	Mori
63.	Atalbiharipura
64.	Kanwarpura

Village Code	Village Name
65.	Barh Jahota
66.	Jahota
67.	Chimanpura
68.	Bhatton Ki Bali
69.	Dwarkapura
70.	Mukandpura
71.	Mohanbari
72.	Jairampura
73.	Govindpura
74.	Datawata
75.	Chatarpura
76.	Achhojai
77.	Harchandpura
78.	Rojda
79.	Singolai
80.	Sardarpura
81.	Dalpura
82.	Kishanpura
83.	Hardattpura
84.	Subhrampura
85.	Khora Beesal
86.	Benar With Daulatpura
87.	Nangal Siras
88.	Maheshpura Rawan
89.	Akeda Chod
90.	Rampura
91.	Tantyawas
92.	Dabri
93.	Doodthal
94.	Degrawas
95.	Risani
96.	Chak Degrawas
97.	Chonp
98.	Israwala
99.	Bilochi
100.	Shri Govindpura
101.	Kalighati
102.	Jaipura Kheenchee
103.	Sangawala
104.	Ladana
105.	Ghatwada
106.	Kiratpura
107.	Kant
108.	Pooth Ka Bas @ Chawa Ka
109.	Manpura Macheri
110.	Chitanu Kalan
111.	Sundarpura
112.	Lamya Mewal
113.	Sundar Ka Bas
114.	Beelpura
115.	Sirohi
116.	Roondal
117.	Nakawala
118.	Chak Manoharpur

(Table 1.4 Contd.)

Table 1.4 (Contd.)

Village Code	Village Name
119.	Deo Ka Harmara
120.	Lakher
121.	Bhuranpura @ Nestiwas
122.	Arniya
123.	Kanwarpura
124.	Harchandpura@Kankarwa
125.	Peelwa
126.	Salarwas
127.	Chandwaji
128.	Jaisinghnagar
129.	Rajpurwas Chandwaji
130.	Chandawas
131.	Kushalpura
132.	Jugalpura
133.	Shyampura
134.	Chak Jaisinghnagar
135.	Rampura@Baniyawala
136.	Syari
137.	Kalwad Kalan & Khurd
138.	Achrol
139.	Ani
140.	Dheengpur
141.	Labana
142.	Gunawata
143.	Chhaprari
144.	Seengwana
145.	Anadpur @ Pokharawala
146.	Chak Pokharawala
147.	Bheempura
148.	Bagwada
149.	Chokhlawas @ Kacherawal
150.	Harwar
151.	Dhand
152.	Rajpur Khanya
153.	Nangal Turkan
154.	Kankrel
155.	Chak Kothiya
156.	Khora Meena
157.	Kookas
158.	Kotra
159.	Daulatpura
160.	Kherwari
161.	Rampura
162.	Chirara
163.	Khora Shyamdas
164.	Badanpura
165.	Chetawala
166.	Chhanwar Ka Bas
167.	Rajarampura
168.	Mothoo Ka Bas
169.	Rajawas
170.	Neendar
171.	Machera
172.	Laxminarayanpura
173.	Jagnnathpura
174.	Udaipuriya
175.	Dweeppura
176.	Ramlyawala
177.	Chak Nangal
178.	Nangal Purohit
180.	Looniyawas
181.	Akhepura
182.	Akeda Doongar
183.	Jaisalya
184.	Maila Bag
185.	Seesiyawas
186.	Bishangarh
187.	Seapura
188.	Baragaon Jarkhya
189.	Nestiwas
190.	Beer Talera
191.	Khurad
192.	Chimanpura
193.	Amer Chak No. 2
194.	Nangal Soosawatan
195.	Amer Chak No. 1
196.	Kishanpura @ Lalwas
Tehsil Jamwa Ramgarh	
1.	Haripura Brahmanan
2.	Ratanpura Haripura
3.	Ratanpura Jatan
4.	Ghatwari Meena
5.	Ghatwari
6.	Bobari
7.	Bamanwas
8.	Brijpura
9.	Gokalyawala
10.	Glo
11.	Todalari
12.	Kela Ka Bas
13.	Chilpali
14.	Doonga Ka Bas
15.	Nekawala
16.	Ajabpura
17.	Bhojpura
18.	Noorpur
19.	Dhaler
20.	Charanwas
21.	Taopura
22.	Bhuranpura
23.	Jaichandpura
24.	Bara Dehra
25.	Ladipura
26.	Arjunpura
27.	Dhaula

(Table 1.4 Contd.)

Table 1.4 (Contd.)

Village Code	Village Name	Village Code	Village Name
28.	Dheerawas	81.	Pawta
29.	Jaisinghpura	82.	Kanikhor
30.	Bahlor	83.	Rasiyanwala
31.	Dhekla	84.	Beer Kanarwas
32.	Datala Gujran	85.	Kali Barkhari
33.	Tala	86.	Bassi
34.	Majipura	87.	Chak Dagota
35.	Rajpurwas Tala	88.	Dagota
36.	Chak Charanwas	89.	Sri Ramgopalpura
37.	Charanwas @ Kalipahari	90.	Neemla
38.	Bilod	91.	Heengawala
39.	Dantala Meena	92.	Kilatpuri
40.	Maliwas	93.	Singpuri
41.	Mathasoola	94.	Rayanwala
42.	Lunetha	95.	Sankotra
43.	Bhatt Ka Was	96.	Patalwas
44.	Jodhrala	97.	Chak Dantli
45.	Raisar	98.	Bhawani Khurd
46.	Devitala	99.	Bhawni
47.	Chainpura	100.	Khard
48.	Darolai	101.	Bamanwati
49.	Kushlpura	102.	Sri Ramjipura
50.	Manhagi	103.	Ghoret @Harrampura
51.	Kooda	104.	Bhiwawas
52.	Anatpura	105.	Anoppura
53.	Gopinathpura	106.	Ghati Ghanshyampura
54.	Gurha Harooka	107.	Vitthalpura
55.	Nangal Tejshingh	108.	Narpatyawas
56.	Rampurabas Samred	109.	Kolyana
57.	Samred Khurd	110.	Khemawas @ Chugalpura
58.	Chainpura Bas Dedwari	111.	Badiyawala
59.	Dedwari	112.	Indragarh
60.	Toda Meena	113.	Chainpurawas Saiwar
61.	Jindon Ki Dhani	114.	Saiwar
62.	Basna	115.	Rampura@Chawa Ki Nanga
63.	Goojron Ka Bas	116.	Ajabgarh@Hari Ka Bas
64.	Palleeton Ki Dhani	117.	Natata
65.	Chhapra	118.	Naradpura
66.	Bhanpur Kalan	119.	Peepalawali
67.	Teelampura	120.	Saipura
68.	Pali	121.	Chakkharchichainpurawas
69.	Bhattawala	122.	Kushalpura
70.	Bisori	123.	Chak Chainpura
71.	Nangal Tulsidas	124.	Chak Mala Ki Nangal
72.	Ghata Jaldhari	125.	Chak Indrabarh
73.	Nimbhi	126.	Heerawala
74.	Kelanwas	127.	Malawala
75.	Surethi	128.	Nayabas
76.	Bhaogarh	129.	Lalee
77.	Godiyana	130.	Neemriyan
78.	Samred Kalan	131.	Chaumukha
79.	Manhagor	132.	Jamwasramgarh
80.	Dantli	133.	Maid Rajsinghpura
		134.	Vishanpura

(Table 1.4 Contd.)

Table 1.4 (Contd.)

Village Code	Village Name	Village Code	Village Name
135.	Gopalgarh	189.	Nayla
136.	Jamwaghat	190.	Ramjipura
137.	Raipura	191.	Kanariyawala
138.	Bhagwanpura	192.	Dyoda Doongar
139.	Saipur	193.	Arwari
140.	Andhi	194.	Jhol
141.	Phootolao	195.	Sarjoli
142.	Rampurawas Thali	196.	Goth Ki Patti
143.	Jagatsar@Rigsya	197.	Palri Kalan
144.	Thali	198.	Kharkara
145.	Guwara	199.	Palri Khurd
146.	Srinagar	200.	Kharana
147.	Ramyawala	201.	Chak Palri
148.	Naghawala	202.	Khemawas
149.	Sekhawala	203.	Gudhawas Nevar
150.	Chatarpur	204.	Gaonli
151.	Dagarwara	205.	Birasana
152.	Ramjipura	206.	Koochawas
153.	Samor	207.	Shankarpura
154.	Ishwarishinghpura	208.	Chak Koochawas
155.	Bhonda Khera	209.	Nangal Bela
156.	Kanwarpura	210.	Sarpura
157.	Chak Kanwarpura	211.	Koliwara
158.	Gopalyawas	212.	Radha Govindpura
159.	Sriramnagar	213.	Barh Rasoolpura
160.	Toloopura	214.	Nangal Gogoriyan
161.	Thaulai	215.	Lalwas
162.	Asthal	216.	Bhanpur Khurd
163.	Barh Thaulai	217.	Sundarpura
164.	Jarunda	218.	Jaisinghpura
165.	Shivpura	219.	Barh Khemawas
166.	Khawa Raniji	220.	Khedawas Newar
167.	Sau	221.	Newar
168.	Sau Sareen	222.	Maksoodanpura
169.	Rampurawas Ramgarh	223.	Booj
170.	Dhaupura	224.	Manota
171.	Moondla	225.	Bhaopura
172.	Roopwas	226.	Deeppura
173.	Palera	227.	Chawandiya
174.	Balkrishnapura	228.	Khatehpura @ Fatehpura
175.	Chawand Ka Mand	229.	Barh Booj
176.	Daloo Ka Barh	230.	Jagmalpura
177.	Langareeyawas	231.	Dhoola Raoji
178.	Guwardi	232.	Heerapura
179.	Mathuradaspura	233.	Rampura Bas Chawandiya
180.	Barh Radhodaspura	234.	Daulatpura
181.	Dangarwara Khurd	235.	Dharmpura
182.	Chak Nondpura	236.	Dhamsya
183.	Raniyawas	237.	Chak Hurela
184.	Rahori	238.	Hurela
185.	Nondpura	239.	Dadiya Patti
186.	Papar	240.	Barh Dhamasya
187.	Harikishanpura	241.	Potli
188.	Meeno Ka Barh		

(Table 1.4 Contd.)

Table 1.4 (Contd.)

Village Code	Village Name
Tehsil Bassi	
1.	Dyorha Chor
2.	Ramratanpura
3.	Harchandpura@Balawala
4.	Vijai Mukandpura@Hirawa
5.	Hardhyanpura
6.	Barh Swami
7.	Geela Ki Nangal
8.	Kuthara Kalan
9.	Chak Ghati
10.	Sevapura
11.	Ghati Meena(Kho Ghati)
12.	Kuthara Khurd
13.	Ghata
14.	Hardi
15.	Dayarampura
16.	Kanota
17.	Hingoniya
18.	Bhatesari
19.	Boorhthal
20.	Kanarwas
21.	Raisinghpura
22.	Jeetawala
23.	Dudawala
24.	Ramsar Palawala
25.	Mansar Kheri
26.	Mangarh Khokhawala
27.	Bhaosar Isharwala
28.	Lasariya Goojaran
29.	Himmatpura
30.	Lasariya Gokulpura
31.	Girdharipura
32.	Shrirampura
33.	Sindoli
34.	Bala Ki Nangal
35.	Sankh
36.	Ralawata
37.	Vishansinghpura
38.	Rooppura
39.	Baseri
40.	Peepla Bai
41.	Barala
42.	Shri Hanumanpura
43.	Khijooriya Brahman
44.	Keshopura
45.	Sambhariya
46.	Shri Jagdishpura
47.	Abhaypura
48.	Rampura
49.	Achalpura
50.	Gangarampura
51.	Khijooriya Ahiran
52.	Khijooriya Jatan
53.	Gurha Phalyawas
54.	Maharajpura
55.	Shyampura Kacholiya
56.	Rajpura
57.	Phalyawas
58.	Ratanpura
59.	Devapura
60.	Trilokpura
61.	Harirampura
62.	Beelwa Khurd
63.	Bainara
64.	Philasan Biharipura
65.	Bhonyawala
66.	Shyampura
67.	Chainpura
68.	Chak Shyampura
69.	Barh Charanwas
70.	Jhar
71.	Doodli
72.	Sujanpura
73..	Mohanpura
75.	Kalyanpura
76.	Rampurawas Doodli
77.	Chorwara
78.	Toda Bhata
79.	Birajpura
80.	Damodarpura
81.	Bhankri
82.	Akhaipura
83.	Bhajoopura
84.	Chak Bhajoopura
85.	Barh Bhajoopura
86.	Manoharpura
87.	Kishanpura
88.	Nayagaon
89.	Chak Shyampura @Dhedpur
90.	Dhindhol
91.	Shyampura@Dhedpura
92.	Peeliya
93.	Palawal Jatan
94.	Chatarpura
95.	Khijooriya Tiwariyan
96.	Barh Mahadeopura
97.	Sawai Jaisinghpura
98.	Brahmpuri
99.	Jheejha
100.	Khera Malookpura
101.	Moondli
102.	Shankarpura
103.	Kashipura
104.	Chattarpura
105.	Bardh Ramrakhpura
106.	Nangal Karna
107.	Rampurawas@Deogaon

(Table 1.4 Contd.)

Table 1.4 (Contd.)

Village Code	Village Name	Village Code	Village Name
108.	Ramrakhpura	162.	Madanpura
109.	Chainpura	163.	Garholi
110.	Ghasipura	164.	Peelarama
111.	Danau Khurd	165.	Kaneti
112.	Danau Kalan	166.	Bhateri
113.	Bimalpura	167.	Kanpura
114.	Deogaon	168.	Prempura
115.	Khatiprua	169.	Ramjipura
116.	Ramsinghpura	170.	Patan
117.	Rooppura	171.	Ugawas
118.	Morandi	172.	Shrinagar
119.	Shri Ramnagar	173.	Dheegar Ka Bas
120.	Kundanpura	174.	Tekchandpura
121.	Chak Naradpura	175.	Charangarh
122.	Naradpura	176.	Rajura Patalwas
123.	Toongi	177.	Kho Rajyawala
124.	Nagarjpura	178.	Rampura@Chandaliya
125.	Kanwarpura	179.	Lalpura
126.	Karanghrh	180.	Tilpatti
127.	Chandpura	181.	Lalawala
128.	Chapriya	182.	Chak Rojwari
129.	Garh	183.	Bhoorla
130.	Lalgarh	184..	Rojwari
131.	Hathipura	185.	Baori Ka Bas
132.	Kishanpura	187.	Dholi
133.	Gurha Meena	188.	Prithvipura
134.	Charanwas	189.	Ramsar
135.	Naika Mahadeo	190.	Chak Madhogarh
136.	Chitori	191.	Rajwas
137.	Baskho	192.	Madhogarh
138.	Nimora	193.	Ratanpura
139.	Malihala	194.	Biharipura
140.	Khori	195.	Gwalini
141.	Gothra	196.	Gumanpura
142.	Jatwara	197.	Doobli
143.	Chak Potli	198.	Kelawala
144.	Dopur	199.	Chak Toonga
145.	Jhajhwar	200.	Toonga
146.	Kaneta	201.	Bhudrpura
147.	Apreta	202.	Ballupura
148.	Kishanpura	203.	Lalpura
149.	Parasoli	204.	Akhaipura
150.	Borai	205.	Siya Ka Was
151.	Peipura	206.	Himmatpura
152.	Nangal Bohra	207.	Anatpura
153.	Barwa	208.	Madhowala
154.	Tahatra	209.	Akhaipura
155.	Meethawas	210.	Sawal Yawala
156.	Laxmipura	211.	Chak Lawan
157.	Chak Dayalpura	212.	Jairam Ka Bas
158.	Barh Babupura	213.	Chak Deori
159.	Dayalpura	214.	Tiddiwala
160.	Kherlawas Jatwara		
161.	Hansmahal		

(Table 1.4 Contd.)

(Table 1.4 Contd.)

Village Code	Village Name
Tehsil Chaksu	
1.	Chak Laxmipura No. 1
2.	Chak Laxmipura No. 2
3.	Raniwala
4.	Shri Jaianand
5.	Najipura
6.	Narya Ka Bas
7.	Chak Chandlai No1
8.	Malwa
9.	Chak Chandali No. 2
10.	Chandlai
11.	Kilkipura
12.	Shivdaspura
13.	Barh Ramzanipura
14.	Khera Jagannathpura
15.	Gordhanpura
16.	Rampura Bas Goner
17.	Chak Shivdaspura No. 1
18.	Pachoora
19.	Bara Maksoodanpura
20.	Bhawanipura @Chatarbhu
21.	Santoshpura
22.	Chak Shivdaspura No.2
23.	Deokinandanpura
24.	Madhosinghpura
25.	Peeplai Ka Barh
26.	Dharmpura
27.	Bhadrwa @ Shri Kishanpur
30.	Bagariya
31.	Achalpura
32.	Sitapura
33.	Narpathipura @ Haripura
34.	Chak Thooni
35.	Ramkishanpura @ Thooni
36.	Harikishanpura @ Barh Bal
37.	Brijrajpura
38.	Bodya Ka Barh
39.	Bhagwatpura
40.	Barh Chandpura
41.	Ramanipura
42.	Chak Chandpura
43.	Roopaheri Kalan
44.	God Ka Bas
45.	Harinarayanpura
46.	Madhopura
47.	Hingoti
48.	Mahadeopura
49.	Koonpa Ka Bas
50.	Tajkhan Ka Bas
51.	Damodar Ka Bas
52.	Mandawari
53.	Mandawarishri Kishanpura No. 2
54.	Shri Kishanpura No. 1
55.	Shri Kishanpura With Chak
56.	Balrampura With Chak Bal
57.	Chak Balrampura No. 2
58.	Chak Tajkhan Ka Bas
59.	Indrapuri
60.	Kot Khawada
61.	Jagrampura
62.	Radoli
63.	Bhagwatsar Ka Sariya
64.	Sawai Jaisinghpura
65.	Barh Moondaheri
66.	Moondaheri
67.	Ugariyawas
68.	Bilaspura
69.	Roopaheri Khurd With Bap
70.	Maharampura
71.	Firozpura@Bibi Ka Barh
72.	Chhadel Khurd
73.	Chhadel Kalan
74.	Ramlaxmanpura @ Thooni
75.	Beer Pinarpura
76.	Ganeshpura
77.	Barh Mahawa Tan
78.	Bhagwanpura
79.	Nimodiya
80.	Akodiya
81.	Kajalpura
82.	Bhawanipura @ Chaturbhu
83.	Nangal Poorna
84.	Rampura Khurd
85.	Jailalpura @ Thooni
86.	Barkhera
87.	Yarlipura @ Sadashivpura
88.	Kathwala @ Laxmipura
89.	Gopirampura
90.	Salagrampura
91.	Dahar
92.	Roopniwas @ Thooni
93.	Hukkan
94.	Sirojya
95.	Shri Lixmipura
96.	Dayapura
97.	Lakhawas
98.	Dadanpura
99.	Jhujharpura
100.	Biharpura (Rural)
101.	Janki Ballabhpura
102.	Beer Suratrampura
103.	Manpur Doongri
104.	Rampura Bujurg
105.	Kalyanpura
106.	Kareda Khurd
107.	Dragpalpura

(Table 1.4 Contd.)

Table 1.4 (Contd.)

Village Code	Village Name
108.	Azamnagar
109.	Chosla
110.	Naharpura
111.	Udaipura
112.	Aleewas @ Urushottampl
113.	Chak Shrikishanpura
114.	Bhojya Dand
115.	Brijnathpura
116.	Prahladpura @ Damakpura
117.	Jachandpura
118.	Seemlawas Watka
119.	Chak Watka
120.	Fatehpura
121.	Kumhariyawas
122.	Bajdoli
123.	Sawai Jaisinghpura
124.	Gogyawas @ Sitarampura
125.	Vinodilalpura
126.	Bhojyara
127.	Surajpura @ Tootoli
128.	Shri Daulatpura
129.	Teetriya
130.	Shri Kishanpura
131.	Deo Kishanpura
132.	Sadarampura
133.	Chak Murarpura
134.	Murarpura
135.	Bhumarkya
136.	Mansar
137.	Kadera
138.	Ankeshpura
139.	Kiratpura
140.	Shri Jaideopura
141.	Khejri Bujurg
142.	Kriparampura
143.	Bhandipura @ Narayanpura
144.	Shri Vallabhpura
145.	Hari Valabhpura
146.	Tamariya
147.	Roopbas
148.	Jaipura
149.	Sewapura
150.	Thali
151.	Hanarajpura
152.	Barh Bagpura
153.	Meerapura
154.	Rasoolpura
155.	Dosari
156.	Shri Ganeshpura
157.	Dalpatpura
158.	Manpura
159.	Deogaon
160.	Anandrampura
161.	Shri Shaipura
162.	Hingoniya
163.	Toomli Ka Bas @ Jagar Shiri
164.	Khera Mukandpura
165.	Ladana Khurd
166.	Sawai Madhosinghpura
167.	Lasariya
168.	Aheeran Thooni @ Shri Niw
169.	Chonp
170.	Shrinagar
171.	Moondiya Khurd
172.	Garhi Ramnagar
173.	Shyami Ka Bas
174.	Barli
175.	Nainwa
176.	Kothoon
177.	Brijrajpura
178.	Mahachandpura
179.	Rampura Bujurg
180.	Jaisinghpura
181.	Tigriya
182.	Girdharilapura
183.	Bhoortiya Kalan
184.	Kishanpura
185.	Deeppura
186.	Sanwaliya
187.	Mahadeopura
188.	Deokinandanpura
189.	Kankata @ Raghunandanpura
190.	Shri Chanadpura
191.	Malpuraiya
192.	Ajmeripura
193.	Govindpura
194.	Anandpura
195.	Jaharipura @ Basra
196.	Bheekarwal
197.	Badrinathpura
198.	Mandoliya Meda
199.	Sanpla
200.	Tajpura
201.	Shakkar Khawada
202.	Ashikpura @ Choriya
203.	Mohammadpura
204.	Nainwa Ki Dhani
205.	Nandgaon Basri
206.	Raghopura
207.	Ramniwas
208.	Roopwas @Bridawanpura
209.	Barodiya
210.	Nandlalpura
211.	Kohlya
212.	Maheshpura
213.	Laxmipra
214.	Khera Jagannathpura
215.	Barh Marlipura

(Table 1.4 Contd.)

(Table 1.4 Contd.)

Village Code	Village Name	Village Code	Village Name
216.	Rajpura	248.	Hirapura
217.	Garoodwasi	249.	Madanmohanopura@Thoon
218.	Yadgarpura	250.	Vimalpura
219.	Barh Yadgarpura	251.	Garh Ka Para
220.	Ralawata	252.	Jhapda Kalan
221.	Nangal Lar	253.	Barh Babanpura
222.	Prithvipura	254.	Barh Fatehpura
223.	Maharajpura Vyasan	255.	Keshopura
224.	Jaitpura @ Kushalpura	256.	Barh Keshopura
225.	Narsinghpura	257.	Ajairajpura@Dehlawala
226.	Grhi Lasshkari	258.	Balmuknadpura
227.	Kanwarpura	259.	Theekariya Goojran
228.	Nenoopura	260.	Babanpura
229.	Shyampura With Barh Shyam	261.	Chak Babanpura
230.	Nasrottampura	262.	Bishanpura
231.	Cheemapuras With Jamin Che	263.	Kankariya
232.	Kushalpurza	264.	Bhidkyawas
233.	Khera Raniwas	265.	Nandkishorpura
234.	Ramchandrapura	266.	Dharampuri
235.	Kagdospura	267.	Chak Sampatpura
236.	Barh Maharajpura	268.	Shri Sampatpura
237.	Maharajpura	269.	Theekariya Meenan
238.	Cham Vinodilalpura No.2	270.	Chak Barh Babanpura
239.	Cham Vinodilalpura No.1	271.	Trilokinathpura
240.	Orangpura	272.	Shri Raghunathpura
241.	Rughanathpura@God Ka	273.	Barh Parmanandpura
242.	Maharajpura	274.	Barh Chauhan
243.	Dobla Kalan	275.	Khejri Khurd
244.	Vinodilalpura	276.	Dwarkapura
245.	Ramnagar Garhi	277.	Shripura
246.	Roopnagar	278.	Goojarhera
247.	Tallukpur Doongri	279.	Parmanandpura@Mandali

REFERENCES

Agarwal, R.K. and Lahiri, A.N. (1981). Evaluation of Soil Fertility Status of Stabilized and Unstabilized Sand Dunes. *Agrochemica* 25:54-60.

Ahmad, E. (1970). *Soil Erosion in India*, Asia Publishing House, New Delhi.

Anonymous, (1986). Prime Minister's Speech at the First Meeting of The National Land Use and Wasteland Development. *Hindustan Times*, Feb.,7.

Bali, J.S. (197). *Ravine Reclamation Needs for India*, New Delhi.

Bharadwaj, B.K. (1979). Distribution and Changing Pattern of Culturable Waste in Gurgaon District, Haryana, *Geog. Rev. of India*, Vol. XXXIII N.2, pp. 120-132.

Bhumbla, D.R. and Arvind Kumar (1984). *Estimate of Wastelands in India; Society for Promotion of Wastelands Development*, New Delhi.

Costin, E.; Babidi, A.S.; Mohammed, E. and Bazara, M. (1974). *Sand Dune Fixation and Afforestation in Semi Desert Countries of the Middle East.* Rep FAO/ Danida Inter Regional Training Centre of Health, Land and Sand Dune Afforestation, pp. 66-78.

Deb Roy, R. and Patil, B.D. (1978). Economic Utilization of Wasteland Through Silvipasture System of Farming, *Proceeding Symposium*, Environment, Adoptation and Distribution, Oct. 25-26, NEHU, Shillong.

Dikshit, K.D. (1969). The Morphological Features of the Khar Lands (Saline Waste) of Gujarat. *Ind. Hr. Geog.*, Jodhpur, IV-VI,2 pp. 21-28.

Doi, R.D. (2005). Interpretation of Ravine Land in Sub-Watersheds of the Morel River, Rajasthan (Ed.) *Geomorphology and Environmental Sustainability.* Concept Publishing Company, New Delhi.

Gupta, J.P. (1976). Studies on Sand Dunes. *In Ann. Prog. rep.*, CAZRI, Jodhpur, pp. 240.

Gupta, J.P. (1986). Moisture and Thermal Regimes of the Desert Oils of Rajasthan, Indian and their Management for Higher Plant Production. *Hydrol Sci.*, J. 31:347-59.

Gupta, N.L. and Maroo, R.L., (1991). *Challenge of Wastelands Utilization Issues and Themes*, Academic Publishers, Jaipur.

Jain, Anita (1982). Wasteland Utilisation in Udaipur District, Unpublished Ph.D. Thesis, M.L.Sukhadia University, Udaipur.

Kalwar, S.C. (1995). "Rajasthan Men Parti Bhumi" *Rajasthan Patrika*, Jaipur 30th July, p. 3.

Kalwar, S.C. (1999). "Wastelands in Rajasthan" (Ed.) *Arid Ecology : Resources, Hazards and Rural Development Policies*, Pointer Publication, Jaipur, Vol. II, pp. 253-271.

Kalwar, S.C. (1996). *"Prayavaran Avam Parti Bhumi"*, Pointer Publishers, Jaipur.

Kalwar, S.C. (1998) Identification and Developments of Wastelands in Semi-Arid Areas of Rajasthan. Unpublished Minor Research Project Report, ICSSR, New Delhi.

Kaul, R.N. (1985). *Afforestation of Dune Areas in Sand Dune Stabilization, Shelterbelts and Afforestation in Dry Zones*, FAO, Rome, pp. 75-85.

Ministry of Environment & Forests, Government of India - National Wasteland Development Board (1985). Guidelines for Action.

Ministry of Environment & Forests, Government of India - National Wasteland Development Board - National Land Use and Wastelands Development Council, First Meeting 6.2.1986, New Delhi - Discussion Papers, Minutes and Decisions.

Ministry of Environment & Forests, Government of India - National Wasteland Development Board - Challenge and Response, New Delhi, pp. 1-8.

Ministry of Food and Agriculture, Government of India (1961). Wasteland Survey and Reclamation Committee Report on the Locational and Utilisation of Wastelands in India, Part X, Uttar Pradesh, New Delhi.

Padmini Pani *et al.* (2001). Delineation and Monitoring of Gullied and Ravinous Lands in a Part of Lower Chambal Valley, India, Using Remote Sensing and GIS, paper presented at the 22nd Asian Conference on Remote Sensing 5-9 November, 2001, Singapore.

Planning Commission, Committee on Natural Resources, (1963), Study on Wastelands including Saline, Alkali and Waterlogged Lands and their Reclamation Measures, New Delhi.

Planning Commission, New Delhi (1965). Study of Survey and Reclamation of Ravines in India.

Rachana (2002). Identification and Utilisation of Wasteland for Sustainable Development - A Case Study of Jhunjhunu district, Unpublished Ph.D. Thesis, University of Rajasthan, Jaipur.

Raheja, R.C. *et al.* (1962). *"Study of Suitable Trees, Grasses and Crops for Saline and Alkali Land"*. Prepared by the Working Group on Wasteland including Saline - Alkali and Waterlogged Lands, Government of India.

Shafi, M. (1968). The Problems of Wastelands in India. *The Geographer*, Vol. XV, No. XXI (Special).

Sen, A.K., (1972) Land Utilization Mapping to Estimate the Wastelands of Arid Zone in Rajasthan by Photo Interpretation Techniques, *Bulletin N.44, Ind. Nat. Sci., Aca.*, pp. 67-71

Sen, A.K., (1989) 'Typology and Mapping Procedures of Wastelands in the Indian Arid Zone' in Yadav H.R. (Ed.) *Dimensions of Wasteland Development*, Concept Publishing Company, New Delhi.

Singh, A.L., (1985). *The Problem of Wastelands in India*, B.R.Pub., New Delhi.

Singh, Gurmel and Bali, Y.P. (1972). Survey and Categorization of Wastelands for their Reclamation and Use in India. In *Proc. Symp. Reclamation and Use of Wastelands in India*, New Delhi.

Yadav, H.R., 1986. *Genesis and Utilisation of Wastelands*, Concept, New Delhi.

2

PHYSICAL AND CULTURAL ENVIRONS

Relief

Interrelationship between relief and wastelands can be observed in any part of the earth e.g. hilly tracts have problem of degraded forest, barren rocky/hills, gullied and/ or ravinous land while peneplained land is affected by salinity. National Atlas and Thematic Mapping Organization (NATMO), Department of Science and Technology, Govt. of India, Kolkata (WB) divided the relief of the district into four categories taking intervals of 150 metres. Approximately three-fourth area of the district belongs to 300 to 400 metre elevation from MSL. In northern part, height is increasing from the central part to northeastern part of the study area whereas in the southern part the height is decreasing continuously.

On the basis of quarter inch topographical sheets, the district can be divided into seven physical divisions i.e. more detailed in comparison to relief map prepared by the NATMO. Fig. 2.1A shows that contour of 388 metre (1250') divides the district into low-land and upland. The southern part is lowland while the norhern part is upland. This district further can be divided into following physical sub-divisions.

UPLAND

As mentioned in preceding paragraph the upland is situated in the northern part of the study area where the height varies from 380 to > 681 metres above MSL. The western and eastern central part of the upland is alomost level having scattered isolated high altitude hills. Besides this, there are high altitude ranges along the eastern and north western boundry of the upland (Fig. 2.1). This upland further can be divided into three physical sub-divisions.

(Chomu) Western Amber and Northern Phulera Upland

This upland lies in the western part especially in Chomu, western Amber and northern Phulera tehsils (Fig. 2.1A). This area has aeolian sandy loam soil with good quality and quantity of groundwater resources. Most of the area of this physical division belongs to sand-desertic land. At some places sand dunes can be observed. This area supplies most of the vegetables, milk and milk cakes to the Jaipur city.

Shahapura - Eastern Amber and Viratnagar Hilly Tract

This hilly tract is scattered in two patches i.e. central and eastern part of the upland especially in Shahapura, eastern Amber and Viratnagar tehsils. This tract is separated by a narrow upland belt. There are numerous parallel hill ranges scattered in south to north direction in this hilly tract.

High Altitude Hill Ranges

Fig. 2.1A shows that high altitude hill ranges are scattered mainly in western Jamwa Ramgarh tehsil, eastern Viratnagar tehsil, along western boundry of Kotputli tehsil and eastern Amber tehsil. The narrow and long hill ranges are scattered from south to north in the western Jamwa Ramgarh tehsil and have became wide in the Viratnagar tehsil. All these hills are covered with dense/degraded forest and also have problem of gullied/ravinous and barren hills/rocky wasteland. Another belt of high altitude ranges is extended along the western boundary of Kotputli tehsil. These hills are almost barren due to more biotic interferences. The hills of central part i.e. Amber hills are covered with dense/ degraded forest. Almost all the highest peaks of the study area are also concentrated in the central part of the upland. (2.1A)

LOWLAND

The southern lowland is in the south of 380 metre contour in Dudu, southern Phulera, Sanganer, Jaipur, northern Phagi, Bassi and eastern Jamwa Ramgarh tehsils. This area is almost peneplained with a few isolated hills in eastern part. This lowland has its lowest area in the south eastern part of the study area. A patch of lowland is also found in the north east of the district. This lowland can be divided into four sub-divisions.

Sambhar Salt Lake Area

This area lies in the western part of the study area (Fig. 2.1A). The bottom of Sambhar lake is flat saucer like and having an altitude of 360 m above MSL and the peripheries are 364 m above MSL. The normal depth of lake in mansoon season ranging between 1.0 to 3 metres, The deepest point is near Mata Pahari. Sambhar inland salt source trending almost east-west and having a semi circular shape covers an area of 234 km^2 and is an elongated fault valley graben within the pre-cambrians. The Sambhar lake is fed by seasonal streams like Mendha, Rupangarh, Khandel, Khari Ka Nala, Bandi Ka nala, etc. Physiographically the basin is situated in a saddle formed by central Aravalli.

Dudu, Western Phulera, Sanganer, North Phagi, Bassi and Eastern Jamwa Ramgarh Plain

Fig. 2.1A shows that this lowland covers almost southern tehsils of the district particularly Dudu, western Phulera, Sanganer, Jaipur, northern Phagi, Bassi and eastern Jamwa Ramgarh tehsils. This long and narrow plain has scattered six hills in its eastern part. This area is

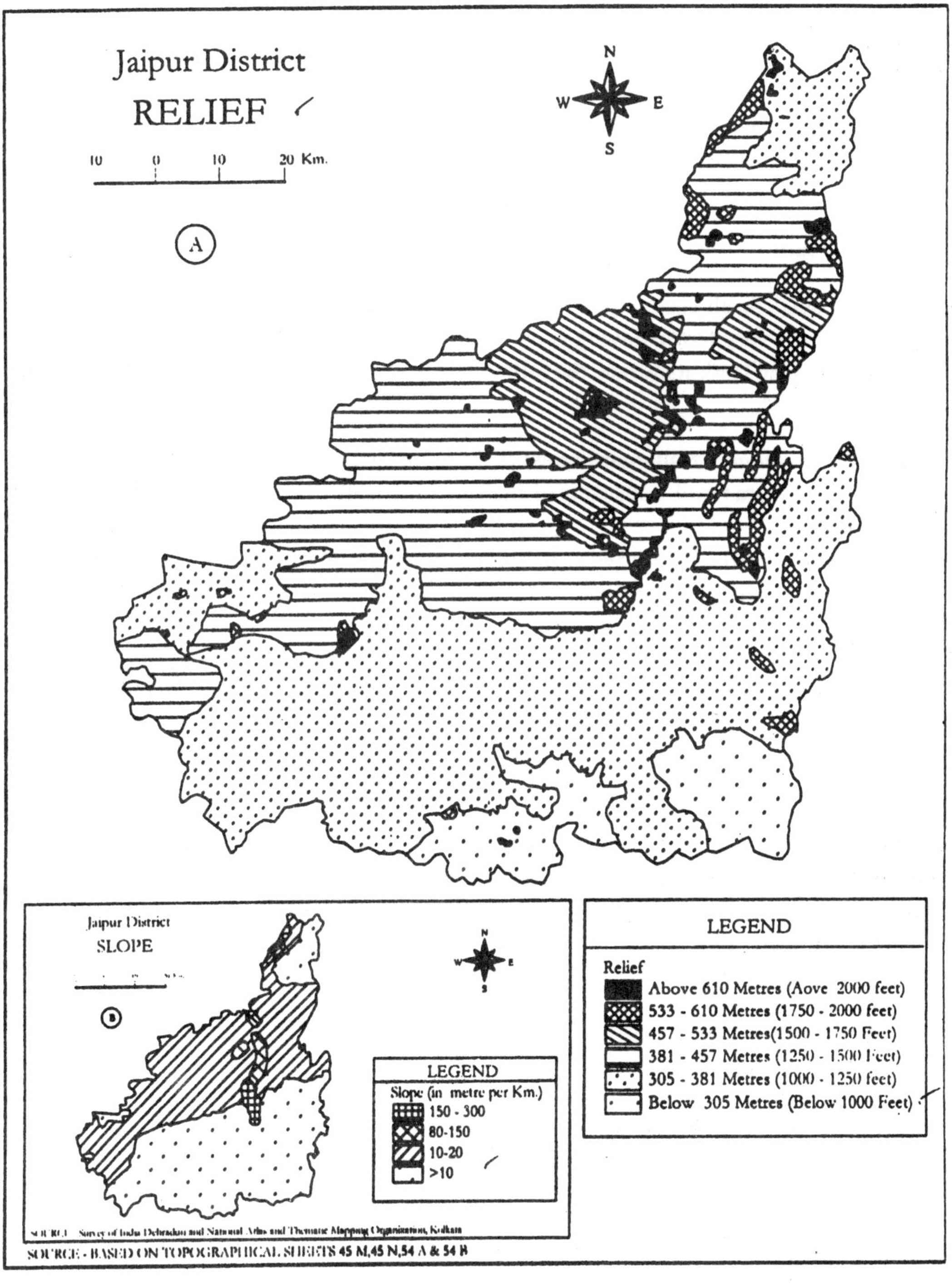

Fig. 2.1A : Relief
Fig. 2.1B : Slope

almost level with poor pedological and hydrological conditions. Therefore this area has problem of salinity/alkalinity.

Phagi–Chaksu Plain

This area is the lowest lowland of the study area having height below 305 metres (Fig 2.1A). In these tehsils, the land is almost level having problem of salinity/alkalinity and degraded pasture/grazing land due to poor pedological, poor quality of ground water resources.

Sota–Sabi Plain

This plain covers north-eastern part of Kotputli tehsil. Due to basin of Sota Nala and Sabi river, this area is very fertile having good quality ground water resources.

On the basis of landsat mosaic, the following hill systems are found in the district. (Saini and Kalwar 1991)

(i) *Puranghat :* Nahargarh range is from Jhalana (near Jaipur city) to Amarsar in Shahapura tehsil, consisting of Jhalana, Ambagarh, Samod, Nahargarh and Bandol hills.

(ii) *Bishangarh :* Baneti range is from Manoharpur in Shahapura tehsil to Baneti in Kotputli tehsil consisting Kairli, Antela, Baneti, Devipura, Balupura and Chatarpur hills.

(iii) *Banera :* Talu range is from Banera in Bassi tehsil to Talu in Viratnagar tehsil consisting Pachhodala, Khan Raipur, Khan Bhankhri, Khan Rahori, Dagota, Bamanwati and Mahnot hills.

SLOPE

The slope plays an important role in formation and reclamation of wastelands. In moderate to steep slope areas, gullied and/or ravinous land is common while in the areas of insignificant slope, waterlogging and salinity/alkalinity problems are dominant.

Survey of India and NATMO divide Jaipur district into four categories on the basis of per kilometre slope in metres.

< 10 metres per kilometre
10-20 metres per kilometre
80-150 metres per kilometre
150-300 metres per kilometre

In the southern part approximately more than half of the district has > 10 metre slope per kilometre especially in Dudu, Phagi, Chaksu, Sanganer, Bassi tehsils, southern Jaipur and southeastern part of Jamwa Ramgarh tehsil. (Fig. 2.1B) These tehsils have problems of salinity/alkalinity, land with scrub or without scrub and degraded pasture/grazing land.

The slope also plays a significant role in the planning of hill area development. Hill Area Development Programme (HADP) was initiated by the Central Government during the Fifth Five-Year Plan (1974-78). In Rajasthan Remote Sensing Division of B.M. Birla Science and Technology Centre, Jaipur highlighted the need of HADP and has delineated the slopes in the Aravalli hills using Henry and Raisz method.

The details of relative relief were finally transferred on district and development block maps to show the hill areas of various types. The hilly areas were categorized into five categories, viz. (i) Hill blocks, (ii) Mini hill tract, (iii) Compact mini hill tract, (iv) Small hill enclaves and (v) Other hill areas.

Hill Block

A development block with 40 per cent of its area with an average slope of 30 per cent or more may be treated as a hill block. Hill block is not found in the district.

Mini Hill Tract

A geographical compact area of 100 sq. km. or more with an average slope of 30 per cent or more may be designated as mini hill tract for the purpose of hill development programme.

Mini hill tracts are scattered over Puranaghat-Nahargarh hill ranges and Banera-Talu hill range in the centre of the district while Bishangarh-Baneti hill range is the northern part of the district.

Table 2.1 gives an idea of the block wise mini hill tract areas in the district.

Table 2.1: Mini Hill Tract in Jaipur District

Sl. No.	Block	Area of Block in sq. km	Hill Area in sq. km. having 30 per cent of more slope	Percentage to Total Area of Block
1.	Jamwa Ramgarh	1029.79	92.21	8.97
2.	Amber	882.64	83.17	9.42
3.	Jhotwara	387.56	7.60	1.96
4.	Kotputli	589.70	58.97	9.77
5.	Viratnagar	674.10	80.83	11.9
	Total	3563.79	322.78	9.06

Source: B.M. Birla, Science and Technology Centre, Jaipur.

Compact Mini Hill Tract

All compact regions have a geographical area of 100 sq. km or more within a block or located in more than one administrative unit may be designated as compact mini hill tract. This type of hill tract is also not found in the study area.

Small Hill Enclave

All compact hill area, having 30 per cent or more slopes with less than 100 sq. km is designated as small hill enclave. This type of slope area is found in small parts of Viratnagar and Shahapura blocks. This category covers 13.18 sq. km area in the district (Table 2.2).

Table 2.2: Small Hill Enclave in Jaipur District

Sl. No.	Block	Area of Block in sq. km	Hill Area in sq. km. having 30 per cent of more slopes with less than 100 km^2 area	Percentage to Total Area of Block
1.	Viratnagar	674.10	1.58	0.25
2.	Sahapura	406.69	11.60	2.85
	Total	1080.79	13.18	3.10

Source: B.M. Birla, Science and Technology Centre, Jaipur.

Other Hill Area

Having less than 30 per cent slope, such areas are ecologically fragile and become target of rackless deforestation. This type of areas require steps for raising resource base in the form of fuel wood plantation, pasture development, silivi pastoral plantation and sand dune stablisation etc.

This type of slope area is extended at all over the foot hills of all the three hill ranges in the district. Total 1001.64 sq. km area in under this category.

Table 2.3 : Other Hill Area in Jaipur District

Sl. No.	Block	Area of Block in sq. km	Hill Area in sq. km. having 30 per cent of more slope	Percentage to Total Area of Block
1.	Bassi	630.21	50.50	9.23
2.	Jamwa Ramgarh	1027.70	297.45	28.94
3.	Viratnagar	674.14	230.75	34.23
4.	Shahapura	406.69	78.70	19.35
5.	Kotputli	589.71	63.61	10.79
6.	Amber	882.64	224.54	25.43
7.	Jhotwara	387.56	32.52	8.41
8.	Dudu	1857.34	23.57	1.26
	Total	6455.99	1001.64	15.51

Source : B.M. Birla, Science and Technology Centre, Jaipur.

GEOLOGY

Mining activities are concentrated in the areas of old rocks which affect the environment, ecology and large areas have been converted into barren hills, degraded forest and mining/industrial wastelands. Similarly geologically recent to sub recent formations such as blown sand and alluvium have problems of wind and water erosion. In the area of wind erosion sand desertic wasteland is common while water erosion/accumulation has created problems of sheet, gully erosion, salinity and waterlogging. Thus geology and wasteland is interrelated.

A large part of the district is covered by a thick mantle of soil, blown sand and alluvium of recent and subrecent age. (Fig. 2.2B) The area to the east and north of Jaipur city is occupied by hill ranges rising to over 200 metres above the surrounding plain. The oldest rocks in the district are the schists, gneisses, magmatites, quartzites and conglamerates of Pre-Delhi formotion. Overlying these rocks with a major unconformity are the rocks of Delhi Super group which are made up of Raialo, Alwar and Agabgarh groups.

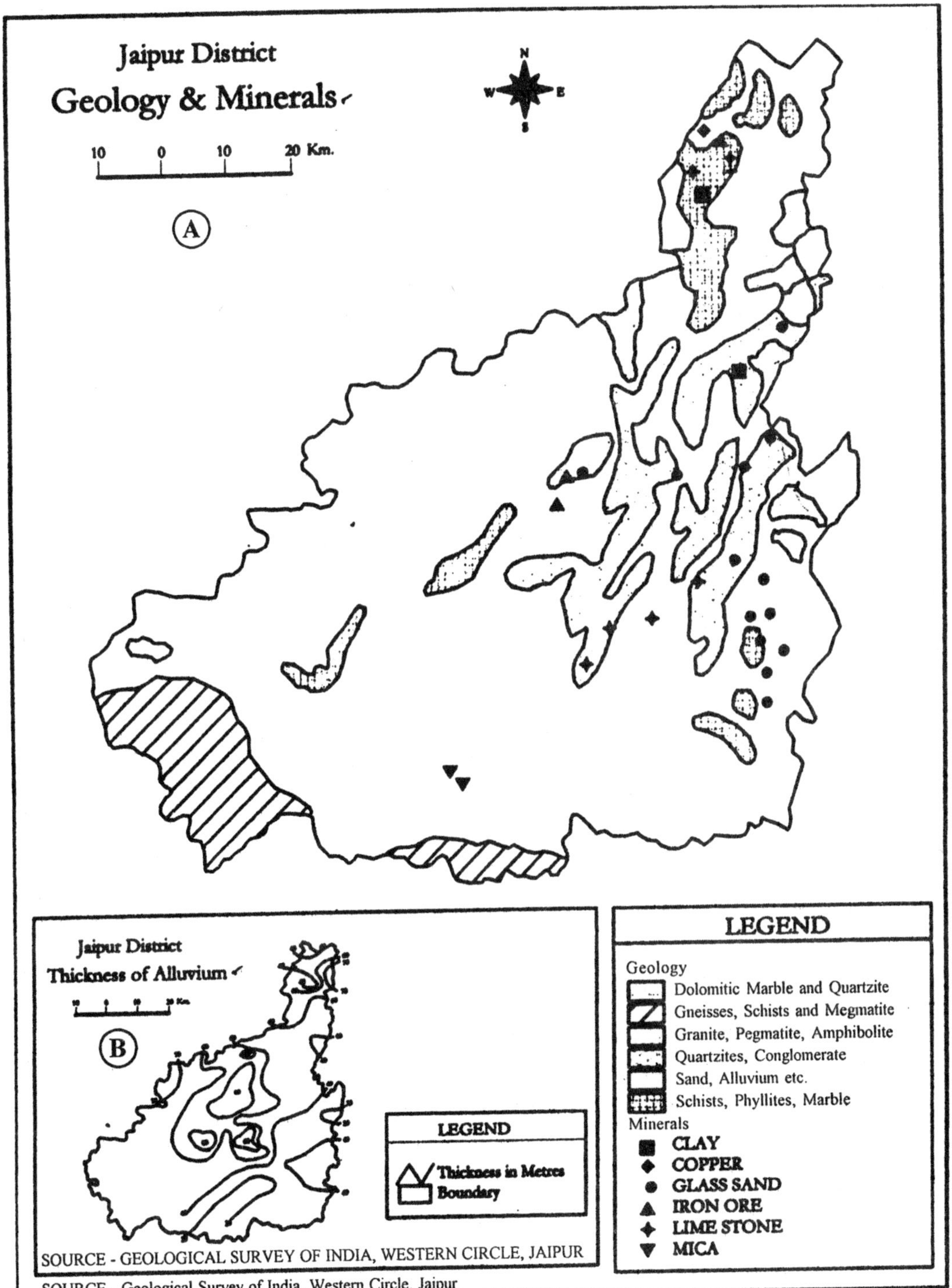

Fig. 2.2A : Geology and Minerals.
Fig. 2.2B : Thickness of Alluvium.

The blown sand is represented by stabilized and drifting sand dunes. The aeolian sand rests on the recent alluvium near river courses or on the older consolidated rocks. The blown sand is fine to very fine grained with silt and little clay. Being loose, unconsolidated and uniform in texture, it has high porosity and permeability. It readily absorbs water in the pore spaces. Blown sand is found in the entire district but is more prominent in the western part of the district.

The sub-surface geology of the district is based on the result of exploratory tube wells and other data available. The areas towards west of north east-southwest trending ridges, are characterised by alluvial thickness of more than 50 metres (Fig 2.2B). The alluvial thickness seams to be gradually increasing from west to east attaining maximum thickness near windward side of ridges. In the area covering south western and southern past of the district, the alluvial thickness is less than 20 metres (Fig. 2.2B). In eastern part of the study area, the alluvial thickness is also less than 20 metres. The granitic gneiss is encountered in dug wells.

The sandy and alluvium have problems of wind and water erosion. The western part of the district is affected by wind erosion as sand dunes can be observed in Chomu, Shahapura and Phulera tehsils. However, these dunes are under cultivation in kharif season (Plates). These soils adjoining to hills, along the Dhund and Banganga river are under gully erosion due to easily erosion by water. The stratigraphical succession in Jaipur district is given in Table 2.4

Agabgarh Group

The Agabgrah formation is predominantly, argillaceous in composition, comprising slates, phyllites, garnetiferous biotitie, schist with bands of quartzite and marble. Outcrops of Agabgarh are seen towards north of Shahapura and west of Kotputli near Antela, Begrana, Dantil, Kilanpur, Mehranpur, Pawana and Sarand (Fig. 2.2). At present most of the Agabgarh group is under the categary of degraded forest land.

The general stratigraphical succession in the district after Geological Survey of India is given in table 2.4.

Table 2.4 : Stratigraphical Succession in Jaipur District

Era	Period	Rank	Lithology
Quaternary	Recent to subrecent	Alluvium	Alluvium soil, sand dune, sand, river, gravels and terraces etc.
	Post – Delhi		Granite, quartz veins, pegmatites, amphibolite (Instrusives)
Proterozoic	Delhi Super Group	Agabgarh Group	Schists, phyllites, marble and quartzites
		Alwar Group	Quartzites, Canglomerate and schists
		Raialo Group	Dolomitic marble and quartzite
Arechaean	Bhilwara Super Group		Gnesisses, schists and migmatites

Source : Geological Survey of India, Jaipur.

Alwar Group

The Alwar formation is predominantly arenaceous in composition and comprise of orthoquartzite, micaceous quartzite and ferruginous quartzite with subordinate bands of quartz-schist and quartz biotite schist. The rocks are exposed as high ridges near Harmara, Nindnar, Samod, Amber, Jobner, Chomu, around Jamwa Ramgarh and Viratnagar. From north of Jaipur city a long but discontinuous ridge of quartzite extends right upto Shahapura and beyond in a north-east to south-west direction (Fig. 2.2).

Raialo Group

The rocks of Raialo group comprise of mainly dolomite marble and minor quartzite. The raialos are exposed in a small patch towards north east of Andhi in eastern part of the district (Fig. 2.2). In Andhi area, mining wateland covers a large tract due to marble mining in large scale. The mining is degrading the environment and ecological balance of the area.

Post-Delhi Intrusives

The Post-Delhi intrusive of the area are amphibolite granite, pegmetite and vein quartze. Amphibolite is found as intrusives in quartzose and schistose rocks in the Viratnagar valley around Rampur and is found in a few well sections close to Kalwar and Ballu Khan – Ki Dhani. The granite occurs as bosses within Delhi in Viratnagar valley near Bawli-ka-Bas and Pahari. Granites of Post-Delhi are exposed around Sankkur and Rahalana in south western part of the district. Veins of pegmatite and quartz traverse the Pre-Aravalli and Delhi rocks in the whole area of the district.

Bhilwara Super Group

The Bhilwara super group of rocks comprising mica-schists and gneisses occupies near Dudu and Sambhar. The area immediately to the south of Sambhar lake is schistose, while the area to the south of Dudu is gneissic. Most of the dug wells in Dudu-Sambhar area are located in these rock units. In the open well sections, the zone of weathering has been noticed down to 10 metres.

MINERALS

Jaipur district is not rich in mineral resources even though a variety of mineral deposits are found. A brief description of minerals is given below:

Iron use

In this district the iron deposits are located mainly in Morija, Rampura, Nimla, Raipur, Moonda, Dabla and Kotputli. The following table shows iron are deposits in Jaipur district:

Table 2.5 : Iron Ore deposits in Jaipur District

Name of Area	Iron Content (% Wt)	Reserve (Million Tonnes)
(a) Morija (Chomu)	64-68	10.1
(b) Rampura		
(c) Nimla and Railao	67	1.0
(d) Dabla		Several scattered deposits
(e) Kotputli :		
(i) Bagwas		
(ii) Tateri	55	0.48
(iii) Bani-Ka-Bas		

Source : Directorate, Mines and Geology, Government of Rajasthan, Jaipur.

Copper

The ores generally occur as veins, disseminations and as bedded deposits. The deposits are of the disseminated type popularly known as Porphyry Copper.

Table 2.6 : Copper Reserve in Jaipur District.

Name of Location	Reserves M.T.	Average Copper Content (Percentage)
(a) Gol Badshahpur	24,000	1.63
(b) Dhania	–	1.00
(c) Ghati Godyana	–	0.5 – 1.0

Source : Directorate, Mines and Geology, Government of Rajasthan, Jaipur.

(i) Gol Prospects

In the Viratnagar and Jamwa Ramgarh tehsils possibilities of copper exploration is quite good and may be taken into consideration.

(ii) Gol Badshahpur Prospects

A fairly extensive zone is located over a strike length of 2 km near Badshahpur. Gol and Badshahpur areas are marked by extensive slag heaps estimated to be around 24,000 tonnes.

(iii) Limestone

In the district limestone deposits occur near Kotputli, the estimated reserves being about 58.6 million tonnes. It is found to be crystalline and grey in colour. Impure limestone deposits are also found near Raori, Naila, Bandhia, Siroli, Harori, Raialo, Nimla and Dabla.

(iv) Mica

Mica is hydrous silicate of aluminium with varying amounts of potassium, sodium, calcium, magnesium and iron. In the district a small part of mica belt with an average width of 100 km extending from Mojamabad (Dudu tehsil) to Kankroli (Udaipur district) has been found. This range is the highest producer of mica in Rajasthan while very little has been explored from Mojamabad.

(v) Quartz and Glass Sand

The main source for quartz and silica sand are sandstones quartzites, pegmatites, quartz veins, etc. In Jaipur district, glass sand occurrences are suitable for utilisation in glass industries.

In the study area, silica sand occurs in quartzites of the Alwar sequence of Delhi group in Banskhoh hill near Jhir (Fig. 2.2A). The silica sand is probably derived by leaching of felspars from the quartzites. The sand is white, fine grained and varies from 0.12 to 0.26 mm in grain size. On the basis of the surface features and prospecting, glass sands are also reported from Khori, Nimora, Baj, Chitori, Gumanpura, Dhuta, Bhankri, Kaloti and Samod (Fig. 2.2A). About 2.8 million tonnes of reserves of silica sand have been estimated in the district.

(vi) China Clay

China-clay occurs at Buchara and Torda. The clays are usually white to milky white in colour, but are occasionally strained reddish, yellowish and brownish. Clay content ranges from 39 to 66 per cent by weight. The clay has a water of plasticity of 34 per cent. The total reserves of China-clay in these deposits have been tentatively estimated 0.712 million tonnes upto a depth of 10 metres.

Table 2.7 : Silica Sand in Jaipur District

Name of Area	Reserve (Million Tonnes)
(a) Jhir Dula Gumanpur	60,1000
(b) Khori	64, 000
(c) Nimora	NA
(d) Narrota	20,000
(e) Palsi	8,000
(f) Samod	2,200

Source : Directorate, Mines and Geology, Government of Rajasthan, Jaipur.

Almost all the production of china-clay is consumed in the indigenous industries such as ceramics, refractory, textile, paper, rubber, pesticides, etc.

(vii) Building Stone

Jaipur is famous for building and decorative stones such as marble, limestone, sandstone, granite, etc. Main deposits of marble are in Moonda Bhainslana, Andhi, Thali, Rayanwala, Dagota, Singhpuri, Kotri, Jugar and Radhonathgarh.

(viii) Felspar

Felspar is an alumino-silicate mineral of potassium, sodium and calcium. Though felspar is among the most widely distributed rock-forming minerals and occurs as a constituent of most of the rocks. Commercial deposits are mainly confined to pegmatites. Felspar is either quarried from the pegmatite veins or is recovered incidental to the mining of mica. Felspar is chiefly used both in the body of the ware and for glazing in the ceramic and glass industries besides insulation manufacture. Main deposits are in Mojamabad and Samod area.

(ix) Other Minerals

(a) *Soapstone* — The best variety of soapstone occurs in Dagota Jharna. Other deposits are at Geejgarh, Khana, etc. Inferred reserves of about 0.25 million tonnes have been recorded in the area.

(b) *Steatite* — Steatite, talc and soapstone are the three terms used in trade for one and the same mineral. Steatite is used for purer variety of compact and massive talc. In this district, prominent deposits are located at Dagota-Jharna, Geejgarh and Khana. Dagota-Jharna deposit is associated with dolomites of Raiolas (Delhi-group) and basic intrusions. Talc occurs as veins in three parallel zones and varies in thickness from 1 to 6 metres. Inferred reserve of 0.25 million tonnes have been indicated in the area.

(c) *Salt* — Salt in one of the most common substances used in our daily life and is an essential constituent of human blood. Salt is mainly obtained by evaporating sea water. Salt also occurs in nature as beds of rock salt which are in fact evaporites derived from ancient basins of highly saline seas. In relatively dry regions like Rajasthan, salt is precipitated from saline ground water at the ground surface in the form of efflorescences.

The important salt producing centre in Jaipur district is the Sambhar Lake. Sambhar salt lake spreads over an area of about 90 sq. kms. in which most of the area about 85 sq. km. lies in Jaipur district alone. The lake is located just at the foot of the central Aravallis. Two non-perennial rivers namely Rupnagar from south-west and Mendha from north-east fall into the lake.

DRAINAGE

Drainage also affects the spatial pattern of wastelands. However, there is not a single perennial river in the study area. The major seasonal rivers are Banganga, Bandi, Dhund, Morel, Mashi, Mendha, Sota and Sabi. Several nallahs origin from the hills have converted the land into gullied and/or ravinous. A brief descriptions of rivers is given below:

Banganga River

The Banganga is an important river of the district. It orginates from the Viratnagar hills, flowing first in a south easterly direction up to the village Ghat and then towards east through partly hilly and partly plain area. It passes through Viratnagar and Jamwa Ramgarh tehsil and then it enters in Dausa district (Fig. 2.3). Catchment area is hilly in its upper reaches with an yield of 9 mcft/km^2. In the intermediate reaches it is partly hilly and partly plain resulting in a yield of 6 mcft/sq. km^2. Hence the catchment area is termed as "good" in the upper reaches and "average" in its lower reaches. In upper and intermediate reaches, the river has formed gullies. On this river a dam is constructed near Jamwa Ramgarh village, supplies drinking water to the pink city Jaipur.

Bandi River

The Bandi is the second most important river of the district. This river originates from the Samod hills of Chomu tehsil. It passes through Shahapura, Chomu, Phulera and Phagi tehsils before entering in Tonk district.

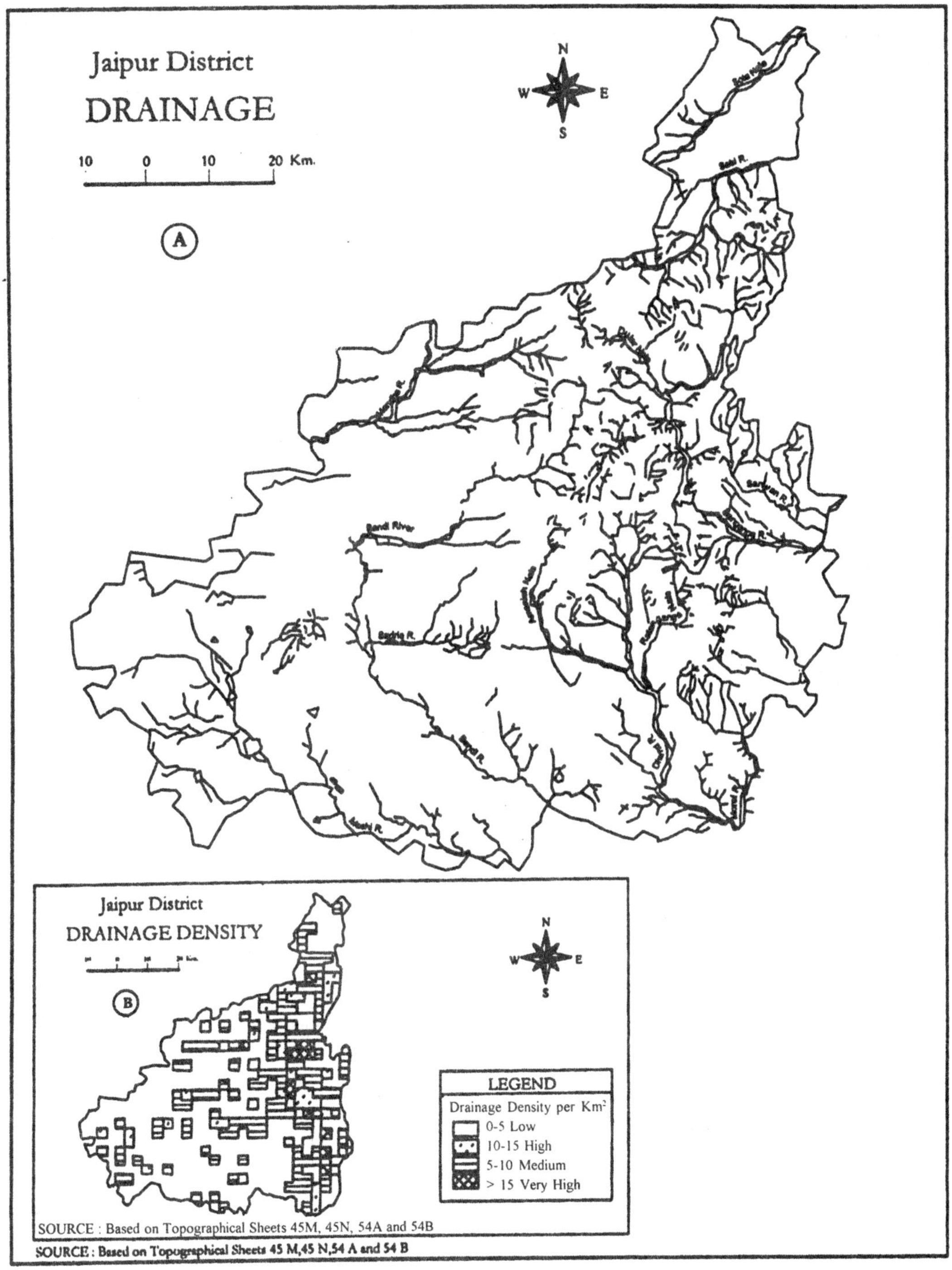

Fig. 2.3A : Drainage

Fig. 2.3B : Drainage Density

Mashi River

The Mashi river, a tributary of Banas, originates near Kishangarh in Ajmer district. Before entering in Tonk district, it traverse through Dudu and Phagi tehsils of Jaipur district (Fig. 2.3). The main tributary of Mashi river is Bandi. This river basin forms an effective and useful source of water to be given proper attention to utilize in its full potential in future.

Morel River

The Morel river orginates from the hills near Dharla and Chainpura villages in Bassi tehsil of Jaipur district.

Sabi River

The Sabi river orginates in Neem-Ka-Thana tehsil of Sikar district and passes through Viratnagar and Kotputli tehsils of Jaipur district (Fig. 2.3). After traversing in north eastern direction, it leaves Kotputli tehsil and enters in Alwar district.

Sota River

The Sota river also originates from Neem-Ka-Thana tehsil of Sikar district and after traversing Kotputli tehsil of Jaipur district it enters in Alwar district and joins the Sabi river (Fig. 2.3).

Mendha River

The Mendha and its tributaries flow in Jaipur district and traverse Chomu and Phulera tehsils after originating from the western slopes of Udaipur wati range near village Deorala in Danta Ramgarh tehsil of Sikar district. It flows in soutwest direction and terminates in Sambhar Salt lake (Fig. 2.3).

SOILS

On the basis of depth, texture, colour, calcareousness and permeability, the soils of Jaipur district have been classified into seven soil associations. The description of each association in given below:

1. Chomu Dune Association

This association dominates in western part of the district. Besides this a small patch of this soil association is also found in southern part of Kotputli tehsil. There is much variations in the soils within short distances due to aeolian depositions. The recent aeolian deposits (sand over burden) on top of older soil materials are very common. In Chomu soils stabilized sand dunes of varying heights are found which are cultivated only in kharif season. The soils of this association are very deep, dominantly coarse textured, light yellowish brown to dark yellowish brown, non calcareous, well drained to excessively drained, non saline and non sodic lying on nearly level to moderately sloping lands.

Low fertility, excessive drainage and low water holding capacity along with severe wind erosion are the principal problems of these soils. Intensive wind aeolian control measures such as growing of wind breaks across the wind direction, bunding strip croping and avoiding grazing etc. may be adopted. Growing of munj (*Saccharum munja*) and phog (*Calligonum polygonoides*) at the top of bunds and sand dunes will help in controlling the wind erosin.

2. Bassi Rajori Association

This association occupies most of the study area particularly southern and eastern part of the district. These soils are deep to very deep, dominantly medium textured (sandy loam to loam), yellowish brown to dark yellowish brown in colour, well drained, calcareous to non calcareous, non-saline, non-sodic and moderately eroded lying on nearly level to gently sloping lands.

Low fertility, slight to moderate erosion and non-availability of irrigation water are the major problems of these soils. Soil conservation measures like bunding with land levelling may be followed to check erosion and conserve soil moisture.

3. Naraina Dudu Association

Soils of this association are found in the south western part of the district. Two patches of these soils are also found in south eastern and eastern part of the district.

The soils of Naraina series are shallow to moderately deep (14-45cm), dominantly medium textured (sandy loam to loam), gray to dark grayish brown in colour, poorly to moderately well drained, strongly calcareous while soils of Dudu series are shallow to moderately deep, dominantly medium textured (sandy loam to loam), dark brown to dark yellowish brown in colour, imperfectly drained, strongly calcareous, moderately to strongly saline sodic and moderately to severely eroded.

Depth, erosion and salinity-alkalinity are the principal limitations of these soils. Growing of deep rooted crops and orchards may be avoided. The soils are kept under native pastures and in the year of good rainfall crops like bajra, jowar, guar and sesamum are taken in kharif. Shallow rooted crops and salt tolerant species should be selected. Grasses must be included in crop rotation.

These soils are shallow to moderately deep and leaching of salt is rather difficult. Addition of tank silt is reported by the cultivators to be beneficial in the reclamation of these soils. Suitable reclamation measures are to be adopted for saline alkaline soils.

4. Rojari Chaksu Association

A small patch of this association is found in south western part of the district (Fig. 2.4A). The soils are deep to very deep, dominantly medium textured (sandy loam to loam), yellowish brown to reddish brown, well drained, calcareous to non-calcareous and slightly to moderately eroded.

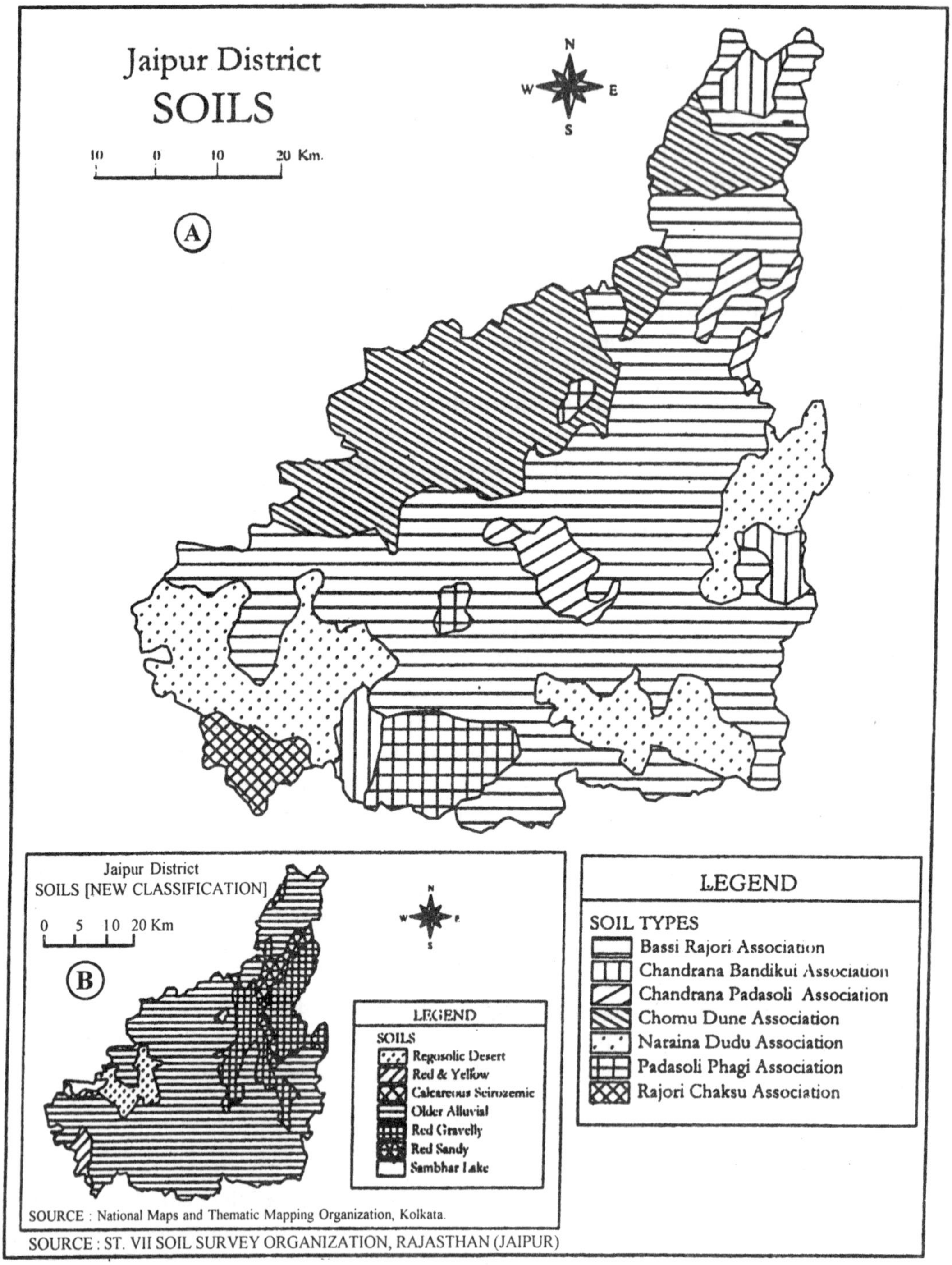

Fig. 2.4A : Soils
Fig. 2.4B : Soils (New Classification)

5. Chandrana Padasoli Association

These soils ocour in the two scattered areas i.e. central and north eastern part of the district. The soils are moderately deep to very deep, dominantly fine textured (clay loam to clay), brown to very dark grayish brown in colour, poorly drained to moderately well drained, neutral to calcareous and slightly to moderately eroded. Soils of Padasoli series lie over a calcareous material which is found at a depth ranging from 40-105 cms.

Poor drainage, slight to moderate salinit-alkalinity in scattered areas and moderate erosion are the main problems of these soils. Growing of very deep rooted crops and orchards in Padasoli series may be avoided.

6. Chandrana Bandikui Association

These soils occur in the three small scattered patches in northern, eastern and south western part of the district (Fig. 2.4A). These soils are very deep, dominantly fine textured (clay loam to clay), yellowish brown to dark grayish brown in colour, poorly drained to moderately well drained, neutral to slightly calcareous and slightly to moderately eroded. The principal limitations of these soils are poor workability, salinity-alkalinity in scattered patches, moderate erosion and non availability of irrigation water. Reclamation measures are necessary to be adopted to keep the salts below root zone.

7. Padasoli Phagi Association

Soils of this association are encountered on alluvial plains of recent and subrecent geological ages located in the southern part of the study area. Besides this two small patches are located in the central and north western part of the study area.

The soils are deep, fine textured (clay loam to clay), dark brown to dark olive gray in colour, poorly drained to moderately well drained, neutral to calcareous and slightly to moderately eroded lying on nearly level to gently sloping lands.

Slight to moderate salinity-alkalinity, non-availability and poor quality of irrigation water and erosion are the principal limitations of these soils.

These soils have a calcium carbonate layer at a depth ranging from 40-100 cms, deep rooted crops and orchards may be avoided on these soils. Soils of this group have a hard calcium carbonate layer in the lower horizons, care must be taken that irrigation water may not be provided in excess otherwise water logging conditions might be created.

CLIMATE

Climate, the synthesis of the weather elements, temperature, rainfall, wind velocity and dust storms etc. are relevant to the wasteland. In this district, rainy season is from July to mid September. The maximum rainfall occurs in July and August. In these months in good drainage areas, more rainfall encourages the sheet, gully and ravinous erosion while on the other side, poor drainage creates the problem of water logging and salinity. Wind erosion and drifting sand dunes can be observed in sandy area due to more wind velocity and dust storms.

Semi-arid type of climate prevails in the district. December to February is the winter season, after which the hot season commences and continues till the third week of June when the south-west monsoon sets in. The southwest monsoon season is comparatively short in this region and lasts only till mid September. The period from the second half of September to the end of November is the post monsoon or retreating monsoon season.

Temperature

The only meteorological observation center in the district is situated in Sanganer town. The data of this station represents the weather conditions in the district as a whole. The period from March to June is of continuous rise in temperature (Table 2.8). The maximum monthly temperature in the area has been recorded in May and June, which varies from 40.3°C to 39.3°C. May and first half of June being the hottest part of the year. During summer the plain as well as upland suffers from extreme heating and hot westerly wind known as *"Loo"*. In summer sandy soil blown with the wind and accumulates adjoining to the obstacles. The sand dunes also drift during this season. January is the coldest month with the mean daily maximum temperature of 22.5°C and mean daily minimum of 7.8°C (Table 2.8).

Rainfall

The average annual rainfall in the district is 673.9 mm. The rainfall generally increases from west to east (Fig. 2.5). But in the Amber region, the rainfall is a little higher than the surrounding parts of the district due to forested hills (Fig. 2.1 A and 2.5). Of the total annual rainfall of the district, 3.6 per cent occurred in winter season, 3.5 per cent in the summer season, 89.8 per cent during the monsoon and 3.1 per cent in the post monsoon and gradual decrease till summer season.

On the average there are 32 rainy days. The number varies from 28 at Mozamabad to 36 at Amber in a year. The monthly rainfall intensity is high in the monsoon months i.e. in June 66 mm, July 216.3 mm, August 231.2 mm and September 80.3 mm and decreases towards the both pre- and post-monsoon months. The high rainfall intensity of July and August in hilly tracts of the northern and central part of the district encourages the sheet, gullied/ravinous erosion.

Relative Humidity

Relative humidity is quite high during the monsoon (July to September) amounting to 68, 76 and 63.5 per cent respectively (Table 2.8). During the remaining months, the area mostly comes under the influence of dry continental air masses and hence in these months relative humidity is lower. In the summer reason, which is the driest part of the year, relative humidity in the afternoon may be as low as 15 to 20 percent. In summer season, due to lowest relative humidity, sandy soil particles become dry and wind erosion takes place.

Winds

The westerly winds are experienced in major part of the year, where as southerly winds have the shortest duration. Normally the wind velocity is high in May (12.6 km/hr), June

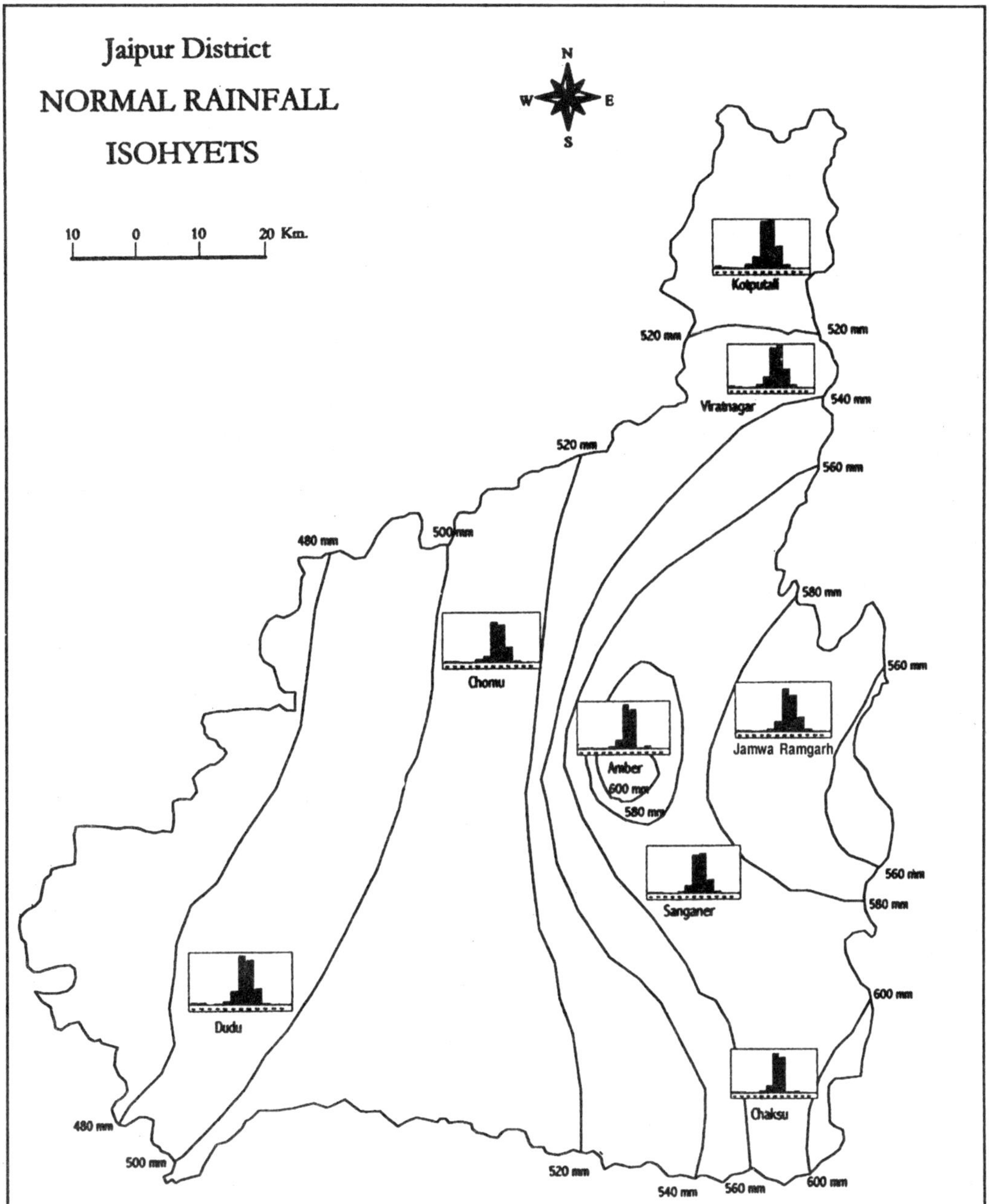

Source : Based on Normal Rainfall of Raingauge Stations of Jaipur District and adjoining areas.

Fig. 2.5 : Normal Rainfall Isohyets

(12.5 km/hr) and July (9.5 km/hr) (Table 2.8). Observations made by Birla Science and Technology Centre, Jaipur in 1980 reveal that Sambhar and Jaipur have 20 and 13 storms during May and June respectively. The average wind speed of 45 kmph was in Sambhar and 45 kmph at Jaipur during the month of May. As strong winds blow from westerly and south westerly direction the sand movement may take place towards east to north-east directions, particularly during the months from March to June.

Table 2.8: Climatological Table

Station : Jaipur (Sanganer) Lt. 25°49′ Long 75°48′ Height above MSL 390 metres

Month		Air Temperature			Rainfall		
		Mean		Humidity	Monthly total	No. of Rainy days	Mean wind speed
		Daily Max.	Daily Min.				
		°c	°c	%	mm		Kmph
January	I	22.5	7.8	63	7.9	0.6	5.6
	II			35			
February	I	25.7	10.7	54	11.7	0.9	5.5
	II			28			
March	I	31.5	15.8	42	6.1	0.7	7.9
	II			19			
April	I	37.0	21.4	30	4.1	0.5	9.7
	II			16			
May	I	40.3	25.4	32	16.2	1.1	12.6
	II			17			
June	I	39.3	27.2	52	66.0	3.6	12.5
	II			32			
July	I	33.9	25.5	75	216.3	10.8	9.5
	II			61			
August	I	32.0	24.3	82	231.2	11.6	8.4
	II			70			
September	I	33.2	22.9	72	80.3	5.1	7.6
	II			55			
October	I	33.4	18.6	51	22.6	1.2	6.0
	II			32			
November	I	29.0	13.1	50	3.2	0.3	3.9
	II			33			
December	I	24.4	9.1	61	3.3	0.4	3.9
	II			38			
Annual Total	I	31.9	18.5	55	673.9	36.8	7.8
Or Mean	II			36			
Number of	I	29	29	29	30	30	10
Year	II			29			

Source: Deputy Director, Indian Meterological Department, Jaipur (Sanganer)

LAND UTILIZATION

Land use of a region is the result of the interaction of various factors such as physical, economic and social and shows the extent to which man has been able to utilize the land resources gainfully. Land is used for multipurpose activities like agriculture, forestry, grazing, recreation, industries, urbanization and mining etc.

The purpose of land use classification is to maximize the productivity and to conserve the land for prosperity. The land use capabilities classification portrays the physical capabilities of land to produce over a long period of time under stated conditions of uses and which can provide land operations with a basis for actual practice on scientific units of land.

The existing pattern of land use is the outcome of past efforts and also evolutionary processes providing a base for future planning of land resources. A brief description of land use in the study area is given below:

Forest land

This category includes all such lands which are occupied by forest notified under the Forest Act. Forest is the greatest renewable natural resource and also of the most striking feature of the landscape indirectly the forest ameliorate the extremes of climate, regulate the flow of rivers, check soil erosion, control floods and other detrimental factors affecting the soil. Thus no one can deny the importance of forest in the regional ecology as well as in the economy.

The study area has only 7.37 per cent forest land to the total geographical area in 2003-04. The density of forests is not equal every where due to several factors such as eroded and rocky slopes on the one hand and less area under hills on the other hand. The maximum area under forest is concentrated in north-eastern part i.e. Viratnagar and Jamwa Ramgarh tehsils (Fig. 2.7) because of hills and rugged areas with greatest slope. Viratnagar is the only tehsil of the study area which occupies its more than one-third area under forest (37.53%) followed by Jamwa Ramgarh tehsil (23.64%). These both tehsils have more than one-half forested area (52.18%) of the district. The lowland areas of the tehsils lying in south and west are generally devoid of forest cover (Fig. 2.7). Hence, the level land has been either entirely brought under plough or under pastures.

Land not Available for Cultivation

It includes hills, barren and unculturable land, land put to non agricultural uses (Area under buildings, railways, roads, rivers, nallahs, tanks/ponds and canals etc). Saline/alkaline and other infertile soils are also included in this category. It covers 10.55 per cent area of the district. The maximum area of land not available for cultivation is in central part of the study area i.e. in Jaipur tehsil due to more area under urban settlements followed by Jamwa Ramgarh tehsil (Fig. 2.6). The latter tehsil is situated in the north eastern part and as stated earlier this part of the district is hilly. Low percentage (10.15%) of land not available for cultivation is found in the central and eastern part of the district due to hilly tracts while in the southern and western part it is low due to peneplained area (Fig. 2.6).

Other Uncultivated Land Excluding Fallow Land

It includes permanent pastures/grazing lands, culturable waste and land under miscellaneous trees and groves. Permanent pastures/grazing lands have been discussed separately. In this study area, culturable wasteland is 3.11 per cent while the area under miscellaneous trees and groves is only 0.08 per cent to the total geographical area. The culturable wasteland is that land which can be used for cultivation, but the same is not being taken up for cultivation at all, or abandoned after the tillage of a few years for one reason or the other. Land once cultivated but not cultivated for more than five years in succession is also included in this category. Such lands are not put to any use and may lie either as fallow or covered with

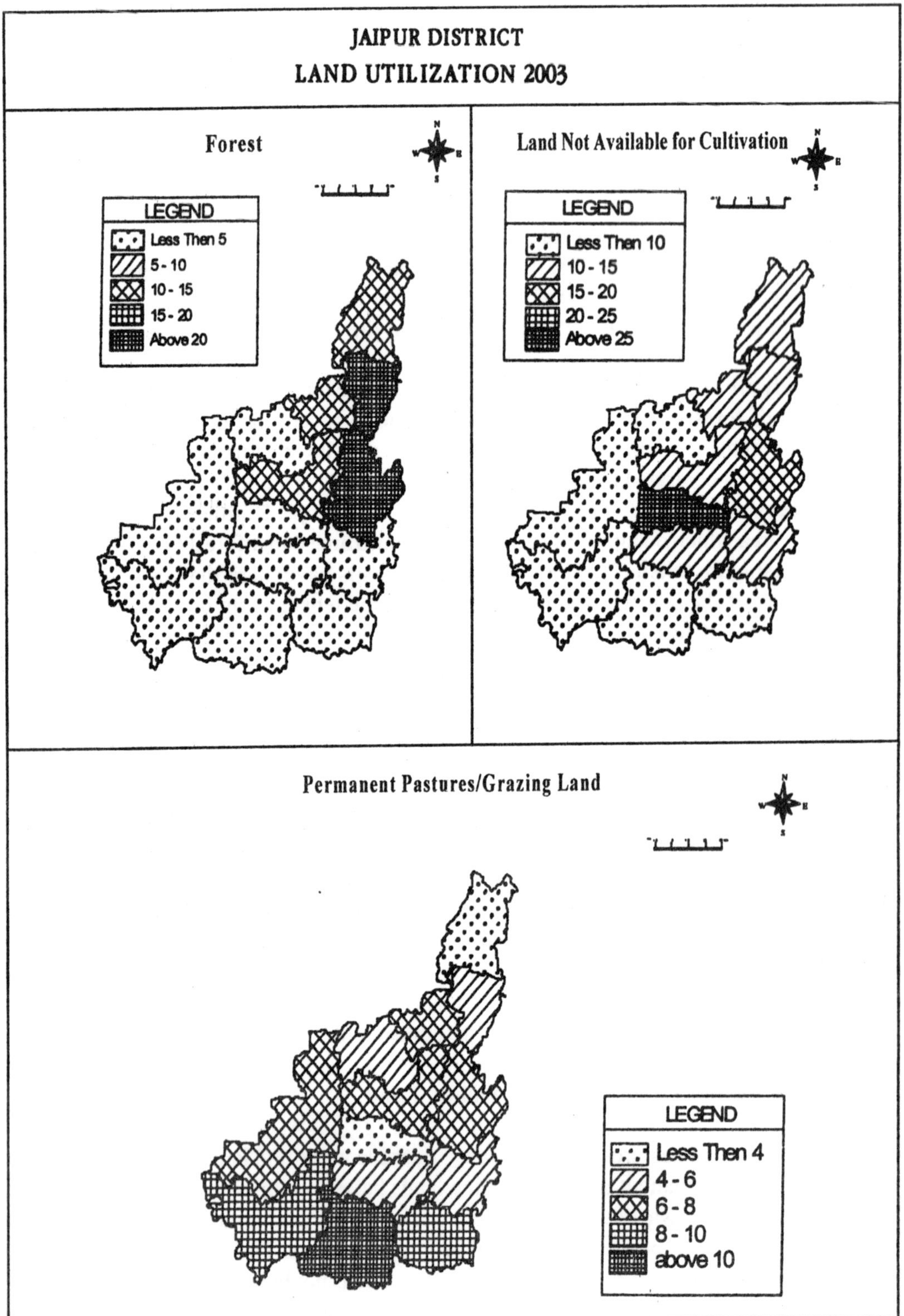

Fig. 2.6 : Jaipur District Land Utilization 2003.

shrubs and scrubs. Most of this category of land lies in isolated blocks or within cultivated holdings. The following table shows tehsilwise culturable wasteland in district.

Table 2.9 : Tehsilwise Culturable Wasteland and Land under Misc. Trees and Groves in Jaipur District, 2003.

S. No.	Name of Tehsil	Percentage to Total Geographical Area	
		Culturable Waste	Miscellaneous Trees and Groves
1.	Amber	1.98	0.31
2.	Bassi	3.57	0.23
3.	Chaksu	3.05	0.00
4.	Chomu	0.64	0.02
5.	Dudu	4.55	0.01
6.	Jaipur	6.09	0.31
7.	Jamwa Ramgarh	3.45	0.05
8.	Kotputli	1.17	0.01
9.	Phagi	3.78	0.00
10.	Phulera	2.53	0.02
11.	Sanganer	4.55	0.17
12.	Shahapura	2.13	0.07
13.	Viratnagar	2.45	0.03
	Total	3.11	0.08

Source : Land Record Section, Collectorate, Jaipur.

The above table reveals that maximum culturable wasteland is in Jaipur tehsil followed by Sanganer and Dudu tehsils. The tehsils having 3 to 4.55 per cent of culturable wasteland are Bassi, Chaksu, Dudu, Jamwa Ramgarh, Phagi and Sanganer. These tehsils are situated in the southern part of the district except Jamwa Ramgarh. The southern part keeps its more land under this category due to poor quality of soil and water. In remaining tehsils it is low and very low.

As stated earlier that only 0.08 per cent land is under miscellaneous trees and groves in the study area. It is maximum in Jaipur tehsil having capital city and its adjoining tehsils viz Amber, Sanganer and Bassi while in other tehsils it is negligible.

According to the settlement rules, the pasture land is earmarked in every village and it is considered to be a criminal offence if anybody violates this rule. But the State Government can convert this type of land for cultivation as and when settlement takes place. Besides, the cultivable pasture land can be exchanged with other poor quality land.

The district has 7.04 per cent of the total area under permanent pastures which is almost equal to the state (7.06%). High and very high percentages of permanent pasture are in the tehsils of southern part of the district (Fig. 2.7). In the study area, maximum land under pastures is in Phagi tehsil (10.35%) followed by Dudu and Chaksu tehsils (Fig. 2.7). These tehsils have large number of animals. Besides this, pedological and hydrological conditions are also not suitable for agriculture in large tracts of the tehsils. These tracts have been kept reserve for grazing purposes. Amber, Phulera, Shahapura and Jamwa Ramgarh tehsils have moderate of permanent pasture i.e. 6 to 8 percent of the total geographical area. Further, the tehsils of Jaipur, Sanganer, Bassi, Chomu and Kotputli have not large animal population in comparison to other tehsils and hence there the area under pasture is kept less. In Sanganer and Jaipur tehsils milk-sellers keep only she buffaloes at home for selling milk in the capital city and they do not utilize pastures for grazing purposes.

Current Fallow

Current fallow is arable land lying uncropped and may remain so for one season or more. According to the practices in Great Britain, current fallow is the land that is well ploughed and harrowed but left uncropped for a whole year or more; it is also called summer fallow as that season is chosen for the sake of killing the weeds. In India current fallow is praised mainly to enable the land to recuperate. In 2003, the current fallow was 10.18 per cent, but unequally distributed throughout the district. The high and very high percentages of current fallow i.e., 12 to 16 and above 16 are in the tehsils of southern part of the district with maximum in Chaksu tehsil (Fig. 2.7). The other tehsils of southern part of the study area having high percentage of this category of land are Dudu, Phagi, Sanganer and Bassi (Fig. 2.7). These tehsils have poor quality water and shallow poor soils, so the most of the land in rabi season is kept as a current fallow. Phulera tehsil of the west and Jamwa Ramgarh tehsil situated in the eastern part and Kotputli of the north, all these three tehsils have medium percentage (8-12%) of current fallow due to sandy nature of soil and undulated hilly tracts while in remaining tehsils the current fallow is low and very low due to more irrigational facilities.

Old Fallow

All such lands which were cultivated but are now lying idle for the last two years. Fig. 2.7 shows that percentage share under this category is maximum in the south central part (Sanganer Tehsil) of the district, while minimum in the north and central part. The very high and high percentages of old fallow are due to the saline soils, low rainfall and deep ground water. These combined with paucity of irrigation water force the farmer to leave the cultivated fallow for long. The low proportion of the old fallow in a major area of the district in the north, and central part is because of the good fertile soils, developed irrigation facilities (Fig. 2.7), enough rainfall which enables the cultivators to take two crops a year, at times even under unirrigated conditions.

Net Sown Area

Net sown area includes the land which is actually under crops during the current year. The net sown area in this district is 52.34 percent to the total geographical area which is almost equal to the state average (52.84 %).

The high and very high percentages (60 to 70 and above 70%) of NSA is in the western part of the district viz in Chomu and Phulera tehsils. Chomu tehsil occupies loamy sand to sandy loam soils with very high intensity of irrigation (Fig.2.8) while, in Phulera if good rains occur most of the cultivated land is sown in kharif season. Thus in this tehsil the percentage of NSA depends on the rainfall in kharif season. It is also interesting to note

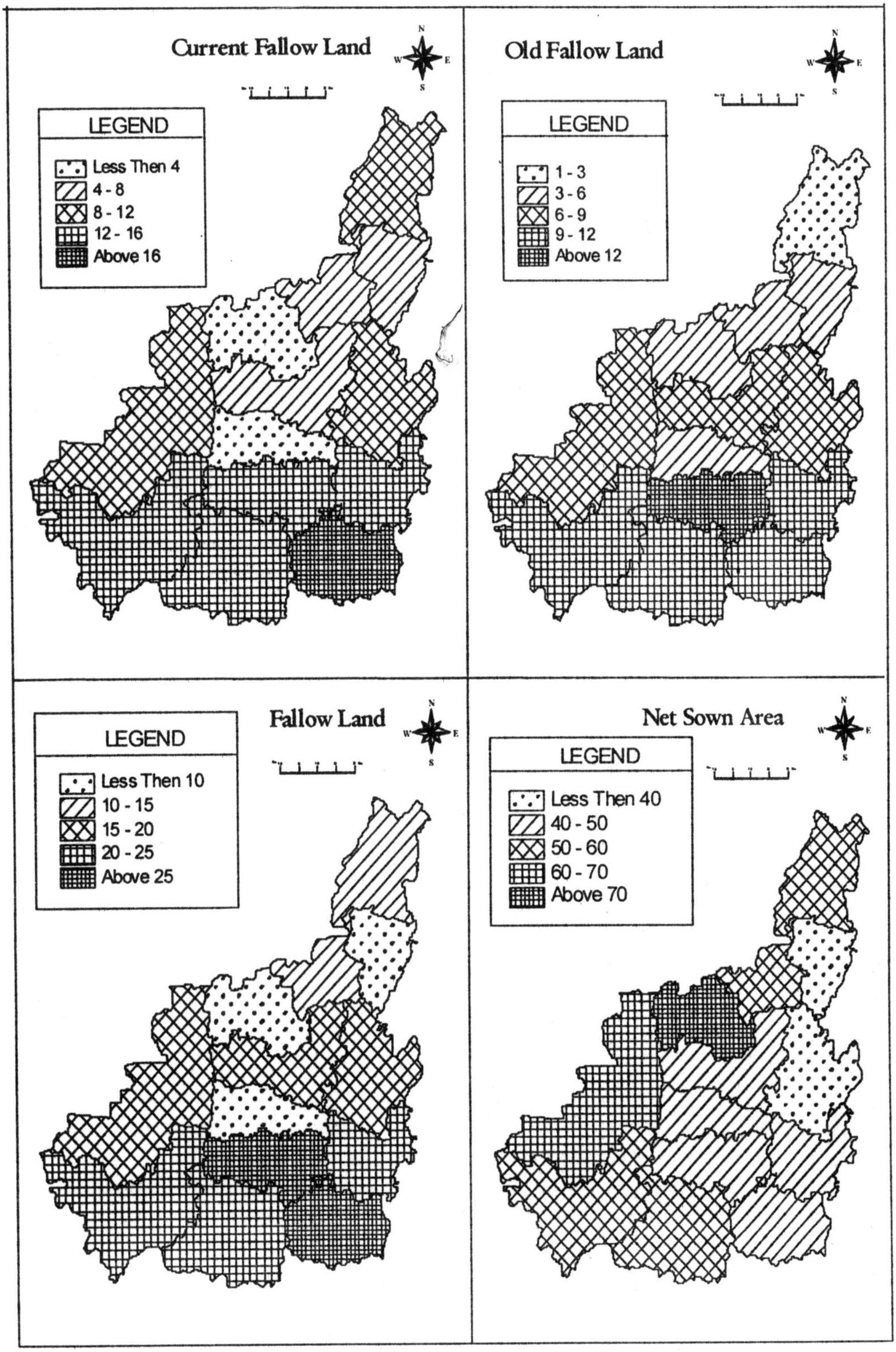

Fig. 2.7 : Jaipur District Land Utilization 2003

that the medium percentage (50-60%) of NSA is also concentrated in northwestern, northern and south western part of the district. The tehsils of northern part have fertile soil with more irrigational facilities. Low percentage of this category is in the central and south eastern part of the study area while it is least in the tehsils of north eastern part viz in Jamwa Ramgarh and Viratnagar due to more area under forest, hilly tracts and gullied/ ravinous land.

IRRIGATION

Water is the life of the plants. Man has to provide water to the plants if rains are deficient. In Indian climate in general and in Rajasthan in particular artificial application of water to the crop land is very necessary as in this state rainfall is not only un-reliable but also deficient. It has already been discussed that almost the whole of east Rajasthan including Jaipur district belongs to the semi-arid climate where the rainfall hardly exceeds 60 cms. Since most of this comes from the summer monsoons, it is never reliable and suffers from the usual vagaries of the monsoons. Contrarily, the crops need water at the right time and on several occasions in varying quantities according to the type of crop, soil characteristics, surface gradient and temperature and other climatic conditions. The crops are so sensitive that if proper supply of water is not available at the right time, their growth is retarded or at times they dry completely.

In general no crops requiring more than 60 cms. of rainfall, are grown in this district. In the absence of irrigational facilities mostly (50.23 %) crops are grown during the monsoon (kharif crops) and the rest in winters (rabi crops).

The following Table 2.10 gives an idea of percentage of crop seasons wise area, irrigated area to the total cropped area and percentage of irrigated area to the gross irrigated area.

Table 2.10 : Seasonwise Percentage of Irrigated Area and Percentage of Irrigated Area to Total Cropped Area in Jaipur District.

Crop Season	Percentage to the total cropped area	Crop Season-wise percentage of irrigated area to the total cropped area	Percentage of irrigated area to the gross irrigated area
Kharif	50.23	20.80	18.78
Rabi	49.31	90.79	80.12
Zaid	0.46	98.60	1.10

The above table shows that four-fifths of the rabi crops are irrigated while 18.78 per cent area of kharif is irrigated. However, when these crops are considered in terms of area, it is found that the picture is not as rosy as it appears. The rabi area is 49.31 per cent and zaid is only 0.46 per cent of the gross cropped area. These figures indicate the precarious condition of the irrigation facilities in this district.

Development of Irrigation Works

Some Indian princes had done monumental work in the field of irrigation in Rajasthan like the Ganga Canal executed by the Maharaja of Bikaner. In some other princely states like

Jaipur, inspite of sufficient resources, very few efforts were made to execute the irrigation works. However, it is worth mentioning that a dam was constructed on the Banganga river in Jamwa Ramgarh tehsil at a distance of 32 kms. north-east of Jaipur. The Banganga passes through a narrow gorge near the village Ramgarh and this site was inspected in 1868 and soon after an earthen dam was constructed to tide over the acute famine conditions prevailing in those times.

Table 2.11 gives some idea of irrigation in Jaipur district from 1875-76 to 1936-37 when it was a princely state. The records for the year from 1876 to 1925 are not available. The earlier figures are not very significant as the state area does not coincide with the present district. However, the increasing area under irrigation indicates the interest of the rulers for the welfare of agriculture in their territory. Fluctuations came in the years 1879-80, 1884, 1887 and 1889 due to the draughts and famines.

Table 2.11 : Irrigation in Jaipur State from 1875–76 to 1936–37

Year	Irrigated Area (in hectares)	Year	Irrigated Area (in hectares)
1875-76	1,364,55	1888	30,516
1876-77	2,489	1889	28,283
1877-78	4,531	1890 to 1925	Data not available
1878-79	3,574	1926-27	1,63,892
1879-80	9,125	1927-28	1,31,861
1980-81	12,452	1930-31	1,07,034
1981-82	11,113	1931-32	1,06,504
1982-83	17,887	1932-33	N.A.
1883	17,371	1933-34	N.A.
1884	12,757	1934-35	1,00,942
1885	15,976	1935-36	85,568
1886	21,592	1936-37	84,997

From 1901 to 1947 was the golden era in the history of irrigation in the district. The major dams of the district, viz., Chhaparwara, Kharkharad, Sainthal Sagar, Madho Sagar, Hingonia, Kalakho Sagar and Buchara, etc., were constructed during this period.

Irrigation After Independence

After independence farmers became land owners. They increased the irrigated area by digging new wells and tube-wells. The government also constructed dams and tanks during the various plans. The following table shows percentage of irrigated area to the total cropped area in different years:

Table 2.12 shows that the area under irrigation has been rising continuously every decade. But during 1971-81, the irrigated area doubled due to more financial assistance by the government to the formers for digging wells.

Table 2.12 : Percentage of Irrigated Area to Total Cropped Area in Different Years (1951-2001) in Jaipur District.

Year	Total Cropped Area (in hectares)	Total irrigated Area (in hectares)	Percentage from columns 2 to 3
1950-51	268576	65277	24.30
1960-61	737839	179087	24.27
1970-71	904608	243079	26.87
1980-81	845295	432174	51.13
1990-91	–	–	–
2000-01	814956	422566	51.85

Table 2.13 shows percentage group of irrigated area according to irrigation intensity in the district in 2003.

Table 2.13 : Percentage Groups of Irrigated Area in Jaipur District 2003-04

Percentage Group	Tehsil	Intensity
Above 60	Amber, Chomu, Jaipur, Kotputli	Very high
45-60	Bassi, Jamwa Ramgarh Sanganer, Shahapura, Viratnagar	High
30-45	Phulera	Medium
15-30	Chaksu	Low
Below 15	Dudu and Phagi	Very Low

Source : Based on data obtained from Land Record Section, Collectorate, Jaipur.

The above Table 2.13 shows the very high intensity of irrigated area (above 60%) is concentrated in the tehsils of northern central and northern part of the district, three tehsils lie in the Sabi-Sota and Bandi river basin having older alluvium and younger alluvium aquifers (yield 50 to 240 m^3/day). Approximately three-fourth cropped area of Chomu and Jaipur tehsils is under irrigation due to good quality irrigation water and fertile soils. Surrounding tehsils of very high irrigation intensity viz Bassi, Jamwa Ramgarh, Shahapura, Viratnagar and Sanganer have high percentage (45-60%) of irrigated area. Three tehsils also have older alluvium acquifer with quartzite and phyllite, so the irrigated area is less in comparison to tehsils having very high irrigation intensity. Phulera tehsil, situated in the western part of the district, has dynamic and stable sand dunes common features of the landscape. This tehsil has only 44-52 per cent irrigated area i.e. medium irrigation intensity. These tehsils having low and very low irrigated area are situated on the southern part of the district with the lowest area in Phagi tehsil (12-96%). These tehsils have scattered patches of saline ground water. Thus poor quality/quantity of ground water is responsible for low and very low percentages of irrigated area. Tehsils of this part have maximum area under land affected by salinity/alkalinity, land with or without scrub land and degraded pasture/grazing land type of wastelands.

Irrigation by Sources and Irrigated Area

There are two sources of water for irrigation, viz., underground water resources or wells and tube-wells (n) surface water resources i.e. dams, and tanks. The following Table 2.14 shows irrigated area by different sources.

Table 2.14 reveals that tube-wells are an important source of irrigation in Jaipur and Shahapura tehsils. Other tehsils having tube well irrigation are Dudu, Chomu and Sanganer tehsils. However, share of tube-well irrigation is only 9.02 per cent to the total irrigated area of the district, wells and tube-wells combinedly irrigate 99.95 per cent of the total irrigated area. Thus groundwater resource is the most important and predominant source of irrigation in the study area. The irrigated area by wells and tube-wells ranges from 99.63 to 100 per cent. Except three tehsils viz Sanganer, Jaipur and Amber in remaining ten tehsils, wells and tube-wells irrigate 100 percent irrigated area i.e. total irrigation depends only on these sources.

Table 2.14: Percentage of Irrigated Area by Different Sources in Jaipur District 2003

S.No.	Tehsil	Tube-wells and wells			Tanks	Canals	Other Sources	Total
		Tube wells	Wells	Total				
1	Amber	—	99.89	99.89	—	0.11	—	100.0
2	Bassi	—	100.0	100.0	—	—	—	100.0
3	Chaksu	—	100.0	100.0	—	—	—	100.0
4	Chomu	5.00	95.00	100.0	—	—	—	100.0
5	Dudu	9.73	90.27	100.0	—	—	—	100.0
6	Jaipur	57.05	42.81	99.86	—	0.14	—	100.0
7	Jamwa Ramgarh	0.20	99.80	100.0	—	—	—	100.0
8	Kotputli	—	100.0	100.0	—	—	—	100.0
9	Phagi	—	100.0	100.0	—	—	—	100.0
10	Phulera	0.03	99.97	100.0	—	—	—	100.0
11	Sanganer	4.33	95.30	99.63	—	—	—	100.0
12	Shahapura	45.98	54.02	100.0	—	—	—	100.0
13	Viratnagar	—	—	100.0	—	—	—	100.0
	Total	9.02	90.93	99.95	—	0.05	—	100.0

Source: Land Record Section, Collectorate, Jaipur.

Wells are indigenous sources of low cost which suit well to the poor peasants. These are the personal property of the farmers from which they can irrigate their fields as and when required. Besides this, their water is rich in soda, nitrates, chlorides and sulphates, which make the land more fertile. on the other hand due to low precipitation, when tanks are not full to their capacity, the supply of adequate water for irrigation is restricted. In 2003 only 0.05 per cent area was irrigated by canals. For tank irrigation farmers are at the mercy of the canal overseers. Many a time they do not release water at the proper time; consequently, the standing crops fail and the poor peasants suffer. This factor increases the suitability of wells as a source of irrigation for poor peasants. It is concluded that only groundwater resources irrigate the cropped area of the district.

POPULATION

Natural environment itself is a dynamic element but without human use it has no importance. Most of the wastelands in this district is man-made e.g. degraded forest, degraded pasture, mining wasteland and extension in saline soils due to irrigation by poor quality groundwater. It is observed that ecological balance has been disturbed due to over use of natural resources. At present more emphasis is being given to sustainable use of resources and control on population growth especially in developing and less developed countries of the world.

In developing countries, with the development of secondary, tertiary and quaternary economic activities, population is also increasing rapidly excluding last one decade. The following Table 2.15 shows growth of population in Jaipur district during the last 100 years.

Table 2.15 : Growth of Population in Jaipur District

Year	Population	Absolute Variation	Percentage decadal variation	Absolute variation over 1901	Percentage variation over 1901
1901	1212812	—	—	—	—
1911	1142522	- 70290	- 5.80	-70290	-5.80
1921	937601	- 204921	- 17.94	-275211	-22.69
1931	1045190	107589	11.47	-167622	-13.82
1941	1189737	144547	13.83	-23075	-1.90
1951	1524493	334756	28.14	311681	25.70
1961	1901756	377263	24.75	688944	56.81
1971	2482385	580629	30.53	1269573	104.68
1981	3436172	953878	38.42	2223360	183.32
1991	4722551	1286379	37.44	3509739	289.39
1991*	3887895	451723	13.15	2675083	220.57
2001	5252388	1364493	35.10	4039576	333.08

* With Dausa District (Dausa District Separated from Jaipur District in 1993-94).
Source: Directorate, Census Operations, Jaipur.

From above Table 2.15 it is clear that population growth during last one century was not uniform. Population growth pattern can be divided into three distinct periods: (1) from 1901 to 1931 (2) from 1931 to 1991 and (3) from 1991 to 2001. During the first period of 30 years, the population of the district decreased continuously due to famine and epidemics. During second period (1931-91), the growth of population has been relatively rapid because of the availability and expansion of medical facilities and control over diseases etc. During this period of six decades, population of the district has increased 4-5 times. The third period (1991-2001) witnessed slightly slow growth (35.10) due to increase in living standard and literacy. Now the tendency of large family is decreasing and educated families adopting one or two children policy. In 1993, Dausa district was carved out from Jaipur district for the convenience of administration.

In general the increase in population was 333.08 per cent during the last century, (1901 to 2001) certainly a high increase against the limited natural resources of the area.

Density of Population

Density of population is the ratio between persons and land. There are various type of density. Arithmetic density is the ratio between the total population and the total geographical area. The arithmetic density of the study area was 471 persons per km^2 in 2001. The very high (above 440) population density is concentrated in the central and north western part of the district as it includes the capital city Jaipur, Chomu and Shahapura tehsil. Most of the northwestern part has fertile soil and good quality irrigation water. High density is found in northern part (360-440) which is occupied by the Sabi and Sota river basins having fertile alluvial deep and non-calcareous soils with high intensity of irrigation. Moderate density (280-360) is in northern, upper central and eastern part of the study area while low arithmetic density (200-280) is found in western, eastern and southern part where sand-desertic, hilly tracts and land affected by salinity, alkalinity are main limitations. Very low arithmetic density, (below 200) is concentrated in south-western part of the study area. This part has *'Kankars'* below 10-60 centimetres depth having poor drainage, sandy loam to loamy texture on the surface with loam to cay loam, and deep calcareous sub soil, pH reaction is strong and permeability is very low.

Rural density is the ratio between rural population and rural areas. The pattern of rural density is almost same as that of arithmetic density except central, north western and northern parts of the district. In the central part the urban population is more concentrated due to the location of the capital city. In the western part Sambhar lake, Phulera towns; in the north western Chomu, Shahapura towns and in the northern part Kotputli town etc. are situated, so the rural density is slightly less than the arithmetic density. Five tehsils viz Amber, Bassi, Dudu, Phagi and Jamwa Ramgarh have no urban population, therefore, in these tehsils rural and arithmetic densities are exactly the same.

Literacy

Literate persons take part in varous type of wasteland developmental activities, e.g. reclamation of land affected by salinity/alkalinity and horticulture development in gullied/ ravinous land. Similarly literate persons take keen interest in the wasteland development through watershed activities in the rural area.

Maximum literacy (above 70%) is concentrated in central and northern parts of the district due to more educational institutions in the capital city. Similarly, high per cent of literacy (65-70%) is found in the western part where more educational infrastructural facilities are available in the towns e.g. Sambhar, Phulera, Jobner, Chomu and Kaladera. Low and very low literacy is in the agriculturally backward tehsils of south western and south eastern part except Amber tehsil.

Scheduled Castes/Scheduled Tribes

These categories of population are found in the tehsils having more areas under wastelands. Generally concentration of Scheduled Tribe population is in the forest clad hilly tracts while the Scheduled Caste populations concentrate in the plains. The same pattern is found in this district. Most of the Scheduled Caste population was enganged in non-agricultural activities to fulfil the requirements of cultivating castes, therefore, it is concentrated in the plain areas. In this study area maximum Scheduled Caste population is found in the tehsils of southern part having almost level land with poor drainage and more land affected by salinity/alkalinity. High percentage (16-20%) of this category of population is also in adjoining tehsils of very high percentage (above 20%) of Scheduled Caste population excluding Phulera tehsil of western part. Scheduled Tribes population was also non-agricultural caste during the British period but with the change in time, now it is a cultivating caste. Maximum concentration of Scheduled Tribes population is in Jamwa Ramgarh tehsil situated in the eastern part of the study area followed by Bassi tehsil having more area under hilly tracts, degraded forest and gullied/ravinous land.

OCCUPATIONAL STRUCTURE

The occupational structure is the true index of the nature of activities practised in the district. Occupational structure of any area is also related with wastelands e.g. if population of a village is engaged in non-agricultural activities, they will not pay any attention for reclamation of their operational holdings wasteland. Population engaged as main and marginal workers has been considered for the calculation of occupational structure. Those who have worked for a major part of that year i.e. for 183 days or more, are categorised as main workers while marginal workers are those who have worked any time at all in the year preceding the enumeration but the period which they have worked is less than 183 days are categorised as marginal workers. In census 2001, the working population was categorised into cultivators, agricultural labourers, house hold industry and other workers.

Cultivators

A person is considered as a cultivator if he/she has been engaged either as an employer, single worker or family worker in cultivation of land owned or held from government or from private persons or institutions for payment in cash, kind or share in cultivation including supervision or direction of cultivation.

In 2001, only 36.47 per cent population was engaged as cultivator in the study area. More than 60 per cent cultivators of the working population are found in Phagi and Chaksu tehsils of southern part where pedological and hydrological conditions are not favourable for the cultivation. These tehsils are economically backward, so most of the working population is engaged in agriculture. Table 2.16 shows tehsilwise occupational structure in the district:

Modrate percentage (55-60%) of cultivators is concentrated in the tehsils of north and eastern parts of the district viz Shahapura, Viratnagar, Amber, Jamwa Ramgarh and Bassi, These tehsils have fertile land with high irrigation intensity. Low percentage of this category of working population is in the western part viz in Chomu, Phulera and Dudu tehsils while the lowest percentage of cultivators is found is Jaipur and Sanganer tehsils i.e. 4.25 and 22.33 per cent of the total working population due to urban agglomeration of capital city Jaipur.

Table 2.16 : Occupational Structure in Jaipur District, 2001

S. No.	Tehsil	Cultivators	Agriculture Labourers	Household Industry Workers	Other Workers	Total
1.	Amber	56.41	4.68	3.35	35.56	100.00
2.	Bassi	58.62	5.31	3.95	32.12	100.00
3.	Chaksu	64.93	5.31	3.07	26.69	100.00
4.	Chomu	54.58	3.92	4.40	37.10	100.00
5.	Dudu	54.61	11.66	2.90	30.83	100.00
6.	Jaipur	4.25	0.60	5.53	86.62	100.00
7.	Jamwa Ramgarh	59.01	7.48	4.45	29.06	100.00
8.	Kotputli	58.16	10.82	2.60	28.42	100.00
9.	Phagi	60.58	10.21	2.66	26.55	100.00
10.	Phulera	50.39	5.90	3.66	40.05	100.00
11.	Sanganer	22.33	3.90	5.08	68.69	100.00
12.	Shahapura	57.22	3.52	4.77	34.49	100.00
13.	Viratnagar	58.14	6.30	4.61	30.95	100.00
	Total	36.47	4.49	4.40	54.64	100.00

Source : Directorate, Census Operations Rajasthan, Jaipur.

Agriculture Labourers

A person who works on another person's land for wages in cash, kind or share is considered as an agricultural labourer. In this study area only 4.49 percent population is working as agricultural labourers. The maximum percentage of agricultural labourers is in southern and northern parts of the district particularly in Dudu, Phagi and Kotputli tehsils (Table 2.16). These tehsils are Industrially backward, so the percentage of agricultural labourers is more. Jaipur and its surrounding tehsils, the percentage of agricultural labourers is less. However in Jamwa Ramgarh and Viratnagar tehsils, the agricultural laboures are slightly more in comparison to Jaipur and its nearby tehsils due to less net sown area.

Household Industry Workers

A household industry is defined as an industry conducted by the head of the household himself/herself and/or mainly by the member of the household at home or within the village. A household industry is further related to production processing, servicing, repairing or making and selling (but not merely selling) of goods.

Only 4.40 per cent is engaged in household industry with maximum percentage is in Jaipur (5.33%) and Sanganer (5.08%) tehsils. In Jaipur tehsil, many families are do their work such as jewellery, embroidery on sarees etc in their houses while in Sanganer tehsil paper making and cloth printing jobs are done in houses. In other tehsils, the percentage of household industry workers ranges between 2.60 to 4.77 per cent (Table 2.16).

Other Workers

This category covers all such workers who do not come under any of the categories mentioned in the fore going paragraphs and also those whose activities have not been adequately described. In the study area. 54.64 percent working population is categorized as other workers. This is the only district in the whole state where the percentage of other workers is very high. The maximum concentration of other workers is in Jaipur tehsil followed by Sanganer and Phulera tehsils (Table 2.16). In capital city Jaipur, many central, state, semi-government offices and NGO's are situated. Besides this, most of the workers are engaged in business, trade, transport, construction and industries etc. Similarly, most of the working population of Sanganer tehsil is also engaged in other works due to adjoining area of the capital city Jaipur. In Phulera tehsil, the largest salt lake of the country is situated near Sambhar town. The salt lake belongs to Hindustan Salt Limited and about three thousand employees work here. In remaining tehsils, the percentage of other workers ranges around 26.55 per cent. The lowest percentage of other workers is in Phagi and Chaksu tehsils i.e. 26.55 and 26.69 per cent of the total working population due to poor resources for industrial development.

REFERENCES

Colonel, S.S. Jacob, *Irrigation in the Jeypore State*, Rajputana, p.2 (1889)

Confidential Report on the Administration of the Jaipur State for 1922-23, 1923-24, 1924-25 and 1925-26. Part I & II: The Pioneer Press, 1927, Allahabad, p.37

Dhabariya, S.S. (1993). *The State of Environment of Aravalli Hill Region in Changing Contours of Arid Ecology*, Vol. I (Ed.) Indra Pal; Dhabariya, S.S.; Kalwar, S.C. Asian Environmental Council, Jaipur.

District Census Handbook, Part XII A&B, District Jaipur, Directorate of Census Operations Rajasthan, 1991 pp. i-iii.

Gardner, J.S. (1971) *Physical Geography*, Harper College Press London, p.154

Gupta, N.L. and Maroo, R.L. (1991) *Challenge of Wastelands Utilization Issues and Themes*, Academic Publishers, Jaipur (Raj.)

Kalwar, S.C. (1971). "Crop Combination Regions of Jaipur District" *Proceedings of Fifth All Rajasthan Geographers Conference*, Udaipur, pp. 45-49.

Kalwar, S.C. (1973). "Methods of Determining Agricultural Efficiency – A Case Study of Jaipur District" *Studies in Geography*, University of Rajasthan, Jaipur, pp. 67-71.

Kalwar, S.C. (1977). Agricultural Land Use in Jaipur District, Unpublished Ph.D. Thesis, University of Rajasthan, Jaipur

Kalwar, S.C. (1984). "Cropping Characteristics – A Case Study of Jaipur District" *Annals of the Association of Rajasthan Geographers*, Vol. IV, pp. 1-11.

Kalwar, S.C. (1990). "Irrigation and Cropping Characteristics in Saline and Alkali Soils" (Ed.) *Geographical Perspectives on Irrigation*, Rawat Publications, Jaipur, pp. 69-80.

Kumar Janendra (1986) *Land Use Analysis: A Case Study of Nalanda District, Bihar*, Inter-India Publications, New Delhi, p.64

Pareek, B.L. and Singh, Richhpal (1976). Report on Soil Survey, Land Classification and Crop Investigation Survey of District Jaipur, State Soil Survey Organisation, Rajasthan, Jaipur.

Report on the Administration of the Jaipur State for 1935-36, Allahabad Law Journal Press, 1937, p.38

Report on the Administration of the Jaipur State for 1936-37, Allahabad Law Journal Press, 1939

Report on the Administration of the Jaipur State for 1933-34, The Pioneer Press, Lucknow, 1935

Report on the Administration of the Jaipur State for 1931-32, The Pioneer Press, Lucknow, 1934, p. 46

Saini R.R. & Kalwar S.C. (1991) *Remote Sensing in Resource Geography*, Pointer Publishers, Jaipur.

Sehgal, K.K. (1977). *Rajasthan District Gazetters*, Jaipur, Directorate of District Gazetteers, Government of Rajasthan, Jaipur.

3

IDENTIFICATION/CLASSIFICATION OF WASTELANDS

A number of Organizations/Central/State Government Departments and individuals have identified various categories of wastelands. Wasteland categories indentified by them are given below: –

Directorate of Economics and Statistics

The Directorate of Economics and Statistics Govt. of India adopted nine fold land use classifications and this classification is also adopted by the Revenue Department and incorporated in a standard performa to be followed right down to the village level record. The nine fold classification is as below: –

1. Forest

This includes all land classed as forest by the Revenue Department. It is not necessary that land is occupied by forest.

2. Barren and Uncultivable Land

Mountains/hills and land affected by salinity (Usar) etc.

3. Land Put to Non-agricultural Use

All lands occupied by roads, railways, water bodies and other lands put to uses other than agriculture.

4. Other Cultivable Lands Excluding Current Fallow

Grazing lands both permanent pastures and meadows.

5. Miscellaneous Tree Crops and Groves not included in Net Sown Area

Land under miscellaneous trees, thatching grass, bamboo bushes and other groves for fuel etc. which are not included under orchards.

6. *Culturable Waste*

Land once cultivated but not cultivated from the last five years in succession and other cultivable lands not cultivated.

7. *Fallow Land other than Current Fallow*

All lands which are not cultivated for a period of not less than one year and not more than five years.

8. *Current Fallow*

Cropped areas, which are kept fallow during the current year.

9. *Net Sown Area*

Area sown with crops and orchards.

In this classification, the data of the following categories of wasteland are collected:

1. Barren and uncultivable land
2. Cultivable waste
3. Old fallow
4. Grazing land and permanent pasture (if the grazing land/pasture are degraded then included in wasteland).

Soil Survey, Directorate of Agriculture, Govt. of Rajasthan 1962

As per report of Planning Commission 30.86 million area of land was lying waste in Rajasthan and Indian Council of Agricultural Research initiated a scheme to survey and categorise of wastelands in the ten districts of the State having rainfall above 60 cms. Accordingly Soil Survey Directorate of Agriculture, Government of Rajasthan has completed work in the three districts viz. Bhilwara, Bundi and Sawai Madhopur. The wastelands have been categorised into four suitability classes as per details given below:

Class A : Lands which are level, deep, non saline, non alkaline with slight erosion, need no reclamation can be brought under cultivation directly.

Class B : Moderately deep lands with gentle slope and slight erosion with moderate salinity or alkalinity and can be brought under cultivation after reclamation or need careful handling.

Class C : Shallow lands with undulation and steep slopes, moderately to severely saline, alkaline and with restricted drainage conditions and active erosion problem, needs prior reclamation, suitable for limited crops and pasture.

Class D : Sloppy and undulated land with gullies and rock outcrop, saline alkaline and not suitable for agricultural use and reclamation is not economical.

All India Soil Survey and Land Use Planning

All India Soil Survey and Land use Planning adopted a classification as follows:

1. ***Forest Area***

   F1. With no canopy
   F2. Thin forest
   F3. Moderate dense forest
   F4. Dense forest and fully stocked top canopy

2. ***Cultivated Land***

   C1. Single cropped
   C2. Double cropped
   C3. Triple cropped

3. ***Terraced Land***

   T1. Poorly bunded land
   T2. Poor terracing measures
   T3. Bench Terraces

4. ***Waste Land***

   W1. Fit for cultivation
   W2. Unfit for cultivation

5. ***Pasture Land***

   P. Pasture and grazing land
   H. Hay lands where the grass is periodically cut
   P1. With young scrub
   T2. Thorny plants with heavy canopy shrubs, weeds.

In above classification, wasteland is divided into two categories i.e. (W1) Land fit for cultivation and (W2) Land unfit for cultivation. Moreover, data on wastelands is difficult to extract out of this scheme of classification because classes are overlapped.

National Commission on Agriculture (1976)

The categories of wastelands and their approximate extent as reported by the National Commission on Agriculture are as below:

Table 3.1: Extent of Wastelands in India

Category	Area (Million ha)	Occurrence
Total area subject to serious water and wind erosion of which 69 million hectare critically affected	150	Water erosion areas in all climatic regions specially in sub-humid and humid areas. Wind erosion areas mostly in arid region of Gujarat, Rajasthan and Haryana.
Riverine land, coastal sandy areas, and high altitude and steeply sloping lands	11.3	Coastal region, interior mountainious regions and steep slopes in Himalayas
Salt-affected lands	7.00	Semi-arid, Indo-Gangetic plain and other semi-arid areas in Penisular region.
Waterlogged areas	6.0	Low-lying areas in high-rainfall regions and irrigated areas, etc.
Ravine land	4.0	Gujarat, Rajasthan, Madhya Pradesh and Uttar Pradesh
Shifting cultivation	3.0	Mostly in north-eastern region
Barren hill ridges or rock outcrops	2.7	Distributed in several states

National Atlas and Thematic Mapping Organization (NATMO)

The NATMO classified the land into major five categories and sixteen sub-categories, the wasteland is known as unproductive land under major categories. The major and sub-categories of land are as below:

1. *Agricultural Land*

    1.1 Irrigated crop land
    1.2 Unirrigated crop land
    1.3 Plantation

2. *Forest*

    2.1 Reserved forest
    2.2 Protected forest
    2.3 Unclassed forest

3. *Non-Agricultural Land*

    3.1 City
    3.2 Mines
    3.3 Settlement with trees

4. *Grazing Land*

   4.1 Grass land
   4.2 Scrubs

5. *Unproductive Land*

   5.1 Sand
   5.2 Rocky
   5.3 Saline
   5.4 Bad land
   5.5 Snow Field

National Atlas and Thematic Mapping Organization (NATMO) has classified the wastelands as an unproductive land under which five categories have been made i.e. sand, rocky, saline, bad land and snow field.

Command Area Development and Water Utilization Department (Wasteland Development Unit)

The CAD and WUD have classified the wasteland into 11 categories. These categories are as below:-

(i) Land with scrub and without scrub.
(ii) Waterlogged land.
(iii) Saline/Alkaline land
(iv) Sand dunes
(v) Mining/Industrial wasteland
(vi) Rocky
(vii) Degraded pasture/Grazing land
(viii) Steep slopping land
(ix) Ravinous and/or gully eroded
(x) Degraded Forest
(xi) Degraded Notified Forest

Bhumbla and Khare

Bhumbla and Khare have indentified these areas under the following seven land use categories :

(i) Forest
(ii) Barren and unculturable land
(iii) Permanent pastures and grazing land
(iv) Culturable waste
(v) Fallow other then the current fallow

(vi) Current fallow and net sown area affected by water and wind erosion.
(vii) Area affected by salinity and alkalinity.

Directorate of Survey (AIR), Survey of India, New Delhi

Serious concern has been expressed over the destruction of forests in India. The need for increasing the forest cover gradually, was being strongly felt due to erratic behaviour of the monsoons, land slides, severe soil erosion and silting of rivers. In this context the establishment of National Wastelands Development Board (NWDB) with the primary objective to (i) devise ways and means to determine the areal extent of wastelands and to bring them under productive use through a massive programme of afforestation and tree plantation and (ii) create an appropriate data base and evolve a computer based monitoring system for social forestry and other afforestation programmes, was a welcome step. But it would take some time to devise suitable methodology for the purpose. It was, therefore, considered appropriate to find out the information available on topographical maps, published by Survey of India could fulfil the requirements of planners or policy makers completely or partly.

Planners and policy-makers are not only interested in the extent of wasteland areas but also in their exact location. Topographical maps published by Survey of India do depict various land areas including built-up area, forest area, cultivated area, water features and other utilised areas as well as various types of wasteland areas such as broken ground and ravines, sandy areas, open scrubs, stony waste areas and rocky barren areas by different nomenclatures and symbols. As the number of topographical maps on 1:50,000 scale covering the country is well over 5000, it would be worthwhile to concentrate on a limited area initially to workout the methodology to determine the extent of wastelands in the country with their locations. It is thought that this study would also reveal the constraints in the procedure followed and indicate the information, which must be picked up during future topographic surveys, so that the topographical maps may depict completely the desired information on wastelands. It is felt that the study would also give a rough estimate of the cost and manpower requirements, if the study is to be completed from the existing topographical maps. Geographical positioning of wastelands in the country together with estimation of their areal extent if taken up district wise would go a long way in planning for optimum utilization of land resources. It is for this reason that present study was taken up. The study aims at depicting the geographical positions of the wastelands by preparing wasteland maps as well as compiling data showing the area of wastelands in hectares. Bharatpur and Dhaulpur districts of Rajasthan state were taken up as the study area, mainly because they are close to New Delhi, the project headquarters, and to enable quick verification of the results of the study in the field. The base material was topographical maps on 1:50,000. The Survey of India divided the land into two broad categories i.e. utilized land areas and wasteland areas. The details of these categories are as below.

Classification of Utilised Land Areas

The following areas were classified as utilised land areas.

(i) ***Built-up area:*** This includes village, town and city blocks, isolated huts, forts and other buildings which are shown in red tint in Survey of India topographical maps.

(ii) ***Forest area:*** This includes protected, reserve and open forests which are shown in green tint in topo maps and gardens, plantations and orchards.

(iii) ***Cultivated areas:*** These have been taken as such from topographical maps which depict cultivation by yellow wash in multicolor maps and by cultivation limits in single colour (black) maps.

(iv) ***Water features:*** These include tanks, lakes and double line streams and rivers which are shown by blue wash in topo maps. Single line streams have been omitted from this category as they were treated as linear features without any area.

Classification of Wasteland Areas

The land areas other than utilised land areas as classified above have been treated as wasteland areas and categorised as follows.

- *Culturable wasteland :* Land which is capable or has the potential for the development of vegetative cover that is not being used due to different constraints of varying degrees is termed as culturable wasteland. This comprises the following categories:-
- *Gullied and/or ravenous land :* This includes broken grounds along streams and rivers and ravines. Broken grounds and ravines falling under forests have not been included in this category but have been included as forest area.
- *Undulating land :* This includes hill ranges, isolated hill tops and other areas of undulating nature prone to degradation.
- *Surface waterlogged land and marsh :* In this category waterlogged marshy areas and swamps have been included.
- *Salt affected land :* Information regarding the soil salinity acquired by the presence of chemical salts are not available in topo maps.
- *Shifting cultivation areas :* Such land is the result of felling trees and burning in forest areas for growing crops. Such areas are indicated in topo maps by giving proper descriptive remarks.
- *Degraded forest land :* Land as notified under the forest act in which denudation of vegetative cover results in degraded land. Vegetative areas which have been reduced to open scrubs have been included in this category.
- *Sands :* Sandy areas are those areas which have accumulation of sand in situ or transported, in coastal or inland areas. These include, sand dunes, flat sand, sand hills, river sands and coastal sandy areas which are depicted in topo maps.
- *Mining and Industrial wasteland :* Information regarding mining and Industrial waste is not available in topo maps. However, quarries including lime and stone quarries which are depicted in topo maps have been included.
- *Wasteland patches along roads and Railway lines :* Generally roads and railway lines have wasteland patches adjoining them. Along roads, the average width of these patches has been taken as 5 m, 10 m being the corresponding figure for railway lines.

Unculturable Wasteland

Land which cannot be developed for vegetative cover is defind as unculturable wasteland. This is divided into the following categories.

- *Barren rocky area :* This includes areas consisting of sheet rocks, boulders and stony waste.
- *Snow covered and/or glacial area :* These are depicted in topographical maps by standard symbols.

Indian Grassland and Fodder Research Institute, Jhansi, Uttar Pradesh

IGFRI has divided the wastelands into eight prominent categories :

(i) Heavily grazed land infested with uneconomic bushes
(ii) Gullied and ravinous land
(iii) Salt infested saline-alkaline land
(iv) Land affected by shifting cultivation
(v) Cho and other riverbed infested area
(vi) Desert land and sand dunes
(vii) Road, rail, canal side areas
(viii) Land affected by water logging

National Remote Sensing Agency (NRSA) 1985

National Remote Sensing Agency, Department of Space has prepared the wasteland maps of all the States and Union Territories on 1:1 million scale in the year 1985. About 190 landsat false colour dispositives on 1:1 million scale of 1980-82, available in the archives of NRSA Data Centre were used for the study. About eight wasteland categories were identified and mapped in this study.

The categories were finalized after interacting with several State and Central Government Departments, Universities and other organizations in the country which are directly or indirectly dealing with the wastelands.

In nation wide wasteland clarification system. The culturable and the non-culturable wastelands have been sub-divided into six and two sub-categories as shown below:—

A. Culturable Wasteland

(i) Salt Affected Land
(ii) Gullied and/or Ravinious Land
(iii) Waterlogged or Marshy Land
(iv) Undulating Upland with or without Scrub.*

---

* Include (a) Foot hill areas, (b) Stony and gravelly land, (c) eroded lands, (d) permanent fallows.

(v) Jhum or Forest Blank.
(vi) Sandy Area (Coastal or Desert)**

B. Non-Culturable Wasteland

(vii) Barren Hill-Ridge or Rock outcrop.***
(viii) Snow Covered or Glacial Area.

Indian Council of Agricultural Research, 1986

From the point of view of establishing vegetative cover, the wastelands have been categorized into different classes as below.

Table 3.2 : Classification of Wastelands by Indian Council of Agriculture Research.

Level – I :	Level II– Based on Causative Agents			
Kinds of Wastelands	1. Water	2. Wind	3. Man	4. Others
1. Utilizable Wastelands	1. Sheet erosion 2. Rill erosion 3. Gullied land 4. Ravinous land 5. Waterlogging 6. Salinity and sodicity (i) Saline soil (ii) Alkali soil 7. Diara land 8. Marshy land 9. Bouldery land	1. Sand dunes, sand bar etc.	1. Shifting cultivation 2. Mine spoils 3. Industrial wasteland 4. Land affected by roads, kilns and borrow pits	1. Shallow soil 2. Landslides

Pillai, V.N.K. Conservator of Forests, North Circle, Haryana (1986)

Wasteland occurs naturally due to geological factors or is the creation of human action.

A. Natural Wastelands

(i) Rocky out crops
(ii) Glacial areas and snow-clad areas
(iii) Sand dunes and sandy wastes
(iv) Saline and Alkali lands

B. Man-made Wastelands

(i) Eroded lands and ravines
(ii) Waterlogged areas

** Include (a) sand dunes (b) other sandy areas like channel islands, sand bars etc.

*** Include (a) barren land with varying lighology (b) mining areas etc.

(iii) Lateritic areas
(iv) Mined areas
(v) Degraded forest areas

CAZRI, Jodhpur (1986)

A.K. Sen, Division of Basic Resources Studies, CAZRI, has given the definition of the classification of wastelands in western Rajasthan as below:—

S. No.	Classification	Definition of the Classification
1.	Sandy waste	These cover barren sand dunes-both stabilized and shifting and sandy plains (barren) which cannot be brought under cultivation unless at a high cost but can be put under grassland and subsequently as a rangeland. These are depleted and degraded lands with high biotic interference where fresh depositions of sand are still going on plantation in the form of shelter belt and wind break are recommended.
2.	Saline waste	These include saline flats, salt infested areas and saline depressions and ranns (depressions) which are not suitable for cultivation but are often used as grazing ground or for extration of slats. In the marginal lands of the saline infested areas, sometimes, like that of the 'Mendha' basin where it joins the Sambar lake salt tolerant crops are grown—these lands however, should be put under saline waste. These are depleted lands and unfit for cultivation. These lowlying areas or depressions (rann) serve as the basin of inland drainage.
3.	Stony waste	These areas are concentrated along the slopping hill sides and piedmont areas where disintegrated rocks due to weathering are the dominating surface feature. Due to agglomeration of stones, cultivation is not possible but grazing may be conducted in the intermittent areas covered with grass and isolated trees. Effective soil depth is poor and a limiting factor for agricultural use. Forestry should be the proper land use unless mining for building stones or others is economically beneficial. These are degraded and highly eroded lands as well as very poor range lands.
4.	Rocky waste	This includes the bare hills and sloping hillsides where the rocks are exposed due to prolonged erosion and weathering. The hills are highly denuded and cannot be put under economic use except quarrying where the rocks are suitable to be used as building materials. Forestry can be recommended.

5. Gravelly waste	These occur in piedmont areas, foothills and plains which are covered by rock fragments caused due to weathering or by drifted pebbles or glaciar during the geological past. Such areas are locally known as *Magra* land. These are not suitable for agriculture and the same is hardly practised unless a depressed area. Silvipastoral is the only land use system that can be suggested.
6. Rocky and stony waste	Often the hills are rocky wastes and the adjacent sloping hillsides and foothills cover very small area to bc mapped in medium scale (upto 1:50,000). Here, the two are grouped together and put under one mapping unit. This is necessary because their development should be considered together. These are highly degraded and eroded land and can hardly be put under cultivation. Forestry and silvipastoral are the alternate land use. Such unit covers small isolated areas.
7. Rocky and gravelly waste	These are quite large areas where Magra lands or gravelly wastelands are associated with isolated hills either monadnocks or inselberge on peneplane or pediplane surface. Soil being shallow is not suitable for cultivation but can be recommended for Silvipastoral and forestry. These are highly eroded and degraded lands.
8. Stony and gravelly waste	These are undulating plains of large areas on piedmont where gravels and stones are equally predominant. These are degraded and eroded and are often covered with grasses and used as grazing land. Silvipasture is the recommended landuse.
9. Sandy waste with open scrub lands	These cover vast areas of idle sandy plains, sandy undulating plain and interdune plains with barchanoid dunes and sandy hummocks. Due to little biotic interference these sandy wastelands are covered with scattered shrubs and wild grasses. These occur extensively on western and northern parts of Jaisalmer district, western Barmer, western Churu and western Bikaner. Fresh sand deposition is common. In many cases the grasses do not survive for more than a few months after the rain. The shrub mostly include *Aerva tomentasa* (Bin), *Calligonum polygonoides* (Phog), *Euphoriba tirucallia* (Phohar), *Panicum turqidum, Eleusine compressa* etc. Prominent grass covers are *Lasiurus sindicus, Fleusine compressa, Cenchrus biflorus, Cymopogon jwarancusa, C. prejpru, Cyperus jaevigatus, Citrullus colonthis, Molligo mudicanllis, Boerharia diffusa* etc.
10. Rocky and gravelly waste with open land.	*Silvipasture is the recommended landuse :* These are the types of lands as described in No. 7 and associated with desert or scattered grasses and scrub lands like that of the previous

one described. These are actually the foothills and gravelly piedmonts with isolated hills in Jaisalmer, Churu, Bikaner and Barmer where it often exists in the form of vast stretches of lands and in isolated patches along the Aravalli foothills in Sikar, Pali and Jhunjhunu districts. Ground flora often consists of *Eleusine compressa, Dactyloctenium sandicu, Aristida, funiculata, Cymbopogon jawarancusa and Lasiurus sindicus Silvipasture* is the alternate landuse.

S.S. Yadav (1986)

Wastelands may be classified in three main categories for standardization of wastelands development in India :

(1) High Altitude Wasteland – its geo-ecology and problems of development :

- (i) Cold deserts, alpine forest and rocky wastelands.
- (ii) Wastelands of hilly areas, their development and environmental impacts of shifting cultivation.
- (iii) Moisture deficiencies in plateau areas and prospects of dryland farming.
- (iv) Wastelands development in river valley projects and their landuse.

(2) Wastelands Development for Desert lands, their Problems and Constraints

- (a) Areal extent of arid wastelands development and problems.
- (b) Appropriate use of Arid Zone :
  - (i) Intensive Irrigation Development.
  - (ii) Development of scrubs, grasses and fodder.
  - (iii) Conservation of sandy areas.
- (c) Development of grazing in wastelands and specialization of animal husbandry regions.

(3) Specific Problem Areas of the Wastelands and their Development Planning

- (i) Flood and drought prone areas.
- (ii) Alkaline or saline lands.
- (iii) Ravines and bad lands.
- (iv) Processes of degeneration and wastelands.
- (v) Rann of Kachch and other salt pans.
- (vi) Tidal forests.
- (vii) Waterlogged areas.

U. P. Bhumi Sudhar Nigam Ltd. Lucknow (1986)

P.D. Bajpai, Managing Director, Bhumi Sudhar Nigam Ltd. Lucknow (U. P.) has divided the wasteland of Uttar Pradesh in the following categories for reclamation/development of wasteland :

Table 3.3 : Categories of Wasteland in Uttar Pradesh

S No.	Category of wasteland
1.	Land infested with shrubs and bushes
2.	Ravine area
3.	Waterlogged lands
4.	Saline and alkalie lands
5.	Riverline lands
6.	Stony and gravelly lands
7.	Thin cover lands

Technical Task Force Group Constituted by Planning Commission (1986)

Confronted by varying estimates by different agencies including data thrown up by latest technological tools like Remote sensing, it became evident that NWDB should lay down a precise definition of wastelands in various categories. Therefore a Technical Task Force Group was constituted by Planning Commission to arrive at precise definition of categories. The Technical Task Group was constituted on December 3, 1985 and its report submitted to National Wastelands Development Board on June 5, 1986. The classification system developed by the Technical Task Force Group is as below :

Table 3.4: Wasteland categories defined by the Technical Task Group

LEVEL I	LEVEL II
Culturable Wasteland	1. Gullied and/or ravinous land
	2. Undulaing upland with or without scrub
	3. Surface waterlogged land and marsh
	4. Salt affected land
	5. Shifting cultivation area
	6. Degraded forest land
	7. Degraded pastures/grazing land
	8. Degraded non-forest plantation land
	9. Strip lands
	10. Sands
	11. Mining/industrial wasteland
Non-culturable wasteland	12. Barren rocky/stony wastes/sheet rock area
	13. Steep sloping area
	14. Snow covered and/or glacial area.

National Wasteland Development Board (NWDB)

The classification system developed by the Technical Task Force Group and subsequently slightly modified by NWDB as below:-

1. Gullied and/or Ravinous land
2. Upland with or without scrub.
3. Waterlogged and marshy land
4. Land affected by salinity/alkalinity
5. Shifting cultivation area
6. Under utilized/degraded notified forest land
7. Degraded pastures/grazing land
8. Degraded land under plantation crops.
9. Sands-Inland/Coastal
10. Mining/Industrial wastelands.
11. Barren Rocky/Stony waste/Sheet rock area
12. Steep sloping area
13. Snow Covered and/or glacial area.

EXPLANATION : Gullied and/or Ravinous Land

Gullied Land

The gullies are formed as a result of localized surface runoff affecting the unconsolidated material resulting in the formation of perceptible channels causing undulated terrain. Gullies are the first stage of excessive land dissection followed by their networking which lead to the development of ravinous land.

Ravinous Land

The word ravine is usually associated not with an isolated gully but a network of gullies formed generally in deep alluvium and entering nearby river, flowing much lower than the surrounding table lands. The ravines then, are extensive system of gullies developed along river courses.

Upland with or without Scrub

This land is generally prone to deterioration due to erosion and may or may not have scrub cover. Such land occupies relatively high topographic locations.

Waterlogged and Marshy Land

Waterlogged land is that land where the water is at/or near the surface and water stands for most of the year.

Marshy land in which gets permanently or periodically inundated by water and is characterised by vegetation which includes grasses and weeds.

Land Affected by Salinity/Alkalinty

Coastal or Inland

Salt affected land is generally characterised as that has adverse effects on the growth of most plants due to the action or presence of excess soluble salts (Saline) or high exchangeable sodium.

Alkali land has an exchangeable sodium percentage (ESP) of about 15 which is generally considered as the limit between normal land alkali soils. The predominant salts are carbonates and bicarbonates of sodium.

Coastal saline soils may be with or without ingress or inundation by sea water.

Shifting Cultivation Area

Such land is the result of cyclical land use consisting of felling of trees and burning of forest areas for growing crops. This results in extensive soil losses, land degradation, and extinction of flora and fauna.

Sands-Inland/Coastal

Sandy areas are those areas which have stabilized accumulation of sand, in coastal, riverine or inland areas.

Wastelands arising out of Mining and Industrial activity:

Mining Wastelands

Lands where mining operations bring about the deterioration of land.

Industrial Wastelands

Lands which have deteriorated on account of large scale industrial effluent discharge.

Barren Hill-ridge/Rock Outcrop

It is defined as the rock exposures of varying lighology often barren and devoid of soil cover and vegetation. They occur amidst hill-forests as openings or scattered as isolated exposures on plateau and plains.

Snow/Glacial Covered Area

Snow is defined as a solid form of water consisting of ice. It includes permanently snow covered areas as on the Himalayas. Glacier is a mass of accumutated ice that occurs in the midst of permanent/snow covered areas.

Degraded Forest Land

Land as notified under the Forest Act and those lands with various types of forest cover, in which denudation of vegetative cover is less than 20 per cent of canopy cover, are classified as degraded land.

Degraded Pastures/Grazing Land

All those grazing lands in non-forest areas, whether or not they are permanent pastures or meadows, which have become degraded due to lack of proper soil conservation and drainage measures, fall under this category.

Degraded non-forest Plantation Land

Degraded lands containing plantation outside the notified forest area :

1. Barren rocky/stony wastes sheet rock area.
2. Steep sloping areas :
   Land with very steep slopes (greater than 35 degrees) prone to erosion and mass wasting (landslides).

National Wastelands Updation Mission, NRSA June 2003

National Wastelands Updation Mission, Land Use Division, NRSA, Hyderabad (A.P.) in the work centres meet on 30th June 2003 discussed existing wasteland classification. On the basis of discussion, the following guidelines were sent to the work centres for wasteland updation.

Wasteland Classes

1. Gullied and/or ravinous land
   (i) Shallow
   (ii) Medium
   (iii) Deep
2. Land with or without Scrub
   (i) Land with Scrub
   (ii) Land without Scrub
3. Waterlogged and Marshy Land
   (i) Permanently
   (ii) Temporarily
4. Land Affected by Salinity/Alkalinity
   (i) Strong
   (ii) Moderate
   (iii) Slight

5. Shifting Cultivation (i) Current Jhum
   (ii) Abandoned Jhum
6. Under Utilized/Degraded Notified Forest Land Scrub Dominated
7. Degraded partures/Grazing land
8. Degraded land under plantation crops
9. Sand (Riverine/Coastal/ Desert)
   Flood Plain
   Levees
   Coastal Sand
   Semi-Stabilized to Stabilized (>40) Sand Dunes
   Major obstacle Dunes
   Semi-Stabilized to Stabilized
   Moderately high (15-40m)
   Minor Obstacle Dune
   Semi-Stabilized to stabilized low (<15m) Dunes
   High Hummocky
   and Shrub- Coppice Dunes
   Closely, Spaced Inter Dune Area.
10. Mining/Industrial wastelands
11. Barren Rocky/Stony Waste/Sheet rock area
12. Steep Sloping area
13. Snow covered and/or glacial area

Identification of Wastelands in Jaipur District

On the basis of satellite imageries of 28 February 2003 the following categories of wastelands are identified in the study area.

1. Gullied and/or ravinous land
2. Land with or without Scrub:
   Land with Scrub
   Land without Scrub
3. Land Affected by Salinity/Alkalinity:
   Strong
   Moderate
   Slight
4. Degraded Notified
   Forest Land
5. Degraded Pastures/Grazing Land
6. Sand Desertic:
   Semi-Stabilized to Stabilized Moderately high (15-40m)Dune and Minor Obstacle Dunes Semi-Stabilized to Stabilized low (<15m) Dunes, High Hummocky and Shrub Coppice Dunes.
   Closely Spaced Inter Dune Area.

7. Mining/Industrial Wasteland:

   Minning
   Industrial

8. Barren Rocky

REFERENCES

Agriculture Chemistry, Directorate of Agriculture, Government of Rajasthan, Jaipur, pp. 43-44.

Anonymous, (1987). Comments on The Technical Task Group Report, Wastelands and Suggested Definition and Classification, ICAR, (Unpublished).

Bachkheti, N.D. (1986). Wastelands Development, National Seminar on Fuelwood and Fodder Production from Wastelands, Forest Research Institute, Dehradun.

Command Area Development and Water Utilization Department (Wastelands Utilization Unit), Govt. of Rajasthan, 1999.

Bajpai, P.D. (1989). 'Wasteland Reclamation and Development in Uttar Pradesh' (Ed.) *Dimensions of Wasteland Development*, Concept Publishing Company, New Delhi-59 p. 320

Bhumbla, D.R. and Arvind Kumar (1984). Estimate of Wastelands in India; Society for Promotion of Wastelands Development, New Delhi.

Classification of Wastelands: Project based on Topograhical Maps and Aerial Photographs, Directorate of Survey (AIR) Survey of India, New Delhi pp.1-4

Kalwar, S.C. (1998). Identification and Developments of Wastelands in Semi-Arid Areas of Rajasthan. Unpublished Minor Research Project Report, ICSSR, New Delhi.

Ministry of Agriculture and Irrigation, Government of India, Report on the National Commission on Agriculture, 1976 Volume-V p. 178.

National Wasteland Development Board (1986). First Meeting of the National Land use and Wastelands Development Council (NLWC).

NRSA, Hyderabad (1985) Mapping of Wastelands in India from Satellite Imagery, 1980-82, Summary Report, Rajasthan.

Pillai, V. N. K. (1989). Wasteland Development in Haryana, (Ed.) *Dimensions of Wasteland Development*, Concept Publishing Company, New Delhi-59.

Rachana (2002). "Identification and Utilisation of Wasteland for Sustainable Development. A Case Study of Jhunjhunu district" Unpublished Ph.D thesis Department of Geography. University of Rajasthan, Jaipur.

Sen, A. K. (1989). Typology and Mapping Procedures of Wastelands in the Indian Arid Zone, (Ed.) *Dimension Wasteland Development*, Concept Publishing Company, New Delhi.

Sen, A. K. (1972) Land Utilization Mapping to Estimate the Wastelands of Arid Zone in Rajasthan by Photo Interpretation Techniques, *Bulletin N. 44, Ind. Nat. Sci Acad.* pp 67-71.

Shankar Narayan, K. A., Sen, A. K. and Balak Ram (1982). Analysis of Wastelands in Arid Zone by Remote Sensing Techniques, Proq-Symp. Res. Surv. for Land use Plan and Env. Conservn, Ind. Soc. Photo Interp./ NRSA., pp. 54-67.

Singh, Panjab (1990). 'Forage and Fuel Production from Degraded and Wastelands' in (T.Ed.) *Technologies for Wasteland Development*, ICAR, New Delhi.

Technical Task Group Report (1986) Wastelands Definition and Classification, National Wastelands Development Board, Ministry of Environment and Forest, Govt. of India, New Delhi.

Yadav, H.R. (1989). (Ed.) *Dimensions of Wasteland Development*, Concept Publishing Company, New Delhi.

Yadav, S. S. (1989) 'Geographic Aspects of Wastelands Development in India'. (Ed.) *Dimensions of Wasteland Development*, Concept Publishing Company, New Delhi-59 p. 33.

4

SPATIAL DISTRIBUTION OF WASTELANDS

At present development activities are being implemented at the village/panchayat/micro-watershed level for the upliftment of rural inhabitants. For development programmes execution, database is required for allocation of funds and monitoring activities by the development authorities etc. Keeping these things in mind wasteland data have been discussed at two levels i.e. (i) Tehsilwise percentage distribution of wastelands. (ii) Village/Townwise wastelands.

Area under Wasteland in Hectares and Percentage to the total Wasteland Area in the District

In the study area following categories of wastelands are found. The area and percentage to the total wastelands under each category is given below:

Table 4.1 : Area of Wastelands in Hectares and Percentage to Total Wastelands in Jaipur District 2003.

S. No.	Wasteland Category	Wasteland Area in hectares	Percentage to the total wasteland
1.	Gullied and/or ravinous land	52987	27.41
2.	Land with or without scrub	23967	12.40
3.	Land Affected by Salinity/ Alkalinity	14186	7.34
4.	Degraded Notified Forest Land	69641	36.02
5.	Degraded Pasture/Grazing Land	7408	3.83
6.	Sands-Desertic	16304	8.43
7.	Mining/Industrial Waste	350	0.18
8.	Barren Rocky	8485	4.39
	Total	193328	100.00

Source : B.M. Birla, Science and Technology Centre, Jaipur (Rajasthan).

The above Table 4.1 and Fig. 4.1 reveal that more than one-third area (36.02%) of total wasteland of the district is under degraded notified forest land followed by gullied and/or ravinous land (27.41%) and land with or without scrub (12.40%). All the three categories of wastelands combinedly consist three fourth (75.83%) wasteland area of the district. In remaining wastelands sands-desertic (8.43%) and land affected by salinity/alkalinity (7.34%)

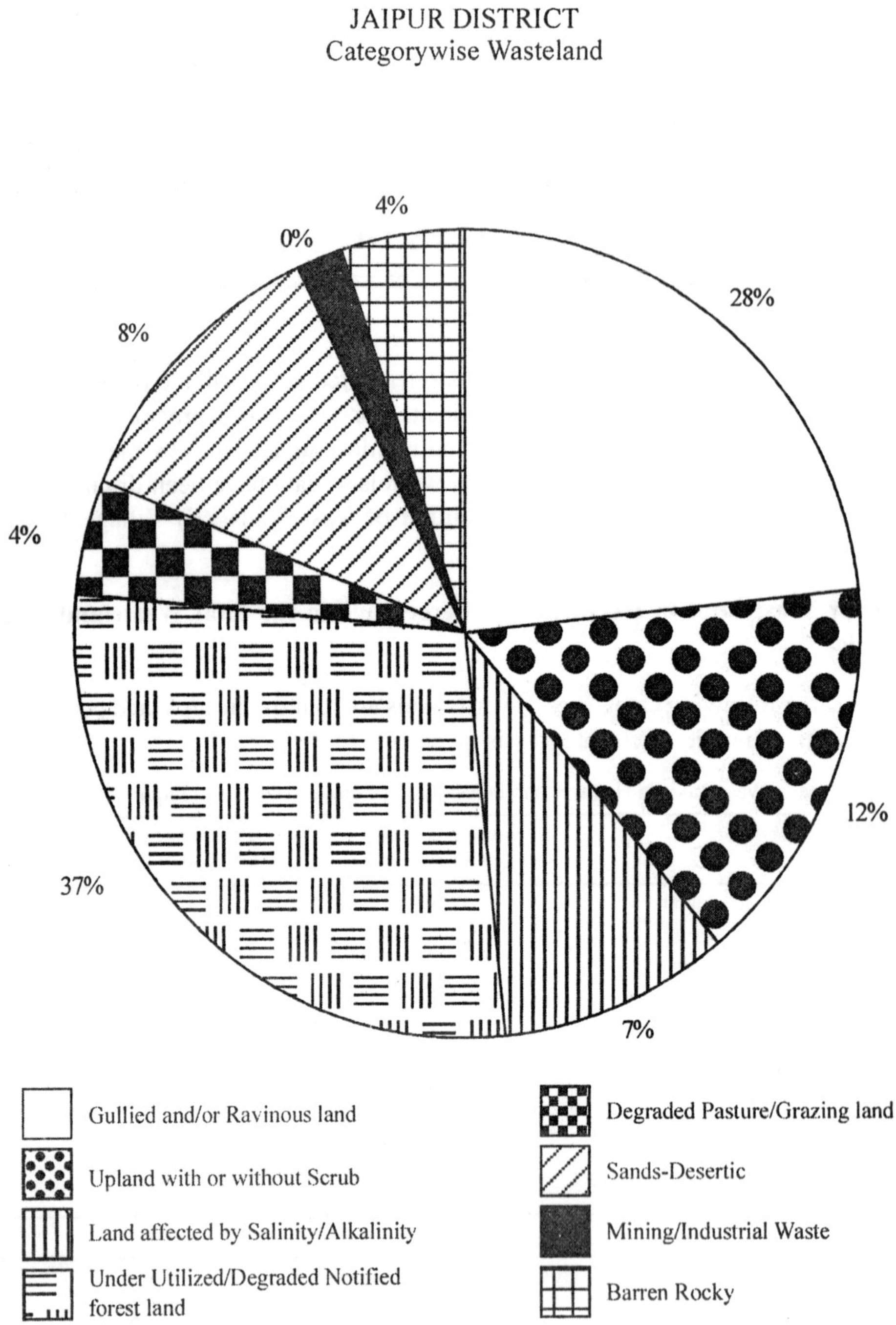

Source : B.M. Birla Science and Technology Centre, Jaipur

Fig. 4.1: Categorywise Wastelands in Jaipur District.

are important. The degraded forest and most of the gullied and/or ravinous land are associated with hilly tracts. Thus the major problem of wasteland is concentrated in the tehsils having more area under hills especially tehsils of eastern part of the district.

Wasteland Pattern in India, Rajasthan and Jaipur District

A comparison of wastelands in India, Rajasthan and Jaipur district is given in Table 4.2 :

Table 4.2 : Wasteland Pattern in India, Rajasthan and Jaipur District (% to total geographical area)

S. No.	Wasteland Category	India*	Rajasthan*	Jaipur district** (2003)
1	Gullied and/or Ravinous land	0.65	1.45	4.76
2	Upland with or without scrub	6.13	7.93	2.15
3	Waterlogged and marshy land	0.52	0.08	0.00
4	Land affected by salinity/alkalinity	0.65	0.79	1.28
5	Shifting cultivation area	1.11	—	0.00
6	Under Utilized/degraded notified forest land	4.44	3.66	6.25
7	Degraded pasture / grazing land	0.82	3.57	0.66
8	Degraded land under plantation crop	0.18	0.006	0.00
9	Sands-inland/coastal	1.58	11.87	1.47
10	Mining/industrial wastelands	0.04	0.04	0.03
11	Barren hills/rocky/stony waste/ sheet rock area	2.04	1.40	0.76
12	Steep sloping area	0.24	0.05	0.00
13	Snow covered and/or glacial area	1.76	0.00	0.00
	TOTAL	20.17	30.87	17.34

Sources : **Wastelands Atlas of India*, 2000, Ministry of Rural Development, Department of Land Resources, Government of India : National Remote Sensing Agency, Hyderabad (A.P.) p.8 and p.41
**B.M. Birla Science and Technology Centre, Jaipur 2003.

On comparing India, Rajasthan and Jaipur district it is observed from the Fig. 4.2 A that the study area occupies lowest percentage of wastelands. However, the state and the district have almost equal wasteland area. It is also very important to know categorywise wasteland pattern in the country, state and the study area. Fig 4.2B shows that there are high percentages of sand-desertic and degraded pasture in the state in comparison to the nation and the study area. It is due to arid conditions in the western part of the state.

The district occupies higher percentage of gullied and/or ravinous land, degraded forest in comparison to the country and the state (Fig. 4.2B and Table 4.2). The district and Rajasthan State both do not occupy any area under shifting cultivation, snow covered and or glacial area.

Gullied and/or Ravinous land

In natural resources, soil is one of the most valuable resources of the world. Food, fodder and fuel production are dependent on agriculture and allied pursuits based on soils. The gullied and/or ravinous land swallows the fertile land and has been reducing the agricultural land.

There are many types of soil erosion but the earth scientists are largely concerned with the relatively important geological erosion and accelerated erosion. Geological erosion is the rate at which the land would normally be eroded without disturbance through human activity. Accelerated erosion is the increased rate of the erosion that often arises when man

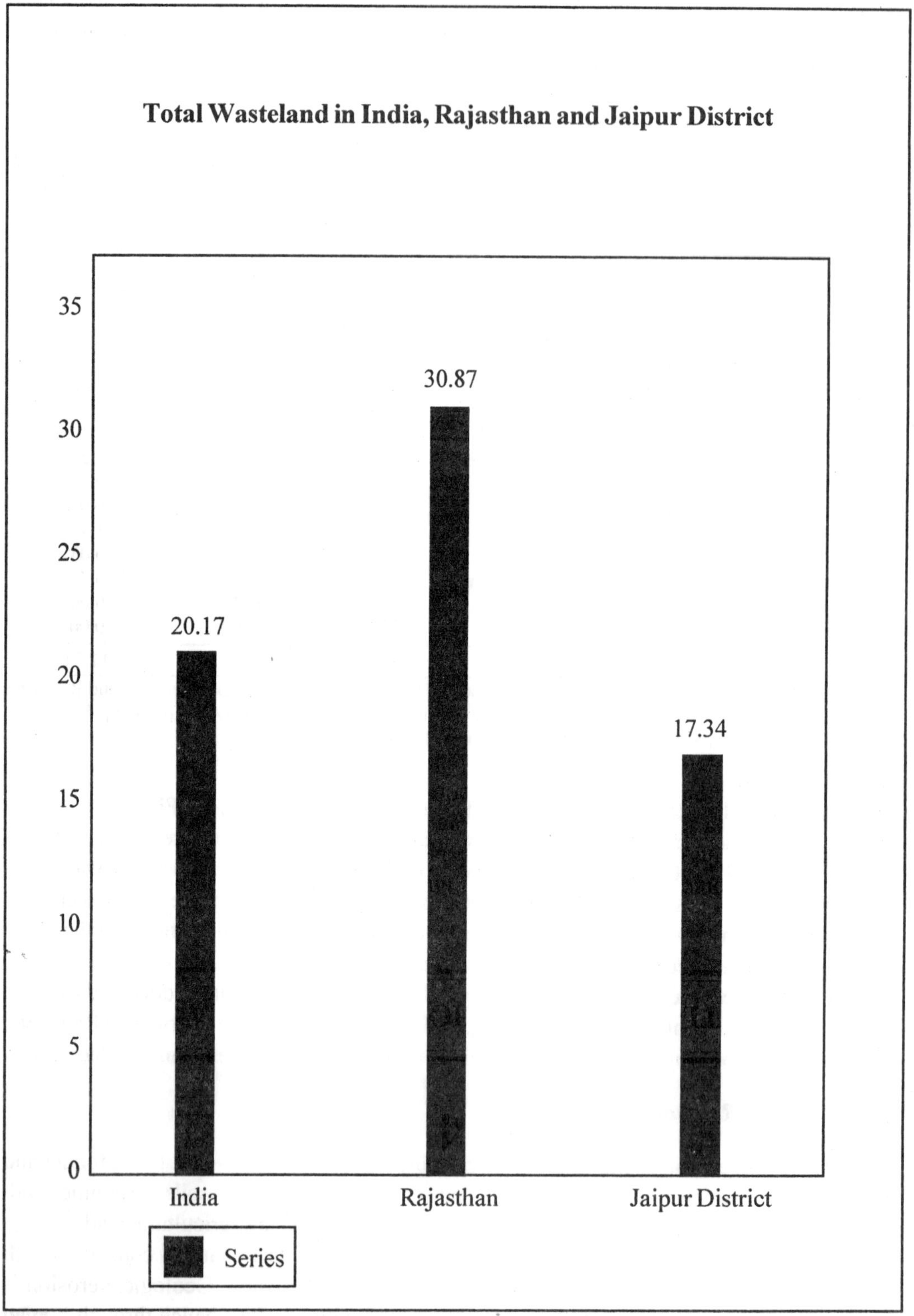

Fig. 4.2A : Total Wastelands in India, Rajasthan and Jaipur District.

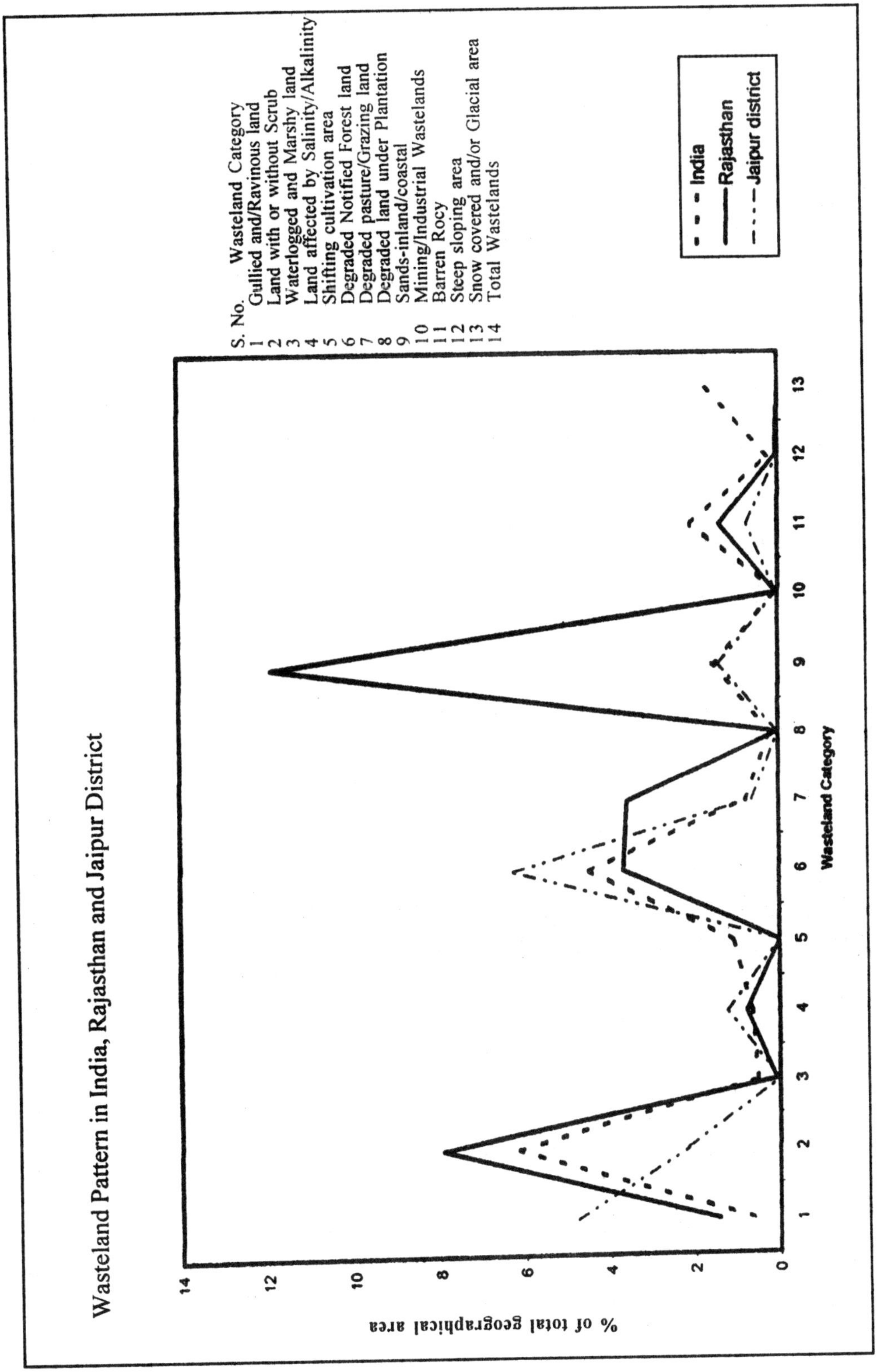

Fig. 4.2B : Wasteland Patterns in India, Rajasthan and Jaipur District.

alters the ecosystem by various land use practices. Ravine erosion is really the problem of accelerated erosion.

Gully initiates along the animal trails, roads and paths on the agricultural uplands. On the contrary, ravine begins along the river sides and encroaches upon the catchment area by headward growth. Hence, ravine is said to be a form produced by river action and gully as the function of catchment area.

The word ravine denotes gullied land containing systems of gullies running more or less parallel to each other and entering a nearby river flowing much lower than the surrounding table lands.

Classification of Gullied and/or Ravinous land

For gullied/ravinous land control/reclamation, classification of ravines is necessary. Tejwani and Ahuja (1956) have classified ravine lands into four classes on the basis of their form, head characteristics, length and width as below:

Classification of Ravines and Gullies

Particulars of the ravines	Description of Symbols of the Gully or Ravine			
	G–1	G–2	G–3	G– 4
Depth in metres	Upto 1	1–3	3 – 9	more than 9
Bed width in metres	Upto 18	Not less than 18	18	varies
Side slope in per cent	Varies	Varies	Uniformly sloping between 6 – 12	Sloping more than 12 steep

All India Soil and Land use Survey has also classified gullies into three grades for mapping purposes. The suggested grades are:

Particulars of the ravines	Symbols of the Gully or Ravines		
	G–1 Narrow	G–2 Medium	G–3 Wide
Width in metres	0.3 – 1.5	1.5 – 3.0	over 3.00

The ravines of the catchment of the Damodar Valley Project have been classified as under:

Particulars of the ravines	Shallow	Medium	Deep
Depth in metres	0 – 1	1– 3	3 and more
Width in metres	0 – 1.5	1.5 – 3.5	3 and more

Sharma (1968) has classified ravines on the basis of their width, depth and slope of side and head scarp into three grades as given below:

Classification of the Chambal Ravines

Particulars of the ravines	Description of Symbols of Ravines		
	G–1	G–2	G–3
Depth in metres	upto 1	1–5	5 – 40
Bed width in metres	upto 18	18 – 25	Above 25
Slope of head scarp	Gently Sloping	Varies	Steep
Slope of scarps	45° – 80°	50° – 90°	50° – 90° but mostly vertical

Stages of Ravine Growth

Tejwani (1960) has distinguished three stages of ravine growth as below:—

Stage I - Development of rills
Stage II - Development of gully
Stage III - Stabilisation of the gully.

Gullied and/or ravinous land is dominant on pediments and foot hill zones particularly on windward side of the Aravalli ranges. Wind drifted loamy sand accumulates along the western side foot hills and rainy water cuts the land and converts the land into gullied and / or ravinous land. In this upper part gullies/ravines are deep due to thickness of wind drifted alluvium deposited on foot hill slopes. Due to this, gullied/ravinous land features are common on the western side of the Aravalli hills. The strong evidences of such land features can be seen in 1 : 50000 topographical sheets of the study area. It is observed during the field study that the depth of gully/ravine depends on the thickness of soil and depth of river channel. It can be said there is a positive relationship between thickness of soil and depth of ravines and channel.

Inspite of peneplained area of south eastern part of the study area, tehsils of this part have gullied and/or ravinous land along the Dhund and its tributaries. It is observed during the field survey that more water erosion is in the areas of calcium carbonate along the Dhund river. The development of ravines also take place through shallow holes. Sharma (1976) has intensively studied this area and has distinguished four stages of ravine growth viz shallow hole stage, tunneling stage, collapsing stage and recession stage.

In this area Gullies/ravines of G1, G2 and G3 categories having linear, bulbous, compound and trellies shape are found. Most of the Gullied/ravines have semi circular head characteristics.

Table 4.3 : Tehsilwise Percentage Distribution of Gullied and/or Ravinous Land in Jaipur district

S. No.	Tehsil	Area under gullied/ravinous in hectares	Percentage of gullied/Ravi-nous to total geog. area	% to Tehsil's total wasteland	Total gullied/ravinous area of the district (%)
1	Amber	5266.25	6.29	28.91	10.62
2	Bassi	4470.70	6.49	46.96	8.41
3	Chaksu	1773.50	2.27	29.70	3.57
4	Chomu	1080.00	1.56	11.13	2.18
5	Dudu	452.50	0.34	2.70	0.91
6	Jaipur	958.00	1.64	15.96	1.93
7	Jamwa Ramgarh	14818.29	14.67	38.90	29.88
8	Kotputli	3309.25	3.97	20.35	6.67
9	Phagi	1630.50	1.52	12.49	3.29
10	Phulera	60.00	0.27	0.27	0.12
11	Sanganer	—	—	—	—
12	Shahapura	7247.15	15.22	54.26	14.61
13	Viratnagar	8823.90	18.58	34.65	17.99
	District	49590.04	4.20	25.01	100.00

Source : Computed from Wasteland Maps, NRSA, Hyderabad (A.P.)

Plate 1 : A ravine approaching culltivated land through headward erosion on left bank of Dhund river in Jamwa Ramgarh Tehsil.

Plate 2 : Reactivated aeolian sand blanketing fertile land near Asalpur-Jobner Railway Station in Phulera Tehsil.

There are 49590.04 hectares of land under gullied and/or ravinous constituting 4.20 per cent of the total geographical area of the district. Maximum concentration of gullied and/or ravinous land is found in the north eastern part of the district. Approximately one-half gullied and/or ravinous land of the district is concentrated in two tehsils viz Jamwa Ramgarh and Viratnagar. Other important tehsils of gullied and/or ravinous land are Shahapura and Amber tehsils (Table 4.3). All the four tehsils constitute three-fourth gullied and/or ravinous land of the district.

Table 4.3 and Fig. 4.3B show tehsilwise percentage of gullied and/or ravinous land to the total geographical area varied considerably in the district depending on their respective surface conditions. It is very interesting to note that eastern part of the district has more area under gullied and/or ravinous land while it is very less in the western part of the district. Its maximum concentration (above 12%) is in north eastern part especially in Viratnagar, Shahapura and Jamwa Ramgarh tehsils (Fig. 4.3 B). These tehsils lie in the hilly tract of the district while tehsils of peneplained area of the western part of the district have very low percentage of gullied and or ravinous land e.g. Sanganer, Phulera, Dudu and Phagi (Fig. 2.1A and 4.3B).

Table 4.3 also reveals that one-fourth area (25.01%) of the total wasteland of the district is under gullied and/or ravinous. Shahapura (54.25%), Bassi (46.96%), Jamwa Ramgarh (38.90%) and Viratnagar (34.65%) tehsils registered larger percentage of their wastelands under gullied and/or ravinous land while the lower percentage is found in Phulera tehsil (0.27%) and Dudu tehsil (3.31%) of the western part of the district.

Fig. 4.3A clearly shows that villages of eastern part of the district have problem of gullied and/or ravinous land while western part of the district has not such problem. The villages having high and very high percentages (45.01 to < 60%) of gullied and ravinous

Table 4.4 : Tehsilwise Distribution of Villages/Towns by Share of Gullied and/or Ravinous Lands in Jaipur District

Tehsil	Percentage wise distribution of villages and Towns of Gullied and/or Ravinous land					Total Villages	% to total Gullied and/or Ravinous villages/towns
	1-15%	12-30%	30-45%	45-60%	Above 60%		
Amber	20	6	3	4	2	35	9.48
Bassi	20	11	7	3	8	49	13.28
Chaksu	22	13	3	—	4	42	11.38
Chomu	2	2	—	—	—	04	1.08
Dudu		01	01	—	—	02	0.54
Jaipur	2	—	01	01	02	06	1.63
Jamwa Ramgarh	29	25	25	13	16	108	29.27
Kotputli	17	4	4	2	—	27	7.32
Phagi	14	4	2	01	—	21	5.69
Phulera	01	—	—	—	—	01	0.27
Sanganer	—	—	—	—	—	—	—
Shahapura	12	3	1	6	4	26	7.04
Viratnagar	13	13	4	10	8	48	13.01
Total Villages	152	82	51	40	44	369	
Percentage	41.19	22.22	13.82	10.84	11.92	100%	100%

Source: Computed from Wasteland Maps, NRSA, Hyderabad (A.P.)

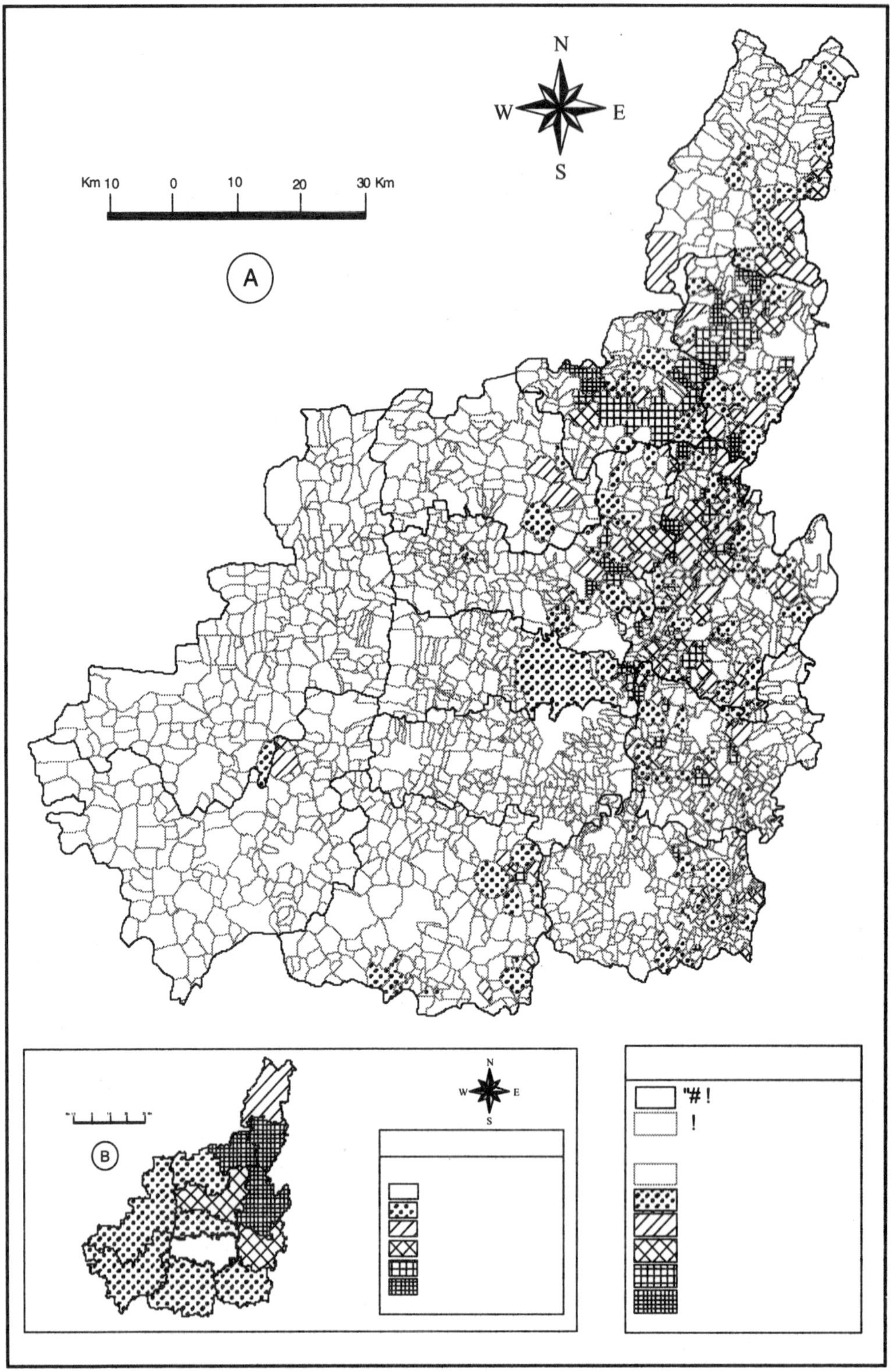

Fig. 4.3A : Gullied and/or Ravinous (Village/Townwise)
Fig. 4.3B : Gullied and/or Ravinous (Tehsilwise)

land are concentrated in a enlongated belt running from south to north. The villages having moderate percentage (30.1 to 45%) are found in two patches i.e. eastern part of Jamwa Ramgarh tehsil and its adjoining area in Amber tehsil. The second patch is in southern part of Shahapura tehsil and central part of Viratnagar tehsil (Fig. 4.3A). The villages of low and very low percentage of gullied and ravinous are also scattered in the eastern part of the district. The distribution of gullied and/or ravinous land at village level is also shown in Table 4.4.

Table 4.4 shows that the villages having very low and low percentages (1 to 15 and 15-30%) to the total geographical area cover approximately two-third gullied and/or ravinous infested villages of the district. The maximum villages of these intensities, (1 to 15 and 15 to 30%) are found in Jamwa Ramgarh (54), Chaksu (35), Bassi (31), Viratnagar (26) and Amber (26) tehsils situated in the eastern part of the district excluding Amber tehsil.

Again Jamwa Ramgarh tehsil leads all the tehsils having villages of moderate intensity (30.45%) of this category of land. Tehsils having more number of villages under high (45-60%) and very high (more than 60%) intensity of gullied/ravinous land are Jamwa Ramgarh (29) and Viratnagar (18) tehsils lie in the hilly tract of the district (Fig. 2.1, 4.3A and B).

Table 4.4 also shows that Jamwa Ramgarh tehsil alone of hilly tract has 108 villages (29.27%) out of total 369 gullied/ravinous villages of the district followed by Bassi (49 villages) and Viratnagar (48 villages) tehsils. All the three tehsils occupy more than half (55.55%) villages of this category of land. Other tehsils having more gullied/ravinous villages are Chaksu, Amber, Kotputli and Shahapura. These tehsils are also situated in the eastern part of the district adjoining to hilly tract except Chaksu tehsil. Sanganer is the only tehsil which does not possess gullied/ravinous land. Other tehsils having negligible problem of gullied/ravinous land are Phulera and Dudu tehsils of western part of the study area. It is concluded that maximum concentration of gullied/ravinous land is in hilly tracts of the district.

Table 4.4 also shows that approximately one-fourth gullied/ravinous villages have high to very high percentages (45 to above 60%) of gullied/ravinous land while two-third gullied/ravinous villages keep their very low and low intensity (less than 30%) of gullied/ravinous land.

Degraded Notified Forest Land

In the study area, cutting of trees for fuel, fodder, furniture, agricultural implements, uncontrolled grazing etc. are main causes of degradation of forest. The problem of forest degradation is worldwide but it is more in developing countries. In degraded forest areas very sparse trees are found. However, several types of shrubs and bushes are common on these lands. With the increasing population and livestock pressure on forestlands, the dense forest is also shrinking rapidly. Due to this, ecological balance and ecosystem have been disturbed and increased wasteland especially degraded forest and gullied and/or ravinous land. According to National Forest Policy, one-third geographical area must be under forest cover but unfortunately this district does not cover desired percentage.

This category covers 64256.13 ha equivalent to 5.44 per cent of the geographical area of the district. Viratnagar tehsil occupies its more than one-third area (33.58%) to the total geographical area under degraded forest. Other tehsils occupying more geographical area of degraded forest are Jamwa Ramgarh (19.53%), Kotputli (11.07%) and Amber (13.13%). All these tehsils are situated fully or partly in the hilly tracts and occupy more than four-fifth area (83.13%) of degraded forests of the entire study area.

The following Table 4.5 shows tehsil wise area under degraded forest, percentage of degraded forest to total geographical area, percentage to tehsils total wasteland and percentage to total degraded forest land in the district.

Table 4.5 : Tehsilwise Percentage Distribution of Degraded Notified Forest land in Jaipur District.

S. No.	Tehsil	Area under Degraded forest in hectares	% of degraded forest to total geographical area	% to tehsil's total waste land	% to total degraded forest of the district
1.	Amber	8479.00	10.13	46.55	13.19
2.	Bassi	2117.51	3.29	23.84	3.29
3.	Chaksu	—	—	—	—
4.	Chomu	1422.00	2.06	14.66	2.21
5.	Dudu	—	—	—	—
6.	Jaipur	3300.13	5.64	54.99	5.13
7.	Jamwa Ramgarh	19753.85	19.53	51.85	30.74
8.	Kotputli	9238.42	11.07	56.65	14.38
9.	Phagi	557.50	0.52	4.27	0.87
10.	Phulera	52.50	0.02	0.23	0.08
11.	Sanganer	405.00	0.64	9.97	0.63
12.	Shahapura	2980.50	6.26	22.31	4.64
13.	Viratnagar	15949.72	33.58	62.64	24.82
	District	64256.12	5.44	32.41	100

Source: Computed from Wasteland Maps, NRSA, Hyderabad (AP).

The above table indicates that Jamwa Ramgarh tehsil alone covers approximately one-third area (30.74%) under degraded forest of the study area followed by Viratnagar tehsil (24.82%). Both the tehsils cover more than one-half (55.56%) degraded notified area of the district. Other tehsils having more area under this category are Kotputli (14.38%) and Amber (13.19%). Fig 4.4A shows that eastern part of Amber tehsil and western part of Kotputli tehsil keep their more area under degraded notified forest. Remaining tehsils occupy nil or negligible area under this category.

Table 4.5 also shows that Viratnagar (62.64%), Kotputli (56.65%), Jaipur (54.99%) Jamwa Ramgarh (51.85%) tehsils occupy more than one-half of their wasteland area under degraded forest. Amber tehsil can also be included in above tehsils. Bassi and Shahapura tehsils also cover approximately one-fourth area under this category to their total wastelands. Other tehsils have low and very low percentage of degraded notified forestland to their total wastelands.

Fig. 4.4B shows tehsilwise high and very high percentages of degraded notified forest land (Above 12%) are concentrated in north eastern and central part of the study area while tehsils of western and southern part of the study area cover low, very low percentage and negligible area under this category Fig. 4.4A shows that the villages having more than 60 per cent of their geographical area under this category are situated mainly in two patches i.e. eastern part of Viratnagar tehsil and north-eastern part of Jamwa Ramgarh tehsil. Besides these three small patches of very high percentage (above 60%) are situated in the south – Eastern part of Amber, Western part of Kotputli and Central part of Jamwa Ramgarh tehsil.

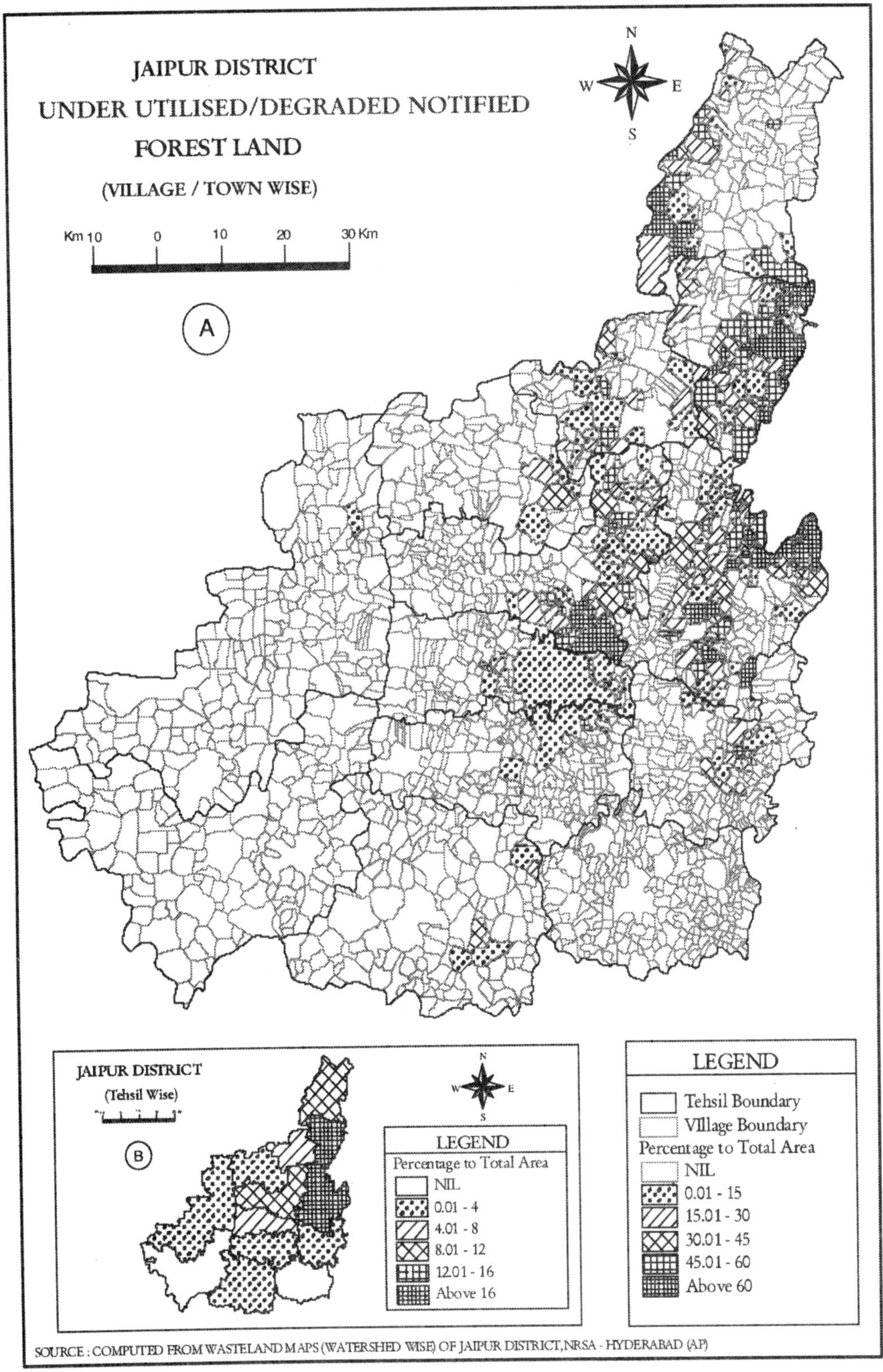

Fig. 4.4A : Under Utilized / Degraded Notified Forest Land (Village/Townwise)
Fig. 4.4B : Under Utilized / Degraded Notified Forest Land (Tehsilwise)

Other percentage intensities under this category of land are also found in the adjoining to the villages having moderate to very high percentages of degraded notified forest land, especially north eastern part of the study area. The intensity of degraded forestland in villages is also uneven. Table 4.6 shows tehsilwise distribution of villages/towns by share of degraded notified forestland in the district:

Table 4.6 : Tehsilwise Distribution of villages/towns by share of Degraded Notified Forest Land in Jaipur District.

S. No.	Tehsil	Percentage wise Distribution of Villages and Towns of Degraded notified Forest land					Total Wasteland Villages/ Towns	% to total degraded notified Forest villages of the district
		1-15%	15-30%	30-45%	45-60%	>60%		
1.	Amber	18	11	7	9	7	52	18.37
2.	Bassi	6	3	4	2	1	16	5.65
3.	Chaksu	—	—	—	—	—		
4.	Chomu	4	1	1	—	—	6	2.12
5.	Dudu	—	—	—	—	—	—	—
6.	Jaipur	9	—	—	2	1	12	4.24
7.	Jamwa Ramgarh	22	17	17	13	19	88	31.09
8.	Kotputli	8	5	2	5	5	25	8.83
9.	Phagi	3	1	1	—	—	5	1.77
10.	Phulera	1	—	—	—	—	1	0.35
11.	Sanganer	5	—	—	—	1	6	2.12
12.	Shahapura	13	7	1	3	—	24	8.48
13.	Viratnagar	10	9	10	8	11	48	16.96
Total Village		99	54	43	42	45	283	
Percentage		34.98	19.08	15.19	14.84	15.90	100.00	100.00

Source : Computed from Wasteland Maps, NRSA, Hyderabad (A.P.).

The above table shows that out of 283 villages having this wasteland, 184 villages have more than 15 percent, 54 villages between 15-30 per cent, 43 villages between 30-45 per cent, 8 villages between 45-60 per cent and 45 villages less than 60 per cent of the geographical area under this category. These villages are mainly concentrated in Jamwa Ramgarh, Amber and Viratnagar tehsils. Remaining 99 villages having less than 15 per cent also are mainly distributed in above mentioned tehsils and one more tehsil Shahapura. This table also indicates that approximately one-third villages having degraded notified forest of the district are situated in only one tehsil Jamwa Ramgarh followed by Amber and Viratnagar tehsils. All these three tehsils combinedly cover two-third villages of this category.

Sands Desertic Land

The sands desertic wasteland is scattered in every tehsil of the district but the maximum concentration is found in the western part of the study area. This part touches the arid/desert districts Nagaur and Sikar of the state (Fig. 1.1). Therefore, western part of the study area has also arid/desert characteristics as adjoining desert districts. This category covers 32318 hectares equivalent to 2.74 per cent of the total geographical area. The maximum area under this category is in Phulera tehsil (13004 ha.) followed by Chomu tehsil (5854 ha.). On the basis of percentages of sands-desertic land to geographical area, Chomu tehsil tops all the tehsils of the study area as this tehsil covers 8.48 per cent to the total geographical area under this category followed by Phulera (5.32%) and Shahapura (3.89%) tehsils. Other tehsils having more geographical under this category are Chaksu and Dudu (Table 4.7). Dudu is adjoining to the Phulera tehsil while in Chaksu Dhund River and its tributaries have sands in their beds. All the tehsils except Chaksu are situated in the western part of the study area.

Table 4.7 shows Tehsilwise area of sand-desertic in hectares, percentage of sand-desertic to total geographical area, percentage of sands-desertic to tehsils total wasteland and per cent to total sand-desertic land of the district.

Table 4.7 indicates that one-sixth area of total wastelands of the study area belongs to sands-desertic lands. Phulera and Chomu tehsils combinedly cover three-fifth area sands-desertic land of the study area as these tehsils occupy approximately 60 per cent area of their total wastelands under this category. Other tehsils e.g. Dudu, Shahapura and Jaipur keep their 21.88, 13.88 and 12.70 per cent sand-desertic area respectively to their total wastelands are situated adjoining to tehsils having more area under this category.

Fig.4.5B shows that on the basis of tehsils, most of the sandy area lies in western tehsils of the study area except Chakshu tehsil. The maximum percentage of this category is in

Table 4.7 : Tehsilwise Percentage Distribution of Sands-Desertic Land in Jaipur District

S.N.	Tehsil	Sand Desertic land in hectares	Percentage of Sand-Desertic toTotal geographical area	% to tehsils total wasteland	% to the total Sands-Desertic area
1.	Amber	1613.00	1.95	8.89	4.99
2.	Bassi	624.50	0.97	7.03	1.93
3.	Chaksu	1926.85	2.47	0.32	5.96
4.	Chomu	5854.00	8.48	60.34	18.11
5.	Dudu	2957.50	2.21	21.88	9.15
6.	Jaipur	762.50	1.30	12.70	2.36
7.	Jamwa Ramgarh	785.50	0.78	2.06	2.43
8.	Kotputli	977.50	1.17	6.01	3.02
9.	Phagi	1085.00	1.01	8.31	3.36
10.	Phulera	13004.00	5.32	58.02	40.24
11.	Sanganer	287.50	0.46	7.08	0.89
12.	Shahapura	1853.00	3.89	13.87	5.73
13.	Viratnagar	587.50	1.24	2.31	1.82
	District	32318.00	2.74	16.30	100.00

Source: Computed from the Wasteland Maps, NRSA,Hyderabad(A.P)

northwestern part i.e. Chomu tehsil followed by Phulera, Shahapura, Chaksu and Dudu tehsils. The Chakshu tehsil lies in the south eastern part of the study area and has river sand in Dhund river and its tributaries.

Fig 4.5 A shows that most of the villages having sands-desertic land are concentrated in the western part of the district. The villages of very high percentage of sands-desertic

(<40%) to their geographical area concentrated in the central part of the Phulera tehsil. As already explained this tehsil is situated adjoining to desert district Nagaur and Sambhar gap in Aravalli hills is also responsible for the more sandy area. The villages of high percentage (30-40%) of sands are also scattered adjoining villages of very high percentage of sands-desertic land and in western part of the Chomu tehsil while the villages of very low, low and moderate percentages of sands-desertic are scattered in most of the tehsils of the district (Fig 4.5A) especially eastern part of Jamwa Ramgarh, Bassi and northern part of Phulera and western part of Dudu tehsil.The following Table 4.8 shows tehsilwise distribution of villages and towns by share of sands-desertic land:

Table 4.8 : Tehsilwise Distribution of Villages/Towns by share of Sands-Desertic Land in Jaipur District

S. No.	Tehsil	Percentagewise distribution of villages and Towns of Sands-Desertic land					Total villages	% to total Sands-Desertic villages of the district
		1-10%	10-20%	20-30%	30-40%	>40%		
1.	Amber	17	8	7	—	2	34	9.31
2.	Bassi	8	4	1	1	1	15	4.10
3.	Chaksu	15	9	10	5	5	44	12.05
4.	Chomu	19	13	8	4	3	47	12.07
5.	Dudu	15	5	1	1	4	26	7.12
6.	Jaipur	6	3	2	1	—	12	3.28
7.	Jamwa Ramgarh	18	4	3	—	1	26	7.12
8.	Kotputli	19	2	3	2	1	27	7.39
9.	Phagi	9	4	2	2	1	18	4.93
10.	Phulera	25	9	7	6	22	69	18.90
11.	Sanganer	9	1	1	—	—	11	3.01
12.	Shahapura	11	9	—	—	5	25	6.84
13.	Viratnagar	5	3	2	—	1	11	3.01
Total Villages		176	74	47	22	46	365	100
Percentage		48.21	20.27	12.87	6.02	12.60	100.00	

Source: Computed from the Wasteland Maps, NRSA Hyderabad.

The above table shows that out of 365 villages having this problem, 176 villages i.e. approximately 50 per cent villages occupy less than 10 per cent of their geographical area under this category in Phulera, Chomu, Jamwa Ramgarh, Kotputli and Amber tehsils while 74 villages (20.33%) between 10-20 per cent. Thus more than two-third (68.68%) sand-desertic villages of the district have low and very low intensity (1 to 20%) of sand. Only 12.36 per cent villages have very high percentage (>40%) under sand desertic land in their total geographical area. On the basis of tehsilwise villages, approximately one-fifth villages of this category are concentrated only one tehsil of western part i.e. Phulera tehsil. Other tehsils having more villages under this category are Chomu, Chaksu, Amber, Kotputli, Dudu, Jamwa Ramgarh and Shahapura while Jaipur, Sanganer and Viratnagar tehsils have less number of villages under sandy-desertic land.

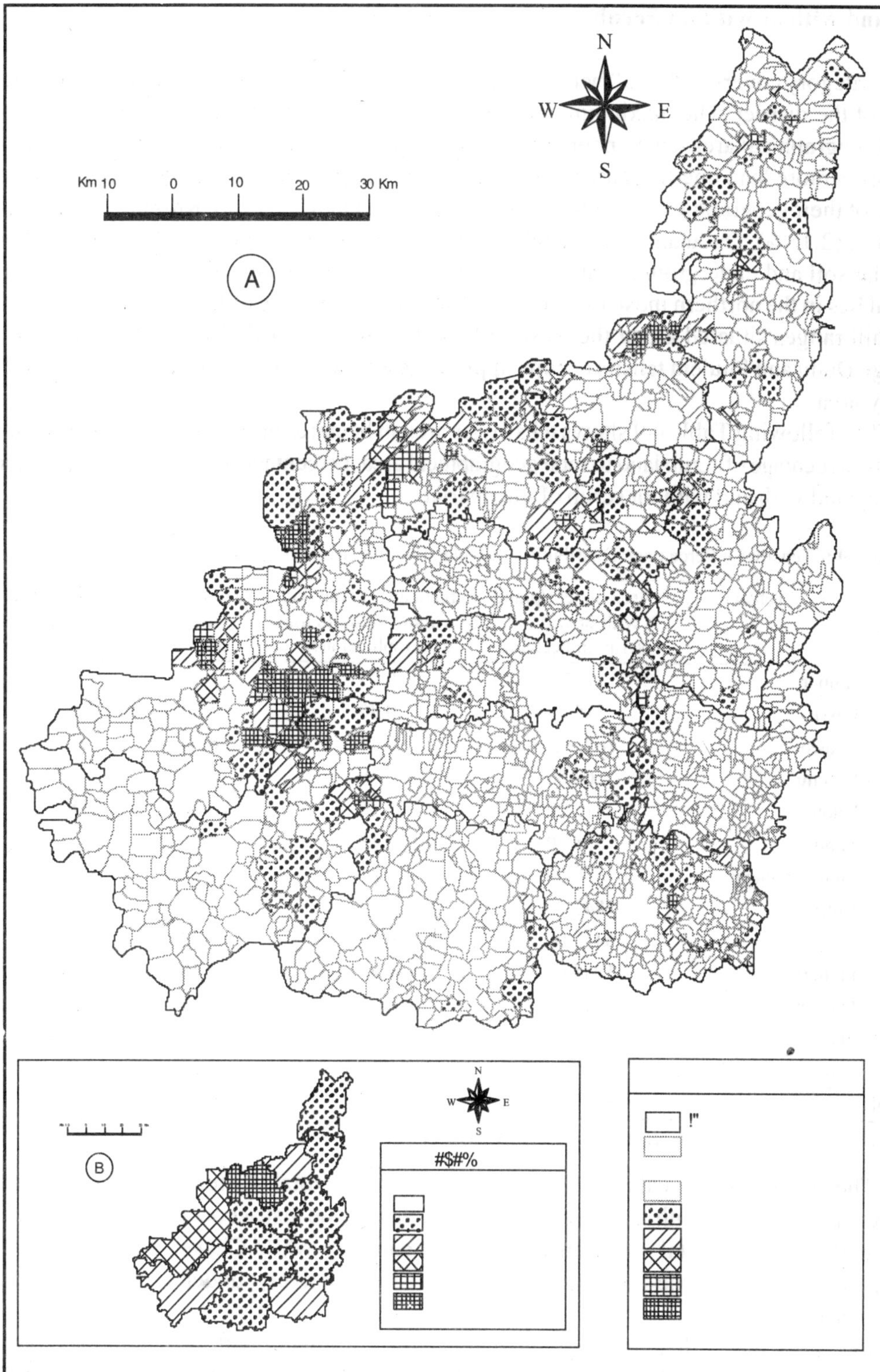

Fig. 4.5A : Sands-Desertic (Village/Townwise)
Fig. 4.5B : Sands-Desertic (Tehsilwise)

Upland with or without Scrub

This category covers 18572.50 hectares equivalent to 1.57 per cent of the total geographical area of the district. The maximum concentration is in Phagi tehsil i.e. 6.01 per cent to the total geographical area due to poor soils and poor groundwater resources. This Tehsil alone occupies more than one-third area of total scrub land in the study area. Other tehsils having more of their geographical area under this category are Dudu (2.55%), Kotputli (2.21%) and Chaksu (2.15%). Dudu and Chaksu tehsils situated adjoining to Phagi tehsil and also have similar soil and underground water characteristics as Phagi tehsil to some extent. Kotputli tehsil lies in the northern most area of the district, where this type of land is very common on the hill ranges situated along the western boundary of the tehsil. Table 4.9 indicates that Phagi, Dudu and Phulera tehsils occupy approximately two-third area of this category of the study area.

The following Table 4.9 shows tehsilwise area in hectares under upland with or without scrub, percentage of scrub land to total geographical area, percentage to tehsils total wastelands and upland with and without scrub of the district.

Table 4.9 : Tehsilwise Percentage Distribution of Upland with or without Scrub in Jaipur District.

S. No.	Tehsil	Area under upland with or without scrub in hectares	Percentage of land with or without scrub to total geographical area	% to tehsil's total wasteland	% to the Total upland with or without scrub
1.	Amber	187.0	0.23	1.03	1.01
2.	Bassi	515.00	0.80	5.80	2.77
3.	Chaksu	1675.50	2.15	28.06	9.02
4.	Chomu	67.50	0.10	0.69	0.36
5.	Dudu	3410.00	2.55	20.36	18.36
6.	Jaipur	398.50	0.68	6.64	2.14
7.	Jamwa Ramgarh	1622.00	1.61	4.26	8.73
8.	Kotputli	1843.00	2.21	11.30	9.92
9.	Phagi	6449.00	6.01	49.39	34.72
10.	Phulera	1945.00	0.80	8.68	10.47
11.	Sanganer	452.00	0.72	11.12	2.43
12.	Shahapura	—	—	—	—
13.	Viratnagar	7.50	0.02	0.03	0.04
Total		18572.50	1.57	9.37	100

Source: Computed from Wasteland Maps, NRSA, Hyderabad.

The above table reveals that 9.37 percent area of the total wastelands of the district is under upland with or without scrub. Only Phagi tehsil of the district occupies approximately one-half area of its total wastelands under this category while Chaksu and Dudu tehsils keep their more than one-fourth and one-fifth area respectively under scrub land to their total wastelands.

Fig. 4.6B shows that very high intensity (> 6%) of upland with or without scrub is in southern part of the study area i.e. Phagi tehsil while tehsils having high intensity of this category (4 to 6%) are also situated adjoining to this tehsil and northern part of the district. As already explained the pedological and hydrological conditions of the Phagi, Dudu and western Chaksu tehsil are almost equal, so the percentage under this category is high. In Kotputli tehsil this category of land is found on the foothills and hill ranges. While in remaining tehsils, it is negligible. Fig 4.6A reveals village wise spatial distribution pattern of upland with or without scrub in the district. This map indicates that problem of upland with or without scrub is concentrated in the south, southwestern part of the study area especially in Phagi, Dudu and south Phulera tehsil. The villages having more than 20 per cent of their total geographical area under this category are concentrated in the southern part of the study area especially in south eastern part of the Phagi tehsil. Other villages of very high to high intensity are scattered in eastern, north western and south western part of the district particularly in Jamwa Ramgarh, Kotputli and Dudu tehsils. The villages of very low and low percentage (1.01 to 10%) of scrubland are also concentrated in the southern part of thc district.

The percentage of land with or without scrub villages is also unevenly distributed. The following table shows tehsil wise distribution of villages/towns by share of upland with or without scrub in the study area.

Table 4.10: Tehsilwise Distribution of Villages/Towns by Share of Upland with or without Scrub in Jaipur District.

S. No.	Tehsil	Percentagewise Distribution of Villages and Towns of Upland with or without Scrub					Total villages	% to total villages having upland with or without Scrub of the district
		1-5%	5-10%	10-15%	15-20%	> 20%		
1.	Amber	01	—	—	—	01	2	0.72
2.	Bassi	5	7	01	—	03	17	5.72
3.	Chaksu	7	8	9	01	10	36	12.12
4.	Chomu	01	01	—	2	—	2	0.72
5.	Dudu	17	14	6	—	5	44	14.81
6.	Jaipur	5	3	3	-2	1	12	4.04
7.	Jamwa Ramgarh	15	9	6	3	6	39	13.13
8.	Kotputli	14	8	—	1	3	26	8.75
9.	Phagi	26	17	13	11	13	80	26.94
10.	Phulera	6	3	4	6	1	20	6.73
11.	Sanganer	7	4	2	3	2	18	6.05
12.	Shahapura	—	—	—	—	—	—	—
13.	Viratnagar	1	—	—	—	—	01	0.36
Total Villages		105	74	44	29	45	297	100
Percentage		35.35	24.92	14.81	9.77	15.15		100

Source: Computed from Wastelands Maps, NRSA, Hyderabad AP.

The table also reveals that three-fifth villages have less than 10 per cent land under this category especially in Phagi and Dudu tehsils while approximately one-fourth villages (24.92%) have their upland with or without scrub under high and very high intensity i.e. 15-20 and >20 per cent to their total geographical area. The villages are distributed mainly in Phagi tehsil.

Table 4.10 also indicates that more than one-fourth villages (24.94%) having this category of land are concentrated in only one tehsil Phagi followed by Dudu (14.81%), Jamwa Ramgarh (13.13%) and Chaksu (12.12%) tehsils. These four tehsils combinedly cover two-third (67%) villages having upland with or without scrub in the study area. Phagi, Dudu and Chaksu

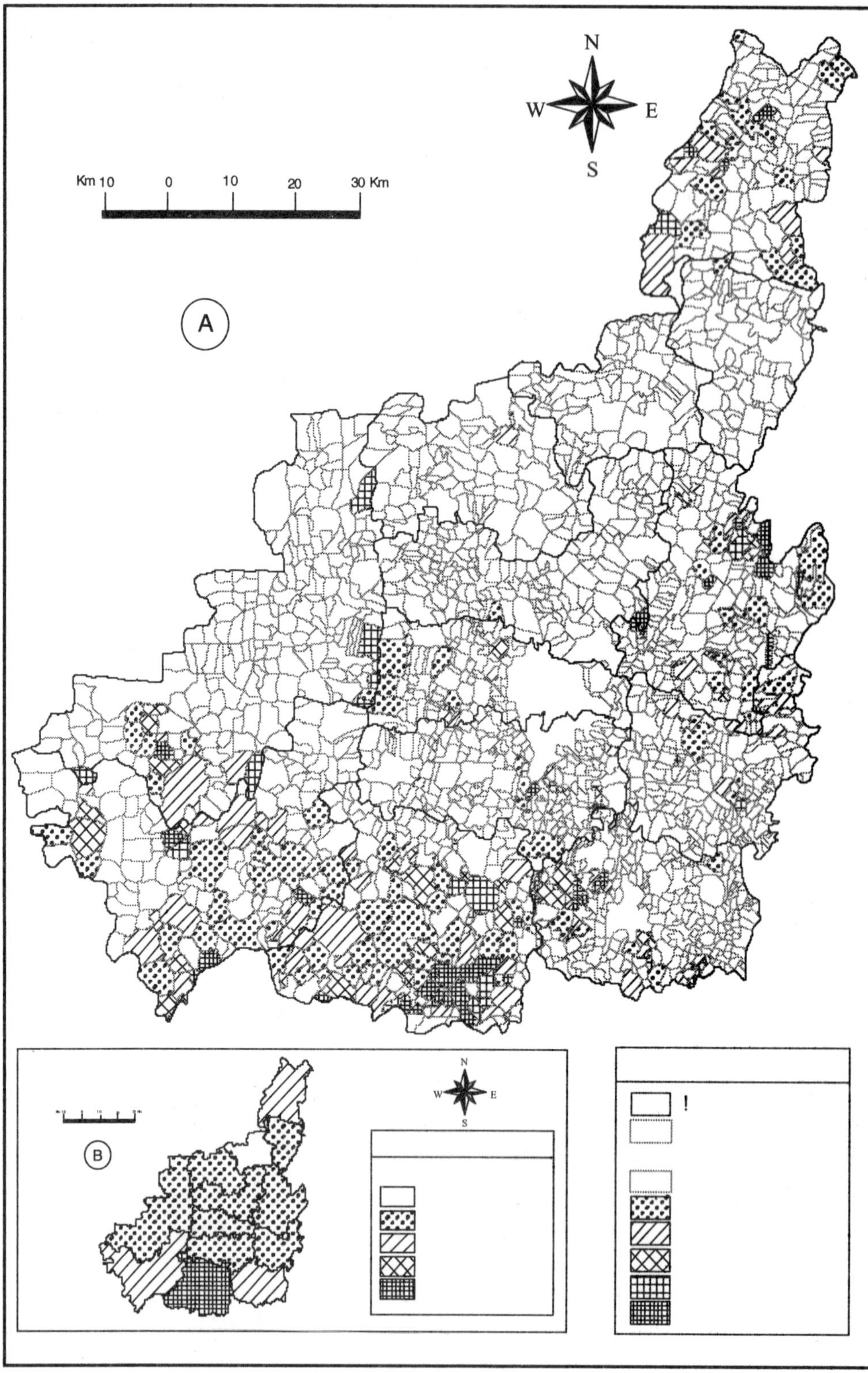

Fig. 4.6A : Upland with or without Scrub (Village/Town wise)
Fig. 4.6B : Upland with or without Scrub (Tehsil wise)

Plate 3 : Land Affected by Salinity and devoid of vegetation on Phulera-Sambhar Road in Phulera Tehsil.

Plate 4 : Wind erosion of a stabilized sand dune on the western margin of 'Smiriti Van' on J.L.N. Marg, Jaipur.

tehsils have poor soils and poor quality and quantity of ground water while in Jamwa Ramgarh and Kotputli tehsils hilly tracts are responsible for more villages under this category.

Land affected by Salinity/Alkalinity

In the study area, salt affected lands are known as *'usar'* which is derived from Sanskrit word *"Ushtra"*, meaning sterile or barren and is usually applied to all kinds of saline and alkali soils.

Land affected by salinity/alkalinity is 18169.51 ha equivalent to 1.54 per cent of the total geographical area of the district. The maximum area affected by salinity/alkalinity is found in Dudu tehsil (6925.50 ha) followed by Phulera (5180.86 ha) and Sanganer (2667.50ha) tehsils. These tehsils consist of 5.18 per cent, 2.12 per cent and 4.24 per cent respectively to their geographical areas. Only two tehsils Dudu and Phulera occupy two-third land under this category of the district (Table 4.11). This type of land is more is these tehsils due to shallow poor soils and poor quality groundwater. Table 4.11 shows salinity/alkalinity area in hectares, percentage of salinity/alkalinity area to tehsil's total wastelands and tehsilwise percentage of salinity/alkalinity land to total salinity/alkalinity affected land of the district.

Table 4.11 shows that 9.16 per cent land of the total wastelands of the district is under this category. Sanagner teshil occupies its two-third wasteland under salinity/alkalinity, although this tehsil occupies very less area under this category to total geographical area. Dudu and Phulera tehsils have 41.35 per cent and 23.12 per cent land of their wastelands under this category. Phagi and Chomu tehsils also keep their 12.17 per cent and 7.13 per cent area respectively under the land affected by salinity/alkalinity to the total wastelands.

Table 4.11: Tehsilwise Percentage Distributions of Land Affected by Salinity/Alkalinity in Jaipur District

S.No	Tehsil	Area affected salinity/ alkalinity in hectares	Percentage of salinity/alkalinity to total geographical area	Percentage to tehsil's total wasteland	Percentage to total land affected by salinity/ alkalinity of the district
1.	Amber	880.00	1.05	4.83	4.84
2.	Bassi	–	–	–	–
3.	Chaksu	–	–	–	–
4.	Chomu	692.15	1.00	7.13	3.81
5.	Dudu	6925.50	5.18	41.35	38.12
6.	Jaipur	235.00	0.40	3.91	1.29
7.	Jamwa Ramgarh	–	–	–	–
8.	Kotputli	–	–	–	–
9.	Phagi	1588.50	1.48	12.17	8.74
10.	Phulera	5180.86	2.12	23.12	28.51
11.	Sanganer	2667.50	4.24	65.67	14.68
12.	Shahapura	–	–	–	–
13.	Viratnagar	–	–	–	–
	TOTAL	18169.51	1.54	9.16	100.00

Source: Computed from Wasteland Maps, NRSA, Hyderabad (AP).

Fig. 4.7 B shows that land affected by salinity/alkalinity is concentrated in the tehsils of western and central part of the study area. The maximum area of this category of land is in Dudu tehsil situated in the south-western part of the district followed by Sanganer and Phulera tehsils. These both tehsils are also situated in the north and east of Dudu tehsil. Other tehsils affected by salinity/alkalinity are adjoining the tehsils having more areas under this category (Fig 4.7B). Fig 4.7 A shows that villages having various intensity of land affected by salinity/alkalinity are concentrated in south western, western and central part of the district. The maximum villages of this category are situated in the south western part particularly western part of Dudu tehsil and southern Phulera tehsil. The table shows tehsilwise distribution of villages/towns by share of land affected by salinity/alkalinity in Jaipur district.

Table 4.12 : Tehsilwise Distribution of Villages/Towns by Share of Land Affected by Salinity/Alkalinity in Jaipur District.

S. No	Tehsil	Percentagewise distributor of villages/towns of land affected by salinity/alkalinity						% to total salinity/ alkalinity villages of the district
		1-6%	6-12%	12-18%	18-24%	24%	Total Villages	
1.	Amber	5	2	1	2	6	16	8.20
2.	Bassi	–	–	–	–	–	–	–
3.	Chaksu	7	–	1	–	–	8	4.10
4.	Chomu	4	2	2	–	3	11	5.64
5.	Dudu	22	15	11	3	8	59	30.26
6.	Jaipur	2	–	–	1	1	4	2.05
7.	Jamwa Ramgarh	–	–	–	–	–	–	–
8.	Kotputli	–	–	–	–	–	–	–
9.	Phagi	21	7	4	3	2	37	18.97
10.	Phulera	23	7	3	2	12	47	24.10
11.	Sanganer	3	1	3	–	6	13	6.6
12.	Shahapura	–	–	–	–	–	–	–
13.	Viratnagar	–	–	–	–	–	–	–
Total		87	34	25	11	38	195	
% to total villages affected by salinity/ alkalinity		44.61	17.43	12.82	5.64	19.49	–	100

Source : Computed from Wasteland Maps, NRSA, Hyderabad (AP).

The above table shows that out of 195 villages, having land affected by salinity/alkalinity, 87 villages (44.61%) between 1-6 per cent, 34 villages (17.43%) between 6 to 12 per cent. Thus approximately two-third villages of the study area belong to very low and low percentages and only one-fifth villages have high and very high percentages (18 to < 24%) of land affected by salinity/alkalinity.

Table 4.12 also indicates that approximately one-third villages of this category are concentrated in Dudu tehsil followed by Phulera and Phagi tehsils. All the three tehsils have three-fourth villages of the district under land affected by salinity/alkalinity.

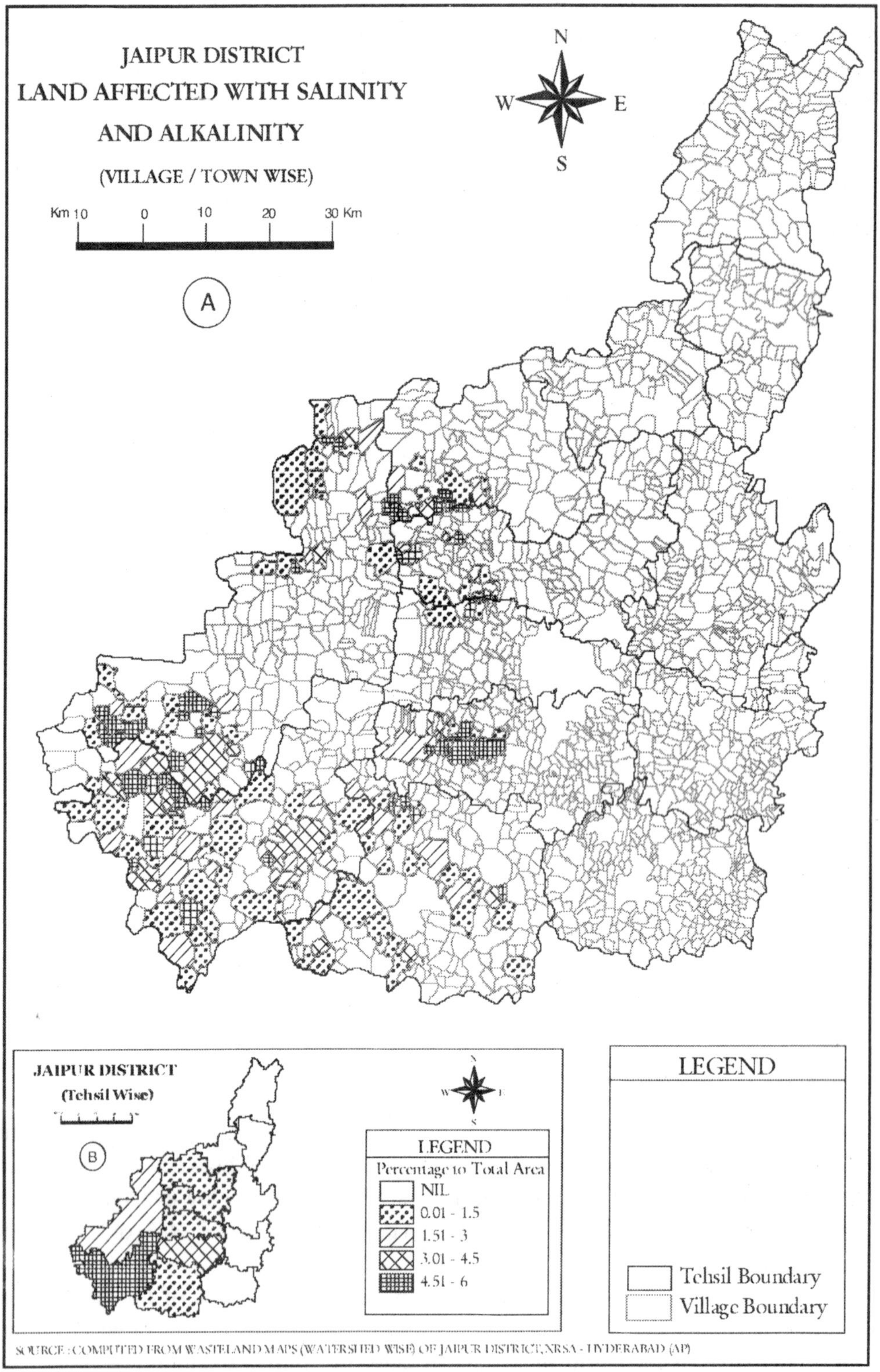

Fig. 4.7A : Land Affected with Salinity/Alkalanity (Village/Townwise)

Fig. 4.7B : Land Affected with Salinity/Alkalanity (Tehsilswise)

Plate 5 : Ploughing on Saline Calcareous Soil near Dudu Town.

Plate 6 : Degraded Pasture/Grazing land in Harsuliya village in Phagi Tehsil.

Degraded Pasture/Grazing Land

This category covers 7648.01 ha equivalent to 0.65 per cent of the total geographical area of the district. The maximum area under degraded pasture/grazing land is in Phagi tehsil (1666.00 ha) followed by Dudu (1242.50 ha) and Bassi (1217.50 ha) tehsils. Phagi tehsil alone covers more than one-fifth (21.78%) area of the district under this category followed by Dudu (16.25%) and Bassi (15.95%) tehsils. In Dudu and Phagi tehsils calcaerous soil, salinity/alkalinity and poor groundwater resources etc. are responsible for more area under this category. These tehsils occupy more than one-half degraded pasture/grazing land of the district. Table 4.13 shows tehsilwise land under degraded pasture/grazing land in hectares, percentage of degraded pasture/grazing land to total geographical area, percentage to tehsils total wasteland and per cent land under this category to total degraded pasture/grazing land of the district.

Table 4.13 : Tehsilwise Percentage Distribution of Degraded Pasture/Grazing land.

S. No.	Tehsil	Area under degraded pasture/ grazing land in hect.	Percentage of degraded pasture/ grazing land to total geographical area	Percentage to tehsil's total wasteland	% to total degraded pasture/grazing land of the district
1.	Amber	587.00	0.70	3.22	7.67
2.	Bassi	1217.50	1.89	13.71	15.92
3.	Chaksu	595.00	0.76	9.96	7.78
4.	Chomu	369.15	0.53	3.80	4.83
5.	Dudu	1242.50	0.93	7.42	16.25
6.	Jaipur	100.00	0.17	1.66	1.31
7.	Jamwa Ramgarh	555.00	0.55	1.46	7.26
8.	Kotputli	307.00	0.37	1.89	4.01
9.	Phagi	1666.00	1.53	12.76	21.78
10.	Phulera	170.00	0.07	0.76	2.22
11.	Sanganer	95.00	0.15	2.34	1.24
12.	Shahapura	717.50	1.51	5.37	9.38
13.	Viratnagar	26.36	–	–	–
	District	7648.00	0.65	3.86	100.00

Source : Computed from Wasteland Maps NRSA, Hyderabad (A.P.)

The above table shows that Bassi, Phagi and Shahapura teshils occupy 1.89 per cent, 1.53 per cent and 1.51 per cent land under degraded pasture/gazing land to the total geographical area. This table also shows that Bassi, Phagi, Chaksu and Dudu tehsils registered larger percentage of their wastelands under this category.

Fig 4.8B shows that only three tehsils of the study area have moderate internity (1.01 to 2%) of degraded pasture/grazing land in the study. These tehsils are situated in southern, eastern and northern part of the district, and occupy more area under this category due to different causes e.g. in southern part poor pedological and hydrological conditions, in eastern part hilly tract undulated land while in north-western part sandy soils with sand dunes.

Fig 4.8A shows village wise spatial pattern of degraded pasture/grazing land in the district. This map reveals that this category of land is scattered in various parts viz southern,

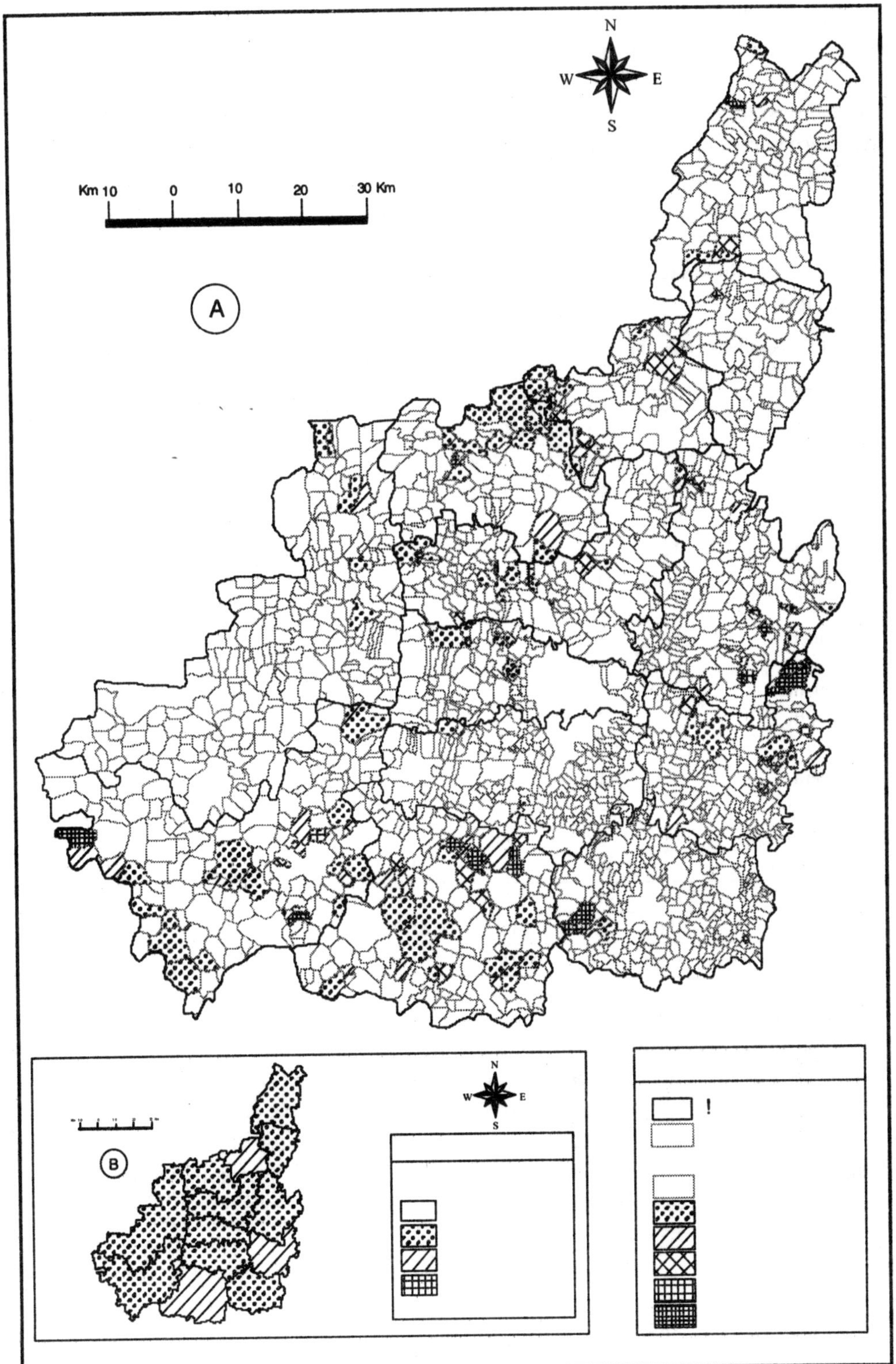

Fig. 4.8A : Degraded Pasture/Grazing Land (Village/Town wise)
Fig. 4.8B : Degraded Pasture/Grazing Land (Tehsil wise)

central and south-eastern part of the district especially in Phagi, Dudu, Bassi and Shahapura tehsils. Besides this, small patches of this category of land is scattered in almost all the tehsils of the study area. This map also shows that village, having very high intensity of degraded pasture i.e. 20 per cent to their total geographical are scattered mainly in southern and eastern part of the district. Similarly villagers of high (15.01-20%) and moderate (10.01-15%) intensities of this category are also unevenly scattered while villages having low and very low percentages of degraded pasture are concentrated in south, south western and north western part of the district particularly in Phagi, Shahapura and Dudu tehsils. The following table shows tehsilwise distribution of villages/towns by share of degraded pasture/grazing land.

Table 4.14 : Tehsilwise Distribution of Villages/Towns by Share of Degraded Pasture/Grazing Land in Jaipur District

S. No	Tehsil	Percentagewise Distribution of Villages/ Towns of degraded pasture/Grazing land					Total Villages	% of Total villages having degraded pasture
		9-5%	5-10%	10-15%	15-20%	7-20%		
1.	Amber	8	3	3	1	4	19	11.24
2.	Bassi	5	4	1	2	6	18	10.65
3.	Chaksu	2	—	—	—	3	5	2.96
4.	Chomu	12	1	—	—	1	14	8.25
5.	Dudu	13	5	3	1	2	24	14.20
6.	Jaipur	6	—	—	—	1	7	4.14
7.	Jamwa Ramgarh	1	6	2	2	4	15	8.87
8.	Kotputli	3	2	1	1	—	7	4.14
9.	Phagi	11	7	6	2	4	30	17.75
10.	Phulera	5	1	—	—	—	6	3.55
11.	Sanganer	2	—	1	1	—	4	2.37
12.	Shahapura	9	5	5	—	—	19	11.24
13.	Viratnagar	—	—	—	1	—	1	0.59
	Total	77	34	22	11	25	169	
	Percentage	45.56	20.12	13.01	6.50	14.79	100	100

Source : Computed from Wasteland Maps, NRSA, Hyderobad (A.P.)

The above table 4.14 shows that the study area has 169 villages under degraded pasture/grazing land i.e. 7.67% villages/towns of the district. Two-third villages occupy very low to low (1-5 and 5-10%) area under this category in Phagi and Dudu tehsils while one-fifth villages have moderate and high percentages of degraded pasture. This table also shows that the maximum villages having such problem are concentrated in Phagi tehsil followed by Dudu, Amber, Shahapura and Bassi tehsils. These tehsils cover approximately two-third villages of degraded pasture/grazing land of the study area.

Barren Hill/Rocky

Barren rocky covers 7363.20 hectares equivalent to 0.62 per cent of the total geographical area of the district. The maximum hectareage is in Phulera tehsil (1999.20 ha.) followed by Dudu (1762 ha.) and Amber (1202.50 ha.) tehsils i.e. 0.82 per cent, 1.32 per cent and

1.44 per cent respectively to their total geographical area. Phulera and Dudu tehsils occupy very less area under hills and due to more pressure of rural population for their fuel wood and fodder. These hills have been converted into rocky barren while in Amber tehsil also at some places the above conditions are found. Table 4.15 shows tehsilwise percentage distribution of barren rocky.

Table 4.15 : Tehsilwise Percentage Distribution of Barren Hill/Rocky in Jaipur District.

S. No.	Tehsil	Area under Barren Rocky in hectares	Percentage of Barren Rocky to total geographical area	Percentage to tehsil's total wasteland	% to total Barren Rocky area of the district
1.	Amber	1202.50	1.44	6.60	16.33
2.	Bassi	236.50	0.37	2.66	3.21
3.	Chaksu	–	–	–	–
4.	Chomu	217.50	0.32	2.24	2.95
5.	Dudu	1762.00	1.32	10.52	23.93
6.	Jaipur	87.50	0.15	1.46	1.19
7.	Jamwa Ramgarh	519.50	0.51	1.36	7.05
8.	Kotputli	589.50	0.71	3.61	8.00
9.	Phagi	80.00	0.07	0.61	1.08
10.	Phulera	1999.20	0.82	8.92	27.15
11.	Sanganer	40.00	0.06	0.0002	0.54
12.	Shahapura	559.50	1.17	4.19	7.60
13.	Viratnagar	69.50	0.15	0.27	0.94
	District	7363.20	0.62	3.71	100.00

Source : Computed from Wasteland Maps, NRSA, Hyderabad (A.P.)

The above table shows that Phulera tehsil alone covers more than one-fourth area of the study area under this category followed by Dudu and Amber tehsils. All the three tehsils have more than two-third barren rocky area of the district. The percentage share of this category to the total wastelands is very low in comparison to other categories of wastelands. It is only 10.52 per cent in Dudu, 8.92 per cent in Phulera 6.60 per cent Amber tehsils.

Fig 4.9B shows that barren rocky is more in two areas viz south western and northern middle part of the study area particularly in Dudu, Shahapura and Amber teshils while it is less in remaining tehsils excluding Chaksu tehsil. Fig. 4.9A shows that villages having more barren rocky are found mainly in a belt stretched from southwest to north east direction in the study area with maximum concentration in upper middle part of the belt. This figure also indicates that barren rocky is almost negligible in Phagi, Chaksu, Sanganer and Viratnagar tehsils situated in the south and north eastern part of the district. The villages having very high and high percentages (12.01 to above 16%) of barren rocky are upper middle part especially northern part of Amber, south Shahapura tehsil, north and south western part of Dudu tehsil. The distributional pattern of villages having high intensity (8.01-12%) is also same as very high intensity of this category. The villages of very low and low percentages (0.01 to 8%) are concentrated in the northern part of the study area especially is Shahapura, south eastern part of Chomu, Amber and western part of Kotputli tehsils. Besides these, two patches are in the south west and along the north west boundary of Dudu tehsil. Some villages of these categories are also found in scattered form in eastern part particularly in

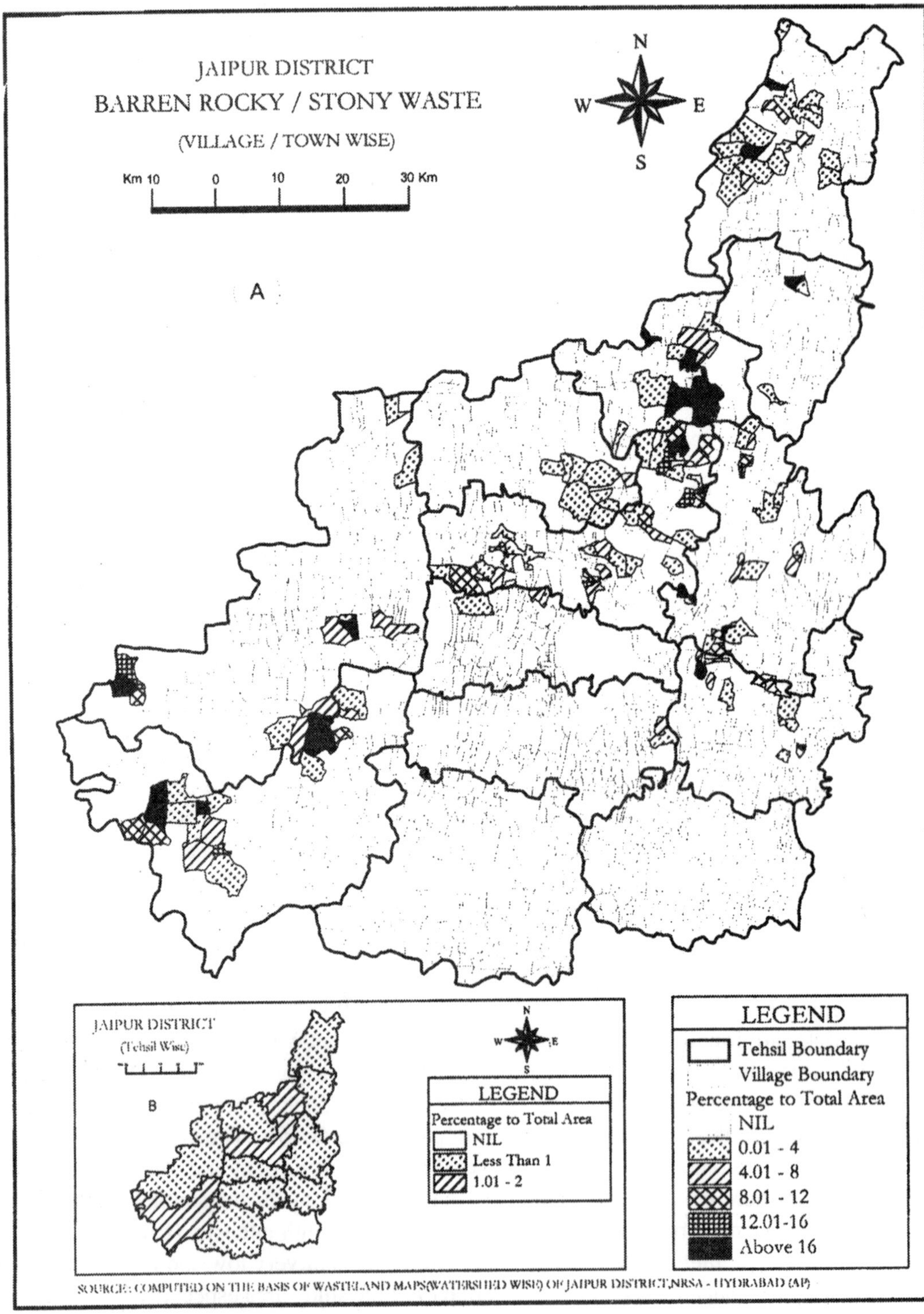

Fig. 4.9A : Barren Rocky/Stony Waste (Village/Townwise)
Fig. 4.9B : Barren Rocky/Stony Waste (Village/Townwise)

Plate 7 : Barren hill near Kawlar village is being used for quarrying.

Plate 8 : Sheep grazing on a fallow land in Phagi Tehsil.

Jamwa Ramgarh and Bassi tehsils. The following table gives tehsilwise distribution of villages/ towns by share of barren rocky land.

Table 4.16 : Tehsilwise Distribution of Villages/Towns by Share of Barren Rocky Land in Jaipur District

S. No.	Tehsil	Percentagewise distribution of villages/towns of Barren Rocky land			Total Villages/ Towns	% of total villages of the district
		0.01-8%	8-12%	12-16%		
1.	Amber	16	8	13	37	24.18
2.	Bassi	6	4	4	14	9.15
3.	Chaksu	—	—	—	—	—
4.	Chomu	8	1	—	9	5.88
5.	Dudu	7	3	8	18	11.76
6.	Jaipur	2	1	—	3	1.96
7.	Jamwa Ramgarh	11	5	5	21	13.72
8.	Kotputli	16	3	4	23	15.03
9.	Phagi	—	—	1	01	0.65
10.	Phulera	4	4	4	12	7.84
11.	Sanganer	1	1	—	2	1.31
12.	Shahapura	5	2	3	10	6.53
13.	Viratnagar	2	-	1	3	1.96
	Total	78	32	43	153	100.00
	Percentage	50.98	20.91	28.10	100	-

Source : Computed from Wasteland Maps, NRSA, Hyderabad (A.P.)

The aove table shows that out of 153 villages, 78 villages i.e. more than one- half (50.98%) villages have low intensity of degraded pasture mostly in Amber, Kotputli and Jamwa Ramgarh teshils while 28.10 per cent villages have their < 8 per ent land under this category. These villages are scattered mostly in Amber and Dudu tehsils. Amber tehsil alone has one-fourth villages having barren rocky of the study area followed by Kotputli, Jamwa Ramgarh and Dudu tehsils. These tehsils occupy two-third villages of the entire study area.

Mining/Industrial Wasteland

This district is not rich in mineral resources. Pink city Jaipur is one of the metropolitan cities of Indian Republic. To fulfil the requirement of masonry stones of the city, stone quarrying was concentrated in the nearby hills in Jaipur and Sanganer tehsils. An environmentalist made an appeal to the High Court to save the environment adjoining the city and the High Court gave the direction to the State Govt. to stop the mining activities on the hills surrounding the capital city. Due to old quarries, the maximum area under this category is in Jaipur tehsil i.e. more than 50 per cent mining wasteland of the district. Now quarries of masonry stone have started in the hills far away from the city in Kalwar, Jamwa Ramgarh area and other places. Four lanes construction of N.H. 8 from the state capital Jaipur to national capital Delhi and Kishangarh (Ajmer) is also one of the causes for the mining wasteland along the National Highway. From the last several years, marble mining has also developed in the foot hills of Aravallis in Jamwa Ramgarh tehsil. Table 4.17 gives an idea of tehsilwise percentage distribution of mining/industrial wasteland in the study area.

This category covers only 315 hectares equivalent to 0.03 per cent to the total geographical

Table 4.17 : Tehsilwise Percentage Distribution of Mining/Industrial Wasteland in Jaipur District

S. No.	Tehsil	Mining/Industrial wasteland in hectares	% of mining/ industrial waste land to total geographical area	% to tehsil's total wasteland	% to total mining/industrial wasteland villages of the district.
1.	Amber	–	–	–	–
2.	Bassi	–	–	–	–
3.	Chaksu	–	–	–	–
4.	Chomu	–	–	–	–
5.	Dudu	–	–	–	–
6.	Jaipur	160	0.27	2.67	50.79
7.	Jamwa Ramgarh	40	0.04	0.10	12.70
8.	Kotputli	–	–	–	–
9.	Phagi	–	–	–	–
10.	Phulera	–	–	–	–
11.	Sanganer	115	0.18	2.83	36.51
12.	Shahapura	–	–	–	–
13.	Viratnagar	–	–	–	–
	District	315	0.03	0.03	100.00

Source : Computed from Wasteland Maps, NRSA, Hyderabad (A.P.)

area. The maximum area is in Jaipur tehsil followed by Sanganer and Jamwa Ramgarh tehsils. On the basis of percentage to the geographical area, Jaipur tehsil covers 0.27 per ent, while Sanganer and Jamwa Ramgarh tehsils occupy 0.18 and 0.14 per cent only. As already explained stone quarrying was important adjoining to the metropolitan city Jaipur due to more requirement of builidng materials in the city. Due to this reason, 87.36 per ent quarrying was in Jaipur and Sanganer tehsils. In Jamwa Ramgarh tehsil especially in Andhi area, marble mining is being done in many mines. But due to stoppage of mining activities in Aravalli area, at present all the mines are closed down.

Fig.4.10 B shows that maximum mining wasteland is in the central part of the district i.e. in Jaipur tehsil followed by Sanganer and Jamwa Ramgarh tehsils. Fig.4.10A shows village wise mining wasteland in the study area. As already explained here stone quarrying was being done for supplying stone for building constructions in city while in the villages of eastern part of the study area have marble mining. But at present these are closed as per directions of the Supreme Court.

Total Wastelands

There are 198232.39 hectares land under the wastelands constituting 16.78 per cent to the total geographical area of the district. Maximum concentration of this category of land is found in the north eastern and western part of the study area. Approximately one-half wastelands of the district is concentrated in only three tehsils viz Jamwa Ramgarh, Viratnagar and Phulera (Table 4.18). In Jamwa Ramgarh and Viratnagar tehsils, maximum area under degraded forest and gullied/ravinous land is found due to hilly tracts and undulated land while Phulera tehsil occupies maximum area under sand desertic land due to adjoining desert

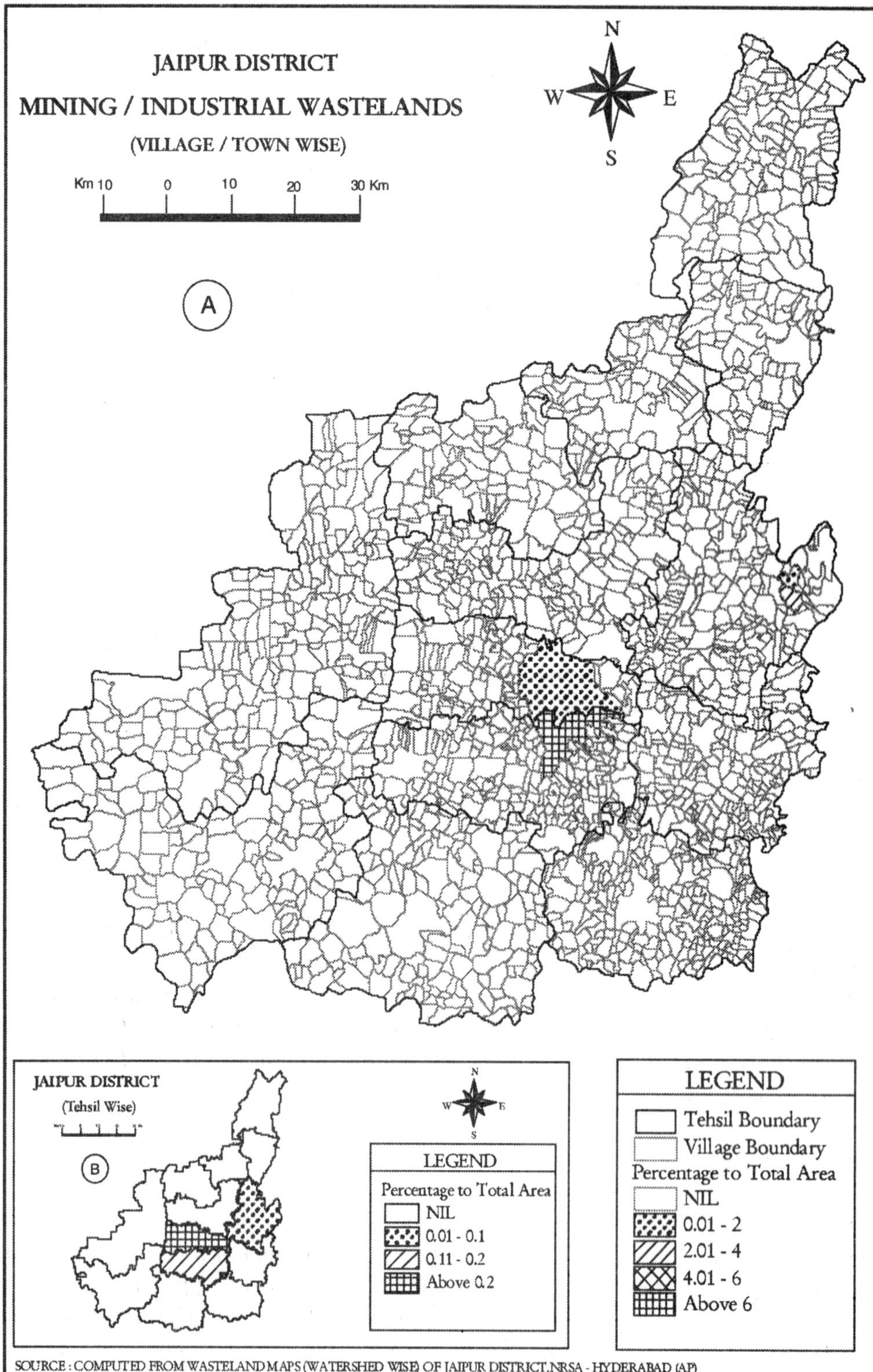

Fig. 4.10A : Mining/Industrial Wastelands (Village/Townwise)
Fig. 4.10B : Mining/Industrial Wastelands (Tehsilwise)

Plate 9 : A view of marble mining near Andhi Village in Jamwa Ramgarh Tehsil.

Plate 10 : Mining Wasteland : Quarrying on Jhalana hill near.Pinkcity Jaipur.

districts of the state. Other important tehsils having more total wastelands are Amber, Dudu and Kotputli. The following Table 4.18 shows tehsilwise percentage distribution of totalwastelands.

Table 4.18 : Tehsilwise Percentage Distribution of Total Wastelands in Jaipur District.

S. No.	Tehsil	Area under total wastelands in hectares	Tehsilwise percentage of total wastelands to total geographical area.	Tehsilwise percentage share of wastelands, of the district
1.	Amber	18215.25	21.77	9.189
2.	Bassi	8881.71	13.81	4.480
3.	Chaksu	5970.50	7.65	3.012
4.	Chomu	9702.30	14.05	4.894
5.	Dudu	16750.00	12.53	8.449
6.	Jaipur	6001.63	10.25	3.027
7.	Jamwa Ramgarh	38094.14	37.70	19.217
8.	Kotputli	16264.67	19.49	8.205
9.	Phagi	13056.50	12.17	6.586
10.	Phulera	22411.56	9.17	11.305
11.	Sanganer	4062.00	6.45	2.049
12.	Shahapura	13357.65	28.04	6.738
13.	Viratnagar	25464.48	53.62	12.845
	TOTAL	198232.39	16.78	100.00

Source : Computed from Wasteland Maps, NRSA, Hyderabad (A.P.)

The Table 4.18 shows that Viratnagar and Jamwa Ramgarh tehsils have severe problem of wastelands as these tehsils occupy more than one-half (53.62%), more than one-third (37.70%) and more than one-fourth (28.04%) of their geographical area under wastelands. Other tehsils having more their area under wasteland are Amber and Kotputli. All these tehsils are situated partly/fully in hilly tracts of the district. Due to their location is undutated hilly tracts, these tehsils have maximum area under degraded forest and gullied/ravinous land. Almost all the tehsils of the western and southern part of the study area lie in peneplained area, occupy less area under this category of land.

Fig. 4.11B shows that moderate (20-30%), high (30-40%) and very high (above 40%) percentages of wastelands are found in the tehsils of north eastern part of the distract i.e. Viratnagar, Jamwa Ramgarh, Shahapura and Amber while in remaining tehsils, the percentage of wastelands is low (10-20%) and very low (0.1 to 10%).

Fig 4.11A also indicates that villages having high (40 to 60%) and very high percentages (Above 60) of wasteland are concentrated in the north eastern part of district especially in hilly terrain. Besides this two small patches of this category are also found is the northwestern and western part of the district. The villages of moderate intensity of wastelands are also found in the areas of high and very high intensities of wastelands. The villages of low and very low percentages of wasteland are concentrated mostly in southern and south western part of the district particularly in Phagi and Dudu tehsils. Small patches of low and very low intensities of wastelands are scattered in remaining tehsils of the district. Table 4.19 shows the tehsilwise villages under various intensities of wasteland.

Table 4.19 shows that approximately two-third villages have very low and low intensities (1-15% and 15-30%) of wastelands of their total geographical area. The maximum villages

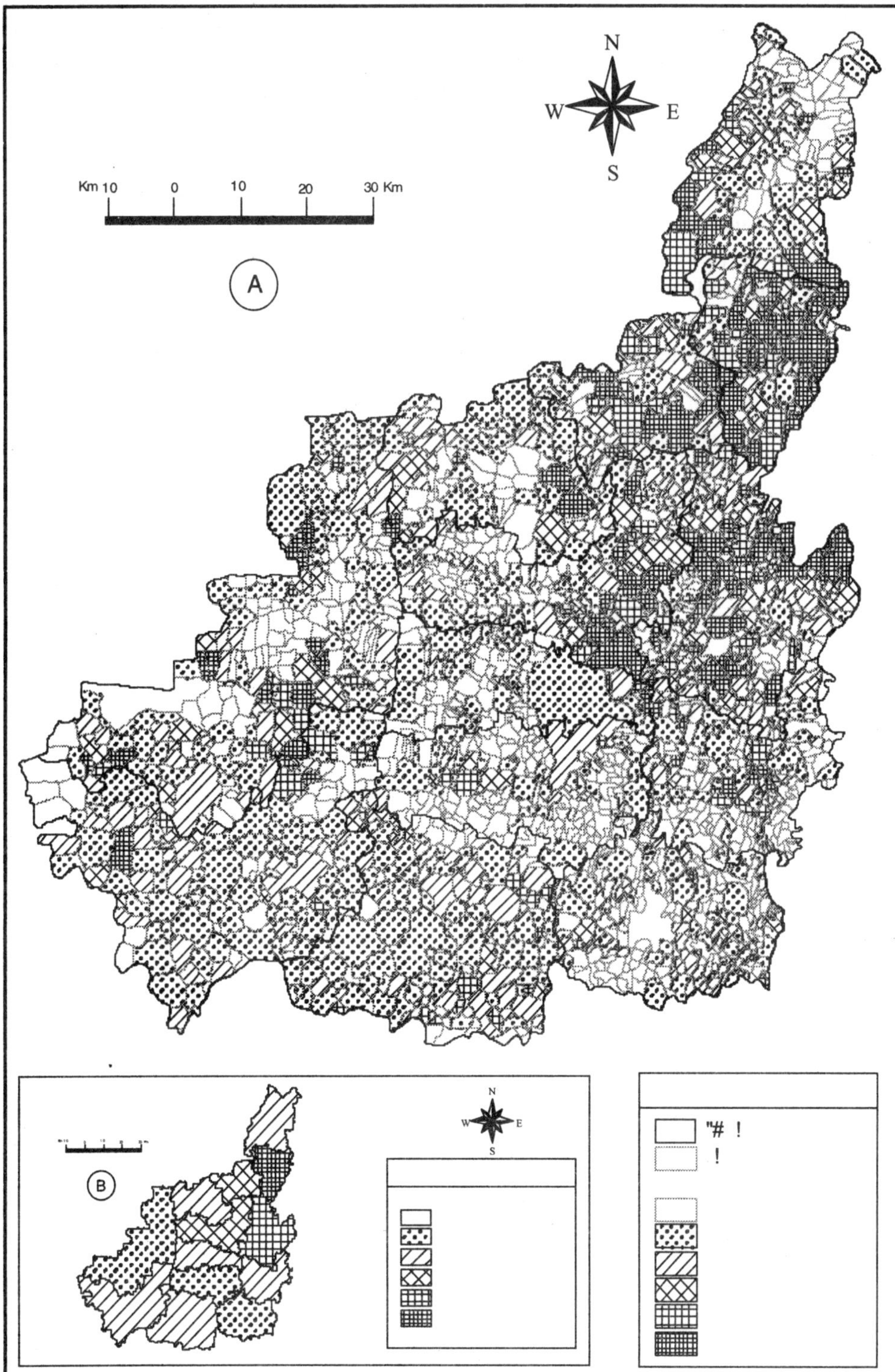

Fig. 4.11A : Total Wastelands (Village/Townwise)
Fig. 4.11B : Total Wastelands (Tehsilwise)

of these categories are found in the tehiles of south western part of the district i.e. Phagi (111) and Dudu (95) tehsils. Both these tehsils occupy more than one-fourth villages (26.55%) of low and very low intensities. These tehsils have more land with scrub and without scrub and degraded pasture due to salinity/alkalinity, brackish ground water and shallow poor soils. Jamwa Ramgarh tehsil leads all the tehsil having villages of moderate intensity (30-45%) of this category of land. Approximately one-third wasteland villages have high (45-60%) and very high percentage (above 60%) of wastelands to their total geographical area. Jamwa Ramgarh tehsil alone occupies more than one-fifth villages (21.47%) of this category followed by Viratnagar tehsil (12%). Both these tehsils are situated in the north eastern part especially hilly terrain of the study area.

Table 4.19 shows that in this district 1250 village/towns are affected by the wasteland i.e. 56.74 per cent of the total villages of the study area. The maximum villages having wasteland

Table 4.19: Tehsilwise Distribution of Villages/Towns by Share of Total Wastelands in Jaipur District.

S. No	Tehsil	Percentagewise distribution of villages and towns of total wastelands					Total villages having wasteland	Percentage of wasteland villages	Percentage to the total wasteland villages
		0.01-15%	15-30%	30-40%	45-60%	Above 60			
1.	Amber	49	29	13	10	23	124	63.26	9.92
2.	Bassi	41	23	11	06	15	63	44.65	7.68
3.	Chaksu	55	37	11	05	07	115	41.07	9.20
4.	Chomu	32	17	06	01	06	62	64.58	4.96
5.	Dudu	70	25	09	05	04	113	76.35	9.04
6.	Jaipur	28	05	03	02	05	43	41.75	3.44
7.	Jamwa Ramgarh	26	42	31	17	61	177	73.44	14.16
8.	Kotputli	41	10	09	05	10	75	54.35	6.00
9.	Phagi	76	35	07	11	03	132	77.19	10.56
10.	Phulera	60	21	16	09	18	124	56.62	9.92
11.	Sanganer	32	09	03	03	02	49	23.22	3.92
12.	Shahapura	25	11	05	10	10	61	67.77	4.88
13.	Viratnagar	12	09	13	09	36	79	84.04	6.32
	Total	547	273	137	88	288	1250	56.74	100.00
	Percentage	43.76	21.84	10.96	7.04	23.04	100		

Source : Computed from wasteland maps, NRSA, Hyderabad (A.P.)

are in Jamwa Ramgarh tehsil (177) followed by Phagi (132), Phulera (124) and Amber (124), while Shahapura (6) and Chomu tehsils (62) have very less number of wasteland villages.

Table 4.19 also indicates that Jamwa Ramgarh tehsil has maximum percentage (14.164%) of wasteland villages in the district followed by Phagi (10.50%), Phulera (9.92%) and Amber tehsils (9.92%). All the four tehsils occupy approximately 50 per cent wasteland villages of the study area. These tehsils have degraded forest, gullied and or ravinous land, land with scrub and without scrub, degraded pasture and sand-desertic wasteland.

All the tehsils of the district have been divided into five groups according to intensity of wasteland villages. Table 4.20 shows intensity group of wasteland villages, number and name of tehsils:

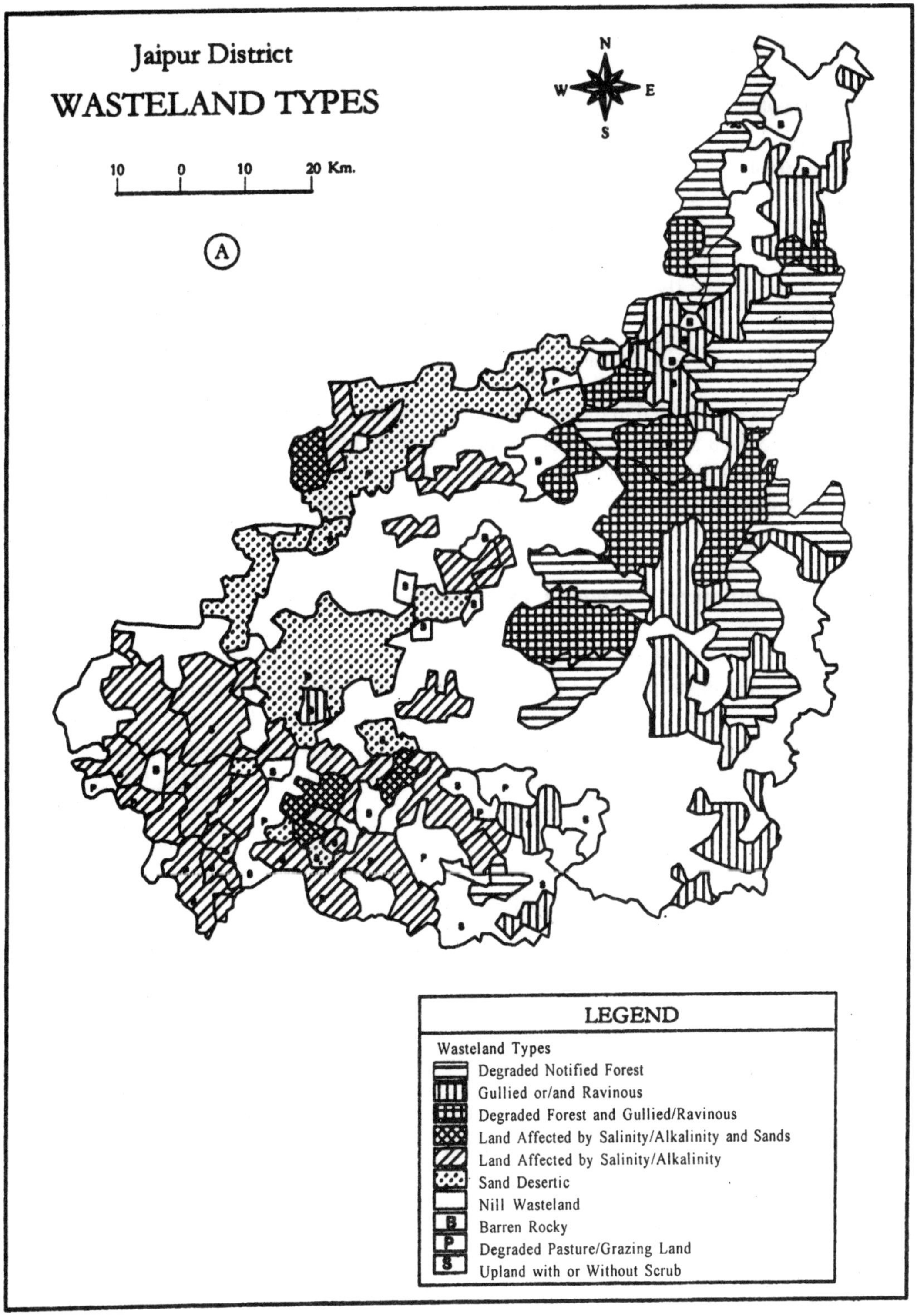

Fig. 4.12 : Wasteland Types

The following Table 4.20 reveals that more than one-half tehsils (53.84%) of the dirstrict have high and very high percentage of villages having wastelands.

Table 4.20 : Percentage of Villages having Wasteland, Intensity Group and Name of Tehsils in Jaipur District

Percentage of villages having wasteland	Intensity group	Number of tehsils	Percentage of total tehsils	Name of the tehsils
Less than 40	Very low	01	7.69	Sanganer
40-50	Low	03	23.07	Jaipur, Chaksu, Bassi
50-60	Average	02	15.38	Kotputli and Phulera
60-70	High	03	23.07	Shahapura, Chomu, Amber
More than 70	Very High	04	30.77	Viratnagar, Phagi, Jamwa Ramgarh and Dudu

Source : Computed from Wasteland Maps, NRSA, Hyderabad (A.P.)

These tehsils are situated in the northern and south western part of the district. In northern part degraded forest and gullied and/or ravinous eroded land are dominant while in the south western part saline/alkaline, land with scrub and without scrub and degraded pasture are significant. Approximately one-third tehsils have very low and low percentage of wasteland villages.

Spatial Distribution of Wasteland Types (Different Categories of Wastelands)

Fig 4.12 shows that degraded forests, degraded forests and gullied/ravinous land are concentrated in the eastern part of the district while in western part sand desertic land is concentrated and scattered patches of land affected by salinity are also found. As mentioned earlier, southwestern part of the district is peneplained with calcareous soil and poor to moderate drained. This area is affected by salinity, degraded pasture and land with or with our scrub. However at some places barren hills are also found.

REFERENCES

Anonymous, (1972). Rep. Survey of Ravine Lands in Rajasthan 1968-70, Forest Department, Government of Rajasthan, Jaipur.

Bharadwaj, B.K. (1979). Distribution and Changing Pattern of Culturable Waste in Gurgaon District, Haryana, *Geog. Rev. of India,* Vol. XXXIII N.2, pp. 120-132.

Bhargava, G.P. and Bhattacharji, J.C. (1982). "Morphology, Genesis and Classification of Salt Affected Soils". In *Review of Soil Research in India Part II,* 12th Inter Congress of Soil Science, New Delhi.

Chouhan, T.S. (1993). Intensity of Desertification Hazards in Rajasthan (Ed.) *Changing Contours of Arid Ecology*, Vol. I. Asian Environmental Council, Jaipur.

Doi, R.D. (2005). Interpretation of Ravine Land in Sub-Watersheds of the Morel River, Rajasthan (Ed.) *Geomorphology and Environmental Sustainability.* Concept Publishing Company, New Delhi.

Forest Department, Government of Rajasthan, Jaipur (1969). Report on Survey of Ravine Lands in Rajasthan 1962-65.

Gupta, N.L. and Maroo, R.L., (1991). *Challenge of Wastelands Utilization Issues and Themes,* Academic Publishers, Jaipur.

Kalwar, S.C. (1995). "Rajasthan Men Parti Bhumi" *Rajasthan Patrika*, Jaipur 30th July, 1995 p. 3

Kalwar, S.C. (1996). *"Prayavaran Avam Parti Bhumi"*, Pointer Publishers, Jaipur.

Kalwar, S.C. (1998) Identification and Developments of Wastelands in Semi-Arid Areas of Rajasthan. Unpublished Research Project Report, ICSSR, New Delhi.

Ministry of Rural Development, Department of Land Resources, Government of India; National Remote Sensing Agency Hederabad, Wastelands Atlas of India, 2000, p. 9 and p. 41.

Padmini Pani *et al.* (2001). Delineation and Monitoring of Gullied and Ravinous Lands in a Part of Lower Chambal Valley, India, Using Remote Sensing and GIS, Paper Presented at the 22nd Asian Conference on Remote Sensing 5-9 November, 2001, Singapore.

Sharma, H.S. (1980). *Ravine Erosion in India*, Concept Publishing Co., New Delhi.

Tejwani, K.G. and Ahuja (1956). Report on Ravine Reclamation in Madhya Pradesh, New Delhi : Central Water and Power Commission.

Tejwani, K.G. *et al.* (1960). Control of Gully Erosion in the Ravine Lands of Gujarat, *Journal of Soil and Water Conservation in India*, 8, 65-74.

5

DETERMINANTS, REGRESSION AND TIME SERIES ANALYSIS OF WASTELANDS

There are various causes of formation and distribution of wastelands in the district. The spatial distribution of wastelands at village and tehsil level may be analysed taking environmental, human/social, economic and technological factors into consideration. Following are the independent variables chosen for the village level wasteland analysis:

Environmental Determinants

(a) ***Morphometric***

X_1 Slope
X_2 Ruggedness number
X_3 Dissection index

(b) ***Hydrological Factor***

X_4 Drainage density

(c) ***Social Factors***

X_5 Rural population density per km^2
X_6 Percentage of literacy
X_7 Percentage of Scheduled Tribe population
X_8 Percentage of Scheduled Caste population
X_9 Percentage of population engaged in agriculture

(d) ***Economic Factors***

X_{10} Average size of holding in hectares
X_{11} Percentage of irrigated land to total cultivated land

The analysis of above factors (independent variables) with the help of Karl Pearson's coefficients for different type of wastelands (dependent variables) has been done for fifty sample villages selected from the various categories of wastelands. Three more additional variables have been taken for tehsil level analysis:

(e) *Economic and Technological Factors*

X_{12} Number of livestock population per 100 hectare land
X_{13} Number of pump sets and diesel engines per 100 hectares of NSA
X_{14} Number of tractors per 100 hectares of NSA

Environmental Determinants

(a) *Morphometric — (X_1-Slope, X_2-Ruggedness number, X_3-Dissection index)*

Relief plays an important role in the spatial distribution, utilization and reclamation of wastelands. The north eastern part of the district is hilly which has maximum concentration of degraded notified forest, barren hills and gullied and/or ravinous land. The barren hilly terrain of steep slope with thin soil layer has accelerated soil erosion while the normal erosion is noticeable in the dense forested hilly tracts. Thus, the accelerated erosion is confined to barren hilly tract and degraded forest lands.

To analysis morphometric factors affecting wastelands and its type (Gullied/ravinous Y_1, degraded forest Y_2, sands–desertic Y_3, scrub land Y_4, degraded pasture Y_5, barren rocky Y_6, saline Y_7, alkaline Y_8 and mining Y_9), slope X_1, ruggedness number X_2 and dissection index X_3 have been considered taking 50 villages from 9 sample study areas representing all the categories of wasteland.

Slope, ruggedness number and dissection index are the predominant parameters in determining the various categories of wastelands. The areas of high altitude have more slope, ruggedness number and dissection index. The sample villages having high percentage of degraded forest, barren hills and mining waste also have more slope, ruggedness number and dissection index (Table 5.2, 5.6 and 5.9).

The above assumption is proved from the correlation matrix (Table 5.11) that there is a positive correlation between barren hills (Y_6) and slope (X_1), sand – desertic (Y_3) and slope (X_1). The positive relationship is not strong between slope (X_1) and barren rocky (Y_5). Sand desertic land lies in the areas of low slopes but there is a high positive relationship between sands–desertic land (Y_3) and slope (X_1). It is interesting to note that there is no positive relationship between degraded forest (Y_2) and slope (X_1).

It is also proved from the correlation matrix (Table 5.10) that there is a significant positive correlation between the barren hills (Y_6) and ruggedness number (X_2), barren hills (Y_6) and dissection index (X_3).

(b) *Drainage Density (X_4)*

The high drainage density dissects higher table land and converts the land into bad land topography, washes top layer of soil through accelerated erosion. The soil fertility loss is of no less significance.

Generally drainage density is high in those sample villages where the percentage of gullied and/or ravinous land, degraded notified forest land, barren hills and land affected by saline/alkaline (Tables 5.1, 5.2, 5.9, 5.8 and 5.5) are also high. An alanysis of correlation matrix (Table 5.10) gives a quite different picture. This table reveals that there is a positive relationship only between drainage density (X_4); and saline (Y_7); barren rocky (Y_5); scrubland (Y_4), mining wasteland (Y_9) and gullied/ravinous land. This variable is quite insignificant in explaining the variation in degraded notified forest land.

(c) Human/Social Factors: Pressure of Rural Population per 100 hectare of land (X_5)

It is assumed that the wasteland would be less in those areas where rural population density per square kilometer is high as farmers are forced to bring wasteland under plough to increase their cultivated land and fulfil their requirement.

It is observed from the tables 5.1, 5.2, 5.4, 5.5, 5.6 and 5.9 that pressure of rural population per square kilometer (Y_5) is found low in those sample villages where the percentage of degraded notified forest land (Y_2), gullied/ravinous (Y_4), degraded pasture (Y_5), saline (Y_7), mining wasteland (Y_9) and sands-desertic land (Y_3) are high and *vice versa.*

There is a negative correlation between rural population per square kilometer and land affected by alkalinity, sands-desertic land and land affected by salinity. However, the negative correlation is insignificant between rural population density and saline, sand-desertic land (Table 5.10).

Percentage of Scheduled Caste Population (X_8)

Generally, it is believed that the Scheduled Castes do not use their land efficiently and their concentration is found in the plains instead of hilly tracts as their economy is based on villagers. Thus, it is assumed that along with their increase in total population, the amount of wasteland also increases in the plains. Tables 5.8, 5.9, 5.5 and 5.7 reveal that Scheduled Caste population is more in the sample villages of land affected by alkalinity/salinity, mining wasteland and degraded pasture/grazing land.

The result of correlation matrix (Table 5.10) reveals that there is a positive relationship between percentage of Scheduled Caste population (X_8) and land affected by salinity (Y_7), land with or without scrub (Y_4), sands-desertic land (Y_3), degraded pasture (Y_5). The correlation matrix analysis (Table 5.10) supports the above hypothesis to some extent.

Percentage of Population Engaged in Agriculture (X_9)

In rural areas, most of the population is engaged in agriculture as cultivators and agricultural labourers and it is assumed that the wasteland would be less in those areas where percentage of agricultural population is more or *vice versa.* The concentration of population engaged in agriculture is more in the sample villages of gullied/ravinous land, land with or without scrub, land affected by salinity and degraded pasture/grazing land (Tables 5.1, 5.4, 5.5 and 5.7).

It is evident from the correlation matrix (Table 5.10) that there is a negative correlation between percentage of population engaged in agriculture and degraded notified forest land,

Table 5.1 : Determinants of Gullied and/or Ravinous Land

Name of Village	Percentage of Gullied and/or Ravinous Land	Slope in Degrees	Rugged-ness Number	Dissection Index	Drainage Density	Per Sq. km Rural Population	Percentage of Literacy	Percentage of ST Population	Percentage of SC Population	Percentage of Population engaged in Agriculture	Average Size of Holding	Percentage of Irrigated Land to total cultivated land
	Y_1	X_2	X_2	X_3	X_4	X_5	X_6	X_7	X_8	X_9	X_{10}	X_{11}
Chainpura Bas Dedwani	24.57	10.35	0.05	0.11	4.50	109	34.94	77.78	19.59	81.82	1.61	48.33
Dedwani	19.07	0.00	0.00	0.00	2.50	78	46.85	56.02	0.00	83.72	3.25	48.76
Godiyana	5.88	10.35	0.09	0.20	5.00	122	38.54	51.01	21.79	87.57	0.98	50.00
Rampura Bas Samred	27.82	8.70	0.01	0.05	4.50							17.50
Samred Kalan	15.68	13.35	0.13	0.25	4.00	146	73.95	22.91	14.81	73.35	0.72	50.24
Samred Khurd	28.55	16.05	0.13	0.23	5.75	163	76.38	53.59	6.10	85.02	1.07	47.50
Correlation (Y_1 over X_{11})		0.1411	−0.2101	−0.2856	0.1661	0.2069	0.3543	0.3936	-0.4729	-0.0847	0.1710	-0.4905

Table 5.2: Determinants of Degraded Notified Forest Land

Name of Village	Percentage of Degraded Notified Forest Land to Total Land	Slope in Degrees	Ruggedness Number	Dissection Index	Drainage Density	Per Sq. km Rural Population	Percentage of Literacy	Percentage of ST Population	Percentage of SC Population	Percentage of Population engaged in Agriculture	Average Size of Holding	Percentage of Irrigated Land to total cultivated land
	Y_2	X_1	X_2	X_3	X_4	X_5	X_6	X_7	X_8	X_9	X_{10}	X_{11}
Bundh Muzaffarpur	93.88	24.8	0.090	0.26	2.75	133	6.58	26.52	2.59	53.06	0.67	58.53
Kuhada	82.4	25.9	0.050	0.27	1.60	177	6.05	0.00	24.13	47.47	0.42	56.15
Pachhodala	56.24	31.4	0.153	0.40	3.00	128	57.29	4.38	21.26	82.59	2.13	47.90
Raghunath-pura Talooka Bas	74.51	19.0	0.050	0.18	2.35	142	77.24	0.00	0.00	69.16	1.21	57.71
Correlation (Y_2 over X_{11})		–0.4815	–0.6187	–0.6099	–0.3692	0.3151	–0.7012	0.6042	–0.4325	–0.8906	–0.9065	0.8911

Table 5.3 : Determinants of Sands-Desertic Land

Name of Village	Percentage of Sands – Desertic Land	Slope in Degrees	Ruggedness Number	Dissection Index	Drainage Density	Per sq. km Rural Population	Percentage of Literacy	Percentage of ST Population	Percentage of SC Population	Percentage of Population engaged in Agriculture	Average Size of Holding	Percentage of Irrigated Land to total cultivated land
	Y_3	X_1	X_2	X_3	X_4	X_5	X_6	X_7	X_8	X_9	X_{10}	X_{11}
Bhagawatpura	57.24	1.80	0.00	0.01	0.00	249	60.00	0.00	9.13	63.27	2.56	26.37
Dhani Bora	61.13	1.80	0.00	0.08	0.00	287	64.00	3.00	13.47	61.39	2.01	35.63
Magipura	85.83	1.80	0.00	0.00	0.00	195	52.22	0.00	28.94	41.56	2.96	13.59
Malyawas	45.80	0.00	0.00	0.00	0.00	157	72.19	9.85	17.05	53.04	1.82	60.42
Sauringhpura	84.18	1.80	0.00	0.05	0.00	135	54.98	15.13	6.01	51.85	3.32	28.39
Correlation (Y_3 over X_{11})		0.6709		0.1260		−0.2900	−0.9312	0.0814	0.2099	−0.6327	0.8949	−0.8042

Table 5.4 : Determinants of Upland with or Without Scrubs

Name of Village	Percentage of Upland with or without Scrubs	Slope in Degrees	Ruggedness Number	Dissection Index	Drainage Density	Per sq. km Rural Population	Percentage of Literacy	Percentage of ST Population	Percentage of SC Population	Percentage of Population engaged in Agriculture	Average Size of Holding	Percentage of Irrigated Land to total cultivated land
	Y_4	X_1	X_2	X_3	X_4	X_5	X_6	X_7	X_8	X_9	X_{10}	X_{11}
Ajnota		1.80	0.00	0.00	0.00	77	53.72	0.80	5.58	85.38	5.82	20.13
Chandkalan	36.36	1.80	0.00	0.01	1.00	129	48.57	6.34	17.49	64.56	1.98	20.95
Harsundar-pura	48.9	0.00	0.00	0.00	0.00	57	60.04	14.86	10.18	49.99	3.45	10.51
Nathalpura	26.7	0.00	0.00	0.00	0.00	125	67.35	0.82	8.70	78.02	1.82	6.00
Panwasoo	55.64	1.80	0.00	0.00	1.00	163	46.77	0.00	7.82	73.72	1.64	4.05
Correlation (Y_4 over X_{11})		0.3669		−0.2862	0.3669	0.0139	−0.6092	0.2130	−0.2958	−0.3765	0.2505	−0.2670

Table 5.5: Determinants of Degraded Pasture/Grazing Land

Name of Village	Percentage of Pasture/ Grazing	Slope in Degrees	Ruggedness Number	Dissection Index	Drainage Density	Per sq. km Rural Population	Percentage of Literacy	Percentage of ST Population	Percentage of SC Population	Percentage of Population engaged in Agriculture	Average Size of Holding	Percentage of Irrigated Land to total cultivated land
	Y_5	X_1	X_2	X_3	X_4	X_5	X_6	X_7	X_8	X_9	X_{10}	X_{11}
Harsuliya	19.00	1.71	0.00	0.01	0.00	241	53.28	3.55	32.54	54.67	1.43	6.50
Janakinath-pura	28.17	1.80	0.00	0.00	0.00	75	77.87	0.00	5.28	85.26	5.47	1.83
Khezro Ka Bas	31.71	1.75	0.00	0.00	0.00	103	53.24	0.00	0.00	90.12	3.18	11.36
Raipura	22.05	1.80	0.00	0.00	0.00	101	50.73	0.00	11.91	77.07	4.64	23.00
Correlation (Y_5 over X_{11})		0.3147		−0.7213		−0.7212	0.3625	−0.7213	−0.9136	0.9152	0.4237	−0.2211

Table 5.6 : Determinants of Barren Hill/Rocky

Name of Village	Percentage of Barren hills/Rocky	Slope in Degrees	Ruggedness Number	Dissection Index	Drainage Density	Per sq. km Rural Population	Percentage of Literacy	Percentage of ST Population	Percentage of SC Population	Percentage of Population engaged in Agriculture	Average Size of Holding	Percentage of Irrigated Land to total cultivated land
	Y_6	X_1	X_2	X_3	X_4	X_5	X_6	X_7	X_8	X_9	X_{10}	X_{11}
Arnia	30.69	11.10	0.15	0.06	2.25	311	51.26	18.47	14.58	75.14	0.85	66.26
Beelpur	27.40	10.30	0.03	0.24	1.00	318	74.91	5.74	28.69	40.65	1.04	70.27
Chok Manoharpur	16.17	10.00	0.00	0.00	1.25	285	35.76	10.85	10.09	93.30	1.68	77.25
Chandwaji	28.74	10.30	0.00	0.25	0.00	1891		10.01	6.52	7.32	0.05	70.75
Deoka Harwar	29.25	15.40	0.05	0.22	2.00	370	48.57	8.76	7.43	56.13	0.88	42.22
Peelwa	21.21	10.30	0.00	0.08	0.25	362	47.62	39.84	6.92	67.71	0.56	70.75
Salarwar	25.10	11.10	0.05	0.25	1.75	240	62.61	89.58	1.69	61.63	0.66	76.56
Sunder Ka Bas	28.60	18.30	0.05	0.21	2.25	460	46.31	12.71	0.50	90.32	0.89	88.34
Correlation (Y_6 over X_{11})		0.4265	0.6011	0.6058	0.3443	0.2716	0.4466	–0.1781	0.0849	–0.4147	–0.5269	–0.3046

Table 5.7 : Determinants of Land Affected by Salinity

Name of Village	Percentage of Land Affected by Salinity	Slope in Degrees	Ruggedness Number	Dissection Index	Drainage Density	Per sq. km Rural Population	Percentage of Literacy	Percentage of ST Population	Percentage of SC Population	Percentage of Population engaged in Agriculture	Average Size of Holding	Percentage of Irrigated Land to total cultivated land
	Y_7	X_1	X_2	X_3	X_4	X_5	X_6	X_7	X_8	X_9	X_{10}	X_{11}
Bokrawas	21.97	1.80	0.00	0.01	1.50	84	64.98	15.08	14.56	44.52	5.90	9.27
Bigolav	10.39	1.80	0.00	0.04	1.00	128	37.20	0.00	8.84	70.92	3.63	4.77
Dantra	40.32	0.00	0.00	0.00	1.75	161	48.14	0.00	42.90	48.04	2.52	17.14
Hotupur	15.28	1.80	0.00	0.01	1.00	82	40.69	0.12	14.86	81.94	6.80	6.47
Jhakolar	41.73	1.80	0.00	0.09	2.00	52	42.02	0.00	13.07	75.47	9.94	9.78
Panwaliya	51.67	1.80	0.00	0.00	1.75	84	50.25	0.00	13.85	86.52	7.20	16.16
Correlation (Y_7 over X_{11})		−0.2977		0.0034	0.8932	−0.1337	0.1986	−0.2475	0.3526	0.1430	0.3253	0.8696

Table 5.8 : Determinants of Land Affected by Alkalinity

Name of Village	Percentage of Land Affected by Alkalinity	Slope in Degrees	Rugged-ness number	Dissection Index	Drainage Density	Per sq. kkm Rural Population	Percentage of Literacy	Percentage of ST Population	Percentage of SC Population	Percen-tage of Population engaged in Agricul-ture	Average Size of Holding	Percen-tage of Irrigated Land to total cultivated land
	Y_8	X_1	X_2	X_3	X_4	X_5	X_6	X_7	X_8	X_9	X_{10}	X_{11}
Girdharipura	33.24	0.00	0.00	0.01	2.00	146	55.25	42.38	0.00	73.71	2.74	34.33
Jharna	15.52	1.80	0.00	0.05	0.60	201	46.72	10.20	21.39	58.85	1.43	72.86
Kopriyawas Kalan	49.80	1.80	0.00	0.01	2.25	116	58.00	21.72	11.11	76.67	2.51	5.92
Kotgewar	46.33	1.80	0.00	0.12	1.75	133	60.28	10.54	27.04	58.36	2.68	13.16
Mohlan	19.56	1.80	0.00	0.01	2.00	232	58.71	5.08	37.13	59.69	1.40	42.13
Nasnauta	68.98	0.00	0.00	0.01	1.00	128	57.80	8.35	27.96	65.36	3.13	2.74
Correlation (Y_8 over X_{11})		−0.4690		−0.0264	0.0537	−0.8378	0.5613	−0.0077	−0.0416	0.3539	0.8927	−0.9133

Table 5.9 : Determinants of Mining/Industrial Wasteland

Name of Village	Percentage of Mining Waste	Slope in Degrees	Ruggedness Number	Dissection Index	Drainage Density	Per sq. km Rural Population	Percentage of Literacy	Percentage of ST Population	Percentage of SC Population	Percentage of Population engaged in Agriculture	Average Size of Holding	Percentage of Irrigated Land to total cultivated land
	Y_9	X_1	X_2	X_3	X_4	X_5	X_6	X_7	X_8	X_9	X_{10}	X_{11}
Dagota	2.08	11.10	0.08	0.36	2.00	41	53.04	35.50	36.78	33.52	0.23	64.28
Rayanwala	6.78	10.35	0.06	0.33	2.00	77	79.71	55.40	23.01	64.44	0.84	5.18
Sanakotra	3.96	8.70	0.06	0.32	2.00	126	67.70	58.90	8.52	51.53	2.09	18.47
Singhpuri	2.18	15.40	0.01	0.13	0.00	72	40.00	54.90	45.10	67.02	0.95	10.00
Thali	9.31	3.05	0.00	0.11	2.37	241	74.39	29.09	17.38	65.83	1.15	19.26
Correlation (Y_9 over X_{11})		−0.8318	−0.4307	−0.3444	0.5896	0.8117	0.8237	−0.3759	−0.5931	0.5427	0.1958	−0.4291

Table 5.10 : Correlation Matrix

Name of Village	Slope in Degrees	Ruggedness Number	Dissection Index	Drainage Density	Per sq. km. Rural Population	Percentage of Literacy	Percentage of ST Population	Percentage of SC Population	Percentage of Popula-tion engaged in Agriculture	Average Size of Holding	Percentage of Irrigated Land to total cultivated land
	X_1	X_2	X_3	X_4	X_5	X_6	X_7	X_8	X_9	X_{10}	X_{11}
Gullied Land or Ravinous Land (Y_1)	0.1411	−0.2101	−0.2856	0.1661	0.2069	0.3543	0.3936	−0.4729	−0.0847	0.1710	−0.4905
Degraded Notified Forest Land (Y_2)	−0.4815	−0.6187	−0.6099	−0.3692	0.3151	−0.7012	0.6042	−0.4325	−0.8906	−0.9065	0.8911
Sands-Desertic Land (Y_3)	0.6709		0.1260		−0.2900	−0.9312	0.0814	0.2099	−0.6327	0.8949	−0.8042
Upland with or Without Srubs (Y_4)	0.3669		−0.2862	0.3669	0.0139	−0.6092	0.2130	−0.2958	−0.3765	0.2505	−0.2670
Degraded Pasture/Grazing Land (Y_5)	0.3147		−0.7213		−0.7212	0.3625	−0.7213	−0.9136	0.9152	0.4237	−0.2211
Barren Rocky (Y_6)	0.4265	0.6011	0.6058	0.3443	0.2716	0.4466	−0.1781	0.0849	−0.4147	−0.5269	−0.3046
Land Affected by Salinity (Y_7)	−0.2977		0.0034	0.8932	−0.1337	0.1986	−0.2475	0.3526	0.1430	0.3253	0.8696
Land Affected by Alkalinity (Y_8)	−0.4690		−0.0264	0.0537	−0.8378	0.5613	−0.0077	−0.0416	0.3539	0.8927	−0.9133
Mining Waste (Y_9)	−0.8318	−0.4307	−0.3444	0.5896	0.8117	0.8237	−0.3759	−0.5931	0.5427	0.1958	−0.4291

Table 5.11 : Determinants of Wastelands (At Tehsil level)

S. No.	Tehsil	Gullied Land or Ravinous Land (Y_1)	Degraded Notified Forest Land (Y_2)	Sands-Desertic Land (Y_3)	Upland with or Without Srubs (Y_4)	Degraded Pasture/ Grazing Land (Y_5)	Barren Rocky (Y_6)	Land Affected by Salinity (Y_7)	Mining Waste (Y_9)	Livestock per 100 ha. (X_{12})	Pumpsets per 100 ha. NSA (X_{13})	Tractor per 100 ha. NSA (X_{14})
1	Kotputli	3.97	11.07	1.17	2.21	0.37	0.71	0.00	0.71	167.07	22.62	2.58
2	Viratnagar	18.58	33.58	1.24	0.02	0.06	0.15	0.00	0.15	277.82	59.30	4.18
3	Shahapura	15.22	6.26	3.89	0.00	1.51	1.17	0.00	1.17	307.96	29.77	4.75
4	Chomu	1.56	2.06	8.48	0.10	0.53	0.32	1.00	0.32	364.29	30.67	4.58
5	Phulera	0.02	0.02	5.32	0.80	0.07	0.82	2.12	0.82	145.86	11.00	2.11
6	Dudu	0.34	0.00	2.21	2.55	0.93	1.32	5.18	1.32	278.77	16.01	6.58
7	Phagi	1.52	0.52	1.01	6.01	1.50	0.07	1.48	0.07	151.16	10.04	3.58
8	Sanganer	0.00	0.64	0.46	0.72	0.15	0.06	4.24	0.06	151.26	15.30	5.72
9	Jaipur	1.64	5.64	1.30	0.68	0.17	0.15	0.40	0.15	229.03	15.83	6.23
10	Amber	6.30	10.14	1.93	0.22	0.70	1.44	1.05	1.44	278.62	30.62	6.28
11	Jamwa Ramgarh	14.67	19.55	0.78	1.61	0.55	0.51	0.00	0.51	206.84	24.01	3.30
12	Bassi	6.49	3.29	0.97	0.80	1.89	0.37	0.00	0.37	237.09	23.43	3.43
13	Chaksu	2.27	0.00	2.47	2.15	0.76	0.00	0.00	0.00	182.35	18.48	3.90

Table 5.12 : Correlation Matrix at Tehsil Level

	Correlation of Gullied Land or Ravinous Land (Y_1) over X..	Correlation Degraded Notified Forest Land (Y_2) over X..	Correlation Sands-Desertic Land (Y_3) over X..	Correlation Upland with or Without Srubs (Y_4) over X..	Correlation Degraded Pasture/Grazing Land (Y_5) over X..	Correlation Barren Rocky (Y_6) over X..	Correlation Land Affected by Salinity (Y_7) over X..	Correlation Mining Waste (Y_9) over X..
Correlation Y... over X_{12}	0.355343677	0.211158469	0.509271682	−0.5167860	0.169839665	0.356057719	−0.12435352	0.356057719
Correlation Y... over X_{13}	0.772390432	0.834707407	0.045761593	−0.5230593	−0.165660128	0.016516085	−0.418081925	0.016516085
Correlation Y... over X_{14}	−0.13479002	−0.117278739	−0.10525022	−0.2184543	−0.041492961	0.252629795	0.458355461	0.252629795

land with or without scrub, sands-desertic land, barren hills and gullied/ravinous land. Thus most of the wasteland categories have negative correlation with the percentage of population engaged in agriculture.

Percentage of Literacy (X_6)

Literate persons have more knowledge about new techniques and wasteland reclamation/ development programmes sponsored by Central/State Government and other agencies. It is assumed that the wasteland would be more in those sample villages where the literacy is low and vice versa.

Tables 5.2, 5.1, 5.3 and 5.5 show that the sample villages of high percentage of degraded notified forest land (Y_2), gullied/ravinous land (Y_1), sands-desertic land (Y_3), land affected by salinity (Y_7) and land with or without scrub (Y_4) have low percentage of literacy. It is evident from Table 5.11 that there is a negative correlation between percentage of literacy and degraded notified forest land, sands-desertic land, land with scrub or without scrub and degraded pasture/grazing land.

Percentage of Scheduled Tribe Population (X_7)

It is observed in the study area that Scheduled Tribe population is generally concentrated in the areas of hilly tract and undulated land. It is assumed that Scheduled Tribe population should be higher in those wasteland areas which are concentrated in the hilly tract i.e. degraded notified forest land, gullied/ravinous land, barren hilly and mining wasteland.

Scheduled Tribe population is more in the sample villages of gullied/ravinous land and mining wasteland (Tables 5.1 and 5.9). The result of the correlation matrix (Table 5.10) proves the above assumption to some extent indicating thereby a positive relationship between percentages of Scheduled Tribe population (X_7) and degraded notified forest land (Y_2), gullied/ravinous land (Y_1) and upland with or without scrub (Y_4). Thus, the above hypothesis is statistically proved (Table 5.10).

(d) Economic Factor

Average Size of holding in Hectare (X_{10})

It is assumed that the areas of large size holdings have high percentage of wastelands while sample villages having low percentage of wastelands have small size of holdings. It is found from Tables 5.3, 5.5, 5.6 and 5.7 that sands-desertic land, land affected by salinity/alkalinity and degraded pasture/grazing land have large size holdings.

From the analysis of correlation matrix (Table 5.10) it is evident that there is a positive correlation between average size of holding (X_{10}) and sands-desertic land, (Y_3) land affected by salinity/alkalinity (Y_7 and Y_8) and degraded pasture/grazing land. Thus the hypothesis "Large size holdings have high percentage of wasteland" is statistically proved.

Percentage of Irrigated Land to Total Cultivated Land (X_{11})

The variable has been chosen keeping in mind that there would be high percentage of wasteland in those sample study areas where the percentage of irrigated land to the total cultivated is less. It is found from Tables 5.3 to 5.7 and 5.9, that the percentage of irrigated land is low in sands-desertic land, land with scrub or without scrub, land affected by salinity/alkalinity, degraded pasture/grazing land and mining wasteland.

It is clear from the correlation matrix Table 5.10 that there is moderate to high negative correlation between irrigated land and land affected by alkalinity, degraded pasture/grazing land, sands-desertic, scrub land and mining wasteland. Again it is statistically proved that there is more wasteland in those areas where percentage of irrigated land is low and very low.

Number of Livestock Population per 100 hectare Land (X_{12})

Livestock plays an important role in economy of rural areas as the animals i.e. cattle like camel, sheep and goats provide power, manure and an additional income to the farmers. Generally, it is believed that the wastelands are kept by the farmers for grazing their cattle or for fodder (hay) for their livestock.

It is evident from the table that there is a positive relationship between livestock population (X_{12}) and sands-desertic land (Y_3), gullied/ravinous land (Y_1) barren rocky (Y_6), mining waste (Y_9) and degraded pasture (Y_5). It indicates that the above hypothesis has its validity up to some extent.

Number of Pump sets and Diesel Engines per 100 hectare N.S.A. (X_{13})

Pump sets and diesel engines provide the facilities of irrigation. It is assumed that more pump sets and diesel engines reduce the amount of wasteland by irrigating the land. The result of correlation matrix (Table 5.10) reveals that there is negative correlation between pump sets (X_{13}) and scrub land (Y_4) while very low negative relationship is found between the pump sets (X_{13}) and land affected by salinity and alkalinity.

Number of Tractors per 100 hectare N.S.A. (X_{14})

Tractor plays an important role in agricultural activities. It is very useful in ploughing, sowing, threshing and transportation. This variable indicates the level of technology in agricultural sector. It may be assumed that the more is the level of technology the lesser would be the amount of wasteland. The result of the correlation matrix depicted in Table 5.10 shows that there is insignificant negative relationship between the tractors and various categories of wastelands. Thus the above assumption is rejected up to some extent.

Regression Analysis

Regression analysis is a statistical device with the help of which we are in a position to estimate (or predict) the unknown values of one variable from known values of another variable. The variable which is used to predict the variable of interest is called the independent variable or explanatory variable and the variable we are trying to predict is called the dependent variable or "explained" variable. The independent variable is denoted by X and the dependent variable by Y. The analysis used is called the simple linear regression analysis – simple because there is only one predictor or independent variable, and linear because assumed linear relationship means that an equation of a straight line of the Y = a+bx, where a and b are constants, is used to describe the average relationship that exists between the two variables.

Regression Lines

If we take the case of two variables X and Y, we shall have two regression lines as the regression of X on Y and the regression of Y on X. The regression line of Y on X gives the most probable values of Y for given values of X and the regression line of X on Y gives the most probable values of X for given values of Y. However, when there is either perfect positive or per cent negative correlation between the two variable ($r = \pm 1$) the regression lines will coincide, i.e., we will have only one line. The farther two regression lines from each other, the lesser is the degree of correlation and the nearer the two regression lines to each other, the higher is the degree of correlation. If the variables are independent, r is zero and the lines of regression are at right angles, i.e. parallel to OX and OY.

Regression Equations

Regression equations, also known as estimating equations are algebraic expression of the regression lines. Since, there are two regression lines, there are two regression equations – the regression equation of X on Y is used to describe the variations in the values of X for given changes in Y and the regression equation of Y on X is used to describe the variation in the values of Y for given changes in X.

Regression Equation of Y on X

The regression equation of Y on X is expressed as follows:

$$Y = a+bx$$

It may be noted that in this equation 'Y' is a dependent variable, i.e., its values depends on X. 'X' is independent variable, i.e., we can take a given value of X and compute the value of Y.

Regression Equation of X on Y

The regression equation of X on Y is expressed as follows:

$$Xc = a+bY$$

To determine the values of a and b, the following two normal equations are to be solved simultaneously:

$$\Sigma X = Na + b\Sigma Y$$
$$\Sigma XY = a\Sigma Y + b\Sigma Y^2$$

Table 5.13 : Calculation of Regression Coeffient Between Population and Wasteland in sample villages of Bassi Tehsil, Jaipur

S. No.	Name of Village	Population Density per km^2	AX = 203 (X-203) dx	d^2x	Waste land	Ay = 27 (y – 27) dy	d^2y	dxdy
1.	Ramsingh Pura	103	-100	10000	22.57	-4.43	19.62	443
2.	Borai	124	-79	6241	46.37	+19.37	375.2	-1530.23
3.	Philsan Biharipura	145	-58	3364	24.84	-2.16	4.67	125.28
4.	Baseri	125	-78	6084	58.32	+31.32	980.94	-2242.95
5.	Dhingar Ka Bas	251	+48	2304	47.32	20.32	412.90	975.36
6.	Dhindhol	39	-164	26896	65.32	38.32	1468.42	-6284.48
7.	Kanota	283	80	6400	16.32	-10.68	114.06	-854.40
8.	Khokhawala	159	-44	1936	30.29	3.29	10.82	144.76
9.	Benara	264	61	3721	12.83	-14.17	200.79	-864.37
10.	Jatwara	227	24	576	13.55	-13.45	180.90	-322.80
11.	Deogaon	191	-12	144	8.25	-18.75	351.56	225.00
12.	Toonga	407	204	41616	15.19	-11.81	139.48	-2409.24
13.	Sambharia	201	-2	4	11.61	-15.39	236.85	30.78
14.	Lalgarh	177	-26	676	16.08	-10.92	119.25	283.92
15.	Banskho	357	-154	23716	16.15	-10.85	117.72	-1670.90
	Total							

Regression Coefficient

X on Y

$\Sigma dxdy = [(\Sigma dx)(\Sigma dy)] / N$

$bxy = \Sigma d^2y - [(\Sigma dy)^2] / N$

$bxy = -14440.8 / 4733.18 - [(0.01)^2]/15$

$bxy = -14440.8 / 4733.18$

$bxy = -3.05$

Mean

$X = \Sigma x / N$

$X = 3053 / 15$

$X = 203.53$

Y on X

$\Sigma dxdy = [(\Sigma dx)(\Sigma dy)] / N$

$Byx = \Sigma d^2x - [(\Sigma dx)^2] / N$

$Byx = -14440.8/133678 - [(8)^2]/15$

$byx = -14440.8/133673.74$

$byx = -0.108$

Mean

$Y = \Sigma Y / N$

$Y = 405.01 / 15$

$Y - 27$

Regression Equation

X

$X - X = bxy\ (y-y)$

$X - 203.53 = -3.05\ (y-27)$

Y

$Y - Y = byx\ (x-x)$

$Y - 27 = -0.108\ (x - 203.53)$

X

X = 3.05 Y = 203.53 + 82.35
X = + 3.05 y = 285.88
Regression Equation of X on Y
X + 3.05 y = 285.88
X = - 3.05y + 285.88

Given Y

- 3.05 x 22.57 + 285.88 = 217.04
- 3.05 x 24.84 + 285.88 = 144.45
- 3.05 x 24.84 + 285.88 = 210.11
- 3.05 x 58.32 + 285.88 = 108.11
- 3.05 x 47.32 + 285.88 = 141.55
- 3.05 x 65.32 + 285.88 = 86.65
- 3.05 x 16.32 + 285.88 = 236.10
- 3.05 x 30.29 + 285.88 = 193.49
- 3.05 x 12.83 + 285.88 = 246.75
- 3.05 x 13.55 + 285.88 = 244.55
- 3.05 x 08.25 + 285.88 = 260.72
- 3.05 x 15.19 + 285.88 = 239.55
- 3.05 x 11.61 + 285.88 = 250.47
- 3.05 x 16.08 + 285.88 = 236.84
- 3.05 x 16.15 + 285.88 = 236.62

Y

Y = +0.108 x = 27 + 21.98
Y = 0.108 x = 48.98
Regression Equation of Y on X
Y + 0.108 x = 48.98
Y = -0.108 x + 48.98

Given X

-0.108 x 103 + 48.98 = 37.85
-0.108 x 124 + 48.98 = 35.59
-0.108 x 145 + 48.98 = 33.32
-0.108 x 125 + 48.98 = 35.48
-0.108 x 251 + 48.98 = 21.87
-0.108 x 039 + 48.98 = 44.77
-0.108 x 283 + 48.98 = 18.42
-0.108 x 159 + 48.98 = 31.80
-0.108 x 264 + 48.98 = 20.47
-0.108 x 227 + 48.98 = 24.46
-0.108 x 191 + 48.98 = 28.35
-0.108 x 407 + 48.98 = 5.02
-0.108 x 201 + 48.98 = 27.27
-0.108 x 177 + 48.98 = 29.86
-0.108 x 357 + 48.98 = 10.42

On the basis of above calculations, the regression lines of population and wasteland are shown in Fig. 5.1A. Similarly regression lines of wasteland and net sown area, irrigated area and wasteland, S.T. population and wasteland, size of holding and wasteland are drawn in Fig. 5.2B, 5.1C, 5.2A to 5.2C.

The lines show that the correlation of wasteland with population density, N.S.A. and irrigated area is negative while it is positive with S.T. population and size of holdings. There is no correlation between tractors and wasteland.

Analysis of Time Series

One of the most important tasks before economist and social scientist these days is to make estimates for the future. In this connection one usually deals with statistical data which are collected, observed or recorded at successive intervals of time. Such data are generally referred to as 'time series'. Thus, when we observe numerical data at different points of time the set of observations is known as time series.

The analysis of time series is great significance not only to the economist and businessman but also to the scientist, geographers, geologist, research workers etc. for the understanding past behaviour, planning future operations etc.

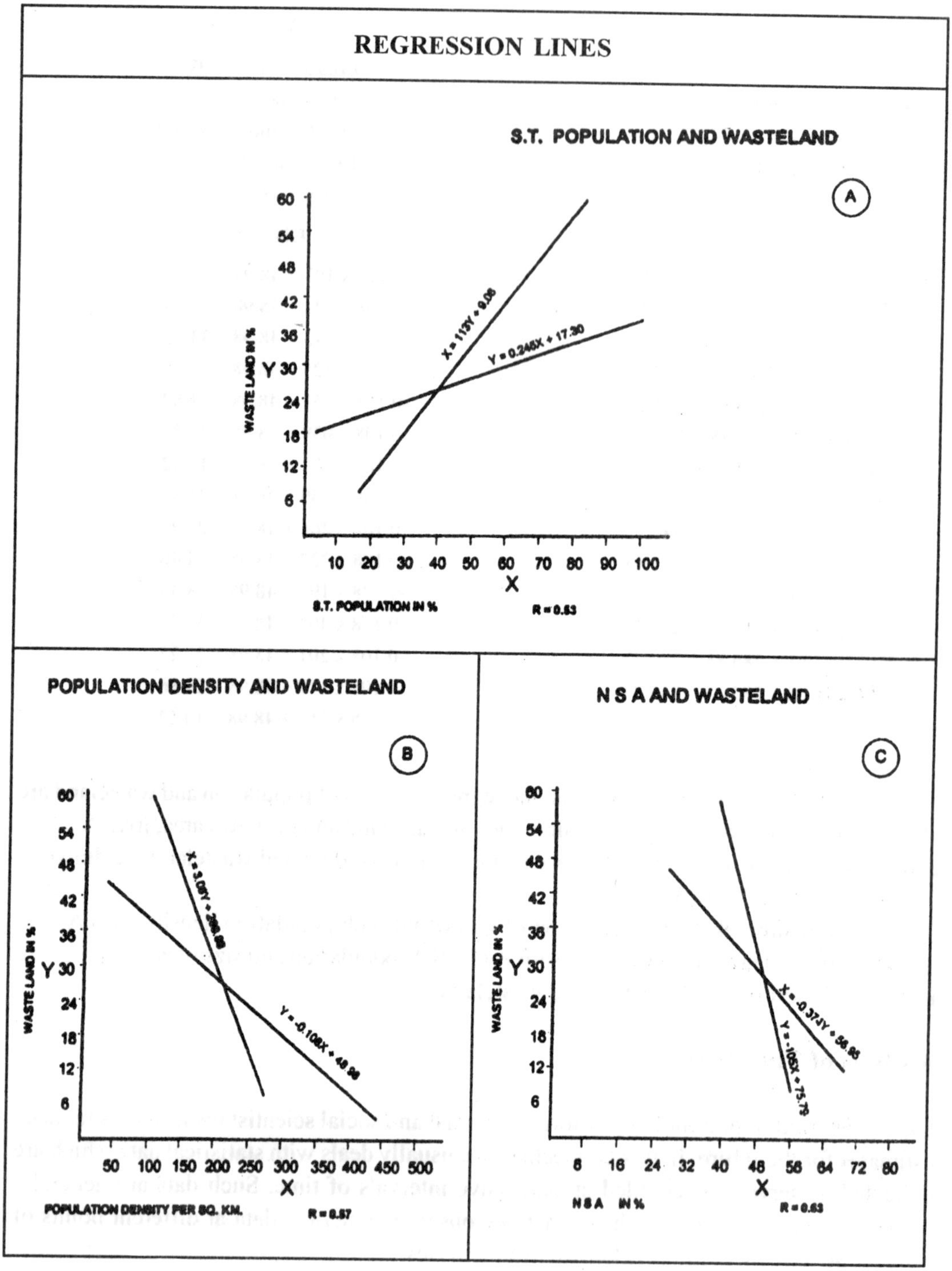

Fig. 5.1A : Regression lines between S.T. Population and Wasteland
Fig. 5.1B : Population Density and Wasteland
Fig. 5.1C : NSA & Wasteland

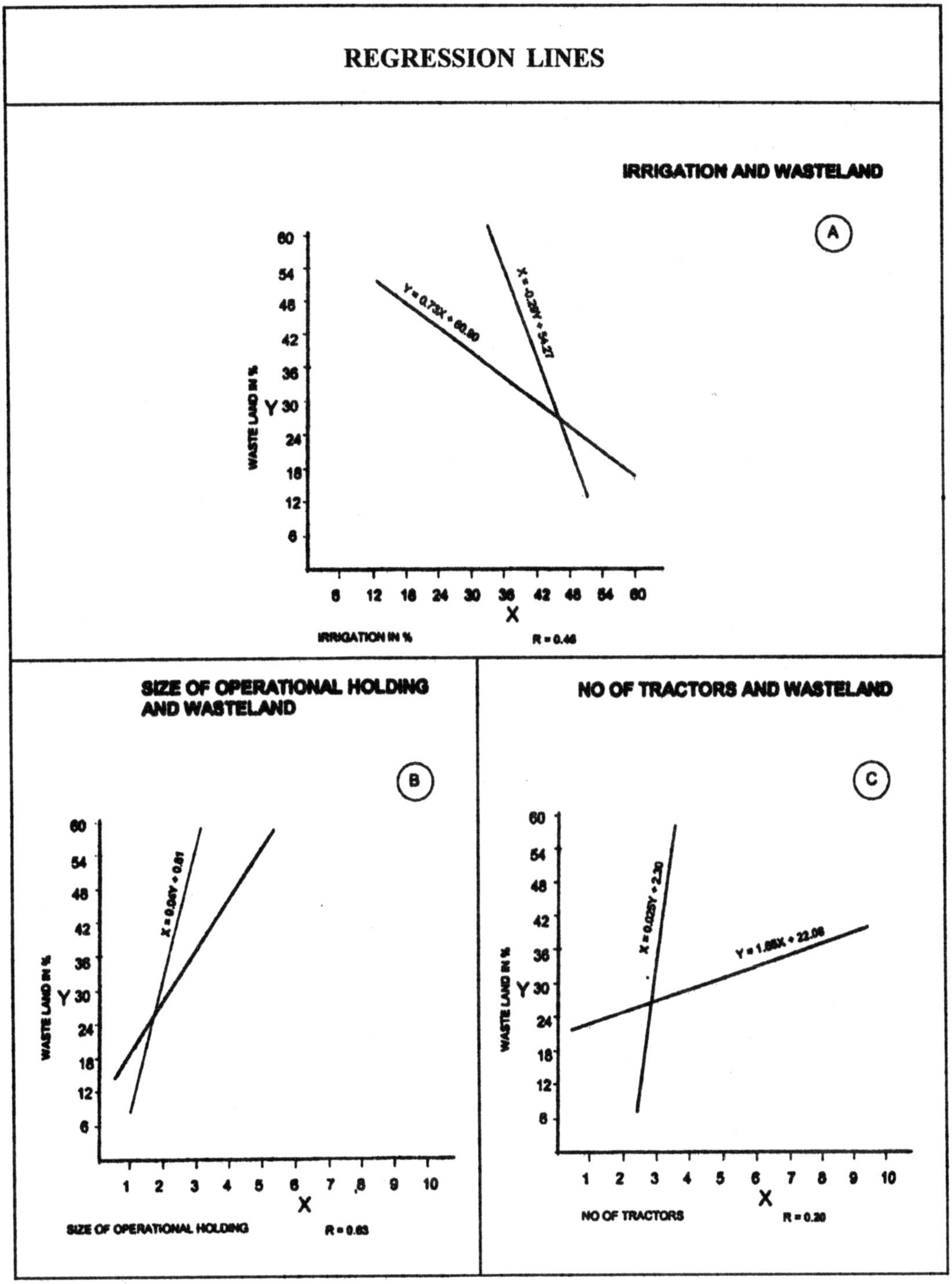

Fig. 5.2A : Irrigation ands Wasteland
Fig. 5.2B : Size of Operational and Wasteland
Fig. 5.2C : Number of Tractors and Wasteland

The various methods that can be used for determining trend are ;

1. Free hand or graphic method
2. Semi-average method
3. Moving average method
4. Method of least squares

The last method has been used for the analysis of time series of Jaipur district. This method is most widely used in practice. It is a mathematical method and with its help a trend line is fitted to the data in such a manner that the following two conditions are satisfied:

1. Σ (y – y) = 0 i.e. the sum deviations of the actual values of y and the computed values of y is zero.
2. $\Sigma (y - y)^2$ is least i.e. the sum of the squares of the deviations of the actual and computed values is least from this line and hence the name method of least squares.

The method of least squares may be used either to fit a straight line trend or a parabolic trend. The straight line trend is represented by the equation —

Yc = a+bx

where Yc is used to designate the trend values to distinguish them from the actual Y values, a is the Y intercept or the computed trend figure of the Y variable when X = 0. b represents the slope of the trend line or the amount of change in Y variable that is associated with a change of one unit in X variable. The X variable in time series analysis represents time.

Table 5.14 : Calculation of Trend Values for Jaipur District

Year	Time deviation from 1997-98	Waste land in thousand hectares (y)	X^2	xy	Trend value a+bx = ye
1993-94	–4	291.4	16	–1165.6	284.16 – 3.43x – 4 = 297.88
1994-95	–3	300.7	9	–902.1	284.16 – 3.43x – 3 = 294.45
1995-96	–2	305.4	4	–610.8	284.16 – 3.43x – 2 = 291.02
1996-97	–1	287.6	1	–287.6	284.16 – 3.43x – 1 = 287.59
1997-98	0	274.5	0	0	284.16 – 3.43 x 0 = 284.16
1998-99	+1	275.9	1	–275.9	284.16 – 3.43 x 1 = 280.73
1999-2000	+2	281.4	4	+562.8	284.16 – 3.43 x 2 = 277.30
2000-01	+3	263.4	9	+790.2	284.16 – 3.43 x 3 = 273.87
2001-02	+4	254.4	16	+1017.6	284.16 – 3.43 x 4 = 270.44
2002-03	+5	289.3	25	+1449.0	284.16 – 3.43 x 5 = 267.00
Total	Σx=+5	Σy^2=2824.5	Σx^2=+85		Σyc = 2824.45

Y = a+bx

Σy = Na+bΣ x ——————————— (1)

Σxy = Σax + bΣ x^2 ——————————— (2)

Hear

$3x = +5, \; 3x^2 = +85, \; 3y = 2824.5$

$xy = 1129.4$ and $yc = 2824.45$

Substituting the value of equation (1) and (2)

$2824.5 = 10a + 5b$ ———————— (1)

$1129.4 = 5a + 85b$ ———————— (2)

Multiplying the second equation by 2

$2824.5 = 10a + 5b$ ———————— (3)

$2258.8 = 10a + 170b$ ———————— (4)

Deducting

$-165b = 565.7$

$b = -3.43$

Substituting the value of b ($b = -3.43$) in equation (1)

$2824.5 = 10a + 5 \text{ x } -3.43$

$a = 284.16$

The calculation of time series shows that during the last one decade, the wasteland has a decreasing tendency in Jaipur district.

REFERENCES

Gupta, N.L. and Maroo, R.L., (1991). *Challenge of Wastelands Utilization Issues and Themes*, Academic Publishers, Jaipur.

Gupta, S.P. (1969). *Elementary Statistical Methods,* Sultan Chand & Sons, 23, Daryaganj, New Delhi- 110002

Hammond, R. and McCullagh, P., (1978). *Quantitative Techniques in Geography : An introduction,* Clarendon, Oxford.

Johnston, J. (1972). *Economics Methods*, Mcgraw Hills, London pp. 8-16

Mahmood, A., (1977). *Statistical Methods in Geographical Studies,* Rajesh, New Delhi.

Mandal, R.B., (1981). *Statistics for Geographers and Social Scientists*, Concept Publishing Company, New Delhi.

Yadav, H.R. (1987), (Ed.) *Wastelands – Diagnosis and Treatment*, Concept Publishing Company, New Delhi.

6

SAMPLE STUDY AREAS/SAMPLE VILLAGES

There are various factors involved in genesis/formation of wastelands and similarly the techniques for reclamation/development of wastelands are also quietly different from one another. Wasteland statistics at village/townwise had been calculated with Digital Planimeter from the wasteland maps on 1:50,000 obtained from National Remote Sensing Agency, Hyderabad (AP). These data are very significant for depicting spatial pattern at the lowest level i.e. village/town level. But this information provides a partial picture of the wasteland problem as statistics calculated at this level are not sufficient to fulfil the objective and purpose. Hence, for the detailed study stratified sampling has been adopted as the study area is heterogeneous. On the basis of physiography, pedology, hydrology and wasteland type, at least one sample study area has been selected from each type of wasteland category and LISS III satellite images of February 28, 2003 of the selected sample areas have been processed by B.M. Birla Science and Technology Centre, Jaipur (Rajasthan) (A work centre of NRSA, Hyderabad). The satellite images and data obtained from the classified image were also used for the interpretation of wastelands. Satellite image help to know the causes of genesis/formations of wastelands and are useful for the planning of reclamation/development of wasteland within village. In all nine sample study areas, one from each category have been selected for the detailed study. A list of these areas is given in Table 6.1 and Fig. 6.0.

SAMPLE VILLAGES FOR GULLIED AND OR RAVINOUS LAND

Samred Khurd, Dedwari, Chainpura Bas Dedwari, Rampura Bas Samred, Godiyana and Samred Kalan sample villages for gullied and/ or ravinous land lie between $27^\circ 5'14''$ to $27^\circ 9'11''$ North latitude and $76^\circ 1'58''$ to $76^\circ 60'22''$ East longitude (Fig. 6.3) at a distance of 32 km from Jaipur city in western part of Jamwa Ramgarh tehsil of Jaipur district (Fig.6.1). These villages occupy 29.87 km^2 with 3749 persons (2001).

This sample study area is roughly square in shape, situated in hilly tracts having elevation from 396 to 561 metres from mean sea level (Fig. 6.1). Aravalli hills are scattered in central part from south to north with small gap, south western and north-western part of the study area (Figs. 6.1A and 6.2). The highest peak is of Samred Kalan (561 m) followed by Samred Khurd (520 m), Godiyana (508 m) and Dhani Bhar (472 m) while the lowest point is near Dhani Shamyali (396 m). The peneplained area is found in eastern and western part of the study area (Fig. 6.3). North-eastern and north-western part of this area is badly dissected by the gullies and or ravinous (Fig. 6.2 and 6.3).

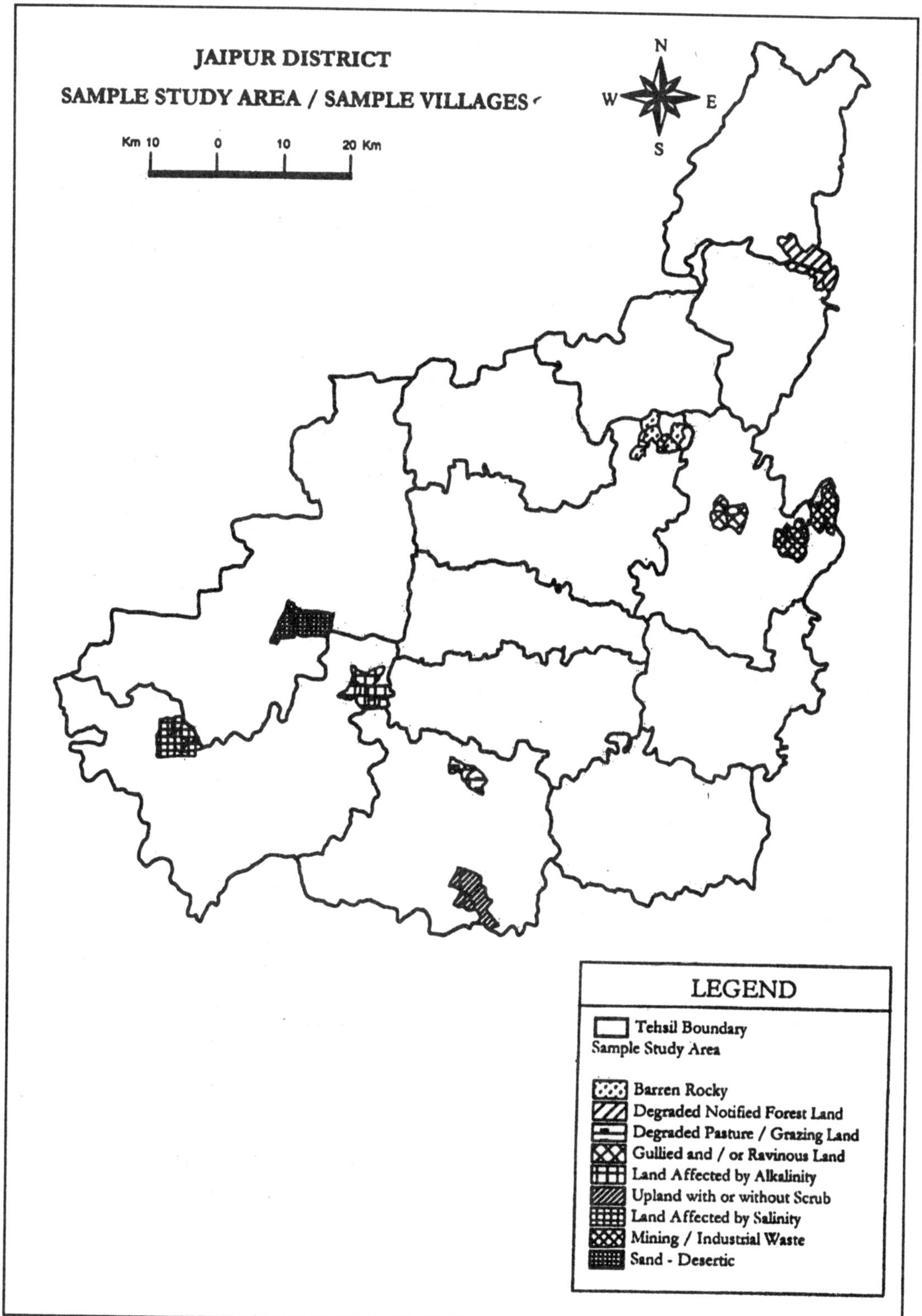

Fig. 6.0 : Location of Sample Study area / Sample Villages

Table 6.1: Sample Study Areas/Villages for Detailed Study

S. No.	Wasteland Type	Number of villages	Tehsil	Name of the villages	Area in km^2	Latitude and Longitude
1.	Gullied and/or Ravinous land	6	Jamwa Ramgarh	(1) Chainpura Bas Dedwari (2) Dedwari (3) Godiyana (4) Rampura Bas Samred (5) Samred Kalan (6) Samred Khurd	29.87	27°5'14"N to 27°09'11"N 76°01'57"E to 76°06'220E
2.	Degraded Notified Forest land	4	Viratnagar and Kotputli	Viratnagar Tehsil: (1) Bandh Muzaffarpur (2) Kuhada (3) Talooka Bas. Kotputli Tehsil: (1) Pachudola	64.34	27°28'15"N to 27°33'35" N 76°8'18"E to 76°14'40"E
3.	Sands-Desertic	5	Phulera	(1) Bhagwatpura (2) Dhani Boraj (3) Majipura (4) Maliyawas (5) Sursinghpura	35.23	26°01'43"N to 26°056'49"N 76°15'49"E to 76°22'13"E
4.	Land with or without Scrub	5	Phagi	(1) Ajnota (2) Chandma Kalan (3) Hatheli (4) Nathmalpura (5) Panwasu	37.40	26°27'51"N to 26°33'24"N 76°36'26"E to 76°41'32"E
5.	Land Affected by Salinity	6	Dudu	(1) Bigolau (2) Dantra (3) Hotupur (4) Jhakolar (5) Pawaliya	47.23	26°42'54" N to 26°46'56"N 75°05'23"E to 75°10'210E
6.	Land Affected by Alkalinity	6	Dudu	(1) Girdharpura (2) Jharna (3) Kapriyawas Kalan (4) Kotjewar (5) Mahlan (6) Nasnota	46.73	26°47'46"N to 26°54'37"N 75°21'52"E to 75°30'40"E
7.	Degraded Pasture/ Grazing land	4	Phagi	(1) Harsuliya (2) Jankinath Pura (3) Khejra Ka Bas (4) Raipura	18.29	26°40'46"N to 26°42'57"N 75°35'42"E to 75°40'05"E
8.	Barren Hill/ Rocky	8	Amber	(1) Arniya (2) Bilpur (3) Chak Manoharpur (4) Chandwaji (5) Deo Ka Harwara (6) Pilwa (7) Salarwas (8) Sunder Ka Bas	33.51	27°11'28"N to 27°16'35"N 75°52'55"E to 75°59'12"E
9.	Mining / Industrial Wasteland	6	Jamwa Ramgarh	(1) Chak Dagota (2) Dagota (3) Rayanwala (4) Sand Koina (5) Singhpuri (6) Thali	76.61	27°02'28"N to 27°10"45"N 76°09'23"E to 76°17'05"E
	Total	50	7		389.21	

The Banganga, an important seasonal river of the district passes through the western part of the sample study area (Figs. 6.2 and 6.3). Several nallahs originate from the hills also join the river (Fig. 6.2). Loamy sand/sandy loam soils of the villages are suitable for producing crops. But irrigation and application of manure/fertilizers are necessary for good harvesting.

This area keeps low population density due to hilly tracts, gullied and/ or ravinous land. The population density varies between 78 to 163 persons per 1.0 km^2. S.T. population in this

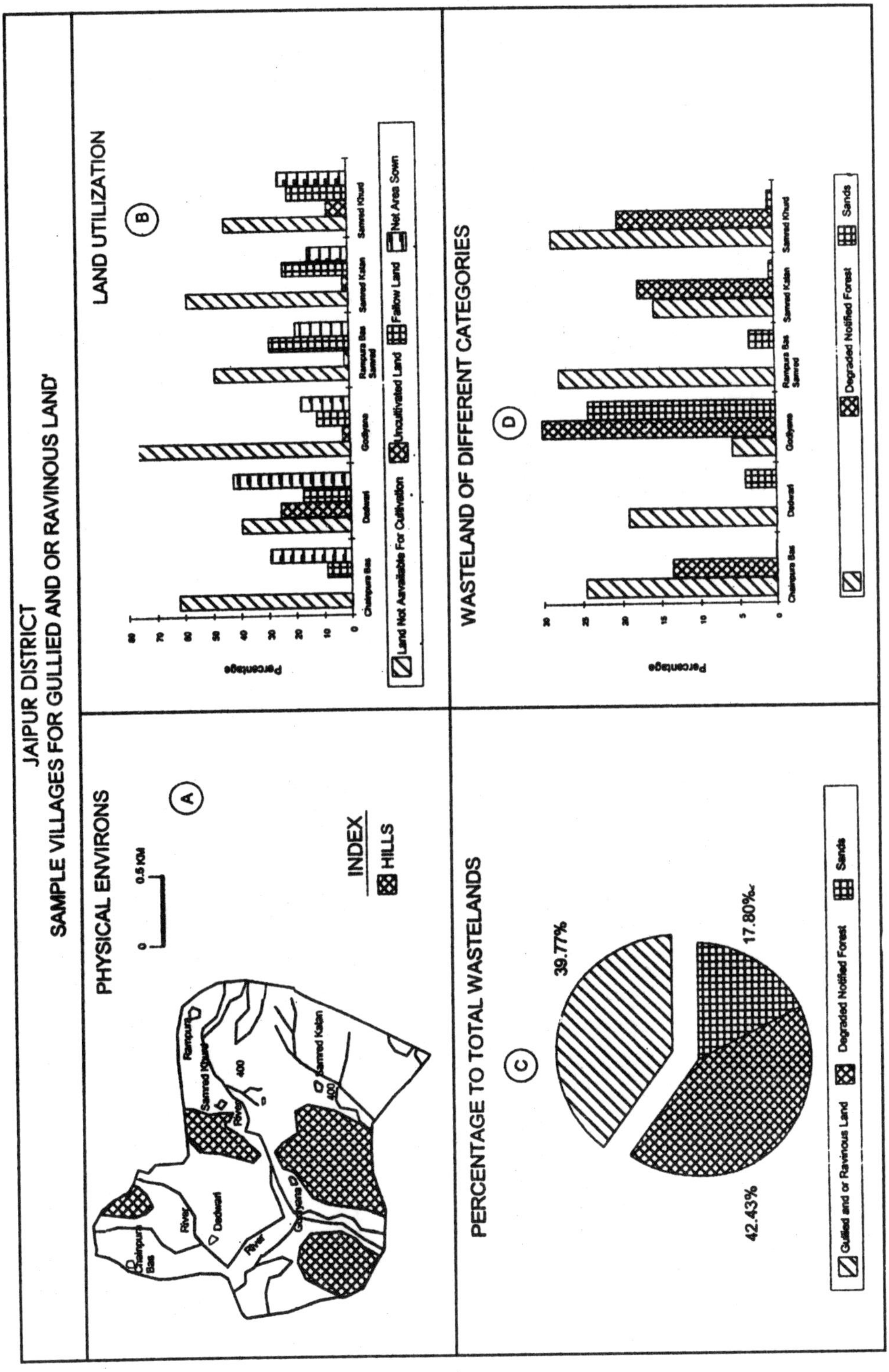

Fig. 6.1 : Sample villages for gullied and ravinous land.

Table 6.2 : Landuse in Sample Study Area for Gullied and/or Ravinous Land 2003-04

S.No	Name of Village	Geographical area in hectares	Percentage to the Total Geographical Area												
			Land Not Available for Cultivation						Other Uncultivated land Excluding Fallow lands			Fallow land			Net Sown Area
			Forest	Hills	Gullied and/or Ravinous Land	Land put to non-agricultural uses	Permanent Pastures	Total	Culturable waste-land	Mice tree & groves	Total	Current fallow	Old Fallow	Total	Irrigated and Unirrigated
1	Chainpura Bas Dedwari	314	50.32	–	11.78	–	–	62.10	–	–	–	3.50	5.09	8.59	29.30
2	Dedwari	245	30.61	–	6.94	0.41	1.22	39.18	25.31	–	25.31	6.53	10.20	16.73	42.44
3	Godiyana	608	54.93	5.92	13.45	–	1.97	76.37	2.96	–	2.96	3.95	8.39	12.34	17.76
4	Rampura Bas Samred	185	32.96	12.96	1.62	1.08	–	48.65	–	2.16	2.16	26.49	2.70	29.19	19.46
5	Samred Kalan	1122	–	32.53	5.52	13.64	6.86	58.55	2.23	–	2.23	15.33	9.09	24.42	14.70
6	Samred Khurd	513	10.13	19.30	5.07	1.36	8.77	44.69	7.80	–	7.80	14.81	7.01	21.82	25.34
	Total	2987	22.76	17.54	5.56	5.49	4.58	55.93	2.88	0.13	3.01	11.65	7.87	19.52	21.59

Source : Land Record Section, Jamwa Ramgarh tehsil, District Jaipur (Raj.)

area 41.98 per cent while S.C. is only 13.92 per cent of the total population. Maximum Scheduled Tribes (ST) population of the study area is concentrated in Jamwa Ramgarh tehsil. Therefore, all the sample villages also have more share of S.T. population in their total population. The S.T. population ranges between 22.91 to 77.78 per cent with maximum in Chainpura Bas Dedwri (77.78%) followed by Dedwari (56.02%), Samred Khurd (53.59%), Godiyana (51.01%) and Samred Kalan (22.91%). The "*meenas*" of this area are more attracted towards education, so two-third population is literate with highest in Samred Khurd (76.38%) and Samred Kalan (73.93%) villages. Approximately four-fifth working population is engaged in agriculture i.e. in Godiyana (87.57%), Samred Khurd (85.02%), Dedwari (83.72%) and Chainpura Bas Dedwari (81.82%) villages.

General Land Use

This area is dominantly under degraded forest, gullied and/or ravinous land and its land use pattern is also controlled by its physical environs (Fig. 6.3). Fig. 6.1B, 6.3 and Table 6.2 shows the general land use of sample villages for gullied and/or ravinous land. Table 6.2 reveals that the NSA is only 21.59 per cent to the total geographical area due to forest, hills, gullied/ravinous land and undulated sand dunes on the western flanks of the hills. It is maximum in Dedwari followed by Chainpura Bas Dedwari and Samred Khurd village while it is less than 20 per cent is remaining three villages i.e. Samred Kalan (14.70%), Godiyana (17.76%) and Rampura Bas Samred (19.46%).

Table 6.2 reveals that two-fifth land (40.30%) of this sample study area is under forest and hills. Godiyana and Chainpura Bas Dedwari villages have their more than one-half area under forest while one-third geographical area of Rampura Bas Samred and Dedwari villages is under this category. Hills are another important landscape of the area and maximum area under hills is concentrated in Samred Kalan (32.53%) followed by Samred Khurd (19.30%) and Rampura Bas Samred (12.96%). More than one-half geographical area of this sample study area is recorded not available for cultivation especially under degraded forest, hills and gullied/ravinous land (Table 6.2). Fig. 6.1B shows that maximum percentage of this category is in Godiyana (76.27%) followed by Chainpura Bas Dedwari (62.10%), Samred Kalan (58.55%), Ram Bas Samred (48.65%) and Dedwari (39.18%).

Identification of Wastelands

On the basis of LISS III satellite image (Fig 6.2), the following type of wastelands have been identified in the sample study area for gullied or ravinous land (Fig. 6.3).

Table 6.3 : Identification of Wastelands in Sample Study Area for Gullied and Ravinous Land

S. No.	Wasteland category	Area in hectares	Percentage to the total area	Percentage to the total wastelands
1.	Gullied and/or Ravinous land	556.39	17.10	39.77
2.	Degraded Notified Forest land	593.63	18.24	42.43
3.	Sands Riverine	248.89	7.65	17.80
	Total	1398.91	42.99	100.00

Source : LISS III Satellite image, Feb. 28, 2003.

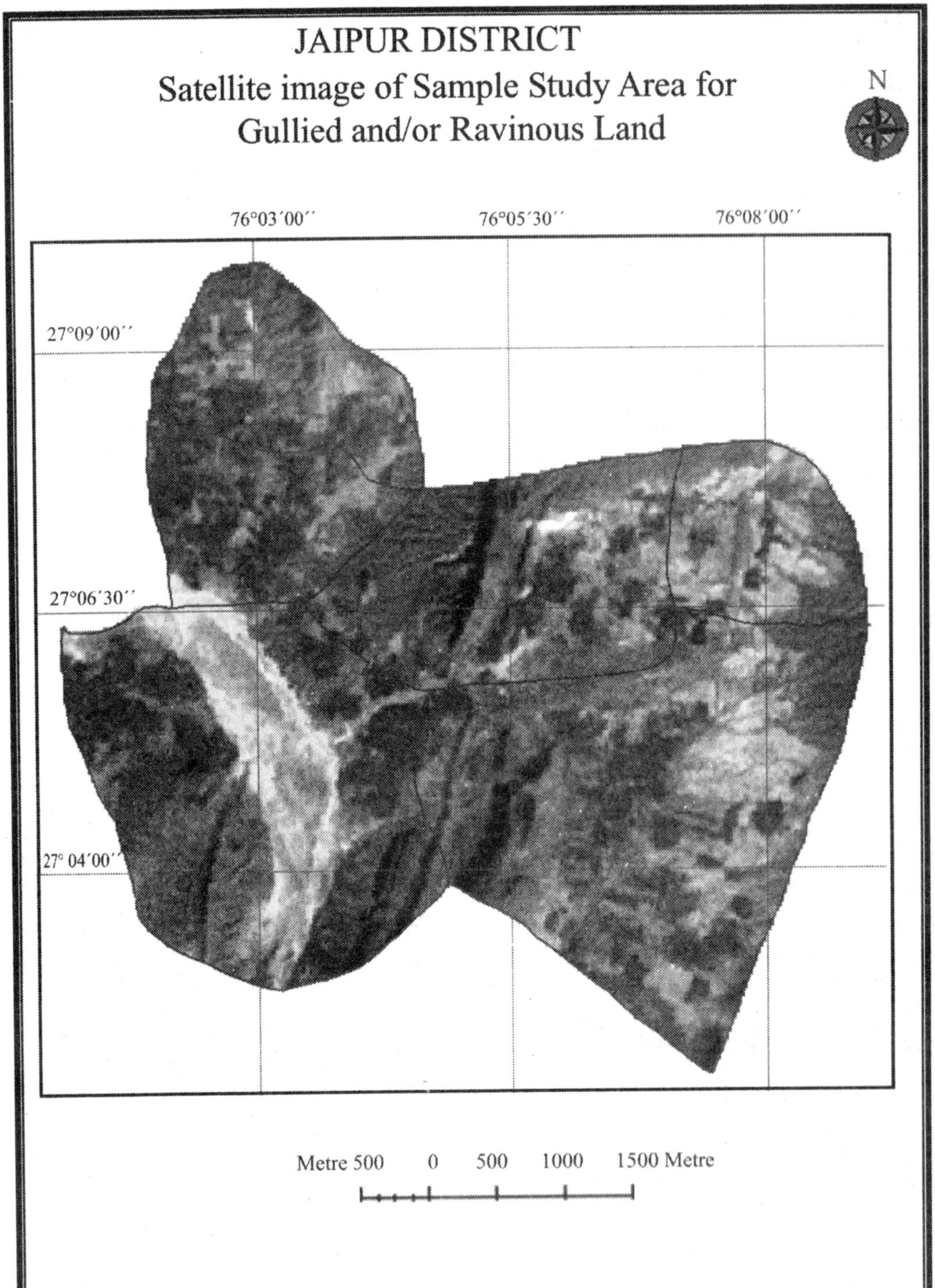

Source : LISS III dated 28th Feb. 2003, Processed at : B.M. Birla Science & Technology Centre, Jaipur

Fig. 6.2 : Satellite Image of Sample Study area by Gullied and/or Ravinous Land

Table 6.3 shows that this sample study area occupies 42.99 per cent land under wastelands. Of the total wastelands, approximately, two-fifth area (39.77%) belongs to gullied and/or ravinous land and almost same area also occupied by the degraded notified forest land (Fig. 6.1C). In the study area most of the gullied and ravinous land is associated with hilly tracts, so the villages having gullied/ravinous land also have problem of degraded forest and sands riverine.

Spatial Distribution of Wastelands

In this study area, the land under gullied/ravinous and degraded forest is almost equal, but it is unevenly distributed in the sample villages (Fig 6.1D). The following Table 6.4 shows village wise wasteland under different categories.

Table 6.4 : Wastelands in Sample Study Area for Gullied and/or Ravinous Land

S. No.	Name of village	Wasteland in % to the total Geographical Area			Total
		Gullied and/or ravinous	Degraded forest	Sands riverian	
1.	Chainpura Bas Dedwari	24.57	13.64	0.24	38.45
2.	Dedwari	19.07	—	4.30	23.37
3.	Godiyana	5.88	30.00	24.11	59.99
4.	Rampura Bas Samred	27.82	—	3.46	31.28
5.	Samred Kalan	15.68	17.63	0.67	33.98
6.	Samred Khurd	28.55	20.16	0.82	49.53
	Total	17.10	18.24	7.65	42.99

Source : LISS III Satellite image, Feb 28, 2003

It is evident from the above table and Fig 6.1D that Samred Khurd, Rampura Bas Samred and Chainpura Bas Dedwari villages occupy one-fourth or more than one-fourth of their area under gullied and/or ravinous land. These villages are situated in the northern and south western part of the sample study area and this category of wasteland is concentrated in the west of hills (Fig. 6.2 and 6.3). The minimum area under this category is in Godiyana and Samred Kalan villages situated in the southern and northern eastern part of the sample study area (Fig. 6.3). In Samred Khurd a hill range is situated in the western part of the village. Similarly, the eastern boundary of Rampura Bas Samred is bounded by the hills running form south to north and a hill range is extended in the same direction in the central northern part in Dedwari village. From these hills, several nallahs originate and flow in the west in rainy season, have dissected land into gullied and or ravinous land (Fig. 6.2)

Degraded forest is also an important wasteland in this area, Fig. 6.2 indicates that hill ranges are spread over in the central, south west and north western part of the sample study area. All these hills are covered by the degraded forest so maximum area under this category is concentrated in Godiyana village followed by Samred Khurd, Rampura Bas Samred and Dedwari village. Godiyana and Rampura Bas Samred are located in the southern part while Samred Khurd and Dedwari village in the northern part of this sample study area (Fig. 6.3).

Banganga, a major river of the study area which passes through Godiyana situated in the western part, has sands in her bed (Fig. 6.3). Other villages also have some area under this category due to tributaries/nallahs that flow from the hilly tracts of this area.

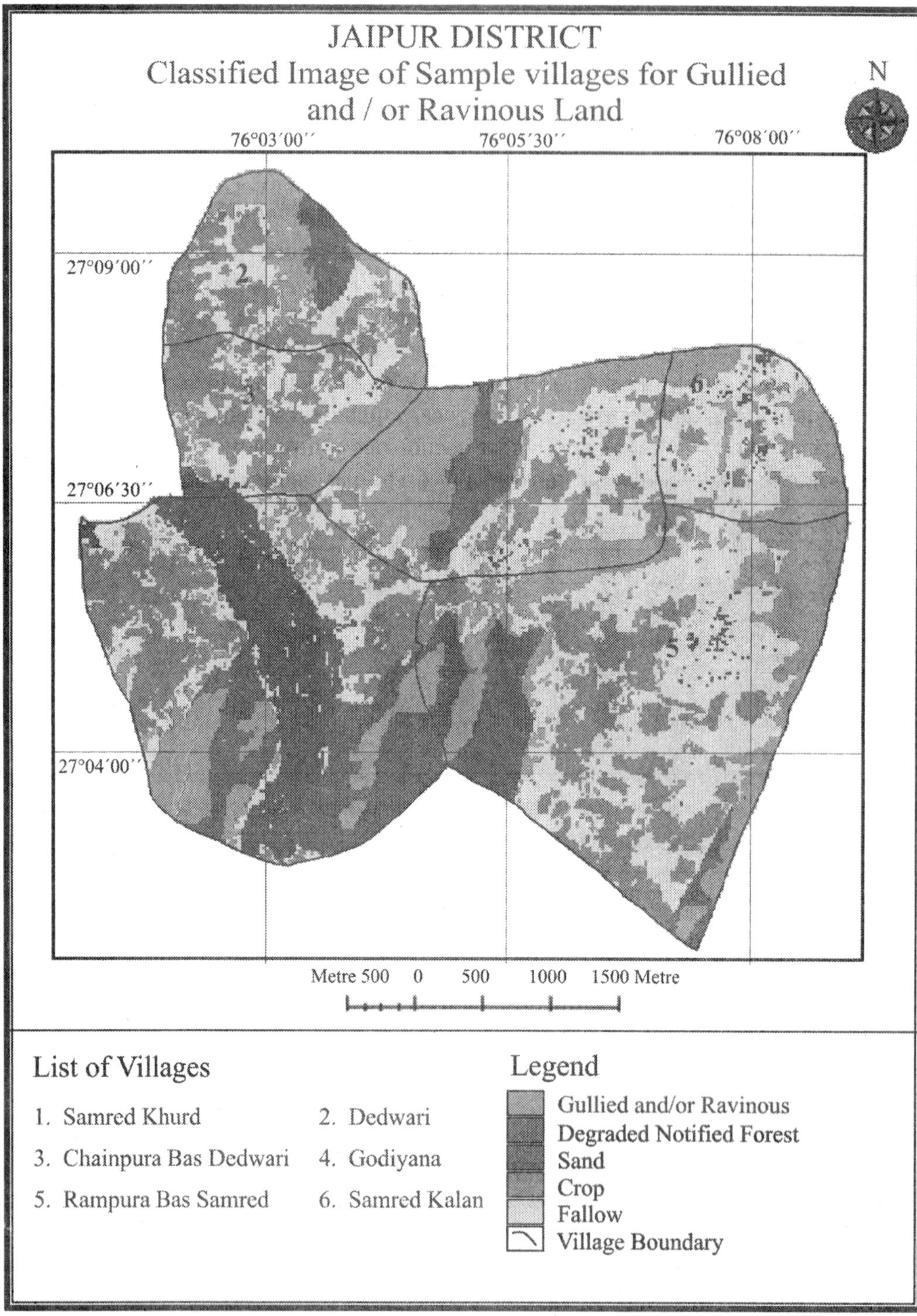

Source : LISS III dated 28th Feb. 2003

Fig. 6.3 : Classified Image of Sample villages for Gullied and/or Ravinous Land

Table 6.4 also shows that 42.99 per cent land of this study area is under wastelands with maximum in Godiyana and Samred Khurd village. In Godiyana it is due to more area under sands and degraded forest while in Samred Khurd village gullied/ravinous and degraded forest land are dominant. Lowest area of wastelands is found in Dedwari village situated in the peneplained area in the north western part of the study area (Fig. 6.3).

Ownership of Wastelands

Out of the total wasteland, 98 per cent is owned by the Government consisting gullied and/or ravinous land, degraded forest and sand riverian in Banganga river bed and its tributaries while the remaining 2 per cent is under private ownership as a few cultivators have been residing in less gullied and ravinous land. They use upper flat land lying between two ravines for producing bajra in kharif season while mustard is produced in gullied /ravinous bed in rabi season.

Characteristics of Wastelands

This area is badly dissected in the western and north-eastern part of the study area due to origin of various nallahs from the Bamanwati hills (Situated along the eastern border of the study area), Samred Khurd hills and Dedwari hills. Besides this, small patches of gullied/ ravinous land are found in the central part along the tributary of Banganga river, western part of Godiyana hills and along western tributary of the Banganga river. Hills of southern part are covered with mixed dhok forest while other hills are occupied by the degraded forest.

Reclamation of Wastelands by the Farmers themselves

No efforts have been made in this area by the government for controlling the soil and water erosion. From the last four years, rich farmers/Govt. officers from out side are taking keen interest in this dissected land. For this, the Govt. land is being allotted to the landless/poor farmers for the cultivation and these farmers sell this land to the rich people of the out side at the rate of Rs. 12,000 to Rs. 20,000 per hectare. During field survey it is observed that three rich farmers have purchased G_1, G_2 categories of gullied and/or ravinous land and levelling was done with GCB machines having chain wheels at the rate Rs. 1.60 lac per hectare. Now this dissected land has been converted into the level land near pucca road passing through this area and rows of very healthy '*Anwala*' plants can be seen with roses on open space between the *anwala* rows. The farmers have their own tube wells on their fields as due to nearness of Jamwa Ramgarh Bund, the groundwater table is high with good quality of water. As 'anwala' takes three years in maturity and during this period the owner of the farm earns approximately Rs. 12,000 per hectare from the sale of rose flowers. Upto the maturity stage of anwala, approximately Rs. 80,000 per hectare is being spent in watering, manuring, weeding, insecticides, pesticides, electricity, labour/employees etc. After three years per hectare yield of anwala will be approximately Rs. 8.00 lac per annum.

During field survey it is found that 5 per cent farmers have 15 to 25 per cent land of their holdings under gullied and or ravinous. Out of these only one farmer has done levelling himself of his G_1 gullied land with his own tractor. But other farmers are not in a position to level their gullied land with GCB machine due to poor economic conditions.

Plate 11 : Levelling of guillied land near Jamwa Ramgarh bund for Horticulture.

Plate 12 : A Scene of ditch fencing on Jaipur-Phagi Road.

Plate 13 : Digging pits for fuelwood plantation/silvipasture in premonsoon period near Phagi Town.

Plate 14 : Anwala and rose crops after levelling of gullied/ravinous land by GCB Machine near Jamwa Ramgarh bund.

More than two-fifth land is lying under gullied/ravinous land and degraded forest in this study area which is an alarming/challenging situation to the environmentalist and ecologist. However, there is a good scope for horticulture development especially '*Anwala*' in gullied/ ravinous croded land due to good quality and quantity of groundwater resources in this area. As mentioned earlier three rich farmers have levelled gully eroded land themselves and healthy 'anwala' plants are standing in place of bad land topography. For this loan should be provided on low interest in easy installments to the cultivators for levelling, digging tube well, other infrastrucural facilities and developing 'anwala' farms.

Besides this, for reclamation of gullied/ravinous land live hedge fencing of Nagar, Ratanjot, Juliflora, Jumta, Israeli Babul, Munja should be done and check dam/spur also should be constructed to control soil erosion. At least 600 saplings per hectare should be planted under reclamation of ravines by state government. For degraded forest, RDF programme of the state government should be implemented in this area.

SAMPLE STUDY AREA FOR DEGRADED NOTIFIED FOREST LAND

This sample study area lies from 27°28´15´´to 27°33´35´´North latitude and from 76°8´18´´ to 76° 14´40´´East longitude covering an area of 6434 hectares (Fig. 6.6). Total population of this area is 8860 including 1700 Scheduled Castes and 459 Scheduled Tribes.

Approximately one-fifth area is covered by the Aravalli hills and gullied and/or ravinous land (Table 6.5). Satellite image (Fig. 6.5) of this area indicates that the hill ranges are extended from south east to north and west to east directions in this area and several nallahs originate from the hills of this sample study area. Out of these two flow from south to north and one from south east to north west, all the three form a tributary of Sabi river (Fig. 6.4A). Fertile plains of north western and west and west central part are under cultivation having multiple cropping (Fig. 6.6).

Average population density is 138 persons per km^2 with highest in Kuhada (177) followed by Talooka Bas (142) village. In other villages it is less than the average density of the study area i.e. 133 in Muzafferpur and 128 in Pachhodala. Maximum concentration of S.T. population is in Bandh Muzafferpur (26.52%) while S.C. population is 24.13 and 21.36 percent in Kuhada and Pachhodala village respectively. Approximately three-fourth population of this area is engaged in agriculture while it is over 80 per cent in Pachhodala (82.55%). Most of the population of Kuhada village (52.53%) is engaged in other activities. Similarly, the population of Muzafferpur village is also almost equally employed in agriculture and other activities. Both these villages have less than 12 per cent land under net sown area due to forest land and hilly tracts.

In western part only one hill range crosses the peneplained area from south to north and its western side is dissected by the gullied and/or ravinous land due to origin of several seasonal nallahs from this hill (Fig. 6.4 and 6.5)

General Land Use

Generally villages of this wasteland category have less net sown area and more land is not available for cultivation. Table 6.5 reveals that approximately two-fifth land is under degraded notified forest. Kuhada and Bandh Muzafferpur villages occupy 80.12 and 79.02 per cent of

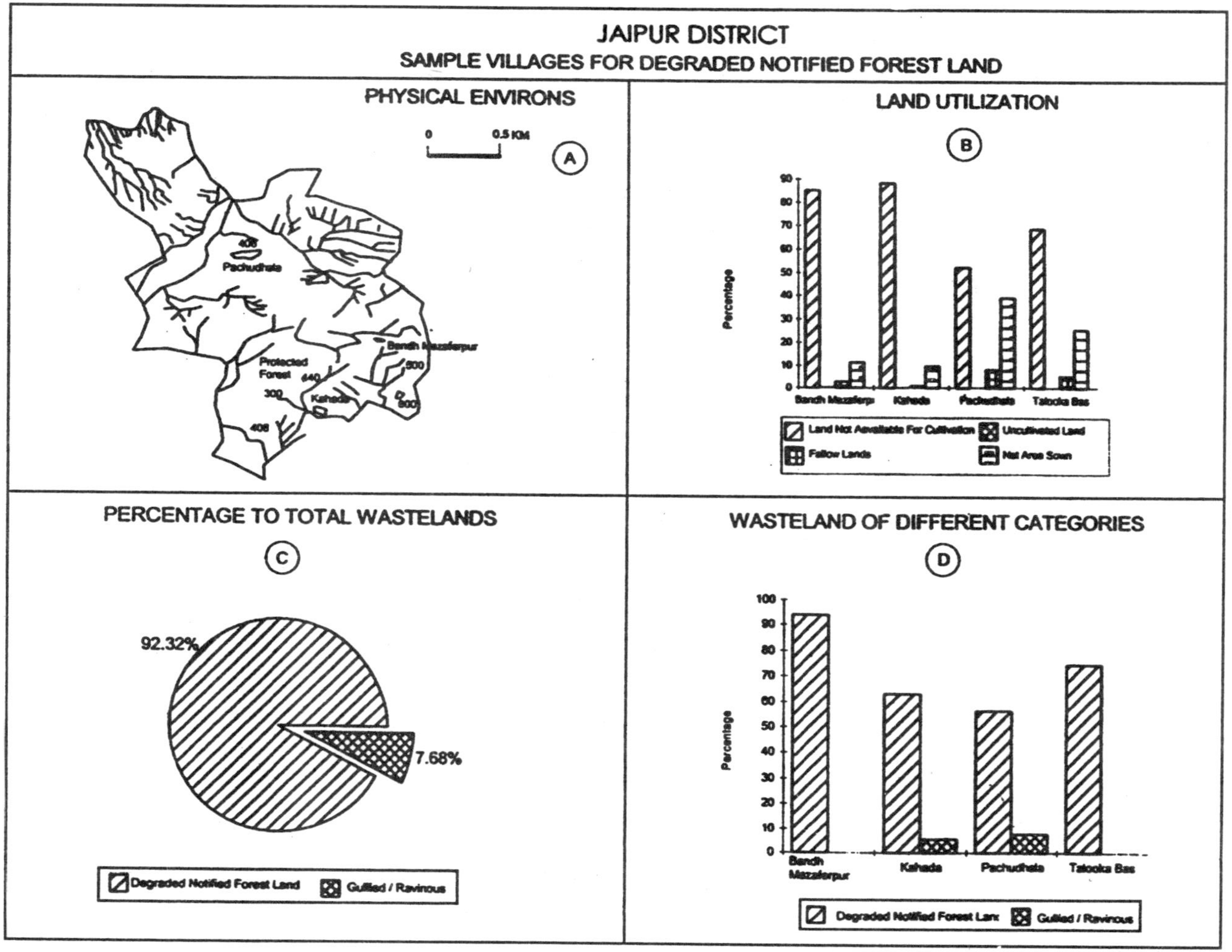

Fig. 6.4 : Sample Villages for Degraded Notified Forest Land.

Table 6.5 : Land Use in Sample Study Area for Degraded Notified Forest Land 2003-04

S. No	Name of Village	Geographical area in hectares	Percentage to the Total Geographical Area												
			Land Not Available for Cultivation						Culturable Waste			Follow land			Net Sown Area
			Forest	Hills	Usar and Barren	Land put to non agricultural uses	Permanent Pasture	Total	Culturable waste	Misc. tree & groves	Total	Current follow	Old Follow	Total	Total Irrigated and Unirrigated
1	Bandh Mazafferpur	583	79.07	0.34	3.43	-	1.54	85.25	0.51	—	0.51	2.57	0.34	2.91	11.32
2	Kuhala	1082	80.12	2.68	0.92	1.82	2.86	88.45	0.37	—	0.37	0.83	0.64	1.47	9.70
3	Pachhodalo	4190	19.50	27.21	1.65	3.22	0.55	52.13	0.38	—	0.38	5.73	2.74	8.47	39.02
4	Talooka Bas	579	56.82	6.73	2.59	0.86	1.73	68.74	0.00	—	0.00	4.83	0.52	5.35	25.90
	Total	6434	38.45	18.81	1.77	2.48	1.13	62.73	0.36	—	0.36	4.54	1.97	6.51	30.40

Source : Land Record Section, Viratnagar tehsil, District Jaipur.

their total geographical area under degraded forest land while it is 56.82 and 19.50 per cent in Raghunathpura @ Talooka Bas and Pachhodala village respectively (Table 6.5). It is also clear from the table that all the hills are not covered with forest. Approximately one-fifth land is occupied by hills with maximum in Pachhodala followed by Raghunathpura @ Talooka Bas. Fig. 6.4B shows that all the sample villages have maximum area under land not available for cultivation. Due to hilly terrain, the net sown area is only 30.40 per cent which ranges from 9.70 to 39.02 per cent to the total geographical area. It is highest in Pachhodala village followed by Raghunathpura @ Talooka Bas as these villages have large patches of plain areas in their western parts amidst degraded forestland while the villages of eastern part have less land under net sown area due to more forested land (Fig. 6.4B and 6.5). It is remarkable that the cropping intensity is very high i.e. 186 in Bandh Muzafferpur village due to very low percentages of net sown area. In remaining villages it is 151, 132 and 124 in Pachhodala, Talooka Bas and Kuhada respectively.

Identification of Wastelands

The following categories of wastelands have been identified from the LISS III satellite image (Fig. 6.5). An area of categories wise wasteland, percentage to total geographical area and percentage to total wastelands are given.

Table 6.6 : Identification of Wasteland in Sample Study Area for Degraded Notified Forest Land

S. No.	Wasteland category	Area in hectares	Percentage to total geographical area	Percentage to total wastelands
1.	Degraded Notified Forest Land	3960.75	65.82	92.32
2.	Gullied and/or Ravinous Land	329.65	4.98	7.68
	Total	4290.43	70.80	100.00

Source : LISS III satellite image, February 28, 2003

The above table indicates that approximately three-fourth area is under wastelands and is mostly occupied by degraded notified forest land (Fig. 6.4C). Main reasons for degraded forest are tree cutting by the local people for fuelwood, fodder and timber etc.

Spatial Distribution of Wastelands in Sample Study area for Degraded Notified Forestland

Village wise distribution of wastelands in sample study area for degraded forestland is given in the following Table 6.7:

Table 6.7 : Wastelands in Sample villages for Degraded Notified Forest Land.

S. No.	Name of Village	Percentage of wasteland to the total Geographical area		Total
		Degraded forest land	Gullied and/or ravinous land	
1.	Bundh Mazafarpur	93.88	–	93.88
2.	Kuhada	63.09	5.59	68.68
3.	Pachudhala	56.24	7.81	64.05
4.	Talooka Bas	74.51	–	74.51
	Total	65.36	5.44	70.80

Source : LISS III Satellite image, February 28,2003

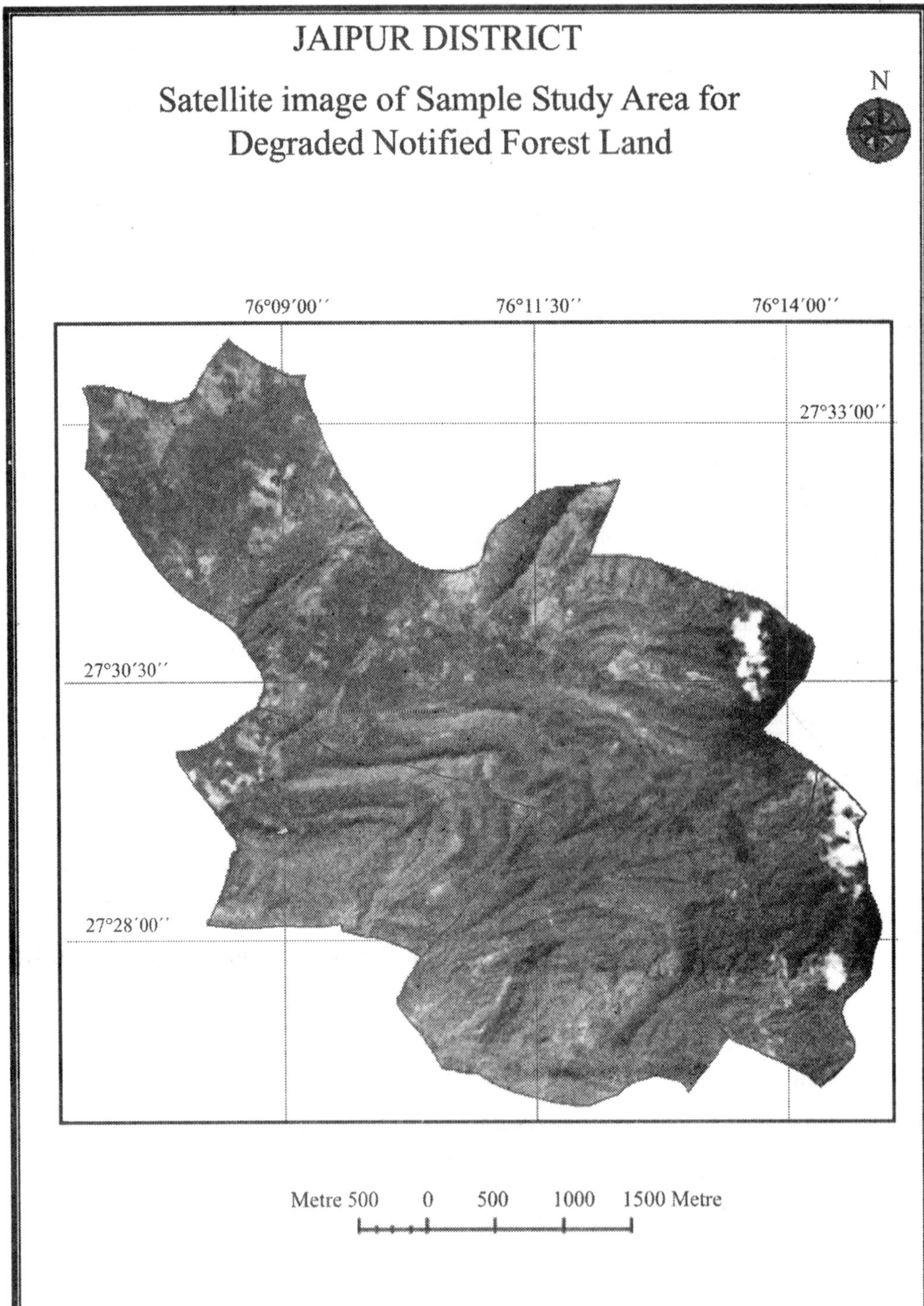

Source : LISS III dated 28th Feb. 2003

Fig. 6.5 : Satellite image of Sample Study Area for Degraded Notified Forest Land.

Table 6.7 reveals that approximately two-third geographical area of this sample study area is under degraded notified forest land. All the hills of this area are covered by the degraded forest with small patches of dense forest (Fig. 6.6). The maximum concentration of this category is found in Bandh Muzaferpur village followed by Talooka Bas and Kuhada villages situated in the southern part of this study area (Fig. 6.6 and Fig. 6.4C) Paehhodala occupies lowest percentage of degraded forest as the central and western part of the village is peneplained while mid-western part belongs to gullied/ravinous land (Fig. 6.6).

Another category of wasteland in this sample study area is gullied and/or ravinous land i.e. only 5.44 per cent to the geographical area with maximum area in Paehhodala followed by Kuhada village (Fig. 6.4D). In both the villages, this category of land is found along the western side of hills running from south to north direction as several seasonal nallahs originate from the hills and dissect the land (Fig 6.5).

No work of RDF has been done in this area by the forest department. Second model of RDF is more appropriate in all the villages of this sample study area. However, farmers of Paehhodala village have done efforts to reclaim G1 gullied land adjoining their cultivated land. In this model, 200 seedlings should be planted in pits and seeds of grass, trees, scrub, medicinal plants on the mounds of trench/ ditch fencing should be sown in rainy season. Restoration of natural regeneration by cut back cultural operation must be done. There should be contour trenches on middle slopes and crescent shaped ridges in lower side of seedlings and saplings.

SAMPLE STUDY AREA FOR SAND-DESERTIC LAND

Sample villages for sand desertic land is situated on relatively upland plain in Phulera tehsil between 26°01' 43" to 26°05' 49" N and 76°15' 49" to 76°22' 13" E (Fig. 6.9) occupying 35.25 km². These villages are selected from the western part of the district where sand-desertic conditions are prevalent due to its proximacy to the desert districts of the state. Phulera tehsil alone covers more than two-fifth sand-desertic land of the study area.

This sample study area is roughly rectangle in shape, having an elevation of 400 metres from MSL as two contours of 400m pass through this area diagonally from west to north east and south to north east (Fig. 6.7 A). The highest point (435m) is on the barren hill near the main settlement of Dhani Boraj village while a small patch having lowest height (below 380m) lies on the north-west boundary of this area near Jaitpura talav. The main feature of the landscape is sand dunes scattered from south-west to north-east direction. Generally, height of sand dunes is 3 metre excluding two sand dunes of 5 and 9m height from the ground (Fig. 6.7). The length of the dunes vary from 50 to 75 metres. There is no seasonal river due to sand-desertic conditions of the area.

This sample study area have 7,766 population i.e. 220 persons per km² in spite of sand-desertic characteristics. Dhani Boraj (287) and Bhagwatpura (249), the villages of eastern part have more population density while it is low in the villages of western part due to more area under sand-desertic land e.g. in Sursinghpura (135), Malyawas (157) and Majipura (195). Population share of S.C. (13.36%) and S.T. (4.44%) is also less in comparison to the average of district. This area has better literacy (62.32) due to its location between Jobner and Phulera towns. In this area, only 57.42 per cent population is engaged in agriculture as cultivators and agricultural labourers. The maximum agricultural population is in Bhagwatpura

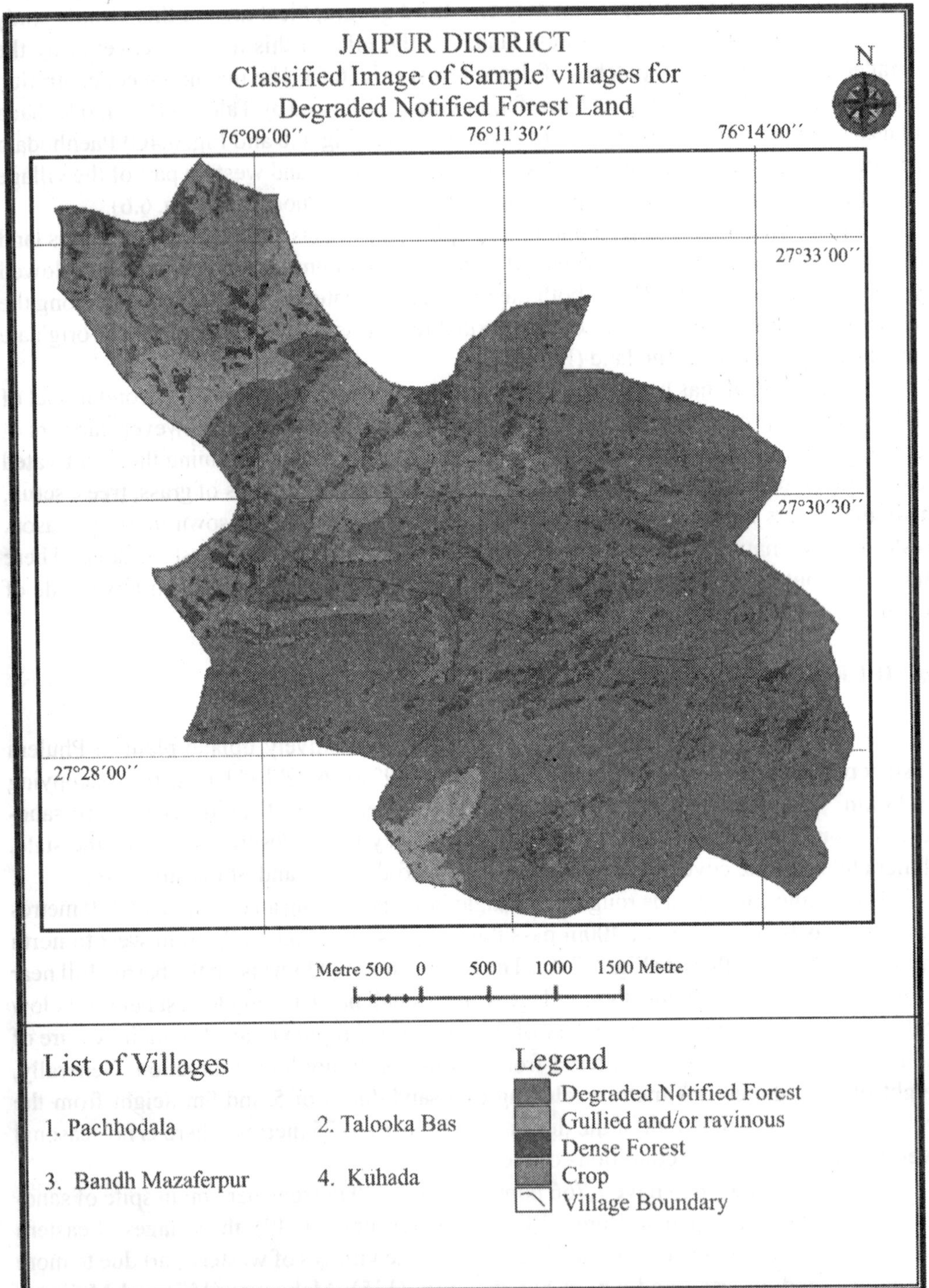

Source : LISS III dated 28th Feb. 2003. Processed at : B.M. Birla Science and Technology Centre, Jaipur

Feb. 6.6 : Classified Image of Sample villages for Degraded Notified Forest Land

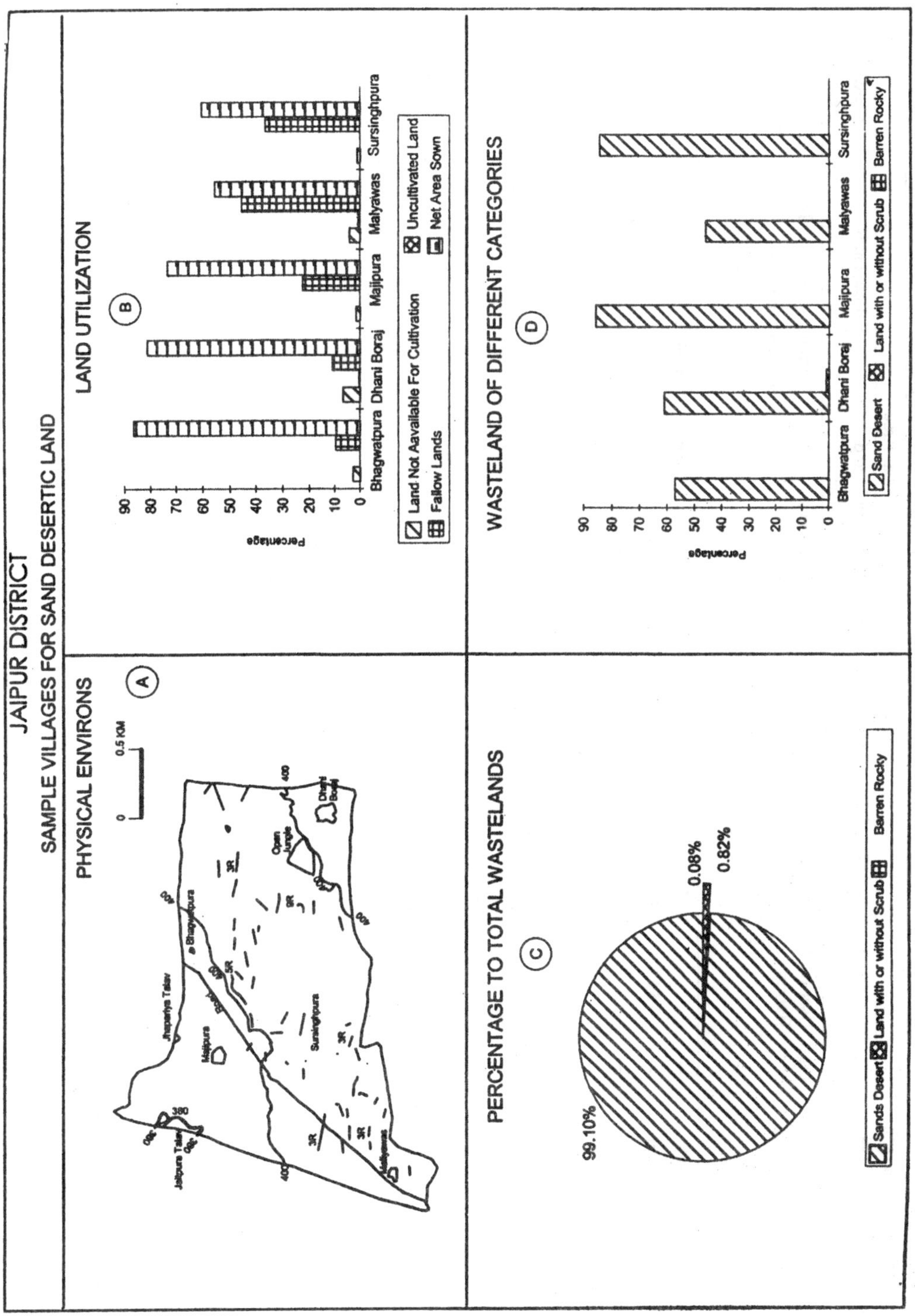

Fig. 6.7 : Sample Villages for Sands-Desertic land.

Table 6.8 : Land Use in Sample Villages for Sands Desertic Land 2003-04

S. No	Name of village	Geographical Area in Hectares	Percentage to Total Geographical Area											
			Land Not Available for Cultivation					Other Uncultivated Land Excluding follow			Fallow lands			Net sown area
			Forest	Usar & Barren	Land Put to non agricultural uses	Permanent Pastures/ Grazing Land	Total	Culturable waste	Misc. trees & Groves	Total	Current Fallow	Old Fallow	Total	Irrigated and unirrigated
1	Bhagwatpura	668	–		3.44	–	3.44	0.60	–	0.60	5.84	3.74	9.58	86.38
2	Dhani Boraj	1116	–	0.54	3.85	2.60	6.99	0.98	–	0.98	7.44	3.31	10.75	81.18
3	Majipura	319	–		1.88	–	1.88	–	–	–	16.93	5.33	22.26	73.35
4	Malyawas	655	–		4.27	–	4.27	1.07	–	1.07	35.72	9.83	45.55	55.42
5	Sursinghpura	765	–		1.70	–	1.70	0.39	–	0.39	28.89	7.58	36.47	60.39
	Total	3523	–		3.21	0.82	4.03	0.71	–	0.71	17.91	4.54	22.45	75.15

Source : Land Record Section, Phulera Tehsil, District Jaipur.

Plate 15 : Afforestation on Sand-Desertic land on Jaipur-Jobner Road in Phulera Tehsil.

Plate 16 : J.D.A. developed a park in a depression surrounded by sand dunes on J.L.N. Marg, Jaipur.

village (62.12%) followed by Dhani Boraj (55.84%) and Malyawas (50.81%). In Majipura village, approximately 60 per cent population is employed in non-agricultural activities while the share of agricultural population is only 40 per cent to the total working population. Majipura village has desertic conditions, less irrigated area and more Scheduled Castes population, so the most of the working population is engaged as labourers in nearby towns Phulera, Jobner and Samhnar. The population employed in other activities vary from 30.95 to 56.49 percent in these sample villages.

General Land Use

In sand desertic area, the land use depends on the rainfall as most of the crops produced in this region are rainfed due to sandy nature of soil and poor quality/quantity of ground water resources. Table 6.8 shows the land use pattern in the sample villages for sand desertic land.

Table 6.8 reveals that 97.60 per cent area is under plough i.e. net sown area and fallow land and it ranges from 90.42 to 94.01 per cent in the sample villages. In this part of the district, more land is kept fallow to maintain the soil fertility due to sandy nature of soil. Fig. 6.7B indicates that maximum NSA is in Bhagwatpura village followed by Dhani Boraj and Majipura villages while the fallow land is more in Malyawas and Sursinghpura villages. In Malyawas, area under rabi crops is more due to irrigation facilities, therefore the farmers keep their land under fallow in kharif season. In these villages land under permanent pasture and land not available for cultivation is almost negligible due to more fallow lands.

Identification of Wastelands

On the basis of LISS-III satellite image (Fig 6.8), the following categories of wastelands have been identified in the sample study area for sands-desertic land.

Table 6.9 : Identification of Wastelands in Sample Study Area for Sands-Desertic Land.

S. No.	Wasteland Category	Area in hectares	Percentage to Total Geographical Area	Percentage to to wastelands
1.	Sands-desertic	2711.75	64.07	99.10
2.	Land with Scrub without Scrub	22.58	0.53	0.82
3.	Barren Rocky	2.07	0.05	0.08
	Total	2736.40	64.65	100.00

Source : LISS III Satellite image, dated February 28, 2003.

The above table shows that approximately two-third land of this sample study area is under sands-desertic land. Of the total wastelands 99.10 per cent belongs to sands-desertic and less than one per cent is occupied by land with or without scrub and barren rocky (Fig. 6.7C). This sample study area is adjoining desert district viz. Nagaur, therefore, more land is occupied by sands-desertic land.

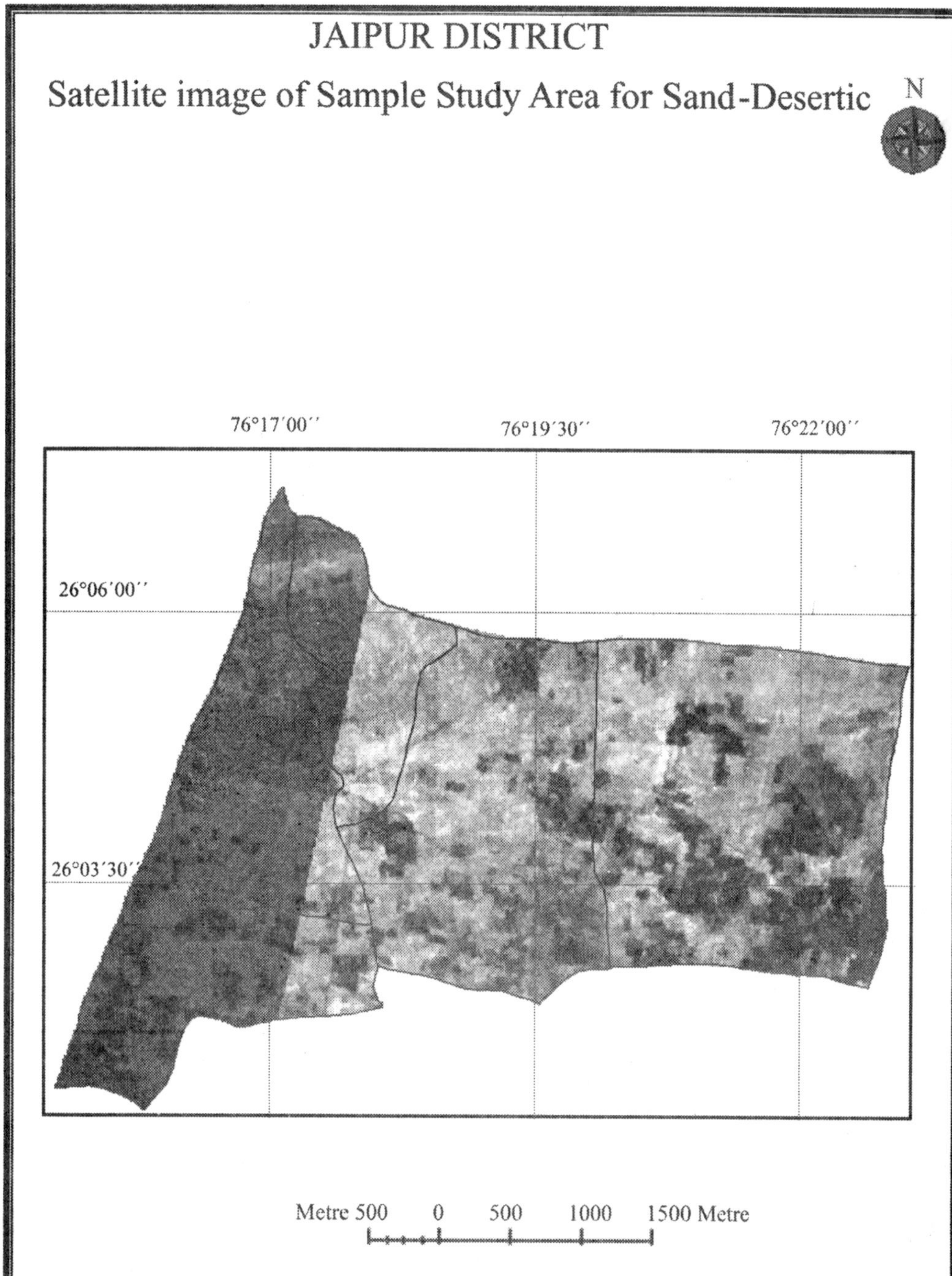

Source : LISS III dated 28th Feb. 2003. Processed at : B.M. Birla Science and Technology Centre, Jaipur

Fig. 6.8 : Satellite image of Sample Study Area for Sand-Desertic

Spatial Distribution of Wastelands in Sample Villages for Sands-Desertic Land

As other categories of wasteland, the area under sands-desertic land is also unevenly distributed. The following Table 6.10 and Fig. 6.7D show villagewise wasteland under different categories:

Table 6.10 : Villagewise Wastelands in Sample Villages for Sands-Desertic Land

S. No.	Name of village	Percentage of wastelands to the total geographical area			Total
		Sands Desertic	Scrub	Barren Rocky	
1.	Bhagwatpura	57.24	–	–	57.24
2.	Dhani Boraj	61.13	1.58	0.15	62.46
3.	Majipura	85.83	–	–	85.83
4.	Maliyawas	45.80	–	–	84.18
5.	Sursinghpura	84.18	–	–	45.80
	Total	64.02	0.53	0.05	64.65

Source : LISS III Satellite image, February 28, 2003

The above table shows that approximately two-third area is under sands-desertic land of the sample study area. Fig. 6.7D shows that all the sample villages have only one type of wasteland i.e. sands desertic excluding Dhani Boraj. The maximum area under this category is in Majipura and Sursinghpura (84.18%) villages. Both these villages are situated in the western part of the sample study area. In Majipura, rabi crops are not produced due to non availability of groundwater while in southern part of Sursinghpura a few hectares are under rabi crops (Fig. 6.9). The lowest percentage of this category occurs in Maliyawas village due to more area under irrigation. Barren rocky and land with or without scrub are found in a small patch lying in the south-eastern part near main settlement of Dhani Boraj (Fig. 6.9).

Ownership of Wastelands

In the sample study area all the sand desertic land is under the private ownership producting crops however barren rocky (0.15%) is under the possession of government.

Characteristics of Sand Desertic Land

Sand desertic land is covered dominantly by sandy soil, which contains less organic matter, more permeability and less moisture. This area is situated in a part of the state where temperatures are high in summers and low rainfall. Soils are less fertile due to leaching of minerals from the surface. Drifting and stabilized sand dunes are scattered in south west to north east direction having 3 to 9 metres height from the ground and very low percentage of cultivated land under irrigation. As a result it is a single cropped area.

Wastelands within Operating Holdings

The average size of holding is eight hectares, which is large size holding in comparison to other sample study areas of the district. Almost all the sand desertic land is utilized for

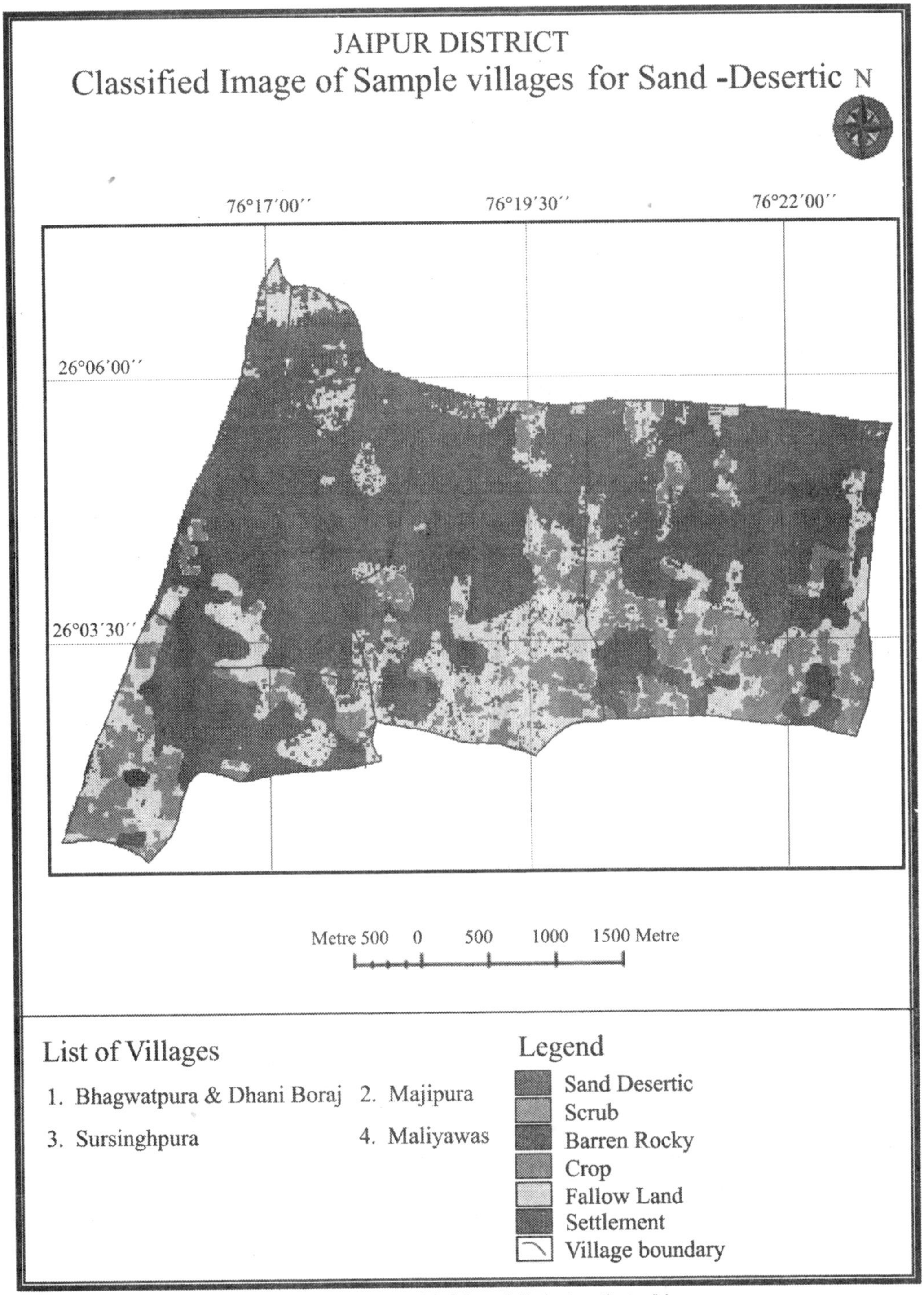

Source : LISS III dated 28th Feb. 2003. Processed at : B.M. Birla Science & Technology Centre Jaipur

Fig. 6.9 : Classified Image of Sample villages for Sand-Desertic

producing rainfed crops. However, the cropped area, yield and production of crops totally depend on the amount of rain and number of rainy days. Approximately two-third land of operational holding is categorized as sand- desertic land.

Causes of Sand-Desertic Wasteland

As already mentioned the western part of the district has sand desertic conditions due to closeness with desert districts (Nagaur and Sikar district) of the state. This area receives aeolion sand from the Aravalli gap continuously. Besides this, rainfall is also less than 50 cm with high temperatures in summers, light sandy/loamy sand soil with more permeability. Various types of sand dunes are common features of this area having 3 to more than 50 metres height.

Reclamation of Wastelands by the Farmers themselves and Cost of Reclamation/ Development of Wastelands

The sand-desertic land is found undulated at some places due to sand dunes. During the field work it is observed that levelling of sand-dunes are not done as other parts of the desert districts, For maintaining soil fertility, the farmers use FYM, produce leguminous crop and keep land fallow after bajra crop.

For getting more yield, deep ploughing is also done by the cultivators annually or biannually. Five per cent farmers having their own tractors generally do deep ploughing every year in their fields while the others adopt this practice at the interval of two or three years. The cost of this ploughing is Rs. 1000 per hectare. Generally, FYM is applied only in those fields which would be utilized for producing bajra or other rabi crops. The cost of FYM per hectare is approximately Rs. 5000 per hectare. Farmers use manure of their own livestocks, however, sometimes farmers purchase manure from the other cultivators of the village.

Utilization of Sand-Desertic Land

The limitations of sand-desertic land are poor light soils having more permeability, low moisture and poor groundwater resources. Farmers of this area adopt such a cropping pattern which is helpful in maintaining the soil fertility. Most of the area is single cropped, mainly kharif crops due to paucity of groundwater. In the sample villages, the area under kharif crops was 93.80 per cent, 82.75 per cent, 78.33 per cent, 68.30 per cent, 55.32 per cent to the total cropped area in Majipura, Sursinghpura, Bhagwatpura, Dhani Boraj and Malyawas villages respectively in 2003-2004. In this season almost all the sand dunes are cultivated. In kharif, bajra occupies 37.24 per cent followed by chaunla (17.70%), guar (13.05%) to the total cropped area and approximately one-fourth cultivated land is under rabi crops viz wheat, barley, gram and mustard. These crops are produced with the help of irrigation. Here bajra is a major crop which requires less moisture and drought resistant. It is also a staple food in this part of the district. All the farmers of this area adopt the crop

Plate 17 : Clusterbean and Pearlmillet on a Sand Dune in Rainy Season.

Plate 18 : Peripheral Bund to check further extension of Gullied/Ravinous land near Bhanpur Kalan village.

rotation to maintain soil fertility. The following crop rotation is common in these sample villages.

Kharif season	*Rabi season*
Bajra	Fallow
Cowpea	Fallow
Moong	Fallow
Guar	Fallow
Fallow	Wheat/barley
Fallow	Mustard
Fallow	Gram

From the above crop rotation it is clear that leguminous crops e.g. cowpea, moong and guar are produced and land is kept fallow to maintain the soil fertility. Rabi crops are produced only those fields where the irrigation facilities are available. In this area, groundwater resources are very poor in quality and quantity so the area under irrigation is also very less.

Sand-desertic soils are very sensitive to wind erosion. For checking wind erosion, most of the farmers keep large number of Khejri tree in their fields, soil ridge boundary, crop residue, *dhamsa* (Jogru), *leptolnia* (Kemp), *lagaria* etc. Another most important problem of this soil is low fertility. To improve fertility, the farmer use manure, grow leguminous crops, and keep land as fallow.

SAMPLE STUDY AREA FOR LAND WITH OR WITHOUT SCRUB

This sample study area is situated in the southern part of Phagi tehsil between $26^0 27' 51''$ N $26^0 33' 24''$ N and $76^0 36' 26''$ E to $76^0 41' 32''$ E, (Fig. 6.10A) occupies 42-44 km^2.

This area is almost level land with poor drainage and salinity/alkalinity problem due to Ca Co_3 layer at a depth of 0 to 1.05 m. All the contour having same height i.e. 300m pass through the sample study area, indicates its average elevation (Fig. 6.10A). A trignometrical station of 314m near Hatheli village is the highest point of this study area. There is no drainage in this area except two very small nallahs lie in the north and south western part of the study area. However, an important seasonal river Mashi demarcates the southern boundary of Chandma Kalan village. The main feature of this area is approximately twenty ponds/ tanks scattered in the five villages including the most important tank of Chandma Kalan (Fig. 6.10A). These are used to drink water to their livestocks, irrigating crops, construction of houses and other domestic purposes. Besides this dug wells are also constructed nearby tank/pond for fetching good quality drinking water as most of the dug wells have brackish water problem, not suitable for drinking as well as irrigation purposes.

This sample study area has 4503 persons having population density only 105 persons per km^2. The maximum population density (163) is in Panwasoo Khera village followed by Nathmalpura (125), and Chandma Kalan (129) villages while very low population density is found is Hotheli (57) and Ajnota (77) due to more salinity/alkalinity land. This area has more S.C. population (12.92%) and less S.T. population (6.35%). Two third population of this sample area is engaged is agriculture while remaining population is employed mainly in other activities. This is one of the sample study area where 12 per cent population of the villages are enganged as agriculture labourer. It indicates two things i.e. unemployment problem and land less people. The maximum population engaged in agriculture is in Ajnota

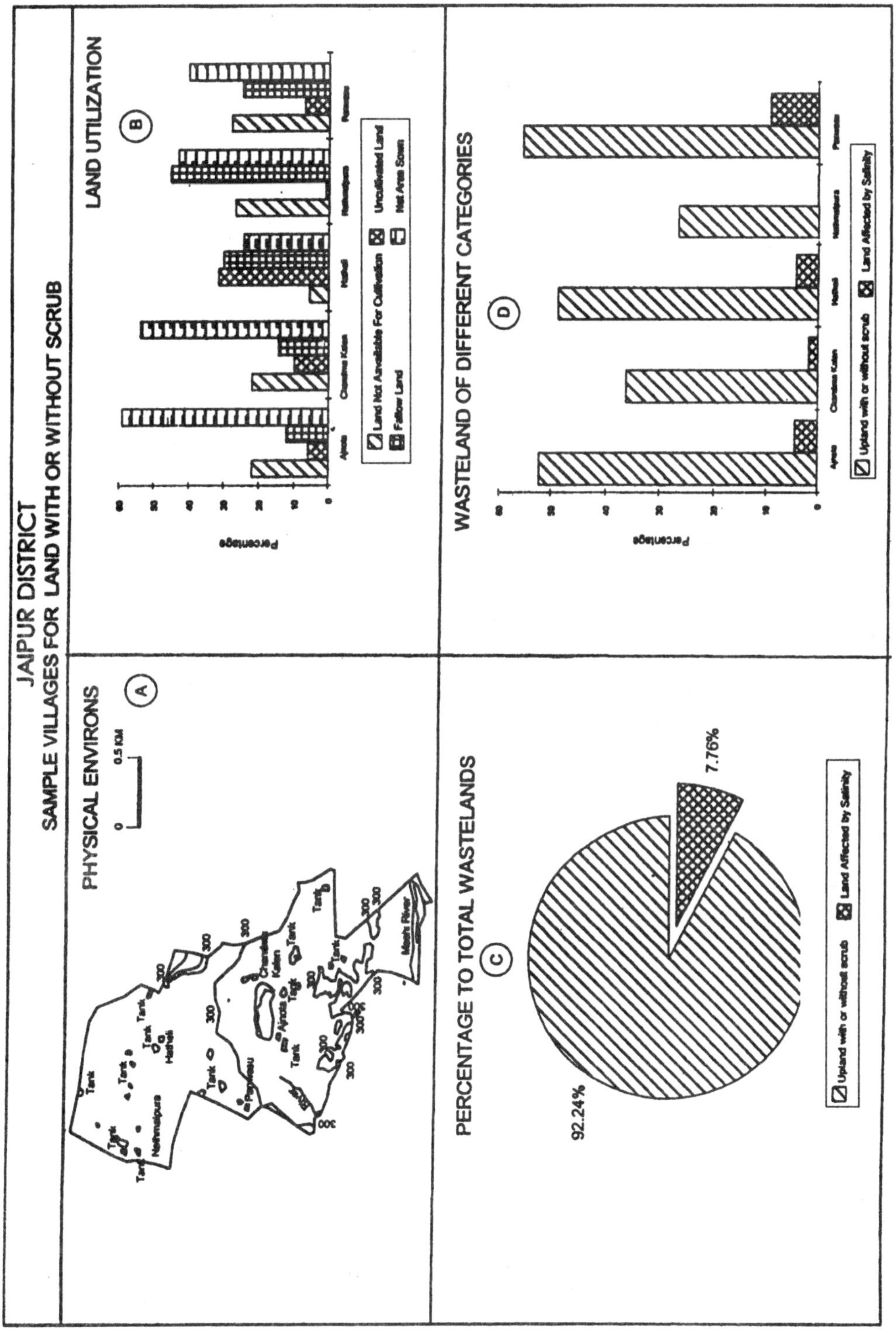

Fig. 6.10A : Physical Environs
Fig. 6.10B : Land Utilization
Fig. 6.10C : Percentage to Total Wastelands
Fig. 6.10D : Wasteland of Different Categories

Table 6.11: General Land Use in Sample villages for Land With or Without Scrub-2003-04

S. No.	Name of village	Geographical Area in Hectares	Percentage to Total Geographical Area												
			Sand Not Available for Cultivation						Other Uncultivated Land Ex. Fallow			Fallow lands			Net Sown Area
			Forest	Hills	Usar and Barren	Land Put to Non - Agricultural uses	Permanent pastures/ Grazing land	Total	Culturable waste	Misc. Tree and Groves	Total	Current Fallow	Old Fallow	Total	Total Irrigated and Unirrigated
1	Ajnota	650	–	–	1.69	7.31	13.00	22.00	6.00	–	6.00	5.69	6.61	12.30	59.08
2	Chandmo Kalan	1209	–	–	1.16	9.71	11.03	21.91	10.04	–	10.04	5.97	8.63	14.60	53.77
3	Hatheli	1094	–	–	1.28	2.65	2.01	5.94	31.44	–	31.44	7.59	22.58	30.17	24.53
4	Nathmalpura	489	–	–	0.20	3.48	23.11	26.79	1.24	–	1.24	16.77	28.42	45.19	42.90
5	Pawansu	298	–	–	–	4.36	23.49	27.85	7.38	–	7.38	15.77	9.06	24.83	40.26
	Total	3740	–	–	1.07	7.21	10.11	18.39	14.21		14.21	8.60	15.01	23.61	43.65

Source : Land Record Section, Phagi tehsil, District Jaipur.

(85.38%) followed by Nathmalpura (78.02%) while lowest population employed in this occupation is in Hatheli village due to livestock rearing and dairy activities in this village. Many cultivators have their own pasture land (Beed) for their livestocks.

General Land Use

In preceding paragraphs it is clear that this sample study area is not suitable for producing crops. Table 6.12 shows village wise land use in the sample villages for land with or without scrub.

On comparison the land utilization of land with or without scrub and degraded pasture/ gazing land, the land use pattern of both the sample study areas is almost identical in their sample villages. Both sample study areas have more land not available for cultivation and fallow lands and less net sown area in their villages (Fig. 6.13B and 6.19B) Table 6.12 shows that maximum scrub land is concentrated in Panwasu (55.64%) followed by Ajnota (52.42%) and Hatheli (48.90%) villages. All the three villages are situated in the western part of the sample study area (Fig 6.12). Chandma Kalan village also keeps her more than one-third land under this category especially in its southern and western part. All the villages have problem of non-availability and poor quality of irrigation water and poor drained to moderately well drained. Soils of this area have calcium carbonate layer at a depth ranging between 30 and 105 cms.

Identification of Wastelands

The following categories of wasteland have been identified on the Satellite image obtained from NRSA, Hyderabad (Fig 6.11).

Table 6.12 : Identification of Wasteland in Sample Study Area for Land with or without Scrub

S. No.	Wasteland category	Area in hectares	Percentage to total geographical	Percentage to total Wasteland
1.	Upland with or without scrub	1794.99	42.30	92.24
2.	Land affected by salinity	150.92	3.55	7.76
	Total	1945.91	45.85	100.00

Source : LISS III Satellite image, Feb. 28, 2003.

The above table shows that more than two-fifth land of the sample study area belongs to land with or without scrub i.e. 92.24 percent of the total wastelands while only 3.55 per cent of the total geographical area i.e. 7.76 per cent to the total wastelands is affected by salinity/ alkalinity. Fig 6.10C indicates that this sample study area is characterised by the land with scrub/without scrub.

Spatial distribution of Wastelands in Sample Study Area for up land with or without Scrub

The villagewise percentage of wastelands has been calculated from the LISS III satellite image (Fig. 6.11) which indicates the uneven distributional pattern of wastelands in sample villages for land with or without scrub (Fig. 6.12):

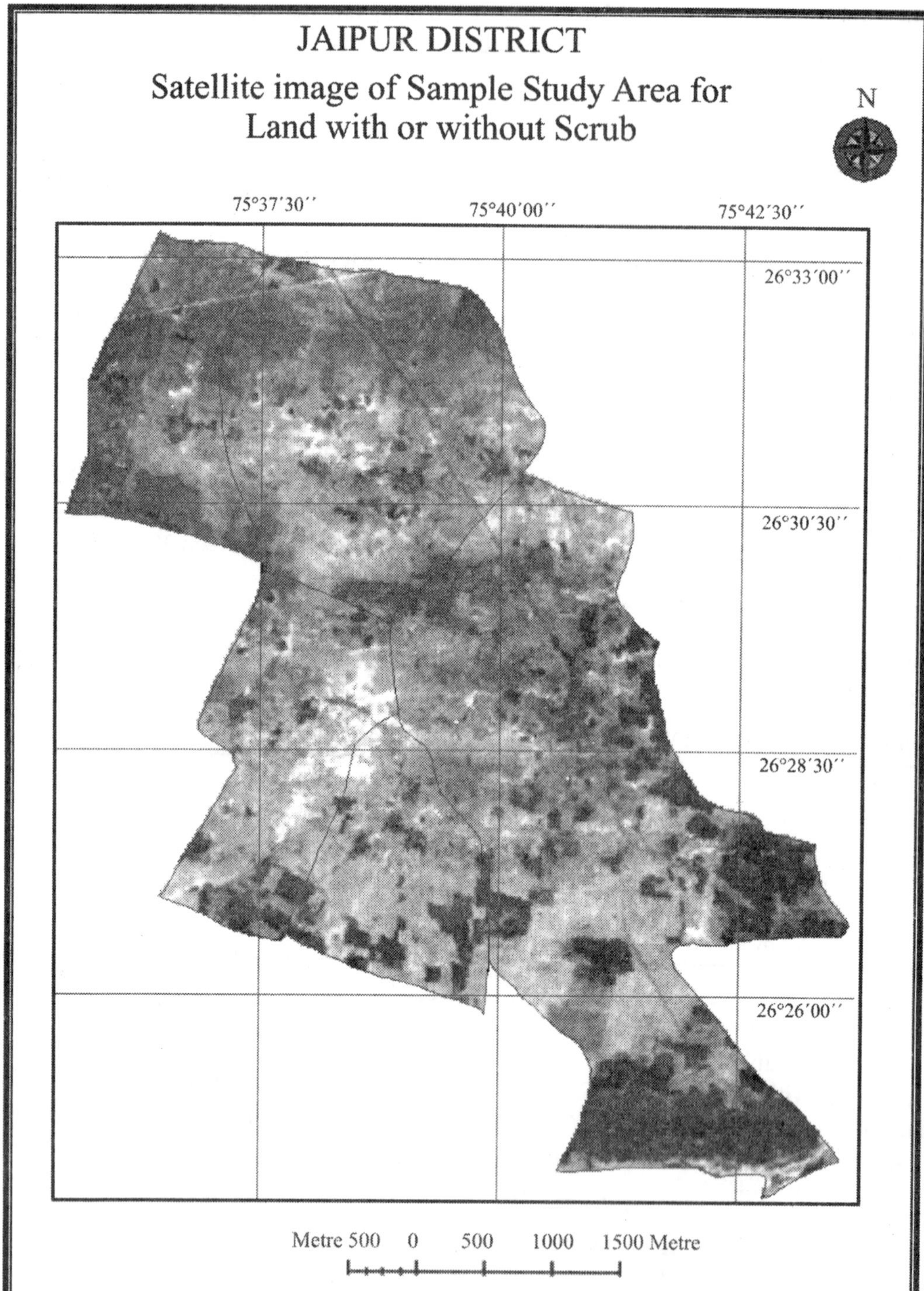

Source : LISS III dated 28th Feb. 2003

Fig. 6.11 : Satellite image of Sample Study Area for Land with or without Scrub

Table 6.13 : Wasteland in Sample Villages for Land with or without scrub

S. No.	Name of the Village	Percentage of wastelands to the total geographical area		Total
		Land with or without scrub	Land affected by salinity	
1.	Ajnota	52.42	4.61	57.03
2.	Chandma Kalan	36.36	1.91	38.27
3.	Hatheli	48.90	4.39	53.29
4.	Nathmalpura	26.70	0.36	27.06
5.	Panwasu	55.64	9.39	65.03
	Total	42.30	3.55	45.85

Source : LISS III Satellite image, Feb. 28, 2003

Ownership of Wastelands

Government wasteland mainly comprise of degraded/grazing land constituting 59.75 per cent of the total wastelands of the area, while remaining wasteland is under the private ownership.

Characteristics of Wastelands

Satellite image of this sample study area (Fig. 6.11) indicates that large saline/alkline patches are scattered in the northern part of Panwasu, Ajnota, Chandma Kalan, southern part of Hatheli and central part of the Nathmalpura villages locally known as *"Kharda"*. Brackish water in dug well is also not suitable for irrigating the rabi crops particularly in the northern part of the sample study area. If cultivators irrigate their field with brackish water, soil becomes hard and compact, therefore once or twice watering is given in barley, wheat and mustard crops. At some places *"Kankars"* can be observed in top surface soil however the soil thickness varies between 30 and 105 cm. It can be said that cultivators of the northern part of the sample study area, face the problems of *'Kharda'* and *'Kadwa'* (brackish water).

In southern part of this study area, the soils are sandy loams to loamy sand and slightly better quality ground water due to mashi river (Fig. 6.11). Farmers of this area earn their cash income throughout the year from the sell of caw/buffalo milk to the Jaipur dairy milk collection centres or owners of restaurants/hotels in nearby towns. Farmers grow green fodder in their fields for their livestocks in summer season. In this area red cows (Reda) are reared as these cows give more milk in comparison to indigenous cows. Now-a-days farmers of this area purchase she buffaloes from Haryana state for getting more income from their livestocks.

Distribution of Wastelands within Operational Holdings

Location, characterstics and size of operational holding play a vital role in determining the economics of reclamation. The average size of holding in this sample study area is 3.38 hectares. More than four-fifth area of the holdings is affected by salinity/alkalinity (Kharda).

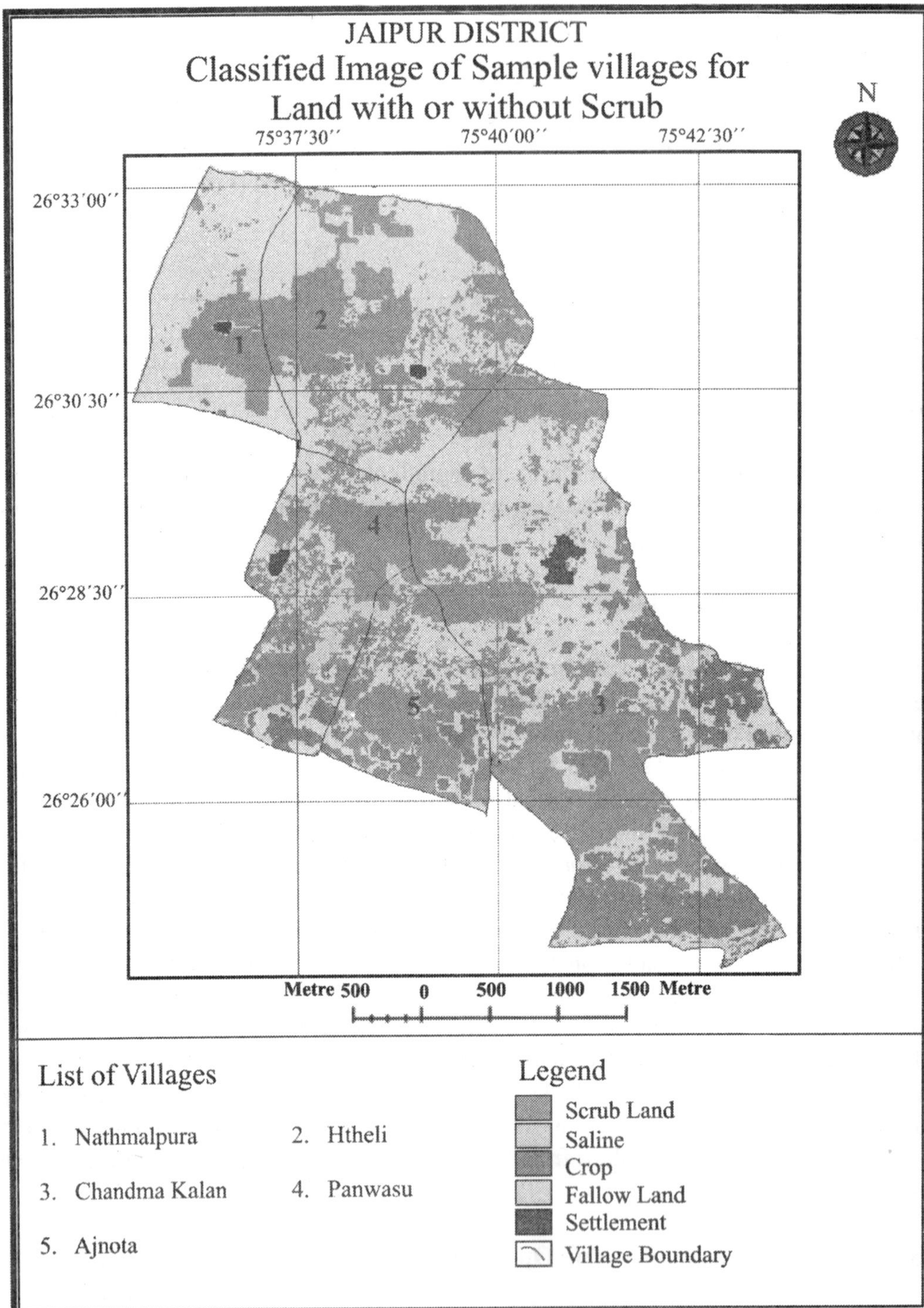

Source : LISS III dated 28th Feb. 2003. Processed at : B.M. Birla Science & Technology Centre, Jaipur

Fig. 6.12 : Classified Image of Sample villages for Land with or without Scrub

The following Table 6.14 sshows the various type of wastelands in operational holdings.

Table 6.14 : Various type of wastelands in sample study area for land with or without scrub

S. No	Type of land	Per household size of land (Hectare)	Percentage of operational holding	Percentage to total wasteland of operational holding
1	Unirrigated affected by salinity/alkalinity	1.81	53.55	65.35
2	Irrigated-salinity/alkalinity affected	0.11	3.25	3.97
3	Unirrigated cultivated land non-saline	0.61	18.05	–
4	Land with or without scrub Salinity/affected (Beed)	0.85	25.15	30.68
	Total	3.38	100.00	100.00

Source : Based on questionnaire filled during field survey, June 2004

The above table shows that approximately three-fifth area of an operational holding is cultivated as rainfed crops in kharif season while irrigated land is very limited due to brackish nature of ground water. Satellite image (Fig 6.11) shows that rabi crops are produced only in southern part while very small patches of rabi crops are scattered in northern part of the sample study area. The irrigated crops are wheat, barley and mustard. In this sample study area approximately one-fourth area is also kept as a reseve for grazing livestocks/cutting fodder grass (Hay) for locally known as "beed" for feeding to livestocks in winter/summer season. Most of the area of beed is generally affected by Salinity/Alkalinity/poor soils and poor quality of water, not suitable for producing crops.

Reclamation of Wastelands

This area is not suitable for agriculture but the farmers are forced to cultivate their fields due to lack of other sources of income. During the field study it was observed that farmers have reclaimed 0.25 hectare per household in their cultivated land themselves without financial assistance from the Government and other agencies.

The farmers of this area adopted only two methods of reclamation i.e. *medbandi* and application of sandy soil in saline/alkaline affected cultivated land. In these reclamation measures, the per hectare cost is approximately Rs. 6000. However, rich farmers use FYM in their fields.

Utilization of Reclaimed Saline Affected Land

As mentioned earlier, the farmers reclaimed their saline/alkaline affected cultivated land themselves to increase crop yield. They adopted the same cropping pattern as earlier practiced. After *medbandi* per hectare yield of jowar increased 15 to 20 times while after use of sandy soil in salinity affected fields, the response was also very encourging, the yield of jowar increased approximately ten times. In this area only one crop is produced in a year. If the land is kept fallow in kharif season, mustard is taken in rabi season as an unirrigated crop. The field depends on rains in rainy season. If the rain occurs in sufficient quantity at proper interval, farmers get good production of grain and straw.

On the basis of preceding paragraphs, it is concluded that the villages of the northern part of this sample study area are affected by salinity/alkalinity. Earlier it was lying waste as land with or without scrub. Now the government has allotted this land to SC, ST and land less people of the villages. Thus most of the land under plough having problem of salinity/ alkalinity, brackish ground water, shallow calcareous soil, causes very low yield. The yield of this area can be increased many times if financial assistance is given to the farmers for remedial measures suggested by them. As almost all the farmers need financial assistance for *medbandi* and mixing of sandy soil in salinity affected cultivated fields. In *medbandi* fields, rainy water can stand so salinity can remove or leached in the subsoil. In these fields, the farmers produce less water requiring rabi crops like gram, barley and mustard etc. Besides this gypsum and DAP should be provided at subsidy rate or free of cost to the poor small holding farmers, SC and ST category of the society as DAP fertilizer keep the soil moisture intact to some extent and farmers can procured more yield per hectare from their fields. There is a good scope for dairy development in this area as most of the cultivated land is utilised for fodder producing kharif crops. However Jat cultivators haveshe buffaloes for supplying milk to milk collection centres run by the Jaipur Dairy Co-operative Federation. From livestock rearing poor farmers get regular income to meet out their expenses. Besides these, an anicut should be constructed on Mashi river, so the water table can be increased in nearby dug wells.

SAMPLE STUDY AREA FOR LAND AFFECTED BY SALINITY

This sample study area is located from 26°42′54″ to 26°56′49″ North latitude and 75°05′23″ to 75°10′21″ East longitude (Fig 6.15) in Dudu tehsil of the study area. This area occupies 4723 hectares with 4236 persons including 17.56 per cent S.C. and 2.10 per cent ST population.

This area, roughly square in shape is situated on a relatively upland plain. Two contours i.e. 380 and 360 metre pass through the western and eastern part respectively, indicate general elevation of the area (Fig. 6.13A). A tributary of the Mashi river along the northern and eastern boundary, indicates the general slope of the area (Fig. 6.13A and Fig. 6.14). Four small nallahs, two each form the right and left join this tributary. Tanks/ponds are the main features of landscape, as one dozen ponds/tanks are concentrated in the southern part of this study area (Fig. 6.13A).

The average population density of the area is only 90 persons per square kilometre with maximum in Dantra (161) and Bigolav (128) villages situated in the central part of this area. Lowest population density is found in Jhokolar (52), Pawaliya (84) and Bokarawas (84). These villages are situated in a salinity affected belt along the seasonal river. Share of SC and ST population is 17.56 and 2.10 per cent to the total population in this sample study area.

It is surprising that 42.90 per cent population of Dantra village belongs to S.C. while in other villages it ranges between 8.84 and 14.86 per cent. Literacy is also low due to poor economic condition of the residents of the area. 69.72 per cent population is engaged in agriculture while remaining population in other non-agricultural activities. Maximum agricultural population is found in Panwaliya (86.52%) followed by Hatupur (81.94%) and Jhakolar (75.47%) villages while more than 50 per cent population of Dantra (51.31%) and Bokarawas (50.38%) villages is engaged in other activities. Both these villages have maximum

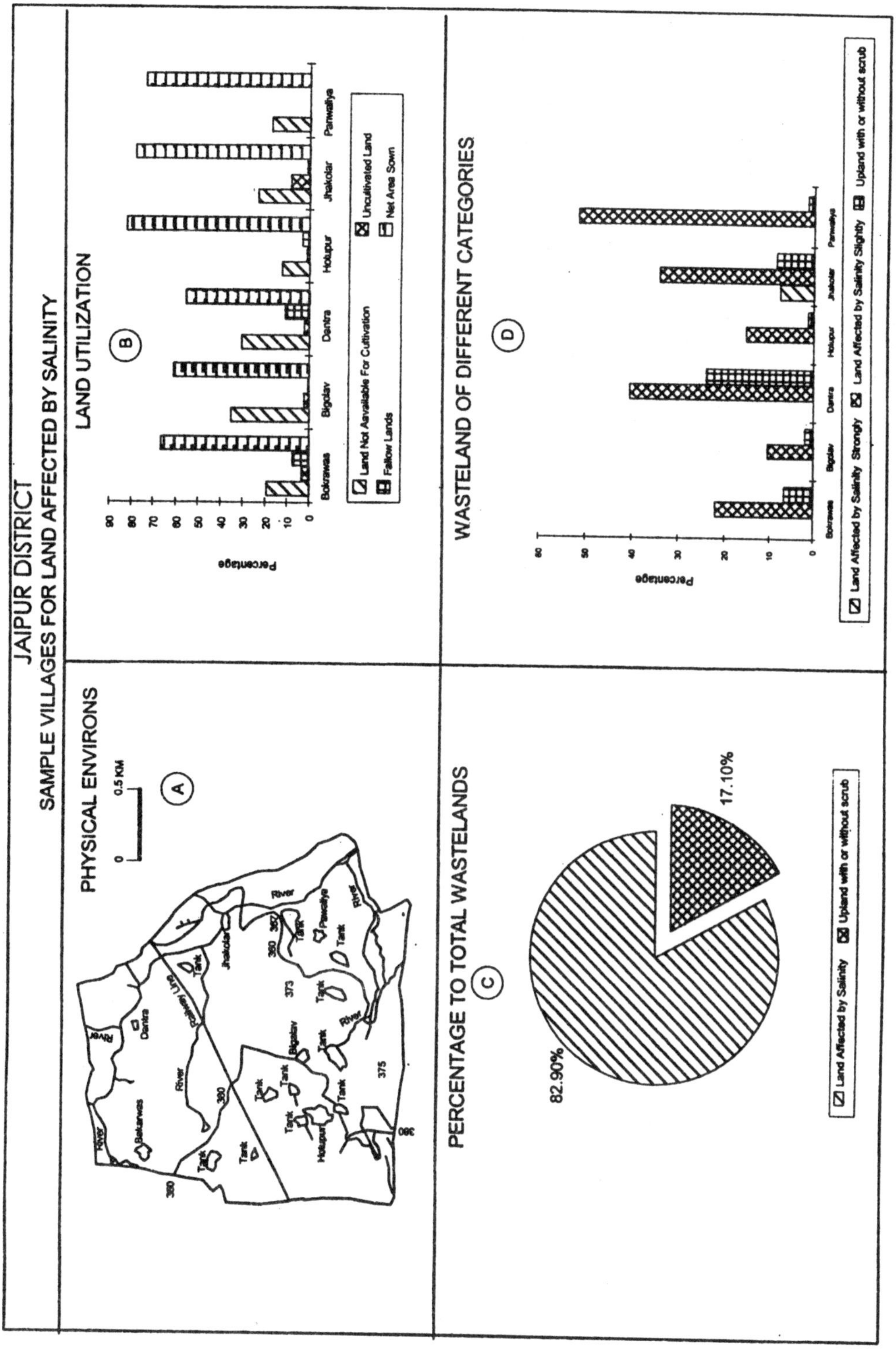

Fig. 6.13 : Sample Villages for Land Affected by Salinity.

Table 6.15 : Land Use in Sample Villages for Land Affected by Salinity 2003-04

S. No	Name of Village	Geographical area in hectares	Percentage to the Total Geographical Area												
			Area Not Available for Cultivation						Uncultivated excluding fallow land			Fallow lands			Net Sown Area
			Forest	Hills	Usar and Barren	Land put to Non Agricultural users	Parmanent Pastures	Total	Culturable wasteland	Mosc. tree & groves	Total	Current fallow	Old Fallow	Total	
1	Bokrawas	683	–	–	0.73	12.00	6.73	19.47	3.51	–	3.51	7.47	3.07	7.54	66.47
2	Bigolav	502	–	–	0.79	5.38	28.88	35.06	2.79	–	2.79	0.40	0.59	0.99	60.75
3	Dantra	367	–	–	3.00	11.99	15.80	30.79	2.72	–	2.72	3.00	8.44	11.44	55.04
4	Hotupur	1962	–	–	1.22	4.38	7.13	12.74	1.68	–	1.68	1.43	2.04	3.47	81.85
5	Jhakolar	627	–	0.32	10.84	4.97	7.33	23.44	8.93	–	8.93	0.81	0.64	1.45	77.67
6	Panwaliya	582	–	–	3.43	5.37	8.59	17.35	0.51	–	0.51	0.17	0.34	0.51	73.02
	Total	4723	–	0.04	2.79	6.37	9.00	19.48	3.00	–	3.00	2.03	2.18	4.21	73.66

Source: Land Record Section, Dudu tehsil, District Jaipur.

S.C. and S.T. population and these categories of the society of this area used to come in Jaipur city to work as labourers in construction and other work.

General Land Use

Table 6.16 shows that three-fourth land of this sample study area is under plough as the cultivators used to produce kharif crops in land affected by salinity. In kharif season, the saline layer washed away with rainy water and growth of plants is less affected Fig. 6.13 B shows that net sown area is maximum in Hotupur (81.85%) followed by Jhakolar (77.67%) and Panwaliya (73.02%) villages while NAS in remaining two villages is low. It is remarkable that in this sample study area, the irrigated area is very low i.e. 4.26 and 6.35 per cent to the total NSA in Bigolav and Hotupur villages respectivery due to poor quality/quantity of ground water.

Fig 6.13B also indicates that Bigolav, Dantra and Jhokolar villages have more area under land not available for cultivation due to large areas under permanent pasture/grazing land and land affected by salinity (Table 6.15) while in other villages it ranges between 12.94 to 19.47 per cent to the total geographical area.

Identification of Wastelands

On the basis of LISS III image (Fig. 6.14) the following categories of wastelands have been identified in Sample Study Area for land affected by salinity.

Table 6.16 : Identification of Wastelands in Samples Study Area for Land Affected by Salinity

Wasteland Category	Area in hectare	% of the Total Area	% to the total wastelands
Land Affected by Salinity	1210.13	27.00	82.90
Upland with or	249.59	5.57	17.10
Total	1459.72	32.57	100.00

Source : LISS III Satellite image, Feb. 28, 2003

The above table shows that this area occupies 27 per cent land under land affected by the salinity of the total geographical area i.e. 82.90 per cent of the total wastelands (Fig. 6.13C). Remaining wasteland is under upland with or without scrub indicates that the dominant wasteland of this area is land affected by salinity.

Spatial Distribution of Wastelands in the Sample Villages for Land Affected by Salinity

The Table 6.17 shows villagewise wastelands in the sample villages for land affected by salinity.

This shows that more than one-fourth land of the sample village is affected by salinity. Pawaliya village has its more than one-half land (51.67%) under salinity. Other important villages having this category of land are Jhokolar (41.73%) Dantra (40.32%) and Bokarawas (21.57%). It is clear from the satellite image (Fig. 6.14) that this category of land is found in

Source : LISS III dated 28th Feb. 2003. Processed at : B.M. Birla Science & Technology Centre, Jaipur

Fig. 6.14 : Satellite image of Sample Study Area for Land Affected by Salinity

wide flat river bed particularly in the north and eastern part along the boundary of the sample study area. In central and south western part of this study area particularly in Bigolav and Hotupur have less land in this category due to less area under river bed (Fig. 6.15).

Table 6.17 : Wastelands in Sample Villages for Land Affected by Salinity

S. No.	Name of Village	Percentage to the total geographical area			Total
		Land affected by salinity		Land with or without scrub	
		Strong	Slightly		
1.	Bokarwas		21.97	6.62	28.59
2.	Bigolav		10.39	2.04	12.43
3.	Dantra		40.32	24.08	64.40
4.	Hotupur		15.28	1.43	16.71
5.	Jhokolar	7.68	34.05	8.35	50.08
6.	Pawaliya		51.67	1.50	53.47
	Total	0.17	26.83	5.57	32.57

Source : LISS III satellite image, Feb 28, 2003

This sample study area occupies only 5.57 per cent under land with or without scrub to the total geographical area with having maximum land (24.08%) in Dantra village of northern part along the southern bank of the river (Fig. 6.15). This type of land is also found along the river especially in Dantra; Jhokolar and Bakarwas villages. It is concluded that this sample study area has problem of wastelands in river beds and along the rivers.

Ownership of Wastelands

Government wasteland mainly comprises of permanent pastures constituting only 38.84 per cent of total wastelands of this smaple study area, while remaining 61.16 per cent is under private ownership including old fallow.

Characteristics of Wasteland

Salt affected land is generally characterised as land that has adverse effects on the growth of most plants due to the action or presence of excess soluble salts (saline) or high exchangeable sodium. Saline soil is defined as a soil whose conductivity of the saturation extract (ECe) is more than 4 mmhos/cm at 25°C and the exchangeable sodium percentage (ESP) is less than 15. The pH of such soils is usually below 8.5. Soluble salts will obviously accumulate wherever evaporation exceeds total percipitation either alone or in combination with irrigation. Salt accumulation is also associated with certain types of relief connected geomorphologically to lowlands and hydrologically to regions of high water tables. At such places surface run off is negligible and drainage water evaporates leaving the salts on the surface. It has been found (Pandey, Sinha and Pal, 1972) that the magnitude of salinization is greater if the water table remains close to the surface for a long period. In this area, wide flat river bed and its tributary bed are vegetation less and barren. Clay/clay soil with $CaCO_3$ layer on the surface/beneath top surface layer and moisture in river bed are responsible for the salinity in the study area. Large tracts of salinity are common in the river and its tributary bed in these sample villages.

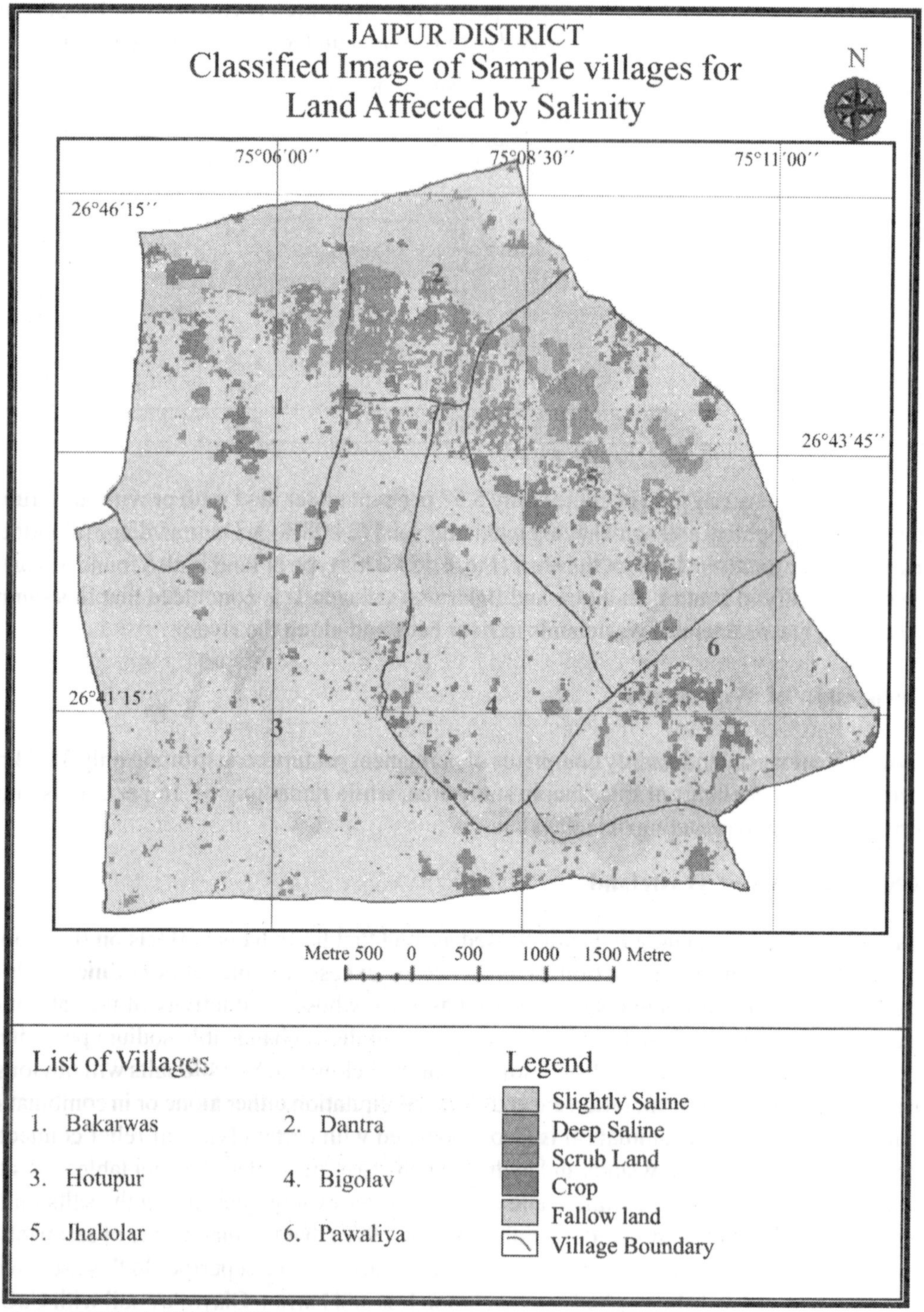

Source : LISS III dated 28th Feb. 2003

Fig. 6.15 : Classified Image of Sample villages for Land Affected by Salinity

Plate 19 : Jowar crop on saline calcareous soil in rainy season on Dudu-Majmabad Road in Dudu Tehsil.

Plate 20 : Afforestation in gullied-ravinous land under Aravalli. Reforestation Programme in Indergarh village (Jamwa Ramgarh Tehsil).

Utilization of Wastelands

Generally saline soils are utilized for producing kharif crops especially jowar. These soils have more moisture holding capacity so cultivators used to grow jowar and 'urd' in rainy season. In this season salt from the surface is washed away with rainy water.

SAMPLE STUDY AREA FOR LAND AFFECTED BY ALKALINITY

This area lies between 27°46′11′′ to 27°30′32′′ North latitude and 75°21′52′′ to 75°29′53′′ East longitude (Fig. 6.18) having an area 132.25 km^2.

Fig. 6.16 shows that contours of 340, 360 and spot heights indicates the general elevation from the MSL. The Bandi an important seasonal river passes through the eastern part of the study area while a small tributary "Sadriya" enters from the south east and finally joins the Bandi river after this sample study area.

The geology of this area has developed in aeolian alluvial materials on nearly level to gently sloping lands. The soils have developed from recent local alluvium of metamorphic and igneous origin from Aravallies. But at few localities of the tract includes coastal and littoral alluvium and aeolian sand.

Generally the soils are light in texture varying from loamy sand to sandy loam having low fertility status. The structure of the soils in general in single grain but alkali soils may have prismatic structure. At some places platy structure is also noted particularly in low permeable soils. There is no perennial river however, Bandi river passes through the area and water flow through it during rainy season.

Total population of this area is 8087 consisting 2275 S.C. and 830 S.T. population. Average population density is 173 per km^2 having maximum in Mahlan (232) and Nasnota (128) villages. About two-fifth population (38.39%) belongs to S.C. and S.T. categories. Maximum percentage of S.C. is concentrated in Mahlan (37.13%) while S.T. in Girdharipura (42.38%). 63.29 per cent population engaged in agriculture with highest in Kapriyawas Kalan (76.67%), Girdharipura (73.71%) and Nasnota (63.36%) villages while it is lowest in Jharna (58.85%) and Mahlan (59.69%) villages. The working population of Mahlan village is almost equally engaged as cultivators (38.92%), agricultural labourers (28.77%) and other workers (39.08%) as most of the population of this village is employed in non-agricultural activities due to its location on N.H. 8 and nearby of Jaipur city.

General Land use

Land use/land cover pattern is almost identical in salinity and alkalinity affected sample villages (Fig. 6.13B and 6.16B). However, the formation and characteristics are quietly different of both the categories. Table 6.19 shows the land use/land cover pattern of the sample villages for land affected by alkalinity.

Table 6.18 reveals that this sample study area occupies more area under permanent pastures, culturable waste and land put to non-agricultural uses due to poor quality of soils and groundwater resources for the development of agriculture. Maximum permanent pasture is recorded in Kapriyawas Kalan village followed by Kotjewar, Jharna and Nasnota villages while highest percentage of culturable waste is concentrated in Girdharipura and Jharna villages therefore these villages occupy more area under land not available for cultivation. It

Table 6.18 : General Land Use in Sample villages for Land Affected by Alkalinity 2003-04

S. No	Name of the village	Geographical area in hectares	Percentage to the Total Geographical Area													
			Area Not Available for Cultivation						Uncultivated Land Excluding Fallow			Follow lands			Net sown Area
			Forest	Hills	Usar and Barren	Land Put to Non Agricultural Uses	Parmanent Pasture	Total	Culturable wasteland	Mics. Tree & Groves	Total	Current fallow	Old Fallow	Total	Total irrigated and unirrigated
1	Girdharipura	265	–	–	–	3.40	7.17	10.57	19.24	–	19.24	7.92	6.41	14.33	55.85
2	Jharna	601	–	–	–	5.82	15.81	21.63	14.14	–	14.14	1.16	15.97	17.13	47.22
3	Kapriyawas Kalan	961	–	–	–	16.79	18.52	35.31	6.66	–	6.66	4.05	6.50	10.55	43.56
4	Kotjewar	540		5.18	–	13.70	16.11	35.00	–	–	–	4.44	8.52	12.96	52.03
5	Mahlan	1613	–	–	–	12.71	7.62	20.33	7.38	0.56	7.94	5.83	9.05	14.88	52.20
6	Nasnota	963	–	–	–	8.93	14.64	22.84	6.64	-	6.64	1.56	9.34	10.90	58.88
	Total	4673	–	060	–	11.23	12.69	24.37	7.79	0.19	7.98	4.11	10.40	14.51	51.87

Source: Land Record Section, Dudu tehsil, District Jaipur.

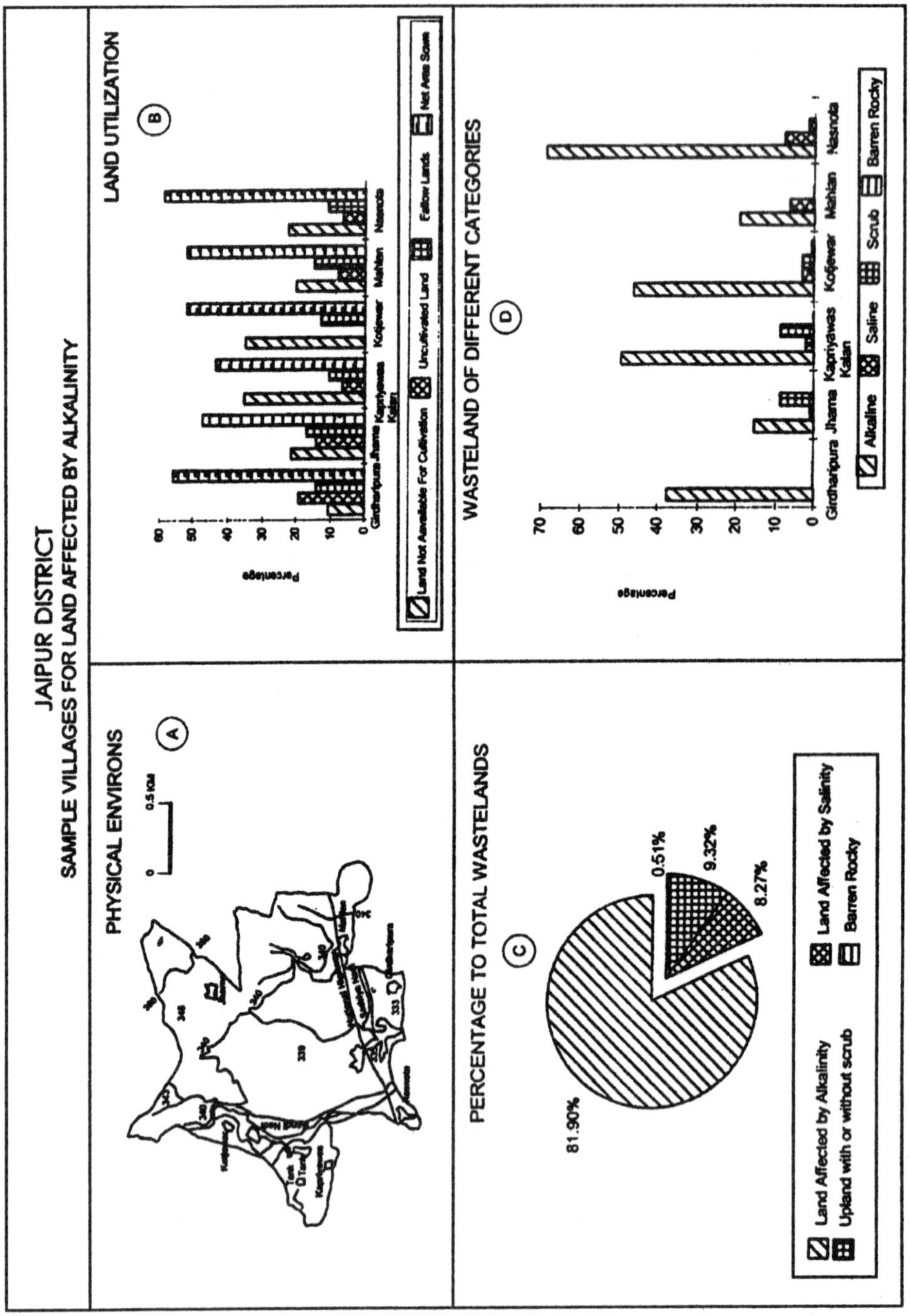

Fig. 16 : Sample Villages for Land Affected by Alalinity.
Fig. 16A : Physical Environs.
Fig. 16B : Land Utilization
Fig. 16C : Percentage to Total Wastelands.
Fig. 16D : Wasteland of Different Categories.

is maximum in Kapriyawas followed by Kotjewar, Nasnota and Jharna villages (Fig. 6.16B). In this sample study area, approximately one-seventh land is kept as fallow to maintain soil fertility. Due to unfavourable pedological and hydrological conditions, average net sown area is only 51.87 percent to the total geographical area (Table 6.18). The maximum net sown area is found in Nasnota village followed by Girdharipura Mahlan and Kotjewar while it is lowest in Kapriyawas Kalan (43.56%) and Jharna villages (Fig. 6.16B).

Out of the six, the three villages have very low percentages of irrigated area i.e. Nasnota (3.51%), Kapriyawas Kalan (5.97%) and Kotjewar (14.93%) villages due to poor quality and quantity of ground water resources.

Identification of Wastelands in Sample Study Area for Land Affected by Alkalinity

Satellite image of this area (Fig. 6.17) indicates the following categories of wastelands.

Table 6.19 : Identification of Wasteland in Sample Study Area for Land Affected by Alkalinity

S. No	Wasteland category	Area in hectares	Percentage to total geographical area	Percentage to the total wastelands
1	Land affected by alkalinity	1581.06	37.55	81.90
2	Land affected by salinity	159.66	3.79	8.27
3	Land with scrub of without scrub	179.94	4.27	9.32
4	Barren Rocky	9.79	0.23	0.51
	Total	1930.45	45.84	100.00

Source : LISS III Satellite image, Feb. 28, 2003

The above table shows that 37.55 per cent of the total geographical area is under land affected by alkalinity i.e. 81.90 per cent of the total wastelands (Fig. 6.16C). Thus land affected by alkalinity is the dominant wasteland followed by land with or without scrub. In this sample study area, major problem in of alkaline and due to this most of the area is without vegetation. Small scattered patches of salinity can also be seen in the area (Fig. 6.18).

Spatial Distribution of Wastelands in Sample Villages for Land Affected by Alkalinity

On the basis of statistics obtained from the classified image (Fig. 6.18) of this sample study area, the following categories of wasteland are found in a cluster of sample villages selected for the detailed study of land affected by alkalinity.

Table 6.20 : Wastelands in Sample Villages for Land Affected by Alkalinity

S. No	Name of the village	Percentage of wasteland of the total geographical area				Total
		Alkaline	Saline	Scrub	Barren Rocky	
1	Girdharpura	37.75	0.46	0.55	–	38.76
2	Jharna	15.52	1.17	8.81	–	25.50
3	Kapriyawas Kalan	49.80	2.43	8.72	0.63	61.58
4	Kotjewar	46.33	3.27	3.14	0.99	53.73
5	Mahlan	19.56	6.42	0.48	–	26.46
6	Nasnota	68.98	7.85	1.73	–	78.56
	Total	37.55	3.79	4.27	–	45.84

Source : LISS III, Satellite Image, February 28, 2003

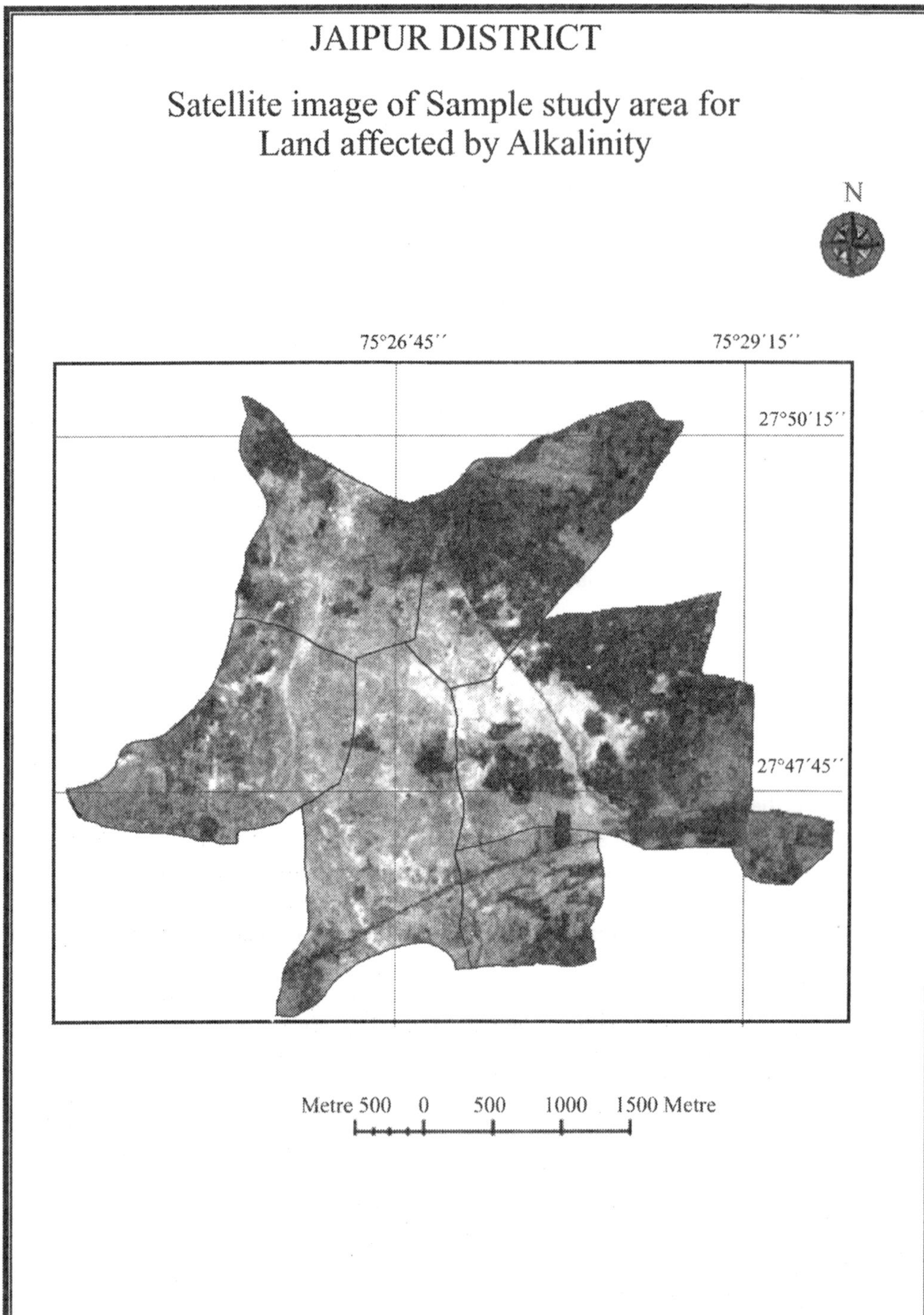

Source : LISS III dated 28th Feb. 2003

Fig. 6.17 : Satellite image of sample study area for land affected by Alkalinity

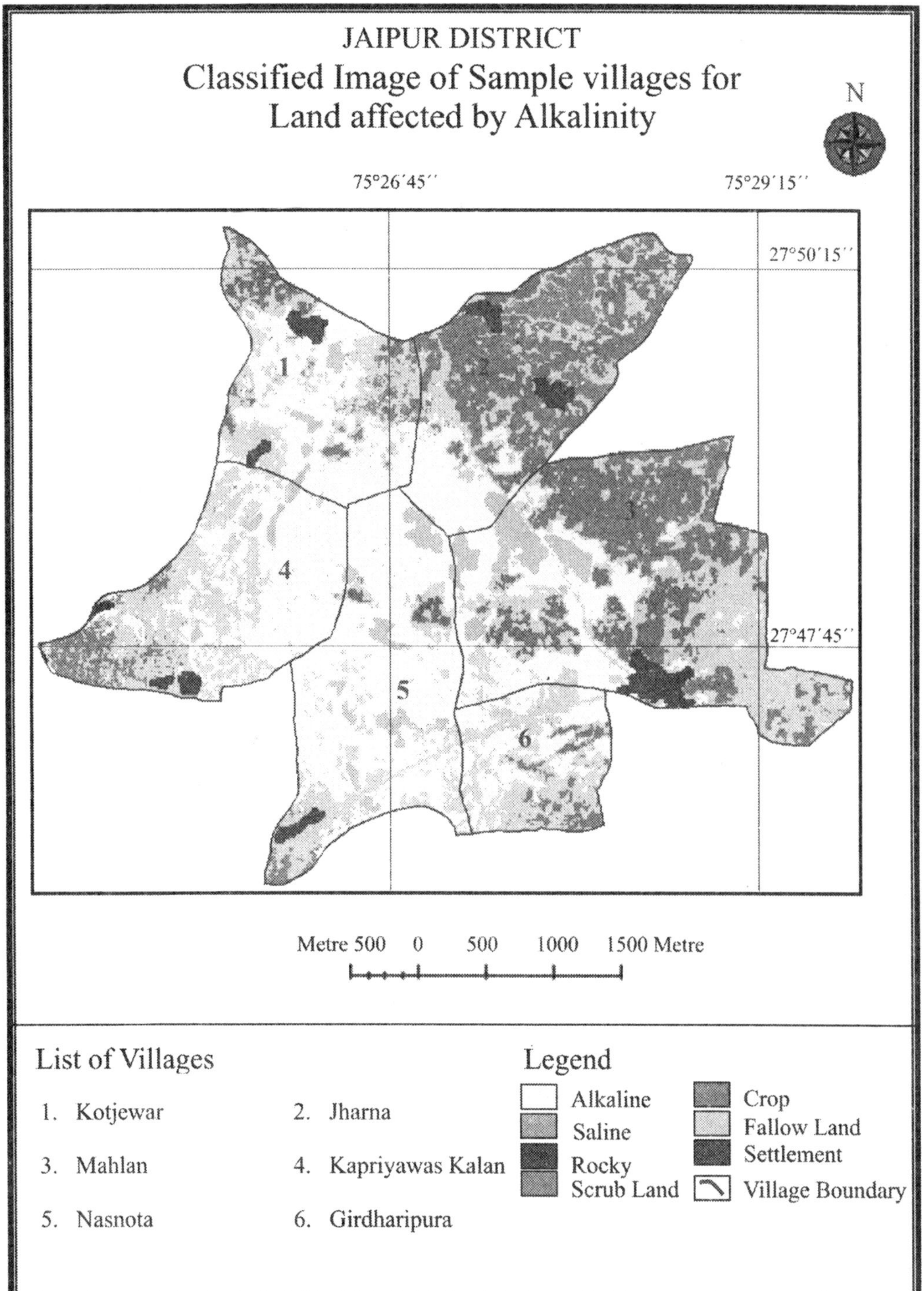

Source : LISS III dated 28th Feb. 2003, Processed at : B.M. Birla Science & Technology Centre, Jaipur

Fig. 6.18 : Classified Image of Sample Villages for Land affected by Alkalinity

Table 6.21 : Alkalinity Hazards and Analysis of Saturation Extract of Soils of Different Profiles

Horizon	Depth (cm)	pH	EC of saturation extract dsm-1 at 25°C	Solicity/ alkalinity hazard	Water soluble cations (me L^{-1})			SAR	SSP (%)	Water soluble anions (Me L^{-1})				RSC me L^{-1}
					Ca^{2+} Mg^{2+}	Na^+	K^+			Co_3^{2-}	HCO_3^-	SO_4^{2-}	Cl^-	
Profile P_1 Mahlan														
A_p	0-27	8.9	1.66	n_1	1.8	13.8	0.6	14.55	85.19	4.4	5.8	2.8	3.2	8.4
B_1	27-49	9.7	1.64	n_2	1.7	13.9	0.4	15.08	86.88	4.2	5.2	3.0	3.4	7.7
BC	49-83	9.6	1.48	n_2	1.5	12.6	0.4	14.55	86.90	3.9	4.6	2.9	3.2	7.0
C_m	83-122	9.3	1.58	n_2	1.4	13.9	0.3	16.61	89.10	3.6	5.0	3.1	3.6	7.2
Profile P_2 Jharna														
A_p	0-30	9.8	1.32	n_2	1.2	11.00	0.8	14.20	84.62	4.3	5.8	1.7	1.2	8.9
B_1	30-63	9.6	1.46	n_2	0.8	12.8	0.6	20.24	90.14	4.2	5.6	2.1	2.5	9.0
BC	63-94	9.2	1.54	n_2	0.6	14.0	0.5	25.56	92.72	3.5	5.1	3.2	3.3	8.0
C_m	94-131	9.0	1.56	n_1	1.4	13.5	0.4	16.14	88.24	3.6	4.0	3.8	3.9	9.0
Profile P_3 Nasnota														
A_p	0-23	8.8	1.66	n_1	1.6	13.8	0.8	15.43	85.19	4.2	5.6	3.1	3.4	8.2
A_2	23-52	8.7	1.72	n_1	1.6	14.7	0.7	16.43	86.47	4.5	6.2	3.0	3.3	9.1
BC	52-88	8.5	1.78	n_1	1.4	15.5	0.6	18.53	88.87	4.6	5.8	3.2	3.8	8.2
C_m	88-136	8.4	1.82	n_1	1.4	15.9	0.5	19.00	89.33	4.1	5.8	3.9	4.1	7.7

Table 6.20 and Fig. 6.16D reveal that maximum land affected by alkalinity is in Nasnota followed by Kapriyawas Kalan, Kotjzewar and Girdharpura villages. These villages have more than one-third to two-third alkaline land, while it is lowest in Mahlan and Jharna villages. Land with scrub is only 4.27 per cent to the total geographical area. It is maximum in Jharna bollowed by Kapriyawas Kalan villages (Fig. 6.16). Land affected by salinity is maximum in Nasnota and Mahlan villages. Maximum wastelands are concentrated in Nasnota, Kapriyawas Kalan and Kotjewar where it ranges between 53.73 to 78.56 per cent to their geographical area. In remaining villages, it is less than one-third in their total area under this category (Table 6.21).

Characteristics of Wastelands

This area has been threatened by the problem of alkalinity and has been rendered uncultivable and unprofitable for cultivation. Land affected by alkalinity is further increasing day by day and many farmers have stopped cultivation on this land.

Soil reaction is one of the most important property of soils because it controls availability of nutrients, microbial activity and physical conditions of soils upto a great extent. The following table shows alkalinity hazards and analysis of saturation extract of soils of different profiles.

Alkalinity Class	*Symbol*	*pH*
Slight to negligible	n0	7.5-8.3
Moderate	n1	8.3-9.0
Strong	n2	9.0-9.8
Severe	n3	>9.8

Table 6.21 shows that pH of soils (1:2 soil water suspension) varies from 8.9 to 9.7, 9.0 to 9.8 and 8.4 to 8.8 in profile no P_1, P_2 and P_3 respectively.

Thus, over all pH values of soils of different profiles ranged from 8.4 to 9.8, therefore, these are alkaline in reaction. Soils of all these profiles are also rich in soluble sodium which is responsible for high pH. The amount of calcium carbonate varies from 4.5 to 8.0, 4.5 to 9.0 and 2.5 to 6.5 per cent in profile no P_1, P_2 and P_3 respectively. An increasing trend of $CaCo_3$ content with depth was observed in all the profiles. The content of Ca^{2+} +mg was low because in the presence of bicarbonate ions and high pH values. The content of bicarbonate in surface soils are 5.8, 5.8 and 5.6 me L^{-1} in profiles number P_1, P_2, and P_3 respectively.

The organic carbon content of these soils had generally been very low (0.030 to 0.141%) because of the absence of natural vegetation, low precipitation and high temperature leading to extremely high oxidising conditions. Soils of this area were rated as medium in available phosphorus (15.38 to 24.62 kg ha^{-1}). The available potassium content in surface horizons of these profiles are observed as 192.64, 197.12 and 174.72 kg ha^{-1} respectively. Soils under study are found medium in available potassium.

SAMPLE STUDY AREA FOR DEGRADED PASTURE/GRAZING LAND

This area (16.41 km^2, 2891 population) is situated between 26°40′50″ N to 26°42′52″ N and 75°36′00″ to 75°39′30″ E (Fig. 6.21) in Phagi tehsil in the southern part of the district (Fig. 6.0). This area is almost levelled with numerous tanks/ponds. Major tanks are

Table 6.22 : General Land Use in Sample Villages for Degraded Pasture/Grazing Land 2003-04

S. No	Name of Village	Geographical area in hectares	Percentage to the Total Geographical Area													
			Area Not Available for Cultivation						Uncultivated Land Excluding Fallow			Fallow lands			Net sown Area
			Forest	Hills	Usar and Barren	Land Put to Non Agricultural uses	Pasture	Total	Culturable wasteland	Mics. Tree & Groves	Total	Current fallow	Old Fallow	Total	Total irrigated and unirrigated
1	Harsuliya	820	–	–	–	5.49	11.58	17.07	2.68	–	2.68	17.68	11.95	29.63	50.61
2	Janakinath-pura	405	–	–	1.48	7.65	21.73	30.86	1.73	–	1.73	22.22	4.69	26.91	40.49
3	Khejra Ka Bas	165	–	–	0.60	3.63	15.75	20.00	0.60	–	0.60	23.64	13.33	36.97	47.27
4	Raipura	439	–	–	1.14	6.83	6.52	14.49	5.46	–	5.46	21.68	11.39	33.07	47.60
	Total	1829	–	–	0.65	6.12	12.96	19.73	2.95	–	2.95	20.06	10.33	30.39	47.34

Source : Land Record Section, Phagi Tehsil, District Jaipur.

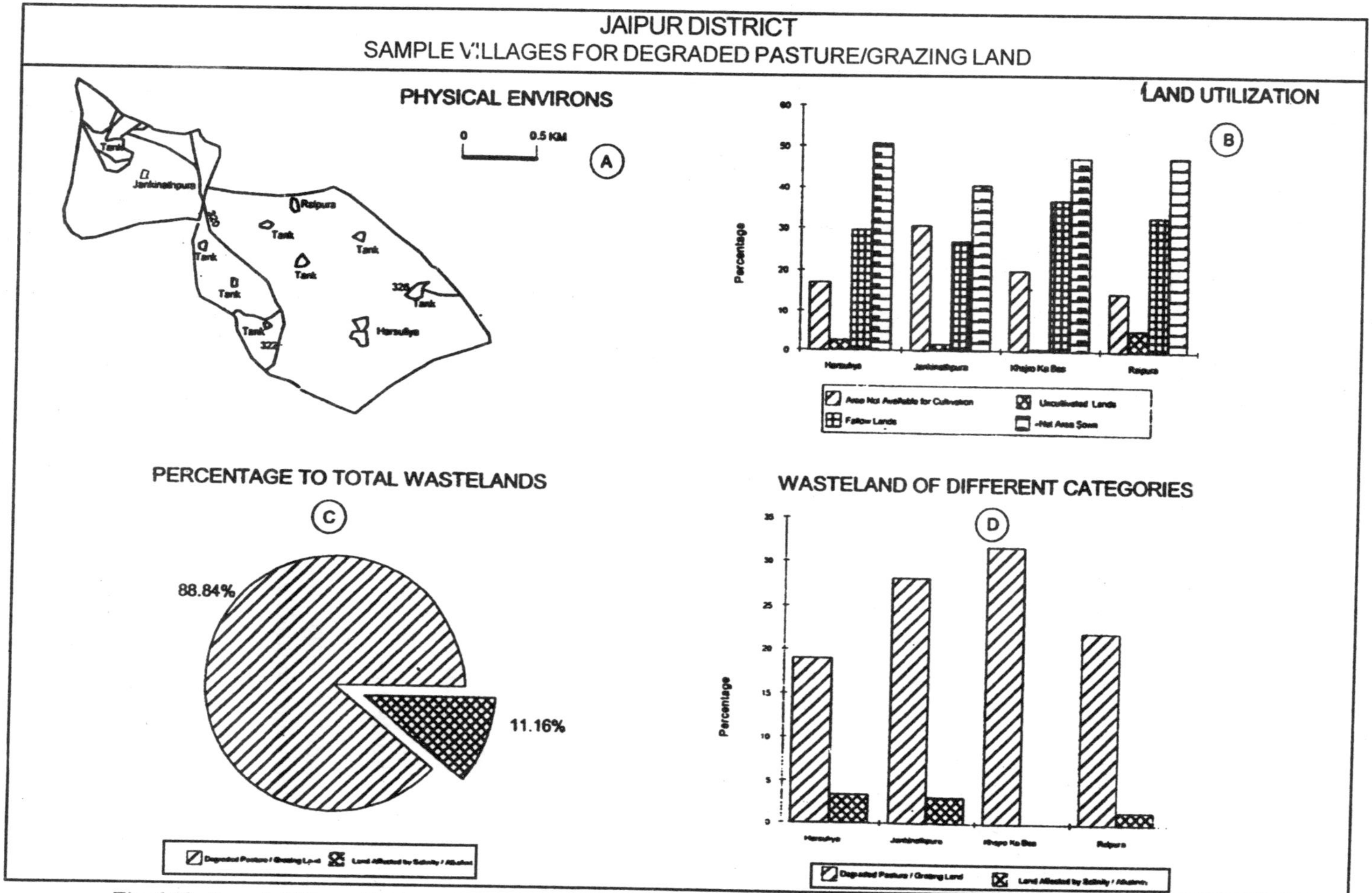

Fig. 6.19 : Sample Villages for Degraded Pasture/Grazing Land.
Fig. 6.19A : Physical Environs.
Fig. 6.19B : Land Utilization.
Fig. 6.19C : Percentage to Total Wastelands.
Fig. 6.19D : Wasteland of Different Categories.

Janakinathpura and Harsuliya while other seven small ponds are scattered in this area (Fig. 6.19A). A contour of 320 metre passes through the middle of the area, indicates its average elevation. The highest point of the area is 326m in the north east of Harsuliya village and lowest point i.e. 317m near the western boundary of Raipura village. There is no perennial river, however several small undefined streams join the tanks/ponds of this area. Soil is dominantly fine textured (clay loam to clay), poorly drained, calcium carbonate layer at a depth ranging between 40 and 105 cm and nearly level to gently sloping land.

Average population density is 158 per square kilometre with maximum in Harsuliya (241) village while it is lowest in Jankinathpura (75) due to problems of water logging and land affected by salinity/alkalinity. One-third population of Harsuliya village belongs to S.C. category. Over 80 percent working population engaged in agriculture with highest in Khejra Ka Bas (90.12%) and Jankinathpura (85.26%) villages.

General Land use

Due to population pressure, poor quality land has been also taken under cultivation. Inspite of this, large tracts of the villages are lying still as open scrub. Table 6.22 shows land use pattern in villages of the sample study area for degraded pasture/grazing land.

This table shows that approximately one-fourth area of the Jankinathpura village is lying as pasture/grazing land followed by Khejra Ka Bas and Harsuliya. As already mentioned that this area has salinity/alkalinity problem due to waterlogging and poor quality ground water resources. Due to this, the cultivators are compelled to adopt dryland farming system and keep their approximately one-third cultivated land fallow for maintaining soil fertility or for producing less water requiring rabi crops like gram and mustard. Fig. 6.19B indicates that Khejra Ka Bas villages keeps her more than one-third area under fallow land followed by Raipura, Harsuliya and Jankinathpura villages. The irrigated land is also very low in these villages i.e. 6.05 per cent in Jankinathpura followed by Raipura (12.84%) causes less sown area. The maximum NSA (50.60%) is in Harsuliya village due to loamy sand soil in northern and southern part of the village which is very clear from the satellite image (Fig. 6.20) of this area. In other villages it is 40 to 47.61 per cent to the total geographical area (Fig. 6.19B).

Identification of Wastelands

From the LISS III satellite image (Fig. 6.20) the following categories of wastelands have been identified in this sample study area.

Table 6.23 : Identification of Wastelands in Sample Study Area for Degraded Pasture/Grazing land

Wasteland category	Area in hectares	% of the total area	Percentage the total wastelands
1. Degraded Pasture/Grazing land	369.09	22.50	88.84
2. Land affected by salinity/ alkalinity	46.3	2.8	11.16
Total	415.46	25.33	100.00

Source : LISS III satellite image, February 28, 2003.

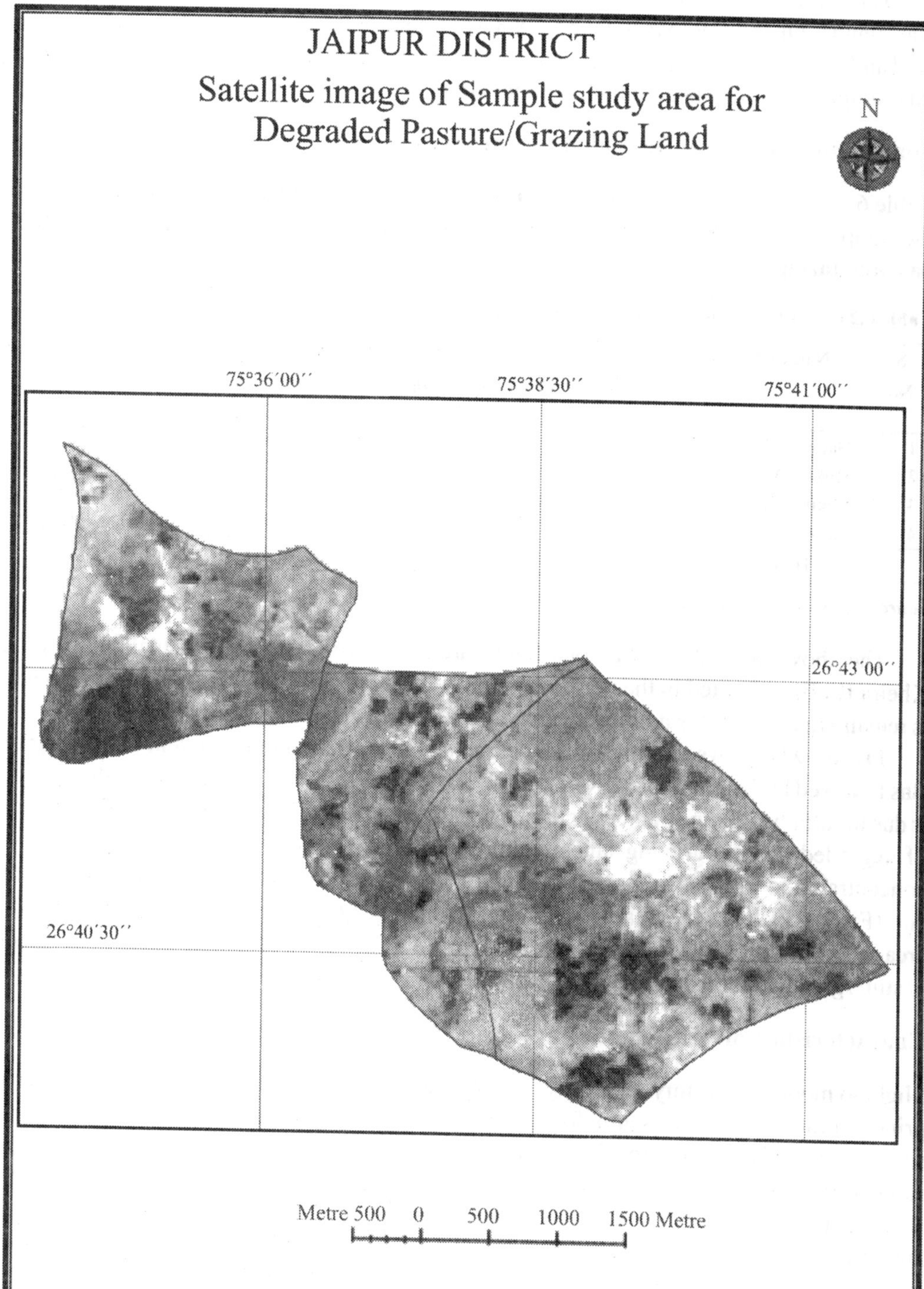

Source : LISS III dated 28th Feb. 2003. Processed at : B.M. Birla Science & Technology Centre, Jaipur

Fig. 6.20 : Satellite image of Sample study area for Land Degraded Pasture/Grazing Land.

Table 6.23 shows that one-fourth land (25.33%) of the sample study area is under wastelands. Of the total wastelands, 88.84 per cent belongs to degraded pasture/grazing land and remaining 11.16 per cent occupies by salinity/alkalinity (Fig 6.19C). It indicates that this sample study area is dominantly under degraded pasture/grazing land.

Spatial Distribution of Degraded Pasture/Grazing Land

Table 6.24 reveals that one-fourth land is under wastelands but it is unevenly distributed in the sample villages. The following table shows wastelands in sample villages for degraded pasture/grazing land.

Table 6.24 : Wastelands in Sample Villages for Degraded Pasture/Grazing land

S. No.	Name of Village	Percentage to the total geographical area		Total Wastelands
		Degraded pasture/grazing land	Saline/alkaline	
1	Harsuliya	19.00	3.43	22.43
2	Jankinathpura	28.17	3.18	31.35
3	Khejra Ka Bas	31.71	–	31.71
4	Raipura	2.05	1.49	23.54
	Total	22.50	2.83	25.33

Source : LISS III satellite image February 28, 2003

The above table shows that one-fourth area is under wastelands in Jankinathpura and Khejra Ka Bas, situated in the north western and western part of the sample study area while is remaining two villages it is approximately one-fourth of the total geographical area.

Fig. 6.19 D shows that maximum percentage of degraded/grazing land is in Khejra Ka Bas followed by Jankinathpura, Raipura and Harsuliya villages. The variation in this category is due to salinity/alkalinity and poor drainage in the sample villages. This distributional pattern of degraded pasture/grazing land is almost same in all the villages as this category is concentrated in the central part of every village except Raipura where it is in the western part (Fig. 6.21). It is very clear from the satellite image of this area (Fig. 6.20) that the saline area is concentrated in a long belt extended from east to west and spatial pattern of degraded pasture/grazing land is also same as saline area.

Characteristics of Wastelands

Slight to moderate salinity/alkalinity, water logging and poor quality of irrigation water are principal limitations in this area for the development of agriculture. As already mentioned soil is clay loam to clay, poorly drained with $CaCo_3$ layer on and below surface. Due to salinity/alkalinity affected land, a large tract of Janakinathpura, central and western part of Raipura and a long belt from east to west in Harsuliya village is under open scrub locally known as 'Kharda'. Trees are almost negligible in southern and eastern part of Jankinathpura and west cenral part of Harsuliya village due to poor quality of soils.

Ownership of Wastelands

Out of the total wastelands in the sample villages, 63 per cent is owned by the government which comprises "Kharda" and permanent pastures while remaining 43 per cent is under

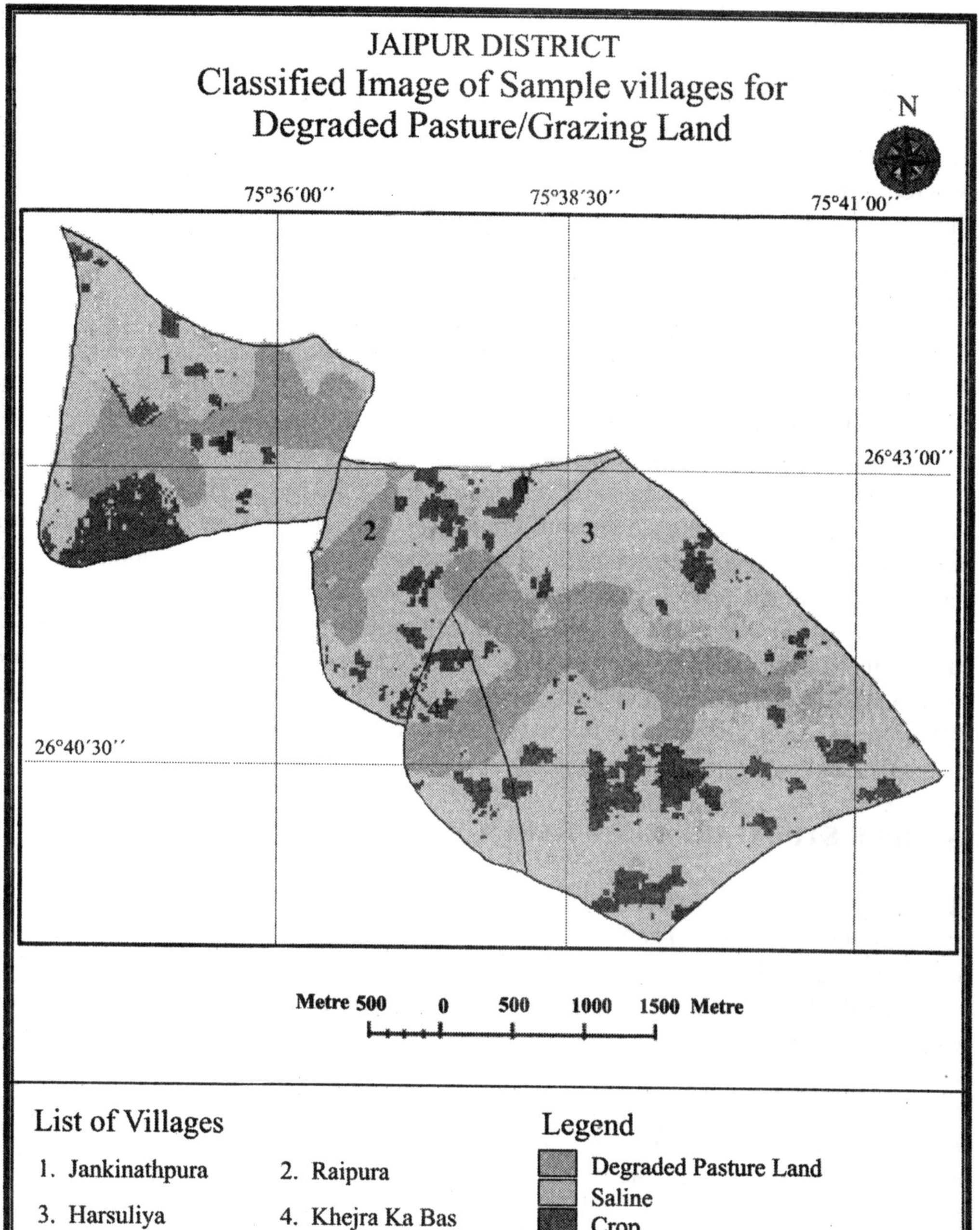

Source : LISS III dated 28th Feb. 2003. Processed at : B.M. Birla Science & Technology Centre, Jaipur

Fig. 6.21 : Classified image of Sample villages for Degraded Pasture/Grazing Land

private ownership. Here greater responsibility lies on government for planning for reclamation/ development of wastelands in this sample study area.

Reasons for Land Lying Waste

Waterlogging due to poor drainage, poor quality soil, poor quality/quantity of groundwater, $CaCO_3$ layer on the surface or below 0.4 to 1.00 metre and erosion hozards are principal limitations in development of wastelands.

Reclamation of Wastelands by Farmers themselves

For increase crop yield, cultivators adopt deep ploughing by disc harrow at the rate of Rs. 640 to 800 per hectare. The reclaimed land is utilized for producing jowar and it is kept fallow is kharf season for sowing gram and mustard in rabi season. However, the rabi crops on unirrigated land depend on the rains in the last week of August or first week of September.

There is good scope for pasture development in eastern part of Harsuliya village due to loamy sand soil. In this area "Dhaman" grass and "Adu" trees can be developed under the watershed development programme. In 1985, silvipasture development programme had been taken in this village, but without co-operation of villagers, this could not be success. Now again silvipasture programme should be taken with peoples participation for getting sufficient fodder, fuel and income from auction "Adu" trees. Other government land lying in "Khardo" is not suitable for silvipasture development due to waterlogged problem/depressions. However "Ronj" trees can be developed in this area. Besides this financial assistance should be given to the BPL cultivators for deep ploughing.

SAMPLE STUDY AREA FOR BAREN HILLS/ROCKY

This sample study area is situated from 27°11′28′′N to 27°16′35′′N and from 76°09′23′′E to 76°17′05′′E (Fig. 6.24) in Amber tehsil of Jaipur district (Fig.6). This sample study area occupies 33.51 km^2 and total population is 12124 (2001).

Aravalli hill ranges viz. Bilpur hills, Sundar Ka Bas hills, Deo-Ka Harwara hills, Chandwaji-Salarwas hills and Arniya hills etc. are running from south east to north east in the sample study area (Fig. 6.22A and 6.23). The height of the hills is decreasing from south to north east. The highest peak of this area is of Beelpur hill range (604 m). Other important peaks are Deo-Ka Harwara (586 m), Sundar Ka Bas (581 m) and Chandwaji (555 m). Hills of southern and eastern part are covered with degraded forest while the remaining hills are almost barren (Fig. 6.24). The general slope of the area is from west to east as a seasonal river "Dhudhala" and its tributaries originate from the hills of this area flow from west to east and join Manoharpur river, a tributary of Banganga river near Pilwa village (Fig. 6.22). This river was perennial before four-five decades as spring water of the hills used to flow in this channel. Four nallahs from the left and three from the right join the river. Soils are 'Kankarili' near foot hills while in remaining area the soil belongs to loamy sand category.

Average population density is 382 persons per square kilometre with maximum in Chandwaji (1891) followed by Sunder Ka Bas (460), Deo Ka Harwara (370) and Peelwa (362) villages while lowest density is in the villages of northern part viz. in Salarwas (240)

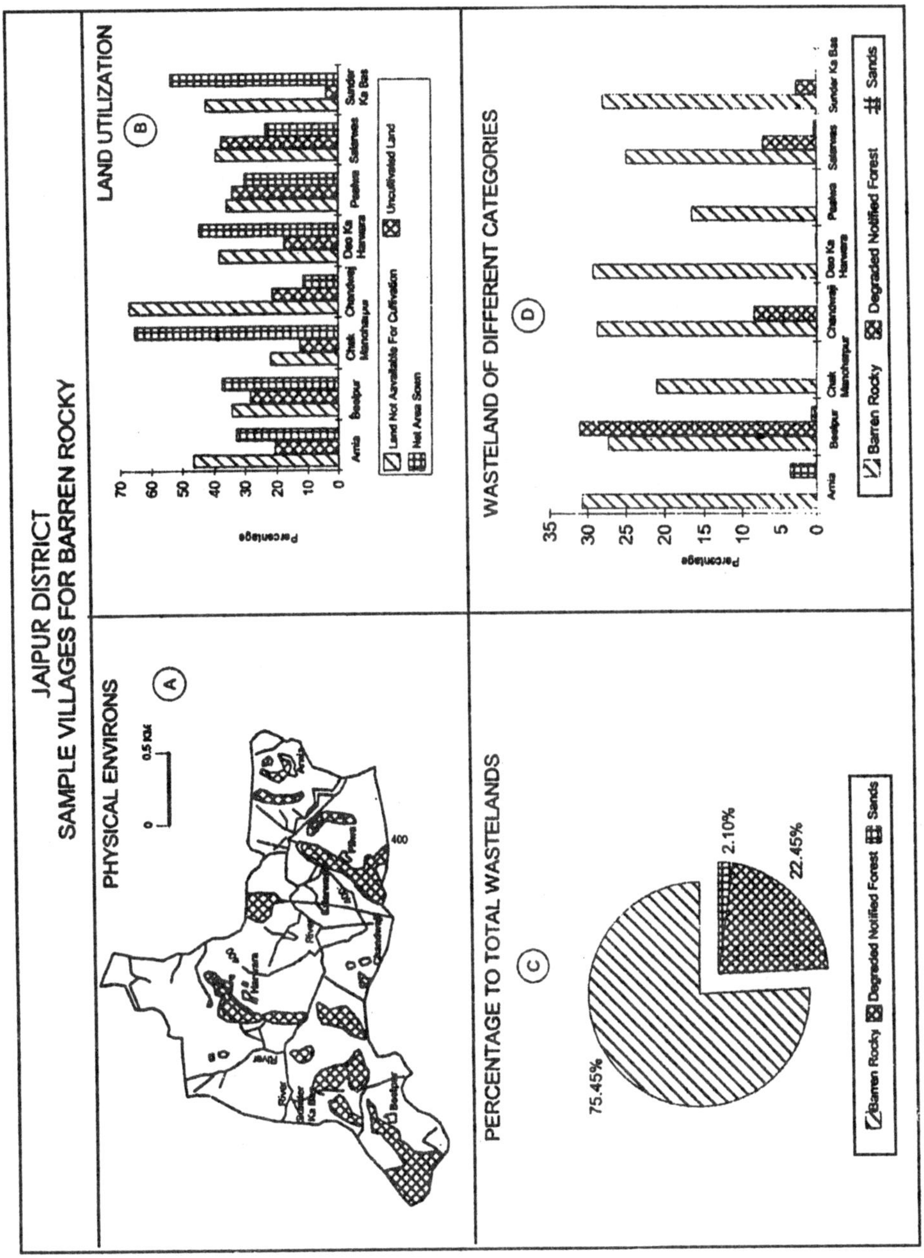

Fig. 6.22 : Sample Villages for Barren Rocky.
Fig. 6.22A : Physical Environs.
Fig. 6.22B : Land Utilization.
Fig. 6.22C : Percentage to Total Wastelands.
Fig. 6.22D : Wasteland of Different Categories.

Table 6.25 : Land Use in Sample Villages for Barren Hill/Rocky 2003-04

S. No.	Name of Village	Geographical area in hectares	Percentage to the total geographical area												Net shown area
			Area Not Available for Cultivation						Uncultivated land Excluding Fallow Lands						
			Forest	Hills	Kankarili Land	Land Put to Non Agricultural users	Pastures/ Grazing land	Total	Current Fallow	Old Fallow	Total	Culturable waste	Misc. tree & groves	Total	
1	Arnia	620	–	12.26	17.58	6.77	9.84	46.45	10.00	6.45	16.45	4.03	–	4.03	33.06
2	Beelpur	439	22.78	4.18	2.73	2.96	11.37	34.17	8.65	5.01	13.66	3.42	11.39	14.81	37.36
3	Chok Manoharpur	550	–	8.73	4.18	5.82	3.27	22.00	5.09	6.18	–	–	1.45	1.45	65.27
4	Chandwaji	103	–	28.15	–	18.45	19.41	66.99	14.56	4.85	19.41	1.94	–	1.94	11.65
5	Deo Ka Harwara	505	–	18.41	2.97	7.72	8.91	38.01	11.09	4.75	15.84	1.58	–	1.58	44.55
6	Peelwa	447	–	13.42	3.15	5.59	13.42	35.79	23.94	10.07	35.01	–	–	–	30.20
7.	Salarwas	248	8.04	8.04	1.21	8.87	12.90	39.11	17.74	17.74	35.48	1.61	–	1.61	23.39
8.	Sunder Ka Bas	439	11.45	20.23	–	10.69	–	42.37	4.20	–	4.20	–	–	0.0	53.43
	Total	3351	4.47	11.85	5.31	6.59	7.22	35.44	10.68	6.38	17.06	1.61	–	1.73	42.40

Source : Land Record Section, Amber tehsil, District Jaipur.

and Chak Manoharpur (285). Scheduled Tribes population is concentrated in Salarwas (89.58%) and Peelwa (39.84%) villages while maximum Scheduled Caste population is in Arnia (14.58%) village. Average literacy in this area is recorded 55.94 per cent with maximum in Beelpur (74.91%), Chandwaji (71.79%) and Salarwas (62.61%) due to more educational institutions in Chandwaji and nearly town Manoharpur. Approximately two-third population of this area is engaged directly in agriculture with highest in Chak Manoharpur (93.30%) followed by Sunder Ka Bas (90.32%) due to more fertile soils and adequate groundwater resources while it is lowest in Chandwaji (7.32%) as Chandwaji, the biggest village has urban characteristics, while in other villages, stone quarrying is also an important economic activity.

General Land Use

Forested area is only 4.47 per cent to the total geographical area in sample villages with maximum in Beelpur (22.78%) followed by Sunder Ka Bas (11.45%) and Salarwas village (8.04%). The first two villages are situated in the western part while the last village is in the eastern part of the study area.

Table 6.25 reveals that barren hills, Kankarili land and pasture/grazing land constitute more than one-third land under the category of land not available for cultivation. The maximum concentration of this category is in Chandwaji village followed by Arania, Salarwas and Deo-Ka Harwara villages. The lowest percentage under this category is in Chak Manoharpur (22.00%) village. One-sixth area is under fallow land due to drought conditions during the last several years. The maximum fallow land is found in Peelwa (34.06%), Salarwas (35.48%) and Chandwaji (19.41%) villages (Fig. 6.22.B).

Only two-fifth area (42.40%) is recorded under net sown area due to more area under barren hills, Kankarili land and pasture/grazing land. The maximum concentration of NSA is in Chak Manoharpur (65.27%) and Sunder Ka Bas (53.43%) villages due to more irrigation from ground water resources. In other villages it varies between 11.65 and 44.53 per cent to the total geographical area (Fig.6.22.B).

Identification of Wastelands

On the basis of LISS III satellite image (Fig. 6.23) the following type of wastelands in the sample study area for barren rocky have been identified.

Table 6.26 : Identification of Wastelands in Sample Study Area for Barren Hill/Rocky

S. No.	Wasteland category	Area in hectares	Percentage to the total geographical area	Percentage to the total wastelands
1.	Bareen Rocky	868.67	26.69	75.45
2.	Degraded Notified Forest land	258.46	7.94	22.45
3.	Sands riverian	24.07	0.74	2.10
	Total	1151.20	35.37	100.00

Source : LISS III Satellite image February 28, 2003.

The above table shows that more than one-third land (35.37%) of the sample study area is under wastelands. Of the total wastelands 75.44 per cent belongs to barren rocky,

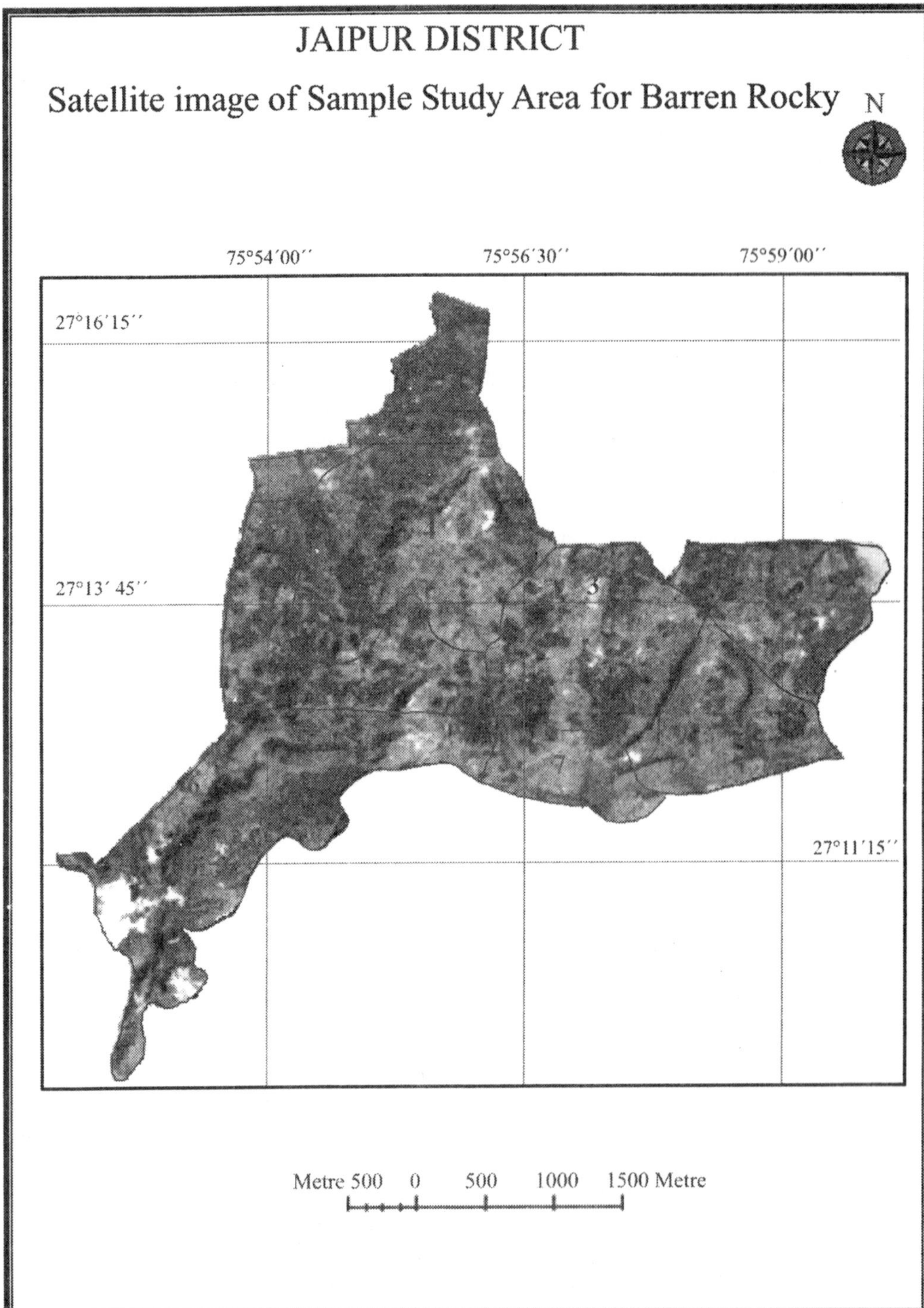

Source : LISS III dated 28th Feb. 2003. Processed at : B.M. Birla Science & Technology Centre, Jaipur

Fig. 6.23 : Satellite image of Sample Study Area for Barren Rocy.

22.45 per ent to degraded forest and reaming 2.10 per cent to sands riverian (Fig. 6.22 C).

Spatial Distribution of Wastelands

The spatial distribution of wastelands in the villages is uneven which is clear from the following Table 6.27.

Table 6.27 : Wastelands in Sample Villages for Barren Hill/Rocky

S. No.	Name of village	Percentage of wasteland to the total Geographical Area			Total waste lands
		Barren rocky	Degraded notified forest	Sands riverian	
1.	Arniya	30.69	–	3.74	34.43
2.	Beelpur	27.40	31.14	0.80	59.34
3.	Chak Manoharpur	21.21	–	0.23	21.44
4.	Chandwaji	28.74	8.51	0.09	37.34
5.	Deo-Ka-Harwara	29.25	–	0.34	29.59
6.	Peelwa	16.47	–	0.17	16.64
7.	Salarwas	25.10	7.28	0.62	33.00
8.	Sunder Ka Bas	28.15	2.84	0.04	31.03
	Total	26.69	7.94	0.74	35.37

Source : LISS III Satellite image February 28, 2003.

The above table shows that more than one-fourth land of the sample villages is under barren rocky. The maximum concentration is in Arniya village followed by Deo-Ka Harwara and Chandwaji villages (Fig. 6.22 D). Satellite image (Fig. 6.23) indicates that in almost all the villages generally Aravalli ranges are spread over in scattered form in the direction of south west to north east. Due to human interference these forested hills have been converted into Bareen hills. However, the hills of south-west and eastern part are still covered by degraded forest. Lowest percentages of barren rocky are in Chak Manoharpur and Peelwa villages, situated in the northern and south eastern part of the sample villages.

As already mentioned approximately one-fifth area is under degraded forest of the total wastelands in the sample villages. The maximum area under this category is in Beelpur village (31.14%) followed by Chandwaji and Salarwas. The former village is situated in the south western part, where most of the hills covered by degraded forest while other villages having this category are located in the eastern part of the sample study area (Fig. 6.24). Almost all the villages have also some area under sand riverion due to origin of nallahs from the hills and these nallahs have sand in their bed. The maximum area under sand is in Arniya village (3.74%) while in remaining villages, it is between 0.04 to 0.80 per cent of the total geographical area.

This area occupies more than one-third area (35.31%) under wastelands of the total geographical area. The maximum area is found in the Beelpur village, where three-fifth (59.34%) land is occupied by the wastelands (Table 6.28). In remaining villages it is approximately one-third to their total area excluding Peelwa and Chak Manoharpur villages situated in north and south eastern part of the sample study area.

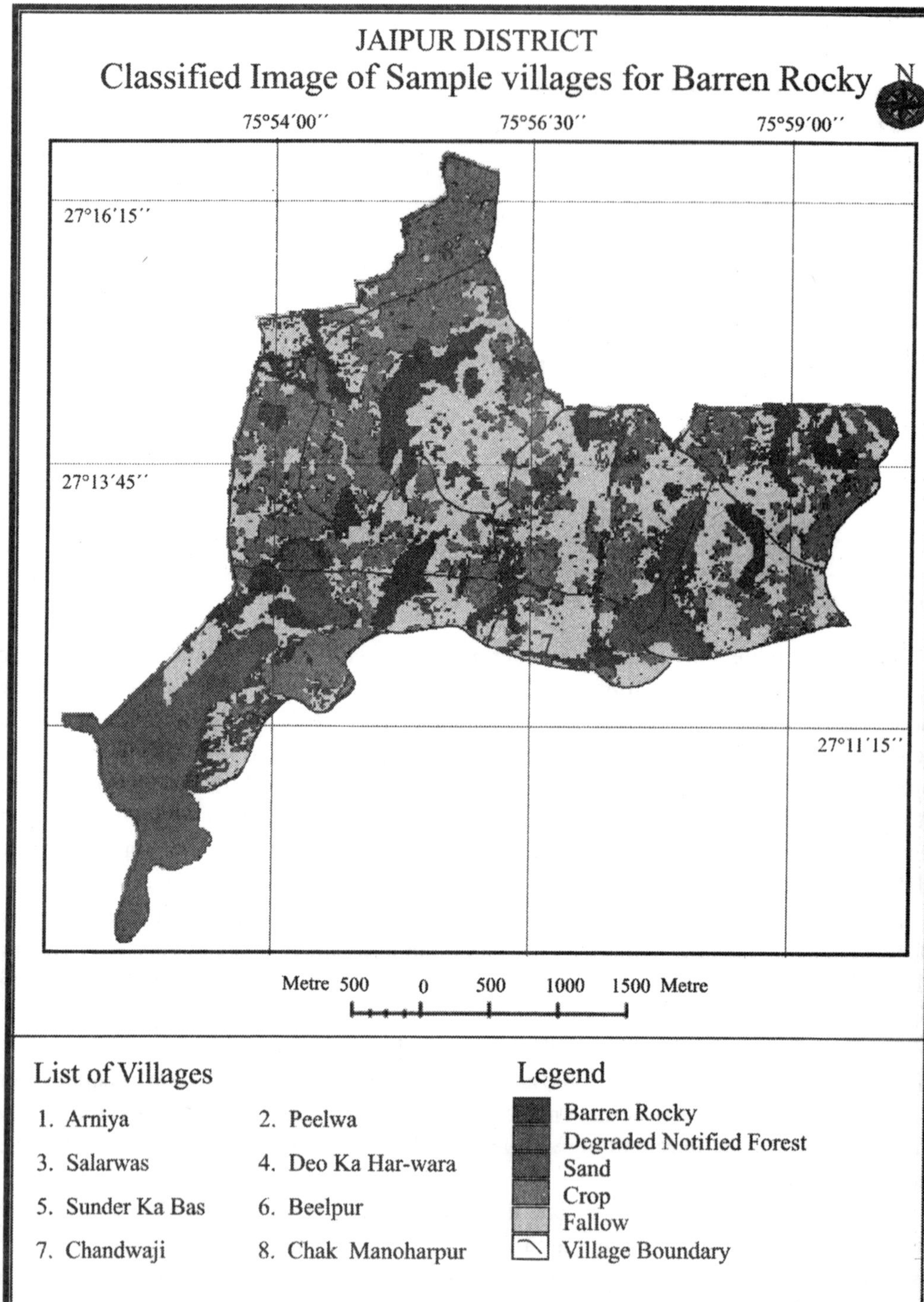

Source : LISS III dated 28th Feb. 2003, Processed at : B.M. Birla Science and Technology Centre, Jaipur

Feb. 6.24 : Classified Image of Sample villages for Barren Rocy

Ownership Pattern

All the wasteland in this sample study area is under the possession of government. Thus development/reclamation of wasteland depends on the government schemes/programmes.

Characteristics of Wastelands

The barren hills are extremely rugged and devoid of any vegetation. Water erosion is continued for the last several decades. As a result these hills have predominance of gravels mixed with soil and stones on the surface. In rainy season, grass seeds grow on the hills but due to grazing the newly born small grass with their roots are lost and finish the species for ever. The hills of south western and eastern part are covered by degraded forest.

Afforestation by the Villages themselves

No efforts have been made by the government for reforestation of barren hills till to date. But "Dev Narain Temple Samiti" (Temple of Gujar caste) developed forest on two hectares near the temple on the foot hills of Deo Narain hill in Deo-Ka Harwara village.

First of all, mining activities must be stopped immediately in this area to save environment and protection from pollution as there are many quarries for grit and massonary stones. Reforestation of these barren hills should be started to improve environment and maintain ecological balance. First of all stone wall/ ditch/wire fencing should be done around all the hills of this area and later on grow thorny trees on upper slopes, sapling in pits, sowing of grass and other seeds between planted pits and regeneration of natural vegetation etc. should be done under peoples participation programmes.

SAMPLE STUDY AREA FOR MINING WASTELANDS

This sample study area is situated between 27°02′28″ to 27°10′45″ North latitude and 76°09′23″ to 76°17′05″ East longitude (Fig. 6.26) in eastern Jamwa Ramgarh tehsil of Jaipur district (Fig. 6.26). These sample villages cover 76.61 km^2 having 7720 persons in 409 households including 3231 Scheduled Tribes and 1513 Scheduled Caste population.

In northern part of this study area, hills are extended from north west to east direction known as Dagtota hills and height of these hills is decreasing in the same direction. The maximum height i.e. 560 m is in the northwest while lowest peak (480m) lies in the southeast. Other intermediate peaks are 540 m and 481m from the MSL. A crescent of ten small hills in the central part of the study area having height of 400 to 480 m is extended in north east direction from Buchara bundh R.F. to the west of Rayanwala bundh and from here take turn from north to southeast direction upto Singhpuri village. The southern part is almost plain having lowest height as contour of 340 metre is passing through southern part in west to south east direction along the Sainthal Sagar river.

Only one perennial river 'Arwari Nadi' flows in northern part of this area. Another important non-perennial river is Sainthal river passes through the southern part. Two small tributaries of western part are coming from north to south, meet each other near Dhani Badon and later on joins Sainthal river on its right bank in southwest of Thali village. In central part, several nallahs origin from the nearby hills, bring rainy water in Rayanwala bundh. Most of the northern part is under reserve forest having fairly dense mixed jungle mainly dhok and degraded forest.

Similar to other areas, this mining area is also situated in the foot hills of Aravalli hills. Due to undulated hilly tracts. The population density is only 101 persons per km^2 with maximum in Thali (241) and Sankotra (126) villages while in remaining villages it is less than 80 (41 to 77 per km^2). This area is also situated in Jamwa Ramgarh tehsil, where S.T. population is dominated. In these sample villages, average percentage of S.T. population is 41 to 85 per cent with maximum in Sankotra (58.90%), Rayanwala (55.40%) and Singhpuri (54.90%) while S.C. population is highest in Singhpuri (45.10%) and Dagota (36.78%) villages. Working population of this area is almost equally engaged in agricultural and mining activities. In Dagota village two-third working population is engaged in mining activities while the population of Sankotra village is equally engaged in both the activities. In remaining villages, ratio of working population is 2:1 in agricultural and mining activities respectively.

General Land use

Aravalli, the oldest mountains/hills of the world are storehouse of the metallic/non-metallic minerals. Almost all the mining activities of the state are concentrated in the Aravalli region. At present most of the marble mining activities are stopped as per the directions of the Supreme Court for the protection of environment of Aravalli hills ecosystem as many mines are located in the forest notified area. Till to date the mine owners are waiting for clearance from the court, so they can restart their work. This mining sample study area situated in the Aravallies, occupies more land under forest and less in net sown area.

Table 6.28 reveals that three-fifth area of the the sample study area under forest. The maximum area under forest is in Dagota village (84.05%) followed by Ranyawala (81.04%) and Singhpuri (75.35%) villages while it is less in Sandkotra (19.46%) and Thali (17.92) villages. The last two villages are situated in the southern plain of the sample study area. The net sown area covers only one-sixth area due to more area under forest, hills and pastures. It is very interesting to note that the villages situated in the northern part of the sample study area have very low percentages of NSA e.g. Dagota village (1.36%), Singhpuri (7.05%) and Ranyawala (9.48%) while it is more in the Thali and Sandkotra villages situated in the southern part of the sample study area.

Identification of Wastelands

Generally mining areas are found in the hilly tract/foothills/ stony land in the district. In this sample study area, all the mining areas are situated in the Aravalli notified forest land. In hilly tracts, degraded notified forest and upland with or without scrub are dominant and same characteristics are found in this sample study area. Table 6.29 shows that more than one-third land is under degraded forest while more than one-half is occupied by the upland with scrubs or without scrub of the total wastelands. Mining wasteland occupies only 4.77 per cent to the total geographical area i.e. less than one-tenth of the total wastelands of the sample study area.

As per the satellite image of February 28, 2003 (Fig. 6.25) the following

Plate 21 : Dumping of mining waste on plain area near Andhi village.

Plate 22 : Cowpea crop on a sand dune in kharif season in Sursinghpura village in Phulera Tehsil.

Table 6.28 : Land Use in Sample study area for Mininsg Wasteland 2003-04

S. No	Name of Village	Geographical area in hectares	Percentage to the total geographical area												Net sown Area
			Area not available for cultivation						Uncultivated excluding fallow land			Fallow land			
			Forest	Hills	Usar and Barren	Land Put to Non Agricultural use	Pastures/ grazing land	Total	Culturable wasteland	Misc. tree & groves	Total	Current Fallow	Old Fallow	Total	
1	Chak Dagota	03	—	—	33.35	—	—	33.33	—	—	—	—	33.33	33.33	33.33
2	Dagota	3449	84.05	8.06	0.49	0.43	0.93	93.97				2.55	1.53	4.08	1.36
3	Ranyawala	823	81.04	0.12	4.86	1.3	1.46	88.70	0.49	1.82	2.31	0.85	0.49	1.34	9.48
4	Sand Kotra	1757	19.46	3.07	0.17	8.99	31.15	44.85	1.99	—	1.99	8.31	11.33	19.64	33.52
5	Singhpuri	284	75.35	—	0.35	1.41	3.52	80.63	0.70	—	0.70	5.98	5.63	11.61	7.05
6	Thali	1345	17.92	0.30	1.26	5.95	8.18	33.60	1.56	—	1.56	17.92	11.97	29.89	34.94
	Total	7661	56.95	3.63	1.79	3.50	5.15	71.03	1.07	—	1.07	6.51	5.99	12.17	15.74

Source : Land Record Section, Jamwa Ramgarh tehsil district Jaipur.

categories of wastelands are identified in the sample study area for mining industrial wasteland.

Table 6.29 : Wastelands Identification of Sample study area for mining/industrial wasteland.

S. No.	Wasteland Category	Area in hectares	Percentage to total geographical area	Percentage to total wasteland
1	Mining	371.64	4.77	8.48
2	Degraded notified forest	1489.48	19.12	34.01
3	Upland with or without scrub	2518.79	32.33	57.51
	Total	4379.91	56.21	100.00

Source : LISS III satellite image, February 28, 2003.

Spatial Distribution of Wastelands in Sample Villages for Mining/Industrial Waste

As mentioned earlier mining areas are situated in the hilly tracts covering dense/degraded forest and upland with scrub or without scrub. The following table shows wastelands in sample villages.

Table 6.30 : Wastelands in Sample Villages for Mining/Industrial Wasteland

S. No.	Name of village	Percentage of wastelands to the total geographical area			Total Wastelands
		Mining/Industrial wasteland	Degraded notified forest land	Upland with or without scrub	
1	Dagota	2.08	35.55	24.57	62.20
2	Rayanwala	6.78	16.30	34.10	57.18
3	Sand Kotra	3.96	0.61	43.87	48.44
4	Singhpuri	2.18	5.04	31.86	39.08
5	Thali	9.31	1.14	39.5	56.22
	Total	4.77	19.12	32.33	56.22

Source : LISS II Satellite image February 28, 2003.

The above table shows that sample villages occupy more than one-half land under wastelands. But the mining wasteland covers only 4.77 per cent to the total geographical area. The maximum area under this category is in Thali and Rayanwala villages, situated in the foothills of Aravalli hill ranges adjoining to the degraded notified forest land. Classified image (Fig. 6.26) indicates that mining activities are concentrted in a narrow long belt extended from south west to north east direction in this study area. At present, all the mining activities are closed due to directions of Supreme Court for stopping mining activities in Aravallies to protect environmental degradation. As discussed in preceding paragraphs, this sample study area is dominated by the other categories of wastelands i.e. upland with or without scrub and degraded notified forest land.

Fig. 6.26 also shows that the southern part of the sample villages is occupied by the upland with or without scrub while the northern part is under degraded forest land due to almost all area under Aravalli hill ranges.

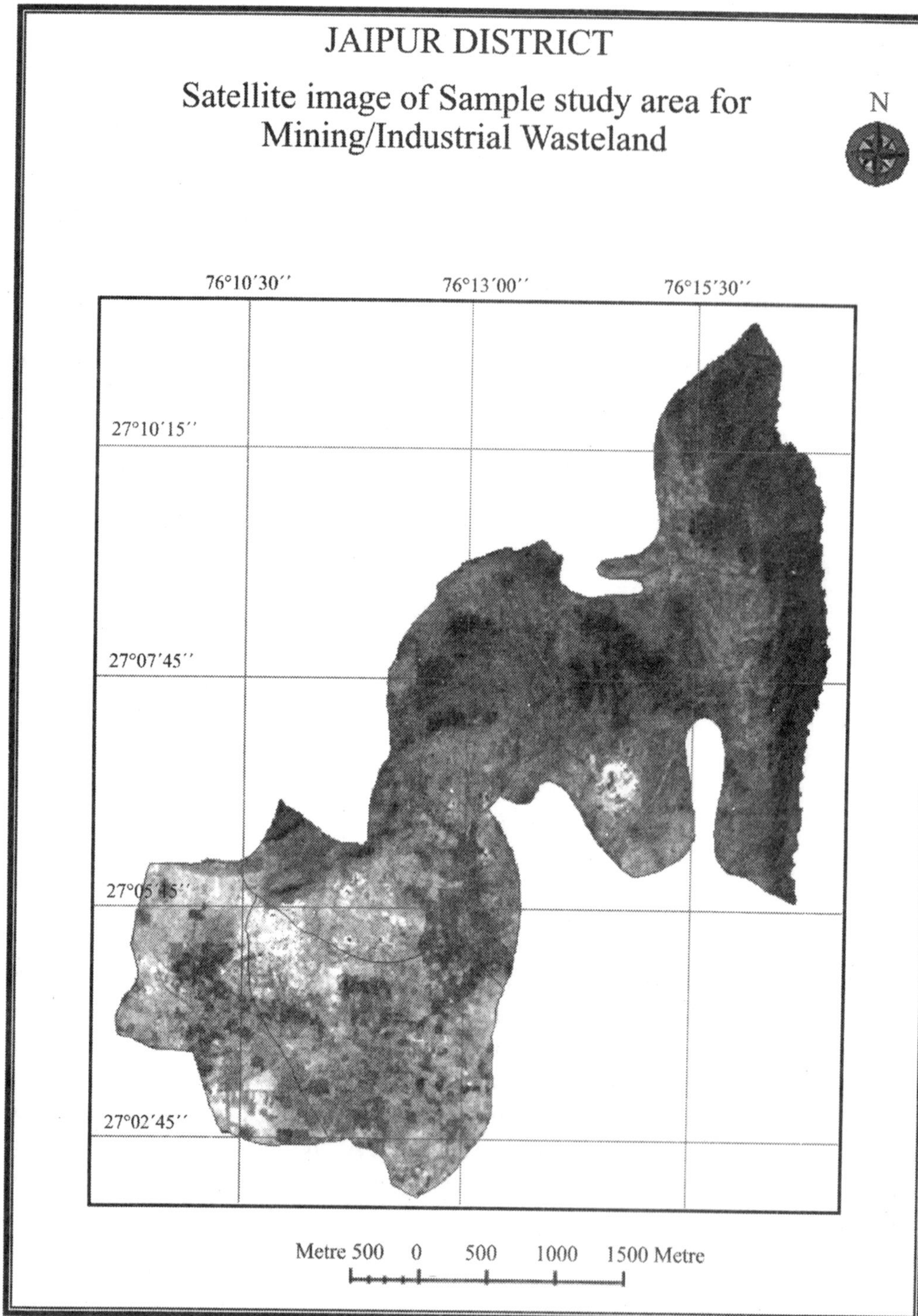

Source : LISS III dated 28th Feb. 2003. Processed at : B.M. Birla Science & Technology Centre, Jaipur

Fig. 6.25 : Satellite image of Sample study area for Mining/Industrial Wasteland.

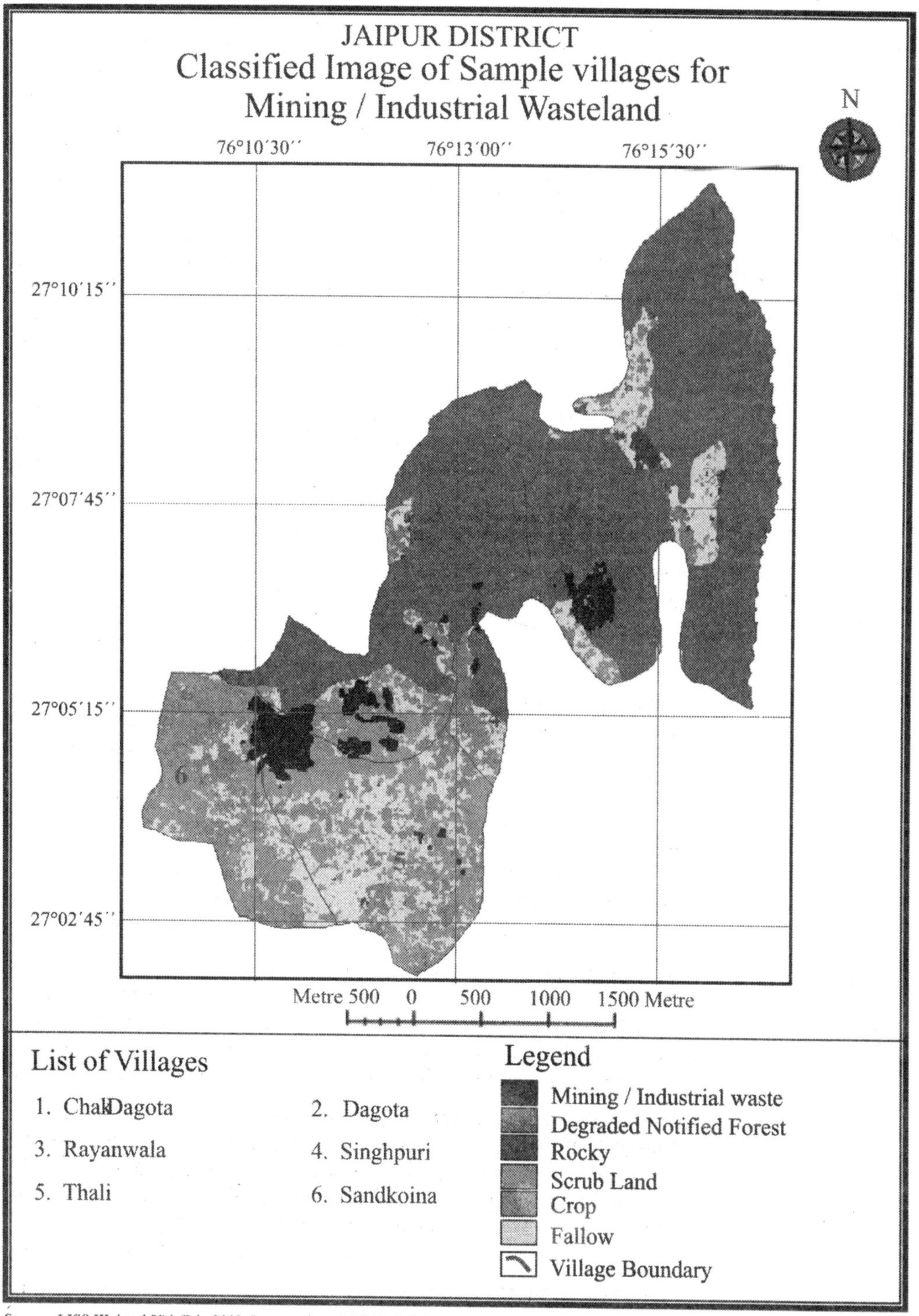

Source : LISS III dated 28th Feb. 2003. Processed at : B.M. Birla Science & Technology Centre, Jaipur

Fig. 6.27 : Classified Image of Sample villages for Mining/Industrial Wasteland.

Reclamation of Mined Lands by Mine Owners

During field survey it is observed that no sincere efforts have been made by the mine owners for rehabilitation of mined lands. However, very small scanty plants are found in this sample study area.

Mining activities disrupts the environment and unscientific mining activities are responsible for loss of level topography, depletion of water resources, denudation of vegetative cover, surface crusting, soil erosion and loss of fertility. These lands, if left as such, should remain unutilized for centuries (Sharma, *et al.* 1998). It is therefore, essential to take appropriate measure for rehabilitation of mined lands.

REFERENCES

Gupta, N.L. and Maroo, R.L., (1991). *Challenge of Wastelands Utilization Issues and Themes*, Academic Publishers, Jaipur.

Kalwar, S.C. (1987). "Forest Cover Monitoring and Management in Jaipur District" Using Remote Sensing Data, *Annals of the Association of Rajasthan Geographers* Vol. VIII, pp. 59-65.

Kalwar, S.C. (1990). "Water Resources Management in Jaipur District" (Ed.) *Ecology of Land and Water Management – Dryland Experiences*, Kuldeep Publications, Jaipur, pp. 69-80.

Kalwar, S.C. (1996). "*Prayavaran Avam Parti Bhumi*", Pointer Publishers, Jaipur.

Kalwar, S.C. (1998). Identification and Developments of Wastelands in Semi-Arid Areas of Rajasthan. Unpublished Research Project Report, ICSSR, New Delhi.

Mukherjee, A.B. (1971). Geographic Patterns of Changes in Agricultural Wastelands in Uttar Pradesh. *G.R. of India*, XXXII, No. 2, pp. 120-32.

N.R.S.A., Hyderabad (1985). Mapping of Wastelands in India from Satellite Imagery, 1980-82, Summary Report, Rajasthan.

Planning Commission, New Delhi (1965). Study of Survey and Reclamation of Ravines in India.

Shafi, M. (1968). The Problems of Wastelands in India. *The Geographer*, Vol. XV, No. XXI (Special).

Yadav, H.R., (1986). *Genesis and Utilisation of Wastelands*, Concept, New Delhi.

7

PLANNING FOR RECLAMATION/DEVELOPMENT OF WASTELANDS AND ECONOMICS OF WASTELANDS

Jaipur district has its 17-34 per cent geographical area under various categories of wasteland. Of the total wasteland degraded notified forest land alone covers 36.02 per cent followed by gullied and or ravinous land (27.41%). Approximately three-fourth wasteland (71.61%) is owned by Government while remaining under the possession of private ownership. In the study area, Central/State Government can play an important role in reclamation/development of wastelands. However, externally aided projects (World Bank US AID and OECF Japan) have been completed in the state.

At present Rajasthan Forest and Biodiversity Project, Forest Department, Government of Rajasthan, Jaipur has specific criterion for site selection for each project component as follows:

Reafforestation of Barren Hills

- Crown density should be less than 10 per cent
- There should be ample scope for planting 600-700 plants per ha.
- The area should be workable.

Rehabilitation of Degraded Forest — Model-I

- Crown density should be between 10-40 per cent
- There should be scope for planting 450-500 plants per ha.

Rehabilitation of Degraded Forest — Model-II

- Crown density should be between 40-70 per cent
- There should be scope for planting about 200 plant per ha.

Fuelwood Plantations

- Plantation be taken on community land of the villages where there is an acute shortage of fuel wood, fodder or both.

- Ample community land is available, so that, closure does not reduce the grazing land, thus preventing any conflict with the villagers.

Biodiversity Conservation

- Under biodiversity conservation the suitable intervention be made in those forest areas which have more than 70 per cent crown density.
- Closers be created for development of translocation centres.
- Eco-tourism site be identified and developed with adequate tourist facilities.

Sand Dune Stabilisation

- The area be selected on the index catchment basis near the threatened habitations, roads, railways and canals.
- The plantation be done on the cluster basis so as to maximize the vegetal cover in the area.

Plantation Along Water Courses

- Plantation be taken up along water courses in the agricultural fields so as to provide effective protection against silting.
- The area be taken up looking to the necessity and willingess of the local people so that their active participation is enlisted.

Pasture Development

- Under this category existing pastures be selected for improvement.
- The sites be selected near the villages as far as possible.
- Those areas be given priority which are highly depleted.

Planning/suggestions for reclamation/development of wastelands in sample study areas at village level, model estimate cost for RDF, RBH, FWP and soil water conservation in gullied and/or ravinous land, financial requirement for reclamation/development of wastelands in the entire study area i.e. Jaipur district, production and income after development of wastelands and cost-benefit ratio etc. are given as follows:

Table 7.1 : Planning for rehabilitation of degraded forest at village level in sample study area for degraded notified forest land

S. No.	Name of Village	Wasteland	Area of Occurrence	Area in ha	Land capability class	Water Potentiality	Soils	Slope	Location	Association	Process of Degradation	Degree of severity	Present Use	Suggestions for Reclamation / Development of wastelands
1	Bandh Mazaferpur	Degraded Forest	Whole Village	547.32	VIII	Poor	Outcrop	Steep	Hilly Tract	Different forest types/sub types	Biotic interference	Moderate	Grazing/ Fuel Wood/ Timber	To adopt RDF model-I guidelines. Fencing either by random rubble stone wall or by trench cum mound fencing. Along fence lines, sowing/ planting seeds of suitable species to act as a live hedge. Cut back operations of degraded root stock in the existing crop. Digging about 200 pits (45cm) 3 per hectare in the blank areas at proper spacing on contours. Planting of suitable indigenous species in the pits and seeds of suitable tree/ shrubs on contour trenches/ V-ditch of size 45cm x 45cm cross section be dug at proper places. For conserve moisture in the area, adequate

(Contd. Table 7.1)

(Table 7.1 Contd.)

S. No.	Name of Village	Wasteland	Area of Occurrence	Area in ha	Land capability class	Water Potentiality	Soils	Slope	Location	Association	Process of Degradation	Degree of severity	Present Use	Suggestions for Reclamation / Development of wastelands
														measures like construction of loose stone check dams with vegetative support to conserve rain water "in situ". With the on set of rainy season, sowing of grass seeds on the ridges of V-ditches and in inter pit spaces. Subsidiary silvicultural operations from time to time as per requirement.
		upland Scrub	Scattered in small patches			Poor	Shallow	Steep	Hill Stlpes	Different forest types/sub types	Biotic interference	Moderate	Grazing	To adopt RBH model.
2	Kuhada	Degraded Forest	Whole village except south western part	681.66	VIII	Poor	Outcrop	Steep slope	Hilly Tract	Different forest types/sub types	Biotic interference	Slight to moderate	Timber/ Fuel wood/ Grazing	To adopt RDF model-II

(Contd. Table 7.1)

(Table 7.1 Contd.)

S. No.	Name of Village	Wasteland	Area of Occurrence	Area in ha	Land capability class	Water Potentiality	Soils	Slope	Location	Association	Process of Degradation	Degree of severity	Present Use	Suggestions for Reclamation / Development of wastelands
		Gullied and Ravinous land	South western part of the village	60.48	VI	Good	Loamy sand	Mode-rate	Along the seasonal flow lines on the hill slopes	On hill slope and pediments	Water erosion along streams and sloping ground	Severe	Nil	Suggested measures as Dedwari Village
		Upland Scrub	South western part of the village		VII	Poor	Outcrop Slop	Steep	Hill slopes	Scattered treens	Biotic Interferences	Severe	Nil	To adopt RBH model-I
3	Taloo Ka Bas	Degraded Forest	Whole village except western part and a long narrow strip in the northern part of the village	650.3	VIII	Poor	Outcrop step	Steep to mode-rate	Hilly tract	Differenct forest types	Biotic interference	Moderate	Nil	To adopt RDF model-II
		Scrub		41.41		Poor	Shallow steep	"	Hilly Tract	Scattered trees	"	Severe	Grazing	To adopt RBH model-I
4	Panchudhala Village	Degraded Forest	Eastern and central part of the village	1701	VIII	Poor	Outcrop	"	Hilly Tract	Different forest type	Biotic interference	Moderate	Timber/ fuel wood grazing	To adopt RDF Model-II

(Contd. Table 7.1)

(Table 7.1 Contd.)

S. No.	Name of Village	Wasteland	Area of Occurrence	Area in ha	Land capability class	Water Potentiality	Soils	Slope	Location	Association	Process of Degradation	Degree of severity	Present Use	Suggestions for Reclamation / Development of wastelands
		Gullied and/ or Ravinous land	Western part of the village	5	VI	Good	Loamy sand	Moderate	Gullied and or ravinous along the seasonal flow lines	Aeolian sand on western hill slope	Water erosion along seasonal streams	Severe	Nil	To adopt soil and water conservation model as Dedwari village.
		Scrub	Scattered patches	190.7	VIII	Poor	Shallow		Hill	Hilly tract	Biotic interference	Moderate	Grazing	To adopt RBH model

Forest Department, Government of Rajasthan has given a model cost estimate for rehabilitation of degraded forest. The following Table 7.2 shows per hectare amount required for rehabilitation of degraded forest as per model cost estimate.

Table 7.2 : Model Cost Estimate for Rehabilitation of Degraded Forest (MODEL-I)

MODEL COST ESTIMATE FOR REFORESTATION OF DEGRADED FOREST					
UNITS : 50 HA					
PERIMETER : 60 M/HA					
LABOUR RATE : Rs. 60/DAY					
COST ESTIMATE : IN Rs. /HA.					
S. No.	Item of Work	Rate	Labour Component	Material Component	Total
	YEAR 0 : ADVANCE ACTION				
1	Collection of Data for Microplanning, preparation of microplan and management plan	165/ha	140	25	165
2	Survey of area, Layout of contour trenches/furrows, Pits and marking of segments/plots	135/ha	110	25	135
3	Fencing by stone wall and or by Ditch.				
	(a) Stone wall fencing 1.20m high 0.80 m at base and 0.60 at top (On an average 30m/ha.)	60/m	1800	0	1800
	(b) Ditch fencing 1.20m Deep 1.50m wide at Top and 0.90 at Bottom (On an average 30m/Ha.)	65/m	1950	0	1950
4	Cost of raising 550 seedlings.	1.60/ plant	633	248	880
5	Digging up 300 rmt. of Staggered Contour trenches 45×45 cm cross section on middle slopes and v-ditch as per site requirement.	7.5/m	2250	0	2250
6	Digging of 300 pits size 0.45×(.4+.5)/2 cum	4.69	1407	0	1407
7	Cost of collection and purchase of Grass and other seeds.	Prorata	0	80	80
	Restoration of natural regeneration by cultural operations and making crescent shaped mounds on the lower side on seedlings.	Prorata	600		600
8	In situ soil and moisture conservation measures like check dam, Nadis, Earthen Bunds etc.	Prorata	1150	0	1150
9	Construction of Thatched cattle Guard Hut.	Prorata	60	18	78
10	Purchase or construction of water storage tank.	Prorata	0	30	30
11	Purchase of tools and plants.	Prorata	0	45	45
12	Labour amenities	Prorata	22	35	57
13	Cattle Guard wages for 4 months	Prorata	125	0	125
14	Misc. and unforeseen expenses including running of vehicles.	Prorata	69	29	98
	TOTAL YEAR 0		10316	535	10850

(Cont. Table 7.2)

(Table 7.2 Contd.)

S. No.	Item of Work	Rate	Labour Component	Material Component	Total
	YEAR 1 PLANATION YEAR				
1	Maint. of 550 seedlings in Nursery.	0.80/ plant	358	83	440
2	Digging of 200 pits size 0.45×(.4+5)/2 Cum	4.69/pit	938	0	938
3	In situ soil & Moisture Conservation measures like Check dam, Nadi, Earthen Bunds etc.	780/ha	680	100	780
4	Digging of 30cm×30cm cross section trench along inner side of stone wall-fencing and seed sowing.	3.30/ rmt	193	5	198
5	Sowing/dibbling of seeds of thorny tree species on the mound of trench and ditch fencing	0.17	51	0	51
6	Purchase of insecticide and fertilizers and its application (Superphosphate/DAP/Aldrine)	0.54/ plant	80	190	270
7	Sowing of pellets of grass pieces/pieces of seed mud cakes in between rows and pits.	Prorata	136	0	136
8	Transport of 500 seedlings from Nursery to planting site.	0.38/ plant	180	10	190
9	Planting of 500 seedlings including refilling of pits.	1.09/ plant	545	0	545
10	Watering and application of insecticides in 500 plants at the time of planting.	0.84/ plant	390	30	420
11	Restoration of natural regeneration by making crescent shaped mounds on the lower slope of 150 seedlings and saplings.	1.09/ Plant	164	0	164
12	Making of crescent shaped mounds below 500 planted saplings after planting and dibbing of 3 seeds of throny tree species.	0.95/ plant	475	0	475
13	Weeding and hoeing of 500 plants Two times with repairing plants mound.	1.91/ plant	955	0	955
14	Weeding on contour trenches/V-diches and espacement/singling	Prorata	140	0	140
15	Raising of 10 per cent plants (50/Ha) in Nursery for casualty replacement in year 2.	1.60/ plant	58	23	80
17	Watch and ward charges for 12 months.	Prorata	375	0	375
18	Labour hut etc.	Prorata	87	20	107
19	Construction of approach roads/inspection path	Prorata	102	0	102
20	Construction of gate and fixing of sign boards.	Prorata	136	34	170
21	Misc. and unforeseen expenses including. (additional watering, fencing running of vehicles and soil conservation measures).	Prorata	56	58	114
	TOTAL YEAR 1		6098	552	6650
	YEAR 2 : MAINTENANCE				
1	Maint. of 50 plants in nursery	0.80/ plant	33	8	40
2	Repair of fencing	Prorata	60	0	60
3	Casualty replacement of 50 plants including (10%) redigging of pits, transportation, planting, watering and application of insecticides.	3.24/ plant	150	12	162
4	Weeding and hoeing in 500 plants.	1.91/ plant	955	0	955

(Cont. Table 7.2)

(Table 7.2 Contd.)

S. No.	Item of Work	Rate	Labour Component	Material Component	Total
5	Watch and ward charges for 12 months.	Prorata	375	0	375
6	Misc. and unforeseen expenses including (Repair of structures, subsidiary silvicultural operations, frost protection, etc.)	Prorata	63	45	108
	TOTAL YEAR 2		1636	65	1700
	YEAR 3 : MAINTENANCE				
1	Watch and ward charges for 12 months	Prorata	375	0	375
2	Expenditure on Maintenance including (Repair of fencing/structures, subsidiary silvicultrual operations, front protection etc.)	Prorata	110	65	175
	TOTAL YEAR 3		485	65	550
	YEAR 4 : MAINTENANCE				
1	Watch and ward charges for 12 months	Prorata	375	0	375
2	Expenditure on Maintenance including (Repair of fencing/structures, subsidiary silvicultrual operations, front protection etc.)	Prorata	110	65	175
	TOTAL YEAR 4		485	65	550
	GRAND TOTAL OF RDF I MODEL YEARS 0-4		19019	1281	20300

Estimation of Financial Requirements for Rehabilitation of Degraded Forest in Jaipur District

The following Table 7.3 gives an idea of Financial requirements for the development of degraded forest land in entire study area i.e. Jaipur district as per estimate cost model RDF I.

Table 7.3 : Tehsilwise Financial Requirement for Rehabilitation of Degraded Forest in Jaipur District.

S. No.	Name of the Tehsil	Financial requirement (Rs. in lakhs)
1	Amber	1721.24
2	Bassi	429.85
3	Chaksu	0.00
4	Chomu	288.67
5	Dudu	0.00
6	Jaipur	669.93
7	Jamwa Ramgarh	4010.03
8	Kotputli	1875.40
9	Phagi	113.17
10	Phulera	10.66
11	Sanganer	82.22
12	Shahapura	605.04
13	Viratnagar	3237.79
TOTAL		13043.99

Source : Financial requirement based on area and model cost estimate.

Table 7.4 : Planning for Reclamation/Development of Wastelands in sample villages for Gullied and Ravinous land

S. No.	Name of Village	Waste land	Area of Occurrence	Area in ha	Land capability class	Water Potentiality	Soils	Slope	Location	Association	Process of Degradation	Degree of sevrity	Present Use	Suggestions for reclamation/ Development of wastelands
1	Dedwari	Gullied and or Ravinous land	Northern central and eastern part	52.36	VI	Good/ Very good	Sandy/ loamy sand	Moderate	Gullies and ravines along the seasonal flow lines on the western hill slope	Aeolian sand on western hill slope and pediments	Water erosion along streams and sloping ground with loose aeolian sand	Severe (G3)	Nil	Water and soil conservation measures through gully plugging, anicuts, crescent shaped ridges, contour trenches and other structures followed by afforestation with shrubs and grasses. Nallah stabilization in the central part of the village. Peripheral bund around gullied and or ravinous land to check the further extension of gullies and/ on ravines. This area should be taken up for the development under wasteland / watershed development programme.
		Degraded Forest	Northern part of the village	11.81	VIII	Poor	Outcrop	Steep	Hills	Different forest typer/sub types	Biotic interference	Degraded Forest (I)	Fuel wood/ timber	Effective enclosures for checking biotic interferences. To adopt RDF model-I. Fencing (Stone wall ditch fencing, live fencing), soil and water structures in the form of check dams and water storage structures like anicuts/V-ditch, sowing of grass seeds, thorn/tree species on the mound of trenches ditch and ditch

(Contd.Table 7.4)

(Table 7.4 Contd.)

S. No.	Name of Village	Waste land	Area of Occurrence	Area in Ha	Land capability class	Water Potentiality	Soils	Slope	Location	Association	Process of Degradation	Degree of sevrity	Present Use	Suggestions for reclamation/ Development of wastelands
														fencing, planting of 700 seedlings per ha and restoration of natural regeneration. Perference should be given to local species and fuelwood species.
2	Chain-pura Bas Ded-wari	Gullied and/ or ravi-nous land	Eastern part of the village	75.34	V	Very good	Loamy sand	Mode-rate	Gullied/ ravinous land	Eroded land with cultivated patches	Water erosion along seasonal streams	Severe	Nil	After levelling horticulture plantation can be developed especially 'anwala' and roses.
3	Godi-yana	Gullied and/ or ravi-nous land	South western and north western part	52.58	VI	Good to very good	Sandy/ Loamy sand	Mode-rate	Gullies and/ or ravines along the seasonal flow lines on the western hill slope in south eastern part and along Banganga river in north western part	Aeolian sand on western hill slope and pediments in south western and cultivated patches in north western part	Water erosion along streams and sloping ground with loose aeolian sand in southwest and water erosion along sea-sonal stre-ams in northern part	Slight to moderate	Nil	(i) Wasteland Development as Dedwari village in south western part of the village. (ii) Farm bunding for mustard cultivation in northern part and suitable for horticulture plantation after levelling. Available good quality/quantity of ground water resources.

(Contd. Table 7.4)

(Table 7.4 Contd.)

S. No.	Name of Village	Waste land	Area of Occurrence	Area in ha	Land capability class	Water Potentiality	Soils	Slope	Location	Association	Process of Degradation	Degree of sevrity	Present Use	Suggestions for reclamation/ Development of wastelands
		River sand	Central part of the village	24.11	IV	Very good	Sandy	Gentle	Banganga river	River sand	Sand deposition in river bed	Slight to moderate	Nil	Zaid crops can be produced in river bed.
		Degraded Forest	Southern part	269.57	VIII	Poor	Outcrop	Steep	Hilly tract	Scattered trees	Biotic interference	Moderate	Grazing/ fuel wood/Timber	To adopt RDF model I as Dedwari village
4	Rampura Bas Samred	Gullied and/ or Ravinous land	North eastern and northern part of the village	69.06	V, VI	Very good	Loamy sand	Moderate	Gullies and/or ravines along the seasonal flow line	Aeolian sand on western hill slope and pediments	Water erosion along streams and sloping ground with loose aeolian sand	Severe	Nil	(i) Soil and water conservation as Dedwari Village (S.N.1) in north eastern part. (ii) Horticulture can be developed in northern part.
		Degraded notified forest	Western and south eastern part of the village			Poor	Outcrop	Steep	Hilly tract	Scattered trees	Biotic interferences	Moderate	Fuelwood/ timber and grazing	To adopt soil and water conservation as Dedwari Village, (S.N. 1)
5	Samred Kalan	Gullied and/ or ravinous land	(i) Eastern part of the village	157.08	VI	Good	Loamy sand	Moderate	Gullied and or ravinous along the seasonal flow lines on the western hill slope	Aeolian sand on western hill slope and pediments		Severe	Nil	Soil and water conservation as Dedwari village

(Contd.Table 7.4)

(Table 7.4 Contd.)

S. No.	Name of Village	Waste land	Area of Occurrence	Area in ha	Land capability class	Water Potentiality	Soils	Slope	Location	Association	Process of Degradation	Degree of sevrity	Present Use	Suggestions for reclamation/ Development of wastelands
6	Samred Khurd	Gullied and/ or ravinous land	Eastern southern and northern part of the village	149.7	V, VI	Good	Loamy sand	Moderate	Gullied and / or ravines along seasonal flow lines	eroded land	Do	Do	Do	(i) Horticulture can be developed after levelling of gullies and or ravines in southern part. (ii) Soil and water conservation as Dedwari villages in eastern and northern part of the village.
		Degraded notified forest	Central part of the village	105.7	VIII	Poor	Outcrop	Steep	Hilly tract	Degraded Forest	Biotic interference	Moderate	Grazing/ fuel wood/ Timber	To adopt R D F model I as Dedwari Village

Plate 23 : Pucca cement wall across gully/ravine eroded land to check further headward erosion.

Plate 24 : Wire fencing to check biotic interference after soil and water conservation activities in gulied/ravinous land.

The following Table 7.5 shows per hectare model cost estimate of soil-water conservation in Gullied and Ravinous land.

Table 7.5 : Model Cost Estimate of Soil/Water Conservation in Gullied/Ravinous Land

MODEL COST ESTIMATE OF SOIL CONSERVATION IN RAVINE AREAS					
UNITS : 50 ha					
PERIMETER : 60 M/ha					
LABOUR RATE : Rs. 60/DAY					
COST ESTIMATE : IN Rs. /ha					
S. No.	Item of Work	Rate	Labour Component	Material Component	Total
	YEAR 0 : ADVANCE ACTION				
1.	Collection of Data for Microplanning, preparation of microplan and management plan	195/Ha	170	25	195
2.	Survey and Layout	159/Ha	134	25	159
3.	Fencing by stone wall and or by Ditch.				
	(a) Stone wall fencing 1.20m high 0.80 m at base and 0.60 at top (On an average 30m/ha.)	60/m	1876	0	1876
	(b) Ditch fencing 1.20m Deep 1.50m wide at Top and 0.90 at Bottom (On an average 30m/Ha.)	65/m	2373	0	2373
4.	Digging 500 pits (45 cm) 3	4.69/pit	2345	0	2345
5.	Soil conservation Digging 200 rmt of contour trenches of cross section 45cm×45cm in compact soil (this will include peripheral bunds also).	8.15/rmt	1630	0	1630
6.	(a) construction of 4 brush wood check dams per ha. Using suitable poles and twigs.	85/unit	680	0	680
	(b) Gully plugging, construction of check dam/earthen bund and diversion drains etc.	Prorata	1150	0	1150
7.	Cost of grass (3 kg.) castor (1 kg.) and thorny species.	120/ha	0	120	120
8.	Purchase or construction of water storage tank.	Prorata	0	30	30
9.	Cost of raising 600 seedlings.	1.60/seedling	960	210	1170
10.	Purchase of tools and plants.	Prorata	0	55	55
11.	Construction of shelter for labour amenities.	Prorata	22	35	57
12.	Construction of thatched cattle guard hut.	Prorata	60	18	78
13.	Cattle Guard wages for 4 months	Prorata	125	0	125
14.	Misc. and unforeseen expenses.	Prorata	40	23	63
	TOTAL YEAR 0				12096
	YEAR 1 PLANATION YEAR				
1.	Maint. of 600 seedlings in Nursery.	0.80/ seedling	480	116	596
2.	Transport of 500 seedlings from Nursery to planting site.	0.38/ plant	144	55	210
3.	Planting of 500 seedlings including refilling of pits.	1.09/ plant	545	0	545

(Contd. Table 7.5)

(Table 7.5 Contd.)

S. No.	Item of Work	Rate	Labour Component	Material Component	Total
4.	Watering and application of insecticides in 500 plants at the time of planting.	0.84/ plant	420	0	420
	Cost of raising agave, Nagar Munja Ratanjot etc. @ 0.80 of per plant	0.80/ plant	712	0	712
5.	Purchase of insecticide and fertilizers and its application	0.54	80	190	270
6.	Weeding and hoeing application of 500 plants (Two times).	1.91/ plant	955	0	9.55
7.	Sowing of castor of grass throny spp.seed on peripheral trenches and cresent shapped ridges below the contour trench.	0.17 m	51	0	51
8.	(a) Vegatative Barrier with Munja, Ipomea, Agave, Nagar, Ratanjot etc. (100 Nos. each unit to consist of 8 plants in two rows each row of 4 plants).	228/ha	228	0	228
	(b) Munja and agave planting on exposed and eroded slopes (250m/s plants).	0.95	475	0	475
9.	Purchase and app. of insecticide and fertilizers and its application (Superphosphate/DAP/Aldrine)	0.54/ plant	0	270	270
10.	Raising of 50 seedlings (for casualty replacement in next year).	1.60/ plant	80	32	102
11.	Maintenance of work charge vehicle	Prorata	0	50	50
12.	Watch and ward charges for 12 months.	Prorata	375	0	375
13.	Misc. and unforeseen expenses	Prorata	127	71	198
	TOTAL YEAR 1		2455	575	5457
	YEAR 2 : MAINTENANCE				
1.	Maint. of 50 seedlings raised in I year for casualty replacement	0.80/ seedling	40	10	50
2.	Casualty replacement of 50 plants (pits digging, transportation, planting, watering).	3.24/ plant	162	0	162
3.	Two weeding and hoeing in 500 plants.	1.91/ plant	955	0	955
4.	Watch and ward charges for 12 months.	Prorata	375	0	375
5.	Misc. and unforeseen expenses including (Repair of structures, subsidiary silvicultural operations, frost protection, etc.)	Prorata	136	61	197
	TOTAL YEAR 2		1000	50	1739
	YEAR 3 : MAINTENANCE				
1	Watch and ward charges for 12 months	Prorata	375	0	375
2	Expenditure on Maintenance including (Repair of fencing/structures, subsidiary silvicultrual operations, front protection etc.)	Prorata	110	65	175
	TOTAL YEAR 3		485	65	550

(Contd. Table 7.5)

(Table 7.5 Contd.)

S. No.	Item of Work	Rate	Labour Compo-nent	Material Compo-nent	Total
	YEAR 4 : MAINTENANCE				
1.	Watch and ward charges for 12 months	1700/ PM	408	0	408
2.	Misc. and unforseen Expenses PM	Prorata	40	0	40
3.	Repair of fencing	Prorata	52	0	52
	TOTAL YEAR 4		500	0	550
	GRAND TOTAL OF RDF I MODEL YEARS 0-4			1145	

Estimation of Financial Requirements for Reclamation/Development of Gullied or Ravinous Land in Jaipur District

The following table shows tehsilwise financial requirements for the development of gullied and or ravinous land in the entire study area:

Table 7.6 : Tehsil wise Financial Requirement for Reclamation/Development of Gullied and/or Ravinous land in Jaipur District

S. No.	Name of the Tehsil	Financial requirement (Rs. in lakhs)
1	Amber	1102.86
2	Bassi	936.25
3	Chaksu	371.41
4	Chomu	226.17
5	Dudu	94.76
6	Jaipur	200.62
7	Jamwa Ramgarh	3103.25
8	Kotputli	693.02
9	Phagi	341.46
10	Phulera	12.57
11	Sanganer	0.00
12	Shohapura	1517.70
13	Viratnagar	1847.90
	TOTAL	1044797.00

Source : Financial requirement based on area and model cost estimate.

As mentioned earlier, forest department, Govt. of Rajasthan has given model cost estimate for the forest development in different areas. Table 7.8 shows model cost estimate per hectare for reforestation of barren hills.

Estimation of Financial Requirements for Barren Hill/Rocky Development in Jaipur District

Barren hill/rocky areas in the district can be developed as sample study area for barren hill/ rocky. Tehsil wise financial requirement is given Table 7.9.

Table 7.7 : Planning for Reclamation/Development of Wastelands in sample villages for Barren Hills/Rocky

S. No.	Name of Village	Waste-land	Area of Occurr-ence	Area in ha	Land capa-bility class	Water Poten-tiality	Soils	Slope	Loca-tion	Asso-ciation	Process of Degrada-tion	Degree of severity	Water potenti-lity	Land use/ Land cover	Suggestions for Reclamation/ Development of wastelands
1	Arnia	Barren hills	North central part	101.3	VII	Poor	Thin layer	Steep	Hills	Barren and exposed rocks	Biotic inter-ference	Severe	Poor	Scatte-tred bushes/ shrubs	Fencing by random rubble stone wall/trench cum mound. Along the fence lines sowing/ planting of seeds/cutting of suitable species to act as a live hedge. Digging 600-700 pits (per ha.) of size (45cm) 3 in the area at proper spacing on contours in addition to it digging 400 running metres of contour trench/V ditch of 45cm × 45cm at proper places per ha. contour dykes on the precipitours slopes, construc-tion of loose stone check dam, construction of crib dams, retaining walls/ outlets etc to conserve rain water "in situ", sowing of grass seeds in rainy season on the ridges of V-ditches and in inter pit spaces. In area of sand deposits on foot hills planting intensive 'munja' Plants in the pits of suitable indigenous species and seeds of suitable tree/ shrubs on contour trenches. Silvicultural operations be taken up from time to time as per requirement.

(Contd. Table 7.7)

(Table 7.7 Contd.)

S. No.	Name of Village	Waste-land	Area of Occurr-ence	Area in ha	Land capa-bility class	Water Poten-tiality	Soils	Slope	Loca-tion	Asso-ciation	Process of Degrada-tion	Degree of severity	Water potenti-lity	Land use/ Land cover	Suggestions for Reclamation/ Development of wastelands
2	Chak Manoharpur	do	South western part and scattered hills	33.58	VIII	do	do	do	do	do	do	do	do	do	Do
3	Deo-Ka Harwara	do	Central part and scattered hills in eastern and western part of the village	197.22	VIII	do	do	do	do	do	do	do	do	do	Do
4	Peelwa	do	North eastern part and scattered hillocks in south wes-tern part	63.94	VIII	do	do	do	do	do	do	do	do	do	Do
5	Beelpur	do	Northern and eas-tern part	170.73	VIII	do	do	do	do	do	do	do	do	do	To adopt RDF model-I as Dedwari village
6	Chandwaji	Barren hills	Central, southern and north western part	53.28	VIII	do	do	do	do	do	do	do	do	do	To adopt RBH model
		Degra-ded Forest	North western part	15.70		do	do	do	do	do	do	do	do	do	To adopt RDF model-I as Dedwari village

(Contd.Table 7.7)

(Table 7.7 Contd.)

S. No.	Name of Village	Waste-land	Area of Occurr-ence	Area in ha	Land capa-bility class	Water Poten-tiality	Soils	Slope	Loca-tion	Asso-ciation	Process of Degrada-tion	Degree of severity	Water potenti-lity	Land use/ Land cover	Suggestions for Reclamation/ Development of wastelands
7	Salarwas	Degra-ded Forest	Along eastern boundary	36.12	VIII	do	do	do	do	do	do	do	do	do	do
		Barren hills	Northern and western part	124.47	VIII	do	do	do	do	do	do	do	do	do	To adopt RBH model as Arnia Village
8	Sunder Ka Bas	do	Eastern, northern part and scattered hills	124.42	VIII	do	do	do	do	do	do	do	do	do	do
		Degra-ded forest	Southern part of the village	12.56	VIII	do	do	do	do	do	do	do	do	do	To adopt RDF model-I as Dedwari Village

As mentioned earlier, Forest department, Govt. of Rajasthan has given model cost estimate for the forest development in different areas. Table 7.12 shows model cost estimate per hectare for reforestation of barren hills.

Estimation of Financial Requirements for Development FWP on Panchayat/common land in Jaipur District

After reclamation, agricultural production would increase ten times in the land affected by salinity/alkalinity.

Table 7.8 : Model Cost Estimate for RBH

REFORESTATION OF BARREN HILLS

UNITS : 50 HA

PERIMETER : 60 M/HA

LABOUR RATE : Rs. 60/DAY

COST ESTIMATE : IN Rs. /HA.

S. No.	Item of Work	Rate	Labour Component	Material Component	Total
	YEAR 0 : ADVANCE ACTION				
1.	Collection of Data for Microplanning, preparation of microplan and management plan	165/Ha	140	25	165
2.	Survey of area, Layout of contour trenches/furrows, Pits and marking of segments/plots	135/Ha	110	25	135
3.	Fencing by stone wall and or by Ditch.				
	(a) Stone wall fencing 1.20m high 0.80 m at base and 0.60 at top (On an average 30m/ha.)	60/m	1800	0	1800
	(b) Ditch fencing 1.20m Deep 1.50m wide at Top and 0.90 at Bottom (On an average 30m/Ha.)	65/m	1950	0	1950
4.	Cost of raising 770 seedlings.	1.60/ plant	886	347	886
5.	Construction of 50m long contour dyes of 30×30cm Cross section	8.15/ rmt	408	0	408
6.	Digging of 400 rmt. of Staggered Contour trenches of cross Sectt. on 45×45 cm on middle slopes contour trenches of cross	7.5/rmt	3375	0	3375
7.	Digging of 300 pits size 0.45×(.4+.5)/2 cum	4.69/ pit	1407	0	1407
8.	In situ soil and moisture conservation measures like check dam, Nadis, Earthen Bunds etc.	Prorata	1150	0	1150
9.	Cost of collection and purchase of Grass and other seeds.	Prorata	0	120	120
10.	Construction of Thatched cattle Guard Hut.	Prorata	60	18	78
11.	Purchase or construction of water storage tank.	Prorata	0	30	30
12.	Purchase of tools and plants.	Prorata	0	55	55
13.	Labour amenities	Prorata	22	35	57
14.	Cattle Guard wages for 4 months	Prorata	125	0	125
15.	Misc. and unforeseen expenses including running of vehicles.	Prorata	40	23	63
	TOTAL YEAR 0		11473	678	12150

(Count. Table 7.8)

(Table 7.8 Contd.)

S. No..	Item of Work	Rate	Labour Component	Material Component	Total
	YEAR 1 PLANATION YEAR				
1.	Maint. of 770 seedlings in Nursery.	0.80/ plant	500	116	616
2.	Digging of 400 pits size 45cm×45cm×45cm	4.69/ pit	1876	0	1876
3.	In situ soil and Moisture Conservation measures like Check dam, Nadi, Earthen Bunds etc.	782/ha	682	100	782
4.	Seed sowings of grasses on V-ditch.	0.17/ rmt	68	0	68
5.	Sowing/dibbling of seeds of thorny tree species on the mound of trench and ditch fencing	0.17/ rmt	68	0	68
6.	Sowing of pillets/pieces of seed mud cakes of grass seeds between rows of planted pits and blank hill slopes.	Prorata	136	0	136
7.	Restoration of natural regeneration by making crescent shaped mounds on the lower slope of 150 seedlings and saplings.	1.09/P	164	0	164
8.	Purchase of insecticide and fertilizers and its application (Superphosphate/DAP/Aldrine)	0.54/ plant	180	414	594
9.	Transportation of 700 seedlings from Nursery to planting site.	0.38/ plant	252	14	266
10.	Planting of 700 seedlings including refilling of pits.	1.09/ plant	763	0	763
11.	Watering and application of insecticides in 700 plants at the time of planting.	0.84/ plant	866	58	924
12.	Construction of crescent shaped mounds on the lower side of planting pits and dibbling 2 or 3 seeds of throny tree species on the mound.	0.95/ plant	665	0	665
13.	Raising of 70 plants in Nursery for casualty replacement in year 2 (10% of 700)	1.60/ plant	81	32	112
14.	Weeding and hoeing of 700 plants (Two times)	1.91/ plant	1337	0	1337
15.	One hoeing of 700 plants.	0.55/ plant	385	0	385
16.	Weeding on contour trenches/V diches and espacement/singling	Prorata	188	0	188
17.	Watch and ward charges for 12 months.	Prorata	375	0	375
18.	Labour hut etc.	Prorata	87	20	107
19.	Construction of approach roads/inspection path	Prorata	102	0	102
20.	Construction of gate and fixing of sign boards.	Prorata	136	34	170
21.	Misc. and unforeseen expenses including. (additional watering, fencing running of vehicles and soil conservation measures).	Prorata	96	56	152
	TOTAL YEAR 1		9007	843	9850
	YEAR 2 : MAINTENANCE				
1	Maint. of 70 plants in nursery	0.80/ plant	46	10	56
2	Repair of fencing	Prorata	55	4	59
3	Casualty replacement of 70 plants including redigging of pits, transportation, planting, watering and application of insecticides.	3.24/ plant	227	0	227

(Contd. Table 7.8)

(Table 7.8 Contd.)

S. No.	Item of Work	Rate	Labour Component	Material Component	Total
4.	Two weeding and hoeing in 700 plants.	1.91/ plant	1337	0	1337
5.	Watch and ward charges for 12 months,	Prorata	375	0	375
6.	Misc. and unforeseen expenses including (Repair of structures, subsidiary silvicultural operations, frost protection, etc.)	Prorata	136	61	197
	TOTAL YEAR 2		2175	75	2250
	YEAR 3 : MAINTENANCE				
1.	Watch and ward charges for 12 months	Prorata	375	0	375
2.	Expenditure on Maintenance including (Repair of fencing/structures, subsidiary silvicultrual operations, front protection etc.)	Prorata	110	65	175
	TOTAL YEAR 3		485	65	550
	YEAR 4 : MAINTENANCE				
1.	Watch and ward charges for 12 months	Prorata	375	0	375
2.	Expenditure on Maintenance including (Repair of fencing/structures, subsidiary silvicultrual operations, front protection etc.)	Prorata	110	65	175
	TOTAL YEAR 4		485	65	550
	GRAND TOTAL OF RBH YEARS 0-4		23625	1726	25350

Table 7.9 : Tehsilwise Financial Requirement for Development of Barren hills in Jaipur District.

S. No.	Name of the Tehsil	Financial requirement (Rs. in lakhs.)
1	Amber	304.83
2	Bassi	59.95
3	Chaksu	—
4	Chomu	55.14
5	Dudu	446.67
6	Jaipur	22.18
7	Jamwa Ramgarh	131.69
8	Kotputli	149.44
9	Phagi	20.28
10	Phulera	506.80
11	Sanganer	10.14
12	Shahapura	141.83
13	Viratnagar	17.62
	TOTAL	1866.57

Source : Amount calculated on the basis of area of Barren hill/rocky and model cost estimate.

Table 7.10 : Planning for Reclamation/Development of wasteland in Sample Villages for Degraded Pasture/Grazing Land

S. No.	Name of Village	Waste land	Area of Occurrence	Area in ha	Land capability class	Water Potentiality	Soils	Slope	Location	Association	Process of Degradation	Degree of severity	Land use/Land cover	Recommendation for Reclamation/development of wasteland
1.	Harsaliya	Degraded Pasture	Cental, Southern and western part of the village	161.45 (Govt. 116.93 private 44.52)	V	Poor (Saline)	Shallow	Nearly level	Plain area	Single cropped area	Low permedility, shallow soil and nearly level land	Moderate	Degraded pasture/ grazing land	(i) Development of silvipasture/ Fuelwood plantation on community land. The indigenous species providing fuelwood and fodder be planted. Fuelwood, grasses, small timber etc fro the silvipasture/ plantation should be available to the local community on preference through village Forest Protection and Management committee. Efforts should be made to introduce either cut and carry system of fodder or grazing should be allowed in rotational pattern in these areas. (ii) Recommended Agro-horticulture/ Horticulture/ Alley cropping on loamy soils having 50-90 cm depth and low water potentiality on private owned areas. The plant species other than the fruit trees prescribed for horticulture are Roonja, Deshi babul and Ardu etc which do not have any adveritse effect on crop production and are recommended for alley cropping. Residents of the area may be encouraged for improvement of their cattle breed and insurance of cattle should also be facilitated to boost the dairy development in the area. Stall feeding should be encounaged. Financial assistance should be provided to the farmers.

(Contd.Table 7.10)

(Table 7.10 Contd.)

S. No.	Name of Village	Waste land	Area of Occurrence	Area in ha	Land capability class	Water Potentiality	Soils	Slope	Location	Association	Process of Degradation	Degree of severity	Land use/Land cover	Recommendation for Reclamation/development of wasteland
		Saline	Scattered patches in Cultivated, and in northern part of the village	29.15	IV	do	do	do	do	do	do	Moderate	Single cropped	Sowing of salt tolerance crops
2.	Janakinathpura	Degraded Pasture	Central part of the village	118.94 (Govt. 95.01, Private 23.93)	V	do	do	do	Do	do	do	do	do	To develop as Harsuliya village
		Saline	Scattered patches in seasonal nallaha bed in north of J.N.P. Bundh	13.42	V	Moderate (saline)	Moderate	Gentle	Nallah bed	Nallah	Moisture in Nallah bed	Moderate	Nil	Planting of salt to tolerance tree species

(Contd.Table 7.10)

(Table 7.10 Contd.)

S. No.	Name of Village	Waste land	Area of Occurrence	Area in ha	Land capability class	Water Potentiality	Soils	Slope	Location	Association	Process of Degradation	Degree of severity	Land use/Land cover	Recommendation for Reclamation/development of wasteland
3.	Raipura	Degraded pasture	Eastern part of the village	59.24 (Govt. 52.59, Private 3.69)	V	Poor (Saline)	Shallow	Nearly level	Plain area	Single cropped area	Low permebility, shallow soil and nearly level land	Moderate	Degraded pasture/ razing land	To develop as Harsuliya village
4.	Khejro Ka Bas	Degraded Pastrue			V	do	do	do	do	do	do	do	do	do

Table 7.11 : Planning for Reclamation/Development of wasteland in Sample Villages for land with scrub or without scrub

S. No.	Name of Village	Waste land	Area of Occurrence	Area in ha	Land capability class	Water Potentiality	Soils	Slope	Location	Association	Process of Degradation	Degree of severity	Present use	Recommendation for Reclamation/development of wasteland
1	Panwasu	Scrub-land	Northern part of the village	310.23 (Govt. 172.1, Privte 138.11)	V	Poor (Saline)	Day loam/ Loamy sand	Nearly level to gentle	Plain area	Single cropped area	Low permeability	Moderate	Land with or without scrub	(I) Silvipasture fuelwood plantation as Harsuliya village on Govt. land (ii) Financial assistance for medbandi, mixing sand/gypsum (iii) Grassland development on private land
		Saline	Eastern part of village in seasonal nallahs	–	V	Poor (Saline)	Clay loam	Gentle slope	Nallah bed	Delir Nallah	Moisture in nallah bed	Moderate	Nil	Salt tolerance tree and shrubs
2	Ajnota	(i) Scrub land	Southern part of the village	222.11 (Govt. 123.50, Private 98.61	V	Poor	Loamy sand	Nearly level to gentle	Plain area	Single cropped area	Overgraded and sheet erosion	Moderate	Degraded pasture	To develop as Panwasu village
		(ii) Saline	Northern upper part of Chandma Kelon Bundh	19.53	IV	Poor	Clay loam	Nearly level to gentle	Plain area	Single cropped area	Low Permeability, shallow soil and nearly level	Moderate	Degraded pasture	Medbandi, mixing sand and use of gypsum

(Contd.Table 7.11)

(Table 7.11 Contd.)

S. No.	Name of Village	Waste land	Area of Occurrence	Area in ha	Land capability class	Water Potentiality	Soils	Slope	Location	Association	Process of Degradation	Degree of severity	Present use	Recommendation for Reclamation/development of wasteland
3.	Hatheli	Scrub-land	A narrow belt in central part with a patch in northern and southern part of the village	470.25 (Govt. 365.94, Private 104.31)	V	Poor	Clay soil	"	"	"	Nearly level and low permeability	Moderate to severe	do	(i) Silvipasture fuelwood plantation as Harsuliya village on Govt. land (ii) Grassland development as private land
		Saline	A large patch in the central part	42.22	do	do	do	"	"	"	"	"	"	Salt tolerance tree and grass species
4.	Chand-mo Kalan	Scrub land	Southern part of the village	670.00 (Govt. 616.36, Private 53.64)	V	Sandy loam	Gentle slope	plain area	Single and double cropped area	Sheet erosion	Slight	Degraded pasture	Open pasture and scrub land	(i) Silvipastue development on Govt. Land (ii) Medbandi, mixing sand and use of gypsum on private land
	Saline	Near Chand-mo Kalan Bundh and northern part of the village	Govt.	35.14	V	Poor	Clayloam		Plain area	Single cropped area	Nearly level & low permeability	Degraded pastrue	Degraded pasture	Salt tolerance trees/shrubs and grasses

(Contd.Table 7.11)

(Table 7.11 Contd.)

S. No.	Name of Village	Waste land	Area of Occurrence	Area in ha	Land capability class	Water Potentiality	Soils	Slope	Location	Association	Process of Degradation	Degree of severity	Present use	Recommendation for reclamation/development of wasteland
5.	Nathmelpura	Scrub land	Southern part of the village	1124.40 (Govt. 119.07 Private 3.3)	—	do	do	do	do	do	do	do	do	To deveop as Panwasu Khera

Table 7.12 : Model Cost Estimate for FWP

FUEL WOOD PLANTATION					
UNITS : 20 HA (500m x 400m)					
PERIMETER : 140 M/HA					
LABOUR RATE : Rs. 60/DAY					
COST ESTIMATE : IN Rs. /HA.					
S. No.	**Item of Work**	**Rate**	**Labour Component**	**Material Component**	**Total**
	YEAR 0 : ADVANCE ACTION				
1.	Collection of Data for Microplanning, preparation of microplan and management plan	165/Ha	140	25	165
2.	Survey of area, Layout of contour trenches/furrows, Pits and marking of segments/plots	135/Ha	110	25	135
3.	Ditch fencing 1.20 m deep, 1.50m wide at Top and 0.90m at Bottom 140 m in length	65/m	9100	0	9100
4.	Digging of 300m contour trenches of 45cm x 45cm cross section	7.50/m	2250	0	2250
5.	Cost of raising 880 seedlings.	1.60/ plant	1012	396	1408
6.	Digging of 400 Pits size 0.45 x (0.4+0.5)/2 cum	3.81/ pit	1524	0	1524
7.	Cost of collection and purchase of grass and other seeds	Prorata	0	80	80
8.	Construction of Thatched cattle guard hut	Prorata	136	74	210
9.	Construction of water storage tank.	Prorata	204	48	252
10.	Purchase of tools and plants.	Prorata	0	90	90
11.	Labour amenities	Prorata	86	80	166
12.	Cattle Guard wages for 4 months	Prorata	312	0	312
13.	Misc. and unforeseen expenses including running of vehicles.	Prorata	74	34	108
	TOTAL YEAR 0		14948	852	15800
	YEAR 1 PLANATION YEAR				
1.	Maint. of 770 seedlings in Nursery.	0.80/ plant	572	132	704
2.	Digging of 400 pits size 45×(0.4+0.5)/2cum	3.81/ pit	1524	0	1524
3.	Sowing/dibbling of seeds of thorny bushes on trench mound V-ditch Fencing in three lines.	0.17/ rmt	51	0	51
4.	Sowing of grass seeds including raking in the interspaces	Prorata	254	60	314
5.	Transportation of 800 seedlings from Nursery to planting site.	0.38/plant	288	16	304
6.	Planting of 800 seedlings including refilling of pits.	1.09/ plant	872	0	872
7.	Watering in 800 plants with appl. of insecticides at the time of planting.	0.84/ plant	624	48	672
8.	Construction of crescent shaped mounds below the planting pits	0.95/ plant	760	0	760

(Contd. Table 7.12)

(Table 7.12 Contd.)

S. No.	Item of Work	Rate	Labour Component	Material Component	Total
9.	Weeding and Hoeing of 800 plants Two times	1.91/ plant	1528	0	1528
10.	One hoeing of 800 plants	0.55/ plant	440	0	440
11.	Cost of raising 80 plants in Nursery for casualty replacement in year 2	1.60/ plant	92	36	128
12.	Watch and Ward charges for 12 months	Prorata	936	0	936
13.	Cost of insecticide and Fertiliser and Superphospate (DAP) & its application	0.54/ plant	144	288	432
14.	Labour amenities etc.	Prorata	25	28	53
15.	Weeding on Contour trenches/V-ditches and espacement/singling	Prorata	188	0	188
16.	In situ Soil and Moisture Conservation measures like check dams/Nadis, Earthern Bunds etc.	Prorata	180	0	180
17.	Construction of approach roads/inspection path	Prorata	65	0	65
18.	Construction of gate and fixing of sign boards	Prorata	140	180	320
19.	Misc. and unforeseen expences including (additional watering, fencing and forest protection measures and running of vehicles etc.)	Prorata	43	36	79
	TOTAL YEAR 1		8726	824	9550
	YEAR 2 : MAINTENANCE				
1.	Maint. of 80 plants in nursery	0.80/ plant	52	12	64
2.	Repair of fencing	Prorata	65	0	65
3.	Casualty replacement of 80 plants including redigging of pits, transportation, planting, watering and application of insecticides.	3.24/ plnat	259	0	259.2
4.	Two weeding and hoeing in 800 plants.	1.91/ plant	1528	0	1528
5.	Watch and ward charges for 12 months.	Prorata	936	0	936
6.	Misc. and unforeseen expenses including (Repair of structures, subsidiary silvicultural operations, frost protection, etc.)	Prorata	53	45	98
	TOTAL YEAR 2		2893	57	2950
	YEAR 3 : MAINTENANCE				
1.	Watch and ward charges for 12 months	Prorata	936	0	936
2.	Misc. and Unforeseen expenses	Prorata	34	30	64
	TOTAL YEAR 3		970	30	1000
	YEAR 4 : MAINTENANCE				
1.	Watch and ward charges for 12 months	Prorata	936	0	936
2.	Misc. and Unforeseen expenses	Prorata	34	30	64
	TOTAL YEAR 4		970	30	1000
	GRAND TOTAL OF RBH YEARS 0-4		28507	1793	30300

Table 7.13 : Tehsilwise Financial Requirements Development FWP on Panchayat common land in Jaipur District.

S. No.	Name of the Tehsil	Area is hectares	Financial requirement Rs. in lkhs
1.	Amber	6165	18.68.00
2.	Bassi	4750	1439.25
3.	Chaksu	7814	2367.64
4.	Chomu	3570	1081.71
5.	Dudu	12948	3923.24
6.	Jaipur	1695	513.57
7.	Jamwa Ramgarh	7212	2185.24
8.	Kotputli	2868	869.00
9.	Phagi	11555	3501.16
10.	Phulera	9442	2860.91
11.	Sanganer	3671	1112.31
12.	Shahapura	4232	1282.30
13.	Viratnagar	2193	664.47
	TOTAL	78120	23670.33

Source : FWP should be done in phases at five years interval.

Table 7.14 : Cost of Estimation for Reclamation of Saline land in Jaipur District

S. No.	Name of the Tehsil	Amount required (Rs. in lakhs)
1.	Amber	88.00
2.	Bassi	—
3.	Chaksu	—
4.	Chomu	69.21
5.	Dudu	692.55
6.	Jaipur	23.50
7.	Jamwa Ramgarh	—
8.	Kotputli	—
9.	Phagi	158.85
10.	Phulera	518.08
11.	Sanganer	266.75
12.	Shahapura	—
13.	Viratnagar	—
	TOTAL	1816.94

Table 7.15 : Planning for Reclamation/Development of wasteland in Sample Villages for land affected by salinity

S. No.	Name of Village	Wasteland	Area of Occurr-ence	Area in ha	Land capabi-lity class	Water Poten-tiality	Soils	Slope	Location	Associa-tion	Process of Degrada-tion	Degree of sever-ity	Land use/ Land cover	Recommendation for Reclamation/Development of wasteland
1.	Hotu-pur	Saline	North eastern and scatered patches in southern part	233.8	III	Poor	Clay loam	Nearly level to gentle	Near pounds and flot land	Seasonal river	Flood plain	Mode-rate	Fallow/ Culti-vated land	Gypsum along with equal quantity of FYM, medbandi (Embanked) to hold rainwater, levelling of the land for uniform spread of water and effective downword leaching of salt, sanding to improve water and air permeability, green manuring especially sesbani aculeata and crop residues as amendments in the reclamation and management of saline soils.
2.	Pawa-liya	Saline	Estern part and a narrow belt along southern boundary	271.07	III	do	Loamy clay	do	Flat seasonal river bed	do	Flood poain	Mode-rate	Fallow/ Cultivat ed dopend on rain	To make seasonal channel narrow and adopt above recommendations.
3.	Bigo-law	Saline	One patch in western part and another patch along southern boundary	54.95	III	Poor	do	Nearly level to gentle	Plain area in western part and in southern part in seasonal river bed	do	Flood plain	Mode-rate	do	To develop as Hotupur village
		Scrub	Nothern part	10.77	V	Poor	do	do	do	do	Water erosion	Mode-rate	Grazing	Silvipasture/Fuelwood plantation

(Contd.Table 7.15)

(Table 7.15 Contd.)

S. No.	Name of Village	Wasteland	Area of Occurrence	Area in ha	Land capability class	Water Potentiality	Soils	Slope	Location	Association	Process of Degradation	Degree of severity	Land use/ Land cover	Recommendation for Reclamation/Development of wasteland
4.	Bokarwas	Saline	Northern part	151.49	III	Poor	do	Nearly level/ gentle	Flat river bed	do	Flood plain	Moderate	do	(i) To develop as Pawaliya village
		Scrub land	Along southern part of seasonal river	45.68	V	do	do	Gentle	Gullied land	Eroded land	water erosion	Moderate	Grazing	Silvipasture/FWP
5.	Dantra	Saline	Northern part	156.04	III	do	do	Nearly level to gentle	Flat river bed	Seasonal river	Flood plain	Moderate	Cultivated	To develop as Pawaliya village
		Scrub land	Southern part	93.2	V	do	do	Gentle	do	do	do	Moderate	Grazing land	Silvipasture/FWP
6.	Jhakolar	Saline	Eastern part	342.78	III	do	do	Gentle	Flat river bed	Seasonal river	Flood plain	Moderate	Fallow/ Cultivated	(i) To develop as Pawaliya village (ii) Afforestation of salt tore rant trees in strong saline area, deep hole (Thalo) system
		Scrub land	North western part and small patches along the both fiver banks	68.6	VI	do	do	Nearly level to gentle	Flot river bed	Seasonal river	Flood plain	Moderate	Grazing	Silvipasture/FWP

Table 7.16 : Planning for Reclamation/Development of wasteland in Sample Villages for land affected by alkalinity

S. No.	Name of Village	Waste-land	Area of Occu-rrence	Area in ha	Land capa-bility class	Water Poten-tiality	Soils	Slope	Location	Associa-tion	Process of Degra-dation	Degree of severity	Land use/ Land cover	Recommendation for Reclamation/development of wasteland
1	Nasnota	Alka-line	Almost entire village except small patches in southerns and northern part	522.89	IV	Poor	Shallow	Near-ly level/ gentle slope	Bandi river and it adjoining area (Flood plain)	Fallow/ single cropped area	Poor drainage	Severe	Cultur-able waste/ single cropped area	(i) Improvement of drainage, organic manures and gypsum may be applied atleast once in three years for sustained crop production. Shallow rooted crop should be sown. Apply little more chemical fertilizers as compared to recommended doses. Avoid flood irrigation with poor quality water. Plants of economic value such as khejri, ber and soobabool may be grown. Salt resistant varieties and salt tolerant crops may be produced after recla-mation. Good quality water for irrigation with frequent but less quantity of water. Afforestation and pasture development on poor soils. This area can be utilized for non-agricultural activities e.g. industries and settlement etc.
		Saline	Scattered patches in entire village	7.85	III	Poor	Shallow	Near-ly level/ gentle	River bed and plain area	Fallow/ single cropped area	Moisture in river bed	Mode-rate	Nil	To apply gypsum
		Scrub	A small patch in south western part	1.73	V	Poor	Mode-rate to deep	Gentle to mode-rate	Stabilized sand dunes	Single croped area	Wind erosion	Mode-rate	Nil	Close growing`kharif crops

(Contd.Table 7.16)

(Table 7.16 Contd.)

S. No.	Name of Village	Waste-land	Area of Occurrence	Area in ha	Land capability class	Water Potentiality	Soils	Slope	Location	Association	Process of Degradation	Degree of severity	Land use/ Land cover	Recommendation for Reclamation/development of wasteland
2.	Kotewar	Alkaline	Central and southern part	260.87	III	Poor	Shallow to moderate	Gentle to moderate	Bandi river and its adjoining area (Flood plain)	do	Poor drainage	Moderate	Blank/ Single cropped	To reclaim or develop as Nasnota village
		Saline	Scattered small patches in central part	18.43	III	Poor	Shallow to moderate	Gentle	Bandi river bed	River	Moisture in river bed	Moderate	Cultivated	Use of FYM/Gypsum and sowing of salt tolerant crops
		Scrub	Eastern part	17.68	V	Poor	Moderate to deep	Moderate	Sand dune	Cultivated land	Sheet erosion	Moderate	Grazing	Horti culture
		Barren	South western part	5.59	VI	Poor	Thin layer	Steep	Hill	Barren	Biotic interferences	Severe	Nil	RBH model be adopted
3.	Kapriyawas Kalan	Alkaline	Eastern part	333.39	III	Poor	Shallow to moderate	Nearly level to gentle	Bandi river and its adjoining area (Flood plain)	Single cropped	Poor drainage	Moderate	Fallow/ Single cropped	To develop as Nasnota village
		Saline	Northern part	16.24	III	Poor	do	do	River bed	Nil	Mositure in river bed	Moderate	Cultivated	Salt tolerant tree/shrubs species
		Scrub	South western part	58.35	V	Poor	Moderate to deep	Moderate	Sandy plain	Single cropped area	Wind erosion	Moderate	Single cropped area	Close growing crops
		Barren	South western part	4.20	VI	poor	Rock exposed	Moderate to steep	Hill	Barren Hill	Biotic interferences	Severe	Grazing	RBH Model be adopted

(Contd.Table 7.16)

(Table 7.16 Contd.)

S. No.	Name of Village	Waste-land	Area of Occu-rrence	Area in ha	Land capa-bility class	Water Poten-tiality	Soils	Slope	Location	Associa-tion	Process of Degra-dation	Degree of severity	Land use/ Land cover	Recommendation for Reclamation/development of wasteland
4.	Girdhari-pura	Alka-line	Northern part	41.24	III	Poor	Shallow to mode-rate	Near-ly level/ gentle	Sadriyo river bed and its adjoining area (Flood plain)	Single cropped area	Poor drainage	Mode-rate	Blank/ Single cropped area	To develop as Nasnota village
5.	Jharna	Alka-line	Southern part	111.17	III	Poor	Shallow	Near-ly level/ gentle slope	Flood plain	Single/ double cropped area	Poor drainage	Mode-rate	Nil	To develop as Nasnota village
		Saline	South eastern part	8.41	III	Poor	Shallow to mode-rate	Gentle	Seasonal river bed	Nil	Moisture in river bed	Mode-rate	Nil	Salt tolerant tree/shrub species
		Scrub	Northern and eastern part	63.07	V	Poor	Mode-rate to deep	Mode-rate	Sand dune	Cultivated land	Wind/ water erosion	Sligt	Nil	Close growing crops
6.	Mahlan	Alka-line	Western part	231.03	III	Poor	Shallow	Near-ly level to gentle	Flood plain	Cultivated land	Poor drainage	Severe	Nil	To develop as Nasnota village
		Saline	Patches in western part	75.86	III	Poor	Shallow to mode-rate	Gentle slope	Seasonal nallah	Nallah	Moisture in nallah bed	Mode-rate	Nil	Salt tolerant trees, shrubs and grasses

Table 7.17 : Planning for Reclamation/Development of Wasteland in Sample Villages for sand desertic land

S No.	Name of Village	Waste-land	Area of Occurrence	Area in ha	Land Capability class	Water Potentiality	Soils	Slope	Location	Association	Process of Degradation	Degree of severity	Land use/Land cover	Suggestions for Reclamation/ development of wasteland
1.	Majipura	Sand desertic	Entire Village	347.56	II	Poor	Sandy loam/ loamy sand	Nearly level	Sondy plain	Single cropped	Sheet erosion	Mode-rate	Cultivated/ Grazing land	(i) FYM/Fertilizers in bajra and rabi crops (ii) Surface mulching to prevent soil from flowing and being washed away, to reduce evoparation, to increase infiltration, to improve soil structure and eventually to increase yield of crops.
2.	Sursing-pura	do	Entire village except southwestern part	587.98	II	do	Loamy sand/ sandy loam	do	Do	do	do	Mode-rate	do	(iii) Bajra should be inter cropped with cowpea, moong and clusterbean to get more yield of grain and forage.
3.	Bhagwat-pura	do	North western and north eastern part	620.87	II	do	do	do	do	do	do	do	do	(iv) Close grawing crops, shelter belts, kanna building, field and contour strip cropping, inter row water harvesting should be adopted.
														(v) Crop rotation : Bajra - Fallow, cowpea - fallow, moong-fallow, Guar-fallow, Fallow-Mustard/Taramira, Fallow-Gram and wheat-barley.
4.	Maliyawas	do	Central part	281.61	II	do	do	do	do	do	Do	do	do	(vi) Crop residues should be left in the field to get benefits as surface mulching.

(Contd.Table 7.17)

(Table 7.17 Contd.)

S. No.	Name of Village	Waste-land	Area of Occurrence	Area in ha	Land Capability class	Water Potentiality	Soils	Slope	Location	Association	Process of Degradation	Degree of severity	Land use/Land cover	Suggestions for Reclamation/ development of wasteland
5.	Dhani Boraj	(i) Sand-desertic	Northern part	873.73	II	do	do	do	do	do	do	do	do	(vii) Deep ploughing by tractor disc plough.
														(viii) Soil ridge boundary on fields to harvest rainwater
		(ii) Scrub land	Southern part	22.58	VI	do	Thin layer	Moderate to steep	Hill	scrub	Biotic interference	Moderate	Grazing	RBH model as bareen hill areas.

Table 7.18 : Planning for Reclamation/Development of Wasteland in Sample Villages for Mining Wasteland

S. No.	Name of Village	Wasteland	Area of Occurrence	Area in ha	Land Capability class	Water Potentiality	Soils	Slope	Location	Association	Process of Degradation	Degree of severity	Land use/Land cover	Recommendation for reclamation/development of wasteland
1.	Thali	(i) Mining wasteland	North-western part	136.92	VI	Poor	Loamy sand	Moderate	Ravinous land	Gullied and/or ravinous land	Mining activities	Severe	Mining area	Rehabilitation of mined lands; Covering mine spoils with good soil material, use of amendments, plantation of vegetation i.e. mixture of trees, shrubs and grasses of indigenous species or exotic species from similar edapho climatic regions of the world.
		(ii) Scrub land	Northern eastern part and scattered patches in cultivated land	582.16	VII	Poor	Loamy sand	Moderate	Ravinous land	Mining and cultivated	Mining spoil	Severe	Grazing	In eastern part soil conservation model in gullied and/or ravinous land be adopted
		(iii) Degraded forest	Northern part	16.76	VIII	Poor	Hill	Moderate	Undulated land	Mining area/Mining spoil	Biotic interference	Moderate	Grazing	To adopt RDF model I
2.	Rayanwala	(i) Mining wasteland	Southern part	121.58	VI	Poor	Loamy sand	Moderate	Undulated eroded land	Mining spoil	Mining activities	Severe	Mining area	To develop as Thali Village
		(ii) Scrub land	Southern part	611.48	V	do	do	do	do	Mining area	Mining spoil	Moderate	Mining area	do
		(iii) Degraded forest	Central and northern part	292.2	VIII	Poor	do	Steep	Hills	Different types of forest	Biotic interference	Moderate	Grazing/ timber and fuelwood	To adopt RDF model I

(Contd.Table 7.18)

(Table 7.18 Contd.)

S. No.	Name of Vill-age	Wasteland	Area of Occu-rrence	Area in ha	Land Capability class	Water Potentiality	Soils	Slope	Loca-tion	Associa-tion	Process of Degrada-tion	Degree of severity	Land use/Land cover	Recommendation for reclamation/development of wasteland
3.	Sand Koina	(i) Mining wasteland	Eastern part	39.8	VI	Poor	do	Mode-rate	Plain area	Scrub and cultivated land	mining activities	Severe	Mining area	To develop as Thali village
		(ii) Scrub land	North-ern and southern part	441.39	VII	Poor	do	Mode-rate	Undula-ted eroded land	Mininng and cultivated land	Ravines	Mode-rate	Grazing	Soil conservation model in gullied and or ravinous land be adopted
		(iii) Degrded forest	Nothern part	6.11	VIII	Poor	do	Steep	Hills	Different types of forest	Biotic interfe-rence	Mode-rate	Grazing/ fuel wood	To adopt RDF model I
4.	Singh-puri	(i) Mining wasteland	Nor-thern part	5.53	VI	Poor	do	Steep to mode-rate	Foothill	Degraded forest and cropped area	Mining activities	Severe	Mining acti-vities	To stop mining activities due to location in forest area.
		(ii) Scrub land	South-ern part	80.87	VII	Poor	Kanka-rili	Mode-rate slope	Foot-hills	Forest and cultivated land	Biotic interfer-ences	Mode-rate	Grazing	To adopt RBH model
		(iii) Degraded forest	Nor-thern part	12.79	VIII	Poor	Hill	Steep slope	Hill	Different types of forest	do	Mode-rate	Grazing	To adopt RDF model I
	Dagota	(i) Mining wasterland	Sout-hern part	67.85	VI	Poor	Kanka-rili	Mode-rate	Foothill	Degraded forest	Mining activities	Severe	Mining area	To develop asThali village
		(ii) Scrub land	Western and central part	802.89	VII	Poor	do	do	do	Scattered trees	Biotic interfe-rence	Severe	Grazing	To adopt RDF model I
		(iii) Degraded forest	Eastern and western part	1161.6	VIII	Poor	Hills	Steep	Hills	Different types of forest	do	Mode-rate	Grazing	do

Table 7.19 : Production and Income from Various Forest Products after Wasteland Development of Barren Hills, Degraded Forest and Degraded Pasture in Jaipur district.

	Area (Ha)	Timber (cum)	Small Timber (cum)	Fuelwood (Quintals)		Grass (Quintals)	Dry/Fallen wood	Munja (Poola)	MFP (kg.)	Fruits (kg.)
Rate Per Unit		5000	4000	150	150	160	130	20	25	20
Harvesting Year		25th	25th	12th	25th	2nd to 25th	12th to 25th	2nd to 25th	6th to 25th	10th to 25th
Reforestation of Barren Hills	7363									
Planted Trees (Per hect.)		10	30	100	400	7.5	20	25	200	100
Natural Trees (Per hect.)		0	0	0	0	0	0	0	0	0
Total Quantity (Per hect.)		10	30	100	400	180	280	600	4000	1600
Total Amount in Rs. (Per hect.)		50000	120000	15000	60000	28800	36400	12000	100000	32000
Total Production (In 25 years) from RBH		73630	220890	736300	2945200	1325340	2061640	4417800	29452000	11780800
Total Income in Lacs from RBH (in 25 years)		3681.5	8835.6	1104.45	4417.8	120.54	2680.13	883.56	736.3	2356.16
Rehabilitation of Degraded Forest	13044									
Planted Trees (Per hect.)		8	20	70	350	5	30	25	200	100
Natural Trees (Per hect.)		22	20	30	150	0	0	0	0	0
Total Quantity (Per hect.)		30	40	100	500	120	420	600	4000	1600
Total Amount in Rs. (Per hect.)		150000	160000	15000	75000	19200	54600	12000	100000	32000
Total Production (In 25 years) from RDF		391320	521760	1304400	6352000	1565280	5478480	7826400	52176000	20870400
Total Income in Lacs from RDF (in 25 years)		19566	20870.4	19566	9528	30.72	7122.04	1565.28	13044	40174.08
Fuelwood Plantation on Panchayat Land	78120									

(Contd. Table 7.19)

(Table 7.19 Contd.)

	Area (Ha)	Timber (cum)	Small Timber (cum)	Fuelwood (Quintals)		Grass (Quintals)	Dry/Fallen wood	Munja (Poola)	MFP (kg.)	Fruits (kg.)
Planted Trees (Per hect.)		0	30	150	700	7.5	20	100	200	100
Natural Trees (Per hect.)		0	0	0	0	0	0	0	0	0
Rate Per Unit		5000	4000	150	150	160	130	20	25	20
Harvesting Year		25th	25th	12th	25th	2nd to 25th	12th to 25th	2nd to 25th	6th to 25th	10th to 25th
Total Quantity (Per hect.)		0	30	150	700	180	280	2400	4000	1600
Total Amount in Rs. (Per hect.)		0	120000	22500	105000	28800	36400	48000	100000	32000
Total Production (In 25 years) from FWP		0	2343600	11718000	54684000	14061600	21873600	187488000	312480000	124992000
Total Income in Lacs from FWP (in 25 years)		0	93744	17577	82026	22498.56	28435.68	37497.6	78120	24998.4

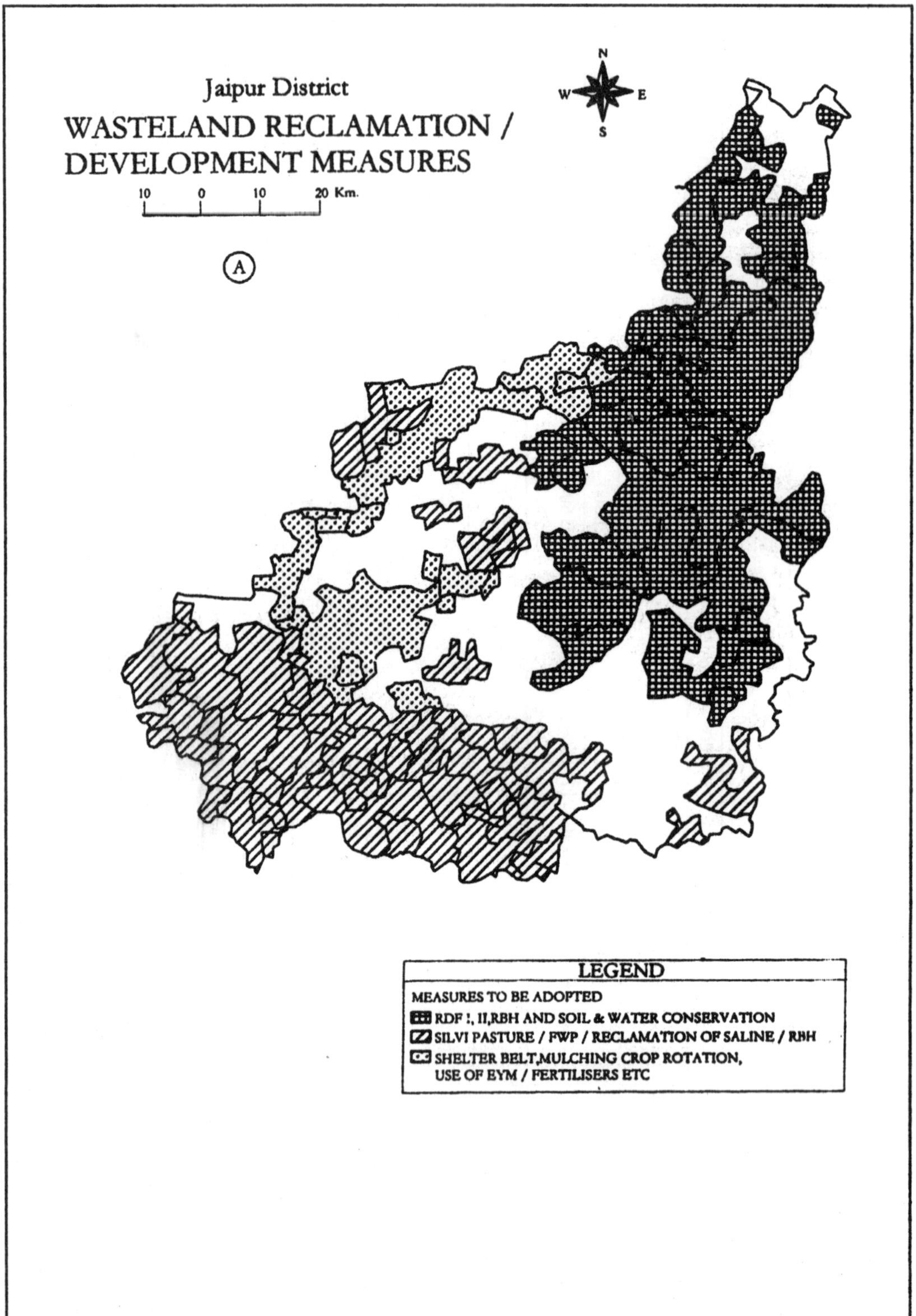

Fig. 7.1: Wasteland Reclamation/Development Measures.

Table 7.20 : Total Expenditure, Income and Cost Benefit Ratio from Development of Wastelands in Jaipur district.

Wasteland Development	Total Expenditure (Including interest @ 8% p.a.) (in Lacs)	Total Income (in Lacs)	Cost Benefit Ratio
Reforestation of Barren hills	11834	26816	1:2.27
Degraded Forest	82699	131467	1:1.59
Fuelwood Plantation on Panchayat Land	150068	384897	1:2.56
Total	244601	543180	1:2.22

Wasteland Reclamation/Development Measures

On the basis of villagewise wasteland distribution, relief, soil and geology the study are can be divided into three wasteland reclamation/development regions as below:-

(i) Eastern hilly tract having degraded forest, barren hills and gullied/ravinous land.
(ii) Western sands-desertic upland.
(iii) South and south western peneplained lowland dominantly affected by salinity/ alkalinity and degraded pasture/grazing land.

Fig. 7.1 also shows that wasteland development is eastern part RDF I, II, RBH, soil and water conservation measures are required while in western part, sand-desertic wasteland is concentrated. This wasteland should be developed as per suggestions given in sample study area for sand-desertic land. In south and south western part of the study area, the main problems are poor pedological and hydrological conditions, Fuelwood plantation, silvipasture and saline/alkaline reclamation measures should be adopted for wasteland development in this region of the district. Besides this there is a good scope for dairy development in this part of the study area.

REFERENCES

Anonymous, (1975). Prog. Report, Dryland Research Project, CAZRI, Jodhpur (Mimeographed)

Anoymous, (1976). Improved Dryland Agriculture for Western Rajasthan, *Tech. Buli, N-1,* pp. 28, CAZRI, Jodhpur.

Bali, J.S. (1972). *Ravine Reclamation Needs for India*, New Delhi.

Bali, J.S. (1985). Problems of Gullied and Ravinous Areas – Policy and Progress. *Proc. National Seminar on Soil Conservation and Watershed Management*, Sept. 17-18, 1985, New Delhi.

Bhimaya, C.P., Kaul, R.N., Jain, M.B. and Ganguli, B.N. (1967). A study of age and habitat differences in the fuel yield of Prosopis Juliftora. *Indian Fmg* 93(6) : 355-58

Chaturvedi, A.C. (1986). Land Use Planning for Wasteland Development, *Proceedings of Foods and Wasteland Management, Organized by Gorakhpur Environmental Action Group*, July 28 to August 2.

Chinnamani, S. (1986). Forestry, Social Forestry and Agro-Forestry in Ravine Reclamation. Lecture delivered at the Summer Inst. Wasteland in Arid and Semi Arid Zones and Technologies for Their Improved Utilization, CAZRI, Jodhpur.

Committee on Natural Resources and Planning Commission, New Delhi (1963). "Study on Wastelands, Including Saline and Alkali and Waterlogged lands and their Reclamation Measures".

Daulay, H.S., Singh, H.P. and Henry, A. (1983). Recommendation and Implementable Practices for Dryland Crop Production in Arid Zone. *Division Bull N. 8, Dry Farming Research Main Centre*, CAZRI, Jodhpur, pp. 32.

Daulay, H.S. and Singh, H.P. (1984). Increasing and Stabilizing Crop Production on Dryland, *Indian Fmg*. 34:23-5.

Daulay, H.S. (1990) "Improving Production of Crop land in the Arid Region" in *Technologies for Wasteland Development* (T.Ed.) Abrol I.P. *et al.* ICAR, New Delhi-12

Deb Roy, R. (1986). Silvipastoral Plantation for Production from Wasteland in respect of Forage, Fuelwood and Fodder, *Proc., Plantation Crop – Opportunities and Constraint*, New Delhi Jan. 31-Feb. 1. Oxford and IBH Pub. Co., New Delhi, pp. 411.

Dhawan, C.L. (1964). *Land Reclamation*, Central Board of Irrigation and Power Publication, No. 48, Vol. II.

Government of Rajasthan, Jaipur (1963). Report on Ravine Reclamation – Kakker Committee.

Gupta, J.P. (1990). *Sand Dunes and their Stabilization in Technologies for Wasteland Development*, ICAR, New Delhi.

Kaul, O.N. (1962). Management of Chambal Ravines in Rajasthan. *Indian Foresters*, 88, pp. 725-30.

Kaul, R.N. (1985). *Afforestation of Dune Areas in Sand Dune Stabilization*, Shelterbelts and Afforestation in Dry Zones, FAO, Rome, pp. 75-85.

Mann, H.S.; Ramana Rao, B.V. and Daulay, H.S. (1981). Maximization of Crop Production in Arid Regions, *Indian J.Soil Water Conservation*. 9 (2 & 3) : 141-53.

Patra Punyatoya and Thakur Baleshwer (2005). Spatial Pattern of Land Degradation in the Northern Highlands of Orissa Sharma H.S. (Ed.) *Geomorphology and Environmental Sustainability*. Concept Publishing Company, New Delhi.

Rajasthan Forestry and Bio-diversity Project, Forest Department, Government of Rajasthan, Jaipur.

Shah, P. (1987). Economics of Wasteland Development Project undertaken by G.S.R.D.C. in Yadav, H.R. (ed.) *Wastelands-Diagnosis and Treatment*, Concept, New Delhi, pp. 175-211.

Sharma, K.D. (1997). Recent Developments in the Reclamation of Surface Mined Lands, *Annals of Arid Zone*. 36 (4) : 311-326.

Singh, A.L., (1978), *Economics and Geography of Agricultural Land Reclamation*, B.R.Pub., New Delhi.

Singh, Rajvir, (2000). *Watershed Planning and Management*, Yash Publishing House, Bikaner.

Tejwani, K.G. *et al.* (1960). Control of Gully Erosion in the Ravine Lands of Gujarat, *Journal of Soil and Water Conservation in India*, 8, 65-74.c

8

SUMMARY AND CONCLUSION

Increasing demand for food, fodder, fuel and fibre has necessitated adoption of scientific measures for increasing land productivity and bringing more areas under cultivation/forest. At the same time land degradation due to desertification, soil salinity, water logging, excessive soil erosion due to deforestation, unscientific agricultural practices etc., has resulted in the creation of vast stretches of wasteland and a decrease in per capita cultivated land besides ecological imbalance. To increase productivity through irrigation at the saturation stage and there is a limited scope for extension of net sown area without reclamation of wastelands. For ecological balance one-third geographical area is desired under forest, which may be achieved by reclaiming wastelands.

The present study is concentrated on identification, spatial distribution and planning for reclamation/development of wastelands. Wasteland has been identified from the soft copies of IRS LIS-III satellite images. Spatial distribution pattern of different wasteland categories at village/tehsil level on district map is based upon the wasteland maps (1:50,000) obtained from National Remote Sensing Agency, Hyderabad (A.P.) in 2002. The unit chosen for spatial distribution of wasteland is village/town. The total villages and towns are 2203 (2187 + 16) in the study area. An area of each category of wastelands of every village/town of the district has been calculated with Digital Planimeter. For the detailed sample study a cluster of 4-6 villages from each category of wasteland has been selected and IRS-LISS III images of February 28, 2003 have been used for identification, spatial distribution and planning for reclamation/development of wastelands in sample villages.

Satellite images of IRS-LISS III have been loaded on computer in Geomatica software for geometic rectification and further land use analysis. These images have mask of each representative areas, as mentioned above have been prepared to demarcate the area of interest. By using these masks 3 bands were used for creating FCC on Geomatica software and files created for each representative area for further analysis. The bit maps of various wasteland categories have been mapped on a single channel to get a composite wasteland map of the each representative area. Appropriate map composition has been prepared for FCC images and wasteland classified images in Geomedia software. Masks have been prepared for each village in each of the representative area for calculating automatic area under the village and each category of wastelands. Areas of wasteland categories were calculated for each village and tables prepared to show areas of different categories in each village. Appropriate map compositions have been prepared for creating output images of raw satellite image (FCC) and classified wasteland categories image. Cartographic techniques including maps and diagrams have been used for the present study to depict the spatial and structural variations of wasteland.

The study area, Jaipur district is situated between 26°23′ and 27°51′ north latitude and 75°55′ and 76°10′ east longitude in the eastern part of Rajasthan state. It occupies an area of 10,876.78 km^2 which is 3.17 per cent to the total area of the state. This district has 4 sub-divisions, 13 tehsils, 16 towns and 2187 villages. National Atlas and Thematic Mapping Organization (NATMO), Department of Science of Technology, Government of India, Kolkata (W.B.) divided the relief of the district into four categories taking interval of 150m. Approximately three-fourth area of the district belongs to 300 to 400 m elevation from MSL. In northern part, height is increasing from the central part to north eastern part of the study area whereas in the southern part, the height is decreasing continuously. On the basis of quarter inch topogrophical sheets, the district can be broadly divided into two physical units i.e. upland and lowland. The upland further can be divided into three physical divisions (i) Chomu-western Amber and northern Phulera upland is situated in the western part of the study area. This area has fertile aeolain sandy loam with good quality ground water resources while hilly tract is scattered in two patches i.e. central and eastern part of the upland especially in Shahapura, eastern Amber and Viratnagar tehsils. High altitude hill ranges are scattered mainly in western Jamwa Ramgarh, eastern Viratnagar tehsil, along western boundary of Kotputli tehsil and eastern Amber tehsil.

The southern lowland is in the south of 380m contour especially in Dudu, southern Phulera, Sanganer, Jaipur, northern Phagi, Bassi and eastern Jamwa Ramgarh tehsils. The lowland can be divided into four sub-divisions. Sambhar salt lake area lies in the western part of the study area. The bottom of Sambhar lake is flat saucer like and having an altitude of 360m above MSL and the peripheries are 364m above MSL. Dudu, western Phulera, Sanganer, north Phagi, Bassi, eastern Jamwa Ramgarh and Phagi, Chaksu plain is almost level land having poor pedological and ground water resources. A small patch of lowland lies in north eastern part of Kotputli tehsil.

In the southern part approximately more than half of the district has > 10m slope per km. especially in Dudu, Phagi, Chaksu, Sanganer, Bassi tehsils, southern Jaipur and south eastern part of Jamwa Ramgarh tehsil. These tehsils have problem of salinity/alkalinity, land with scrub or without scrub and degraded pasture/grazing land. The slope of 10-20m per kilometre is found in the northern part particularly in Phulera, Chomu, Amber, Shahapura and Jamwa Ramgarh tehsils. A narrow long belt of north central part starts from Jaipur city to Triveni (west of Shahapura town) and along the western border of Kotputli tehsil there is very steep slope i.e. 80-150 and 150 to 300m per kilometre. This area occupies sand-desertic, degraded forest, barren hills and gullied and/or ravinous land.

Geologically western and southern part of the study area belongs to sand and alluvium while south western part consists of gneisses, schists and megmatite. Hill ranges of north eastern part comprise of quartizites and conglomerate. Maximum concentration of schists, phyllites and marble is in eastern part of Kotputli tehsil and small scattered patches are also found in the south eastern and western part of the district. Besides these small patches of dolomite, marble, quartizite and granite, pegmatite, amphibolite are found in eastern and north eastern part of the study area.

This district is not rich in mineral resources even though a variety of minerals are found. Iron are, copper, mica, felspar, soapstone deposits are found in various parts of the district. But mining activities related to soapstone, marble and building stones are continued.

Drainage also affects the spatial pattern of wasteland. However, there is not a single perennial river in the study area. The major seasonal rivers are Banganga, Bandi, Dhund, Morel, Mashi, Mendha, Sota and Sabi. Banganga is an important river of the study area. A dam on this river near Jamwa Ramgarh village, supplies drinking water to the Pinkcity Jaipur.

On the basis of depths, texture, colour, calcareousness and permeability the soils of Jaipur district have been classified into seven soil associations, Chomu dune association dominates in western part of the district. Bassi-Rajori association occupies most of the study area i.e. southern and eastern part of the district. These soils are deep, sandy loam to loam, well drained and moderately eroded lying or nearly level to gently sloping land. The soils of Naraina-Dudu association are shallow to moderately deep, imperfectly drained, strongly calcareous and moderately to strongly saline sodic. Soil of Rajori-Chaksu association is found in a small patch in the south western part of the study area. Soils of Chandrana-Padasoli association are found in two areas i.e. central and north eastern part of the district. These soils are moderately deep to very deep, clay loam to clay, poor to moderately drained, netural to calcareous and slightly to moderately eroded. Soils of Padasoli-Phagi association are found in the southern part of the study. These soils are deep, fine textured, poorly drained to moderately well drained and neutral to calcareous. Soils of Chandrana-Bandikui are scattered in three small patches. These soils are also very deep, dominantly fine textured and poorly to moderately drained.

Approximately one-fourth area of the district has very high water potentiality particularly in north, western part of the district and small patches of this zone are also found in Kotputli, Viratnagar, Phulera, Chomu and Sanganer tehsils. In this zone average yield is 200-250m^3/day. High water potential zone (75-150m^3/day) constitutes 2828.96km^2 area in south eastern, north west and central part of the district. About one-third area of the district belongs to medium water potential zone especially north east part of the district. Low and very low water potentiality zones (yield 40-90m^3/day and 2136.57km^2) are found in Chaksu, Dudu, Phagi and Jamwa Ramgarh tehsils.

The fresh to slightly saline water having EC below 2000 us/cm at 25^{0}C occurs in most part of the district. In eastern part of the district around Hastal Ka Bas (Block Jamwa Ramgarh), and Bassi, Jatwara Railway Station (Block Bassi) electrical conductivity of ground water is more than 5000 us/cm at 25^{0}C. In south western part of the district around Mangalwara, Mozamabad, Nosnota (Block Dudu), Pallu Khurd and Jobner (Block Sambhar) electrical conductivity of ground water is more than 5000us/cm at 25^{0}C. Two small patches of this range are one around Kotputli and the other between Shahapura and Amber block. In south west a patch between Phagi, Dudu, Sambhar and Sanganer block also has such type of water.

The average annual rainfall in the district is 556.4mm. The rainfall generally increases from west to east. But in the Amber region, the rainfall is a little higher than the surrounding parts of the district due to forested hills. The period from March to June is of continuous rise in temperature. The maximum monthly temperature in the area has been recorded in May and June which varies from 40:60^{0}C to 39.20. During summer, the plain suffers from extreme heating and hot westly wind known as "Loo". After mid-November both day and night temperatures fall rapidly till January which is the coldest month with the mean daily maximum temperature of 22°C and mean daily minimum of 8.3°C. Relative humidity is quite high during monsoon (July to September) amounting to 68.5, 76.5 and 65.5 per cent respectively.

The existing pattern of land use is the outcome of past efforts and also evolutionary processes providing a base for future planning of land resources. The study area has only 7.37 per cent forest land to the total geogrophical area in 2003-04. The maximum area under forest is concentrated in north eastern part i.e. Viratnagar and Jamwa Ramgarh tehsils because of hills and rugged areas with greatest slope. Viratnagar is the only tehsil of the study area which occupies its more than one-third area under forest (37.53%) followed by Jamwa Ramgarh tehsil (23.64%). Land not available for cultivation covers 10.55 per cent area of the district. The maximum area under this category is in central part of the study area i.e. in Jaipur tehsil due to more area under settlements followed by Jamwa Ramgarh tehsil. Maximum culturable wasteland is in Jaipur tehsil followed by Sanganer and Dudu tehsils. This district has 7.04 per cent of the total area under permanent pastures. High and very high percentages of permanent pasture are in the tehsils of southern part of the district. Maximum land under permanent pasture is in Phagi tehsil (10.35%) followed by Dudu and Chaksu tehsils. These tehsils have large number of animals and poor pedological and hydrological conditions.

High and very high percentages of current fallow i.e. 12 to 16 and above 16 were in the tehsils of southern part of the district with maximum in Chaksu tehsil. The other tehsils of southern part of the study area having high percentage of this category are Dudu, Phagi, Sanganer and Bassi. These tehsils have poor quality of irrigation water and shallow poor soils, so the most of the land in rabi season is kept as a current fallow.

The net sown area in this district is 53.24 per cent to the total geographical area which is almost equal to the state average (52.84%). The high and very high percentages (60-70 and < 70%) of NSA in the tehsils of western part of the district i.e. Chomu and Phulera. The moderate percentage (50-60%) of NSA is also concentrated in north western, northern and south western part of the district. Low percentages of this category is in the central and south eastern part of the study area while it is least in the tehsils of north eastern part viz. in Jamwa Ramgarh and Viratnagar due to more area under forest, hilly tracts and gullied/ravinous land.

From 1901 to 1947 was the golden era in the history of irrigation in the district. The major dams of the district viz. Chhaparwara, Kharkharad, Madho Sagar, Mingonia, Kalakh Sagar and Buchara etc. were constructed during this period. After independence farmers have became land owners. They increased the irrigated area during the Five Year Plans. At present approximately three-fourth cropped area of Chomu and Jaipur tehsils is under irrigation due to good quality irrigation water and fertile soils. Surrounding tehsils of very high irrigation intensity viz. Bassi, Jamwa Ramgarh, Shahapura, Viratnagar and Sanganer also have high percentages (45-60%) of irrigated area. The tehsils having low and very low irrigated area are situated in the southern part of the district. These tehsils have poor quality/quantity of ground water resources.

Population growth pattern can be divided into three distinct periods: (1) from 1901 to 1931 (2) from 1931 to 1991 and (3) from 1991 to 2001. During the first period of 30 years, the population of the district decreased continuously due to famine and epidemics. During second period (1931-91), the growth of population has been relatively rapid because of the availability and expansion of medical facilities and control over diseases etc. During this period of six decades, population of the district has increased 4.5 times. During the third period (1991-2001) witnessed slightly slow growth (35.10) due to increase in living standard and literacy.

The arithmetic density of the study area was 471 persons per km^2 in 2001. The very high (above 440) population density is concentrated in the central and north western part of the district as it includes the capital city Jaipur, Chomu and Shahapura tehsil. Most of the northwestern part has fertile soil and good quality irrigation water. High density is found in northern part (360-440) which is occupied by the Sabi and Sota river basins having fertile alluvial deep and non-calcareous soils with high intensity of irrigation. Moderate density (280-360) is in northern, upper central and eastern part of the study area while low arithmetic density (200-280) is found in western, eastern and southern part where sand-desertic, hilly tracts and land affected by salinity, alkalinity are main limitations. Very low arithmetic density, (Below 200) is concentrated in south-western part of the study area. The pattern of rural density is almost the same as that of arithmetic density except central, north western and northern parts of the district.

Maximum literacy (above 70%) is concentrated in central and northern parts of the district due to more educational institutions in the capital city. Similarly, high per cent of literacy (65-70%) is found in the western part where more educational infrastructural facilities are available in the towns e.g. Sambhar, Phulera, Jobner, Chomu and Kaladera. Low and very low literacy is in the agriculturally backward tehsils of south western and south eastern part except Amber tehsil.

Maximum concentration of S.T. population is in Jamwa Ramgarh tehsil situated in the eastern part of the study area followed by Bassi tehsil having more area under hilly tracts, degraded forest and gullied/ravinous land.

In 2001, only 36.47 per cent population was engaged as cultivator in the study area. More than 60 per cent cultivators of the working population are found in the Phagi and Chaksu tehsils of southern part. Moderate percentage (55-60%) of cultivators are concentrated in Shahapura, Viratnagar, Amber, Jamwa Ramgarh and Bassi tehsils. Low percentage of this category of working population is in the western part viz in Chomu, Phulera and Dudu tehsils while the lowest percentage of cultivators is found in Jaipur and Sanganer tehsils i.e. 4.25 and 22.33 per cent of the total working population due to urban agglomeration of capital city Jaipur. The maximum percentage of agricultural labourers is in southern and northern parts of the district particularly in Dudu, Phagi and Kotputli tehsils. These tehsils are industrially backward, so the percentage of agricultural labourers is more. Only 4.40 percent is engaged in household industry with maximum percentage in Jaipur (5.33%) and Sanganer (5.08%) tehsils. In the study area. 54.64 per cent working population is categorized as other workers. This is the only district in the whole state where the percentage of other workers is very high. The maximum concentration of other workers is in Jaipur tehsil followed by Sanganer and Phulera tehsils.

More than one-third area (36.02%) of total wastelands of the district is under degraded notified forest land followed by gullied and/or ravinous land (27.41%) and land with or without scrub (12.40%). All the three categories of wastelands combinedly consist three-fourth (75.83%) wasteland area of the district. In remaining wastelands, sands-desertic (8.43%)

and land affected by salinity/alkalinity are important. The degraded forest and most of the gullied and/or ravinous land are associated with hilly tracts. Thus the major problem of wasteland is concentrated in the tehsils having more area under hills especially tehsils of eastern part of the district.

On comparing India, Rajasthan and Jaipur district it is found that the study area occupies lowest percentage of wastelands. However, the state and the district have almost equal area under wastelands. The district occupies higher percentage of gullied and/or ravinous land and degraded forest in comparison to the country and the state. The district and Rajasthan state both do not occupy area under shifting cultivation, snow covered and or glacial area.

There are 49590.04 hectares under gullied and/or ravinous constituting 4.20 per cent to the total geographical area of the district. Maximum concentration of gullied and/or ravinous land is found in the north eastern part of the district. Approximately one-half gullied and/or ravinous land of the study area is concentrated in two tehsils viz. Jamwa Ramgarh (29.88%) and Viratnagar (17.99%). Other important tehsils of gullied and/or ravinous land are Shahapura (14.61%) and Amber (10.63%). All the four tehsils constitute three-fourth gullied and/or ravinous land of the district.

The villages having high and very high percentages (45.01 to < 60%) of gullied and ravinous land are concentrated in a enlongated belt running from south to north. The villages of moderate percentage (30.1 to 45%) are found in two patches i.e. eastern part of Jamwa Ramgarh tehsil and its adjoining area in Amber tehsil. The second patch is in southern part of Sahapura tehsil and central part of Viratnagar tehsil. The villages of low and very low percentages of gullied and ravinous are also scattered in the eastern part of the district.

Jamwa Ramgarh tehsil alone covers approximately one-third its geographical area (30.74%) under degraded forest followed by Viratnagar tehsil (24.82%). Both the tehsils cover more than one-half (55.56%) degraded notified area of the district. Other tehsils having more area under this category are Kotputli (14.38%) and Amber (13.19%). Remaining tehsils occupy nil or negligible area under this category.

Villages having more than 60 per cent of their geographical area under this category are situated mainly in two patches i.e. eastern part of Viratnagar and north-eastern part of Jamwa Ramgarh tehsils. Besides these three small patches of very high percentages (above 60%) are situated in the south –eastern part of Amber, western part of Kotputli and Central part of Jamwa Ramgarh tehsil. Other percentage intensities under this category of land are also found in the adjoining to villages having moderate to very high percentage of degraded notified forest land, especially north-eastern part of the study area.

The sands desertic wasteland is scattered in each tehsil of the district but the maximum concentration is found in the western part of the study area. This part touches the arid/desert districts Nagaur and Sikar of the state. Therefore, western part of the study area has also arid/desert characteristics as adjoining desert districts. This category covers 32318 hectares equivalent to 2.74 per cent of the total geographical area. Chomu tehsil tops all the tehsils of the study area as this tehsil covers 8.48 per cent of the total geographical area under this category followed by Phulera (5.32%) and Shahapura (3.89%) tehsils. Other tehsils having more geographical under this category are Chaksu and Dudu. Dudu is adjoining Phulera tehsil while in Chaksu Dhund river and its tributaries have sands in their beds. All the tehsils except Chaksu are situated in the western part of the study area. The villages of very high percentage of sands (<40%) to their geographical area concentrated in the central part of the Phulera tehsil. As already explained this tehsil is situated adjoining desert district of Nagaur and Sambhar gap in Aravalli hills is also responsible for the more sandy area. The villages of high percentage (30-40%) of sands are also scattered adjoining villages of very high percentage of sands-desertic land and in western part of the Chomu tehsil while the villages of very low, low and moderate percentages of sands-desertic are scattered in most of the tehsils of the district especially eastern part of Jamwa Ramgarh, Bassi and northern part of Phulera and western part of Dudu tehsil.

Land with or without scrub covers 18572.50 hectares equivalent to 1.57 per cent of the total geographical area of the district. The maximum concentration of this category is in Phagi tehsil i.e. 6.01 per cent to the total geographical area due to poor soils and ground water resources. Other tehsils having more their geographical area under this category are Dudu (2.55%), Kotputli (2.21%) and Chaksu (2.15%).

Very high intensity (>6%) of land with or without scrub is in southern part of the study area i.e. in Phagi tehsil while tehsils having high intensity of this category (4 to 6%) are also situated adjoining this tehsil and northern part of the district. As already explained the pedological and hydrological conditions of the Phagi, Dudu and western Chaksu tehsil are almost same, so the percentage under this category is high. In Kotputli tehsil this category of land is found on the foothills and hill ranges. In remaining tehsils, it is negligible. Maximum land with or without scrub is concentrated in the south south-western part of the study area especially in Phagi, Dudu and south Phulera tehsil.The villages having more than 20 per cent of their total geographical area under this category are concentrated in the southern part of the study area especially in south eastern part of the Phagi tehsil. Other villages of very high and high intensity are scattered in eastern, north western and south western part of the district particularly in Jamwa Ramgarh, Kotputli and Dudu tehsils. The villages of very low and low percentages (1.01 to 10%) of scrubland are also concentrated in the southern part of the district.

Land affected by salinity/alkalinity is 18169.51 hectares equivalent to 1.54 per cent of the total geographical area of the district. Land affected by salinity/alkalinity is concentrated in the tehsils of western and central part of the study area. The maximum area of this category of land is in Dudu tehsil situated in the south western part of the district followed by Sanganer and Phulera tehsils. Phulera and Sanganer tehsils are also situated in the north and east of the Dudu tehsil. Other tehsils affected by salinity/alkalinity are also adjoining the tehsils having more areas under this category. Villages having various intensity of land affected by salinity/alkalinity are concentrated in south western, western and central part of the district. The maximum villages of this category are situated in the south western part particularly Dudu tehsil and southern Phulera tehsil.

Degraded pasture/grazing land covers 7648.01 hectares equivalent to 0.65 per cent of the total geographical area of the district. Only three tehsils of the study area have moderate intensity (1.01 to 2%) of degraded pasture/grazing land. These tehsils i.e. Phagi, Dudu, Bassi and Shahapura are situated in south, east and northern part of the district, and occupy more area under this category due to different causes e.g. in southern part poor pedological and hydrological conditions, in eastern part hilly tracts while in north-western part sandy soils with sand dunes.

Besides this, small patches of this category of land are also scattered in almost all the tehsils of the study area. Villages having very high intensity of degraded pasture i.e.

20 per cent to their total geographical are scattered mainly in southern and eastern part of the district. Similarly villages of high (15.01–20%) and moderate (10.01–15%) intensities of this category are also unevenly scattered while villages having low and very low percentages of degraded pasture are concentrated in south, south western and north western part of the district particularly in Phagi, Shahapura and Dudu tehsils.

Barren hill/rocky covers 7363.20 hectares equivalent to 0.62 per cent of the total geographical area of the district. Barren rocky is more in two areas viz. south western and northern part of the study area particularly in Dudu, Shahapura and Amber teshils while it is less in remaining tehsils. Villages having more barren hill/rocky are found mainly in a belt stretched from southwest to north east direction in the study area with maximum concentration in upper middle part of the belt. Barren rocky is almost negligible in Phagi, Chaksu, Sanganer and Viratnagar tehsils situated in the south and north eastern part of the district. The villages having very high and high percentages (12.01 to above 16%) of barren hill/rocky are upper middle part especially northern part of Amber, southern Shahapura tehsil, north and south western part of Dudu tehsils. The distributional pattern of villages having high intensity (8.01-12%) is also the same as very high intensity of this category. The villages of very low and low percentages (0.01 to 8%) are concentrated in the northern part of the study area especially is Shahapura, south eastern part of Chomu, Amber and western part of Kotputli tehsils. Some villages of these categories are also found in scattered form in eastern part particularly in Jamwa Ramgarh and Bassi tehsils.

Mining wasteland covers only 315 hectares equivalent to 0.03 percent to the total geographical area. The maximum area is in Jaipur followed by Sanganer and Jamwa Ramgarh tehsils. The maximum mining wasteland is in the central part of the district i.e. in Jaipur tehsil followed by Sanganer and Jamwa Ramgarh tehsils.

Of the total wastelands, approximately one-half wasteland of the district is concentrated in only three tehsils viz Jamwa Ramgarh, Viratnagar and Phulera. In Jamwa Ramgarh and Viratnagar tehsils, maximum area under degraded forest and gullied/ravinous land is found due to hilly tracts and undulated land while Phulera tehsil occupies maximum area under sand desertic land due to proximacy of desert districts of the state. Other important tehsils having more total wastelands are Amber, Dudu and Kotputli.

Viratnagar, Jamwa Ramgarh and Shahapura tehsils have severe problem of wastelands as these tehsils occupy more than half (53.62%), more than one-third (37.70%) and more than one-fourth (28.04%) of their geographical area under wastelands. Other tehsils having more their area under wasteland are Amber and Kotputli. All these tehsils are situated partly/fully in hilly tracts of the district.

Very high (above 40%), high (30-40%) and moderate (20-30%) percentages of wastelands are found in the tehsils of north eastern part of the district i.e. Viratnagar, Jamwa Ramgarh, Shahapura and Amber while in remaining tehsils, the percentage of wastelands is low (10-20%) and very low (0.1 to 10%).

Villages having very high (above 60%) and high (40 to 60%) percentages of total wasteland are concentrated in the north-eastern part of district especially in hilly terrain. Besides this two small patches of this category are also found in the north-western and western part of the district. The villages of moderate intensity of wastelands are also found in the areas of high and very high intensities of wastelands. Villages having low and very low percentages of wasteland are concentrated mostly in south and south-western part of the district particularly in Phagi and Dudu tehsils. Small patches of low and very low intensities of wastelands are scattered in remaining tehsils of the district.

Approximately two-third villages have very low and low intensities (1-15% and 15-30%) of wastelands of their total geographical area. The maximum villages of these categories are found in the tehsils of south-western part of the district i.e. Phagi (111) and Dudu (95) tehsils. Both these tehsils occupy more than one-fourth villages (26.55%) of low and very low intensities. These tehsils have more land under scrub and without scrub and degraded pasture due to salinity/alkalinity, brackish groundwater and shallow soils. Jamwa Ramgarh tehsil leads all the tehsil having villages of moderate intensity (30-45%) of this category of land. Approximately one-third wasteland villages have high (45-60%) and very high percentages (above 60%) of wastelands to their total geographical area. Jamwa Ramgarh tehsil alone occupies more than one-fifth villages (21.47%) of this category followed by Viratnagar tehsil (12%). Both these tehsils are situated in the north eastern part i.e. hilly terrain of the study area.

1250 villages/towns are affected by the wasteland i.e. 56.7 per cent of the total villages of the study area. The maximum villages having wasteland are in Jamwa Ramgarh tehsil (177) followed by Phagi (132). Phulera (124) and Amber (124), while Shahapura (61) and Chomu tehsils (62) have very less number of wasteland villages.

Jamwa Ramgarh tehsil has maximum percentage (14.164%) of wasteland villages in the district followed by Phagi (10.50%), Phulera (9.92%) and Amber tehsils (9.92%). All the four tehsils occupy approximately 50 per cent wasteland villages of the study area. These tehsils have degraded forest, gullied and or ravinous land, upland with scrub and without scrub, degraded pasture and sand-desertic wastelands.

A number of organizations/Central/State Government and individuals have identified/ classified wastelands i.e. Directorate of Economics and Statistics, Soil Survey, Directorate of Agriculture, Government of Rajasthan, Jaipur; All India Soil Survey and Land Use Planning; National Atlas and Thematic Mapping Organization (NATMO); Command Area Development and Water Utilization Department (Wasteland Development Unit); Bhumbla and Khare; Directorate of Survey (AIR), Survey of India, New Delhi; Indian Grassland and Fodder Research Institute, Jhansi, Uttar Pradesh; National Remote Sensing Agency (NRSA) 1985; Indian Council of Agricultural Research, New Delhi: 1986; V.N.K. Pillai, Conservation of Forests, Haryana: CAZRI, Jodhpur; S.S. Yadav; Bhumi Sudhar Nigam Limited, Lucknow (U.P.); Technical Task Force Group Constituted by Planning Commission 1986: National Wastelands Updation Mission, NRSA June 2003. In present study, latest wasteland classification (2003) has been adopted.

Slope, ruggedness number and dissection index are the predominant parameters in determining the various categories of wastelands. There is a positive correlation between barren hills and slope, ruggedness number and dissection index. Generally, it is believed that Scheduled Caste do not use their land efficiently and their concentration is found in the plains instead of hilly tracts as their economy is based on villagers. Thus, it is assumed that along with their increase in total population, the amount of wasteland also increases in the plains. The result of correlation matrix reveals that there is a positive relationship between percentage of Scheduled Caste population and saline, scrub, sand-desertic and degraded pasture. The correlation matrix analysis supports the above hypothesis to some extent. It is observed in the study area that Scheduled Tribe population is generally concentrated in the areas of hilly tracts. The result of the correlation matrix proves the above assumption to some extent indicating thereby a positive relationship between percentage of Scheduled Tribe population and degraded notified forest land and gullied ravinous land. Thus the above hypothesis is statistically proved. It is assumed that the area of large size holdings have high percentage of wastelands while sample villages having low percentage of wastelands have small size of holdings. This hypothesis is statistically proved. It is also statistically proved that there is more wasteland in those areas where percentage of irrigated land is low and very low. The regression lines show that the correlation of wasteland with population density, NSA and irrigated area is negative while it is positive with Scheduled Tribes population and size of holdings. The calculation of time series shows that during the last one decade, the wasteland has a decreasing trend in the study area.

For detailed study nine sample study areas have been selected from different categories of wastelands. Sample study area for gullied and/or ravinous land is situated 32 kilometres away from Jaipur city in western part of Jamwa Ramgarh tehsil. This sample study area occupies 42.99 per cent land under wastelands. Of the total wastelands, approximately two-fifth area (39.77%) belongs to gullied and/or ravinous land and almost the same area is also occupied by the degraded notified forest land. Samred Khurd, Rampura Bas Samred and Chainpura Bas Dedwari villages occupy one-fourth their area under gullied and/ or ravinous land while minimum area under this category is in Godiyana and Samred Kalon villages. The Aravalli hill ranges are spread over in the central, south-west and north-western part of the sample study area. All these hills are covered by the degraded forest so maximum area under this category is concentrated in Godiyana village followed by Samred Khurd, Rampura Bas Samred and Dedwari village. The Banganga river passes through Godiyana village, has sands in her bed.

Sample study area for degraded notified forest (Bandh Muzaferpur, Kuhada, Pachhadala and Talooka Bas villages) lies in north Jamwa Ramgarh tehsil and southern part of Kotputli tehsil. This sample study area has three-fourth land under wastelands especially degraded forest. The maximum concentration of degraded forest is in Bandh Muzaferpur village (93.88%) followed by Talooka Bas (74.51%) and Kuhada (63.09%) villages situated in the southern part of this study area. Pachhadala village occupies lowest percentage of degraded forest as the central and western part of the village is peneplained while mid western part belongs to gullied/ravinous land.

The sand-desertic sample study area has been selected from the western part of the district where sand-desertic conditions are prevalent due to its proximacy to the desert districts of the state. Phulera tehsil alone covers more than two-fifth sand-desertic land of the district. Approximately, two-third of this sample study area is under wastelands and 99.10 per cent of the total wastelands belongs to sands-desertic. The maximum area under this category is in Majipura (85.83%) and Sursinghpura (84.18%) villages both these villages are situated in the western part of the sample study area. The lowest percentage of this category occurs in Maliyawas village due to more area under irrigation.

Sample study area for land with or without scrub is situated in the southern part of Phagi tehsil. More than two-fifth land of the sample study area is under wastelands. Of the total wasteland 92.24 per cent is occupied by the scrub land. Maximum concentration of this category is in Panwasu, Ajnota and Hatheli villages due to problem of salinity/alkalinity while

Chandma Kalan and Nathmalpura villages keep their less area under this category due to slightly better land in their southern and western part respectively.

For saline wasteland, sample study area has been selected from Dudu tehsil situated in the south western part of the district. This sample study area occupies 27 per cent land under land affected by the salinity to the total geographical area i.e. 82.50 per cent of the total wastelands. Pawaliya village has its more than one-half land (51.67%) under salinity. Other important villages having this category are Jhakalar (41.37%), Dantra (40.32%) and Bokarawas (21.57%) villages. It is clear from the satellite image that this category of land is found in wide flat riverbed particularly in the north and eastern part of the sample study area. Sample study area for land affected by alkalinity has been also selected from the Dudu tehsil. This area occupies 37.55 per cent of the total geographical area under land affected by alkalinity i.e. 81-90 per cent of the total wastelands. Maximum land affected by alkalinity is in Nasnota followed by Kapriyawas Kalan, Kotjewar and Girdharipura villages. These villages have more than one-third to two-third alkaline land while it is lowest in Mohlan and Jharna villages. Most of the these villages are situated in the Bandi river bed and its adjoining areas.

Sample study area for degraded pasture/grazing land is situated in the southern part of the district. This area is almost levelled with numerous tanks. Maximum percentage of degraded pasture/grazing land is in Khejra Ka Bas followed by Jankinathpura, Raipura and Harsuliya villages. The variation in this category is due to salinity/alkalinity and poor drainage in the sample villages. It is very clear from the satellite image of this area that the saline area is concentrated in a long belt extended from east to west and spatial pattern of degraded pasture/grazing land is also similar to saline area.

Barren hill/rocky sample study area is situated in Amber tehsil. This area has more than one-third land under wastelands. Of the total wastelands 75.44 per cent belongs to barren rocky, 22.45 per cent to degraded forest and remaining 2.10 per cent to sands riverian. The maximum concentration of barren hill/rocky is in Arniya village followed by Deo-Ka- Harwara and Chandwaji villages. Satellite image indicates that in almost all the villages Aravalli ranges are spread over in scattered form in the direction of south-west to north-east. Due to biotic interferences these forested hills have been converted into barren hills. However, the hills of south-west and eastern part are still covered by degraded forest. Lowest percentages of barren hills are in Chak Manoharpur and Pilwa villages, situated in the northern and south eastern part of the sample villages. No efforts have been made by the Government for reforestation of barren hills to date. But "Dev Narain Temple Samiti" developed forest on two hectares near the temple on the foot hills of Dev Narain hill in Deo-Ka-Harwara village.

Sample study area for mining wastelands lies in eastern Jamwa Ramgarh tehsil of Jaipur district. Almost all the mining areas are situated in the hilly tracts covering dense/degraded forest and upland with scrub. This area covers more than one-half geographical area under wastelands. But the mining wasteland occupies only 4.77 per cent to the total geographical area. The maximum area under this category is in Thali and Rayanwala village situated in the foothills of Aravalli hill ranges adjoining to the degraded forest land. Classified satellite image indicates that mining activities are concentrated in a narrow long belt extended from south west to north east direction in this study area.

Gullied/ravinous land is concentrated in eastern part of the study area. For reclamation/ development of this land peripheral fund around gullied/ravinous land to check the further extension of gullies and ravines, gully plugging, anicuts and other structures followed by afforestation with shrubs and grasses especially local and fuelwood species and effective enclosures for checking biotic interferences etc. should be done. There is also a good scope for gartucyktyre i.e. 'Anwala' near Jamwa Ramgarh bundh in G1, G2 gullied area after levelling with GCB machines and jojuba near Achrol.

Forest Department of the State Government should develop degraded forest land, barren hills and degraded pasture/grazing land under RDF I, II, RBH and FWP programmes. In the area of degraded pasture/grazing land/scrub land, there is a good scope for livestock rearing.

In the area of land affected by salinity, gypsum along with equal quantity of FYM, *Medbandi* (Embanked) to hold rain water, levelling of land for uniform spread of water and effective downward leaching of salt, sanding to improve water and air permeability, green manuring especially sesbania aculeata and crop residues as amendments etc. should be adopted. Similarly, in alkaline areas, improvement of drainage, organic manure and gypsum, shallow root crop, avoid flood irrigation with poor quality water and afforestation of alkaline toleront trees deep hole (Thala) system should be adopted to establish seedlings.

In sand-desertic land, use of FYM/fertilizer, surface mulching, close growing crops, shelter belts, appropriate crop rotation, inter cropping, crop residues, deep ploughing and soil ridge boundary etc. should be done. In mining wastelands, covering of mine spoils with good soil material, use of amendments, plantation of indigenous species should be done by the mine owners themselves.

Financial requirement for rehabilitation of degraded forest, soil/water conservation in gullied/ravinous land, reforestation of barren hills and improvement of pasture/grazing land is Rs. 1305, 1045, 1866, 1817 million respectively. After 25 years, the cost benefit ratio would be 1:2.22.

BIBLIOGRAPHY

Abhichandani, C.T. and Kolarkar, A.S. (1987). Soils of the Wastelands of Rajasthan (Ed.) *Wastelands – Diagnosis and Treatment*, Concept, New Delhi. pp. 69-81.

Abrol, I.P. and Joshi, P.K. (1987). Economic Viability of Reclamation of Alkali Lands with Special Reference to Agriculture and Forestry (Ed.) *Wastelands – Diagnosis and Treatment*, Concept, New Delhi. pp. 149-168.

Agarwal, A.N., (1980), *Indian Agriculture : Problems, Progress and Prospects*, Vikas, New Delhi.

Agarwal, R.K. and Lahiri, A.N. (1981). Evaluation of Soil Fertility Status of Stabilized and Unstabilized Sand Dunes. *Agrochemica* 25:54-60.

Agarwal, R.R. (1957). "Alkali Soils can be Reclaimed" *Indian Farming* 7(9).

Ahmad, E. (1970). *Soil Erosion in India*, Asia Publishing House, New Delhi.

Ahuja, L.D. and Bhimaya, C.P. (1967). Germination Studies of Perennial Grass Seeds, *Ann. Arid Zone* 6(2) : 146-52.

Ahuja, L.D.; Vangani, N.A. and Bhimaya, C.P. (1973). Range Management Studies – Effect of Different Soil Conservation Measures on Range Land Prodction in Arid Zone 43rd Ann. Session, *Nat. Acad. Sci.*, Oct., 1973, Jodhpur.

Ahuja, L.D. and Mann, H.S. (1975). Range Management in Western Rajasthan, *Annals of Arid Zone* 14(1) : 29-44.

Anonymous, (1972). Rep. Survey of Ravine Lands in Rajasthan 1968-70, Forest Department, Government of Rajasthan, Jaipur.

Anonymous, (1976). Rep. Part III, National Commission on Agriculture, Ministry of Agriculture and Irrigation, Government of India, New Delhi.

Anonymous, (1976-B). Improved Dryland Agriculture for Western Rajasthan. Tech. Buli. N.I., pp. 28 CAZRI, Jodhpur

Anonymous, (1982). Inaugural Brochure, Society for Promotion of Wasteland Development.

Anonymous, (1985-A). Comments on the Technical Task Group Rep., Wasteland (Definition and Data Base) – Submitted to National Wastelands Development Board.

Anonymous, (1985-B). Mapping of Wastelands in India from Satellite Imagery 1980-82, Summ. Rep., National Remote Sensing Agency.

Anonymous, (1986-A). Prime Minister's Speech at the First Meeting of The National Land Use and Wasteland Development. *Hindustan Times*, Feb.,7

Anonymous, (1986-B). Institute for Coastal and Offshore Research, Vishakhapatnam, Area Estimation of Wastelands in India.

Anonymous, (1987-A). Comments on the Technical Task Group Rep. Wastelands and Suggested Definition and Classification, ICAR (Unpublished).

Anonymous, (1987-B). Wastelands –Meeting the Challenge ICAR, Special Brochure.

Bachkheti, N.D. (1986). Wastelands Development, National Seminar on Fuelwood and Fodder Production from Wastelands, Forest Reserch Institute, Dehradun.

Bali, J.S. (1972). *Ravine Reclamation Needs for India*, New Delhi.

Bali, J.S. (1985). Problems of Gullied and Ravinous Areas – Policy and Progress. *Proc. National Seminar on Soil Conservation and Watershed Management,* Sept. 17-18, 1985, New Delhi.

Bharadwaj, B.K. (1979). Distribution and Changing Pattern of Culturable Waste in Gurgaon District, Haryana, *Geog. Rev. of India,* Vol. XXXIII N.2, pp. 120-132.

Bhargava, G.P.; Abrol, I.P. and Bhumbla, D.R. (1976). "Nomenclature of some Salt affected soils in the Indo Gangetic Plains", *Journal Ind. Soc. Sci* – 24.

Bhargava, G.P. and Bhattacharji, J.C. (1982). "Morphology, Genesis and Classification of Salt Affected Soils". In review of Soil Research in India Part II, *12th Inter Congress of Soil Science*, New Delhi.

Bhumbla, D.R. and Arvind Kumar (1984). *Estimate of Wastelands in India : Society for Promotion of Wastelands Development*, New Delhi.

Chaturvedi, A.C. (1986). Land Use Planning for Wasteland Development, *Proceedings of Foods and Wasteland Management*, organized by Gorakhpur Environmental Action Group, July 28 to August 2.

Chinnamani, S. (1986). Forestry, Social Forestry and Agro Forestry in Ravine Reclamation. Lecture delivered at the Summer Inst. Wasteland in Arid and Semi Arid Zones and Technologies for their improved Utilization, CAZRI, Jodhpur.

Chouhan, T.S. (1993). Intensity of Desertification Hazards in Rajasthan (Ed.) *Changing Contours of Arid Ecology*, Vol. I, Asian Environmental Council, Jaipur.

Chowdhary, Kamala (1985). On Wastelands, *The Ind. Magazine* 5(10), 66-67.

Committee on Natural Resources and Planning Commission, New Delhi (1963). "Study on Wastelands, Including Saline and Alkali and Waterlogged lands and their Reclamation Measures".

Costin, E.; Babidi, A.S.; Mohammed, E. and Bazara, M. (1974). Sand Dune Fixation and Afforestation in Semi Desert countries of the Middle East. Rep FAO/ Danida Inter Regional Training Centre of Health, *Land and Sand Dune Afforestation*, pp. 66-78.

Daulay, H.S.; Singh, H.P.; Singh, R.P. and Singh, K.C. (1979). Effect of Different Mulihen on Yield and Moisture use of Pearlmillet, *Ann. Arid Zone 8* (1 & 2): 108-15.

Daulay, H.S. and Singh, H.P. (1984). Increasing and Stabilizing Crop Production on Dryland, *Indian Fmg*. 34:23-5.

Daulay, H.S. (1986). Managing Arid Soils for Maximizing Crop Plant Productivity under Rainfed Conditions, *Proc. Nat. Semin. Integrated Management Approach for Maximizing Crop Production in Rainfed and Problem Areas*, Feb. 26-28, 1986.

Datiya, A.K. (1982). *Utilisation of Wastelands, Science Reporter,* CSIR, Pub. New Delhi. Vol. 19. No. 7, July, 1982, pp. 419-420.

Deb Roy, R. and Patil, B.D. (1978). Economic Utilization of Wasteland through Silvipasture System of Farming, *Proceeding Symposium, Environment, Adoptation and Distribution,* Oct. 25-26, NEHU, Shillong.

Deb Roy, R; Patil, B.D.; Pathak, P.S. and Gupta, S.K. (1978). Increasing Production Potential of Wastelands through Silvipastural System, Ann. Rep., IGFRI, Jhansi.

Deb Roy, R; Patil, B.D.; Pathak, P.S. and Gupta, S.K. (1984). Production Potential of Wasteland through Silvipastoral System, Annual Report, IGFRI, Jhansi.

Deb Roy, R. (1986). Utilization of Wasteland through Silvipastoral System for Augmenting Fodder, Fuel and Forage Production. *Proceeding, National Seminar, Wasteland Its Development and Utilisation*. Dec. 11-13, 1986, CAZRI, Jodhpur.

Deb Roy, R. (1986). Silvipastoral Plantation for Production from Wasteland in respect of Forage, Fuel wood and Fodder, *Proc., Plantation Crop – Opportunities and Constraint,* New Delhi Jan. 31-Feb. 1. Oxford and IBH Pub. Co., New Delhi pp. 411.

Department of Rural Development and Panchayati Raj, Government of Rajasthan, Jaipur (1986). Wasteland Development Programme (1986-87).

Dhabriya, S.S. and Saini, R.R., (1986). *Existing Land Use System and Possible Strategy to involve an Optimum Land use Plan, Jaipur District,* Pub. Social Policy Research Institute, Jaipur, p. 11.

Dhabariya, S.S. (1993). The State of Environment of Aravalli Hill Region (Ed.) *Changing Contours of Arid Ecology*, Vol. I, Asian Environmental Council, Jaipur.

Dhawan, C.L. (1964). *Land Reclamation*, Central Board of Irrigation and Power Publication, No. 48, Vol. II.

Dhir, R.P. (1985). Characteristics and Properties of Dune and Associated Soils. *In Sand Dune Stabilization, Shelter belts and Afforestation in Dry Zones*, FAO, Rome, pp. 41-49.

Dikshit, K.D. (1969). The Morphological Features of the Khar Lands (Saline Waste) of Gujarat. *Ind. Hr. Geog.*, Jodhpur, IV-VI,2 pp. 21-28.

Doi, R.D. (2005). Interpretation of Ravine Land in Sub-Watersheds of the Morel River, Rajasthan (Ed.) *Geomorphology and Environmental Sustainability*. Concept Publishing Company, New Delhi.

Fateh, Karan and Qureshi, F.M. (1987). *Usar Bhumi Sudhar* (Hindi), Pub. No. 351, Dire of Exten. Rajasthan Agriculture University, Udaipur, pp. 1-5.

Forest Department, Government of Rajasthan, Jaipur (1969). Report on Survey of Ravine Lands in Rajasthan 1962-65.

Forest Department, Government of Rajasthan, Jaipur (1972). Report on Survey of Ravine Lands in Rajasthan 1968-70.

Gautam, N.C. and Narayan, L.R.A. (1988), *Wastelands in India*, Pink Publishing House, Mathura.

Gemawat, Sadhana (1985). Agricutural Landuse and Population, A Geographical Analysis of Salumbar Tehsil, Unpublished Ph.D. Thesis, Sukhadia University, Udaipur.

Goojar, K.S. (1984). Wasteland Utilisation in Udaipur Basin, M.Phil. Dissertation, M.L.Sukhadia University, Udaipur.

Government of Rajasthan, Jaipur (1963). Report on Ravine Reclamation – Kakker Committee.

Ground Water Potentialities and Development of Water Resources of Jaipur District, Report, C.G.W.B., Jodhpur.

Gupta, J.P. (1976). Studies on Sand Dunes. In *Ann. Prog. rep.*, CAZRI, Jodhpur, pp. 240.

Gupta, J.P. (1979). Some Observations on the Periodic Variations of Moisture in Stablized and Unstablized Sand Dunes of the Indian Desert, *J. Hydrol.* 41:153-56.

Gupta, J.P. (1986). Moisture and Thermal Regimes of the Desert Soils of Rajasthan, Indian and their Management for Higher Plant Production. *Hydrol Sci., J.* 31:347-59.

Gupta, J.P. (1990). Sand Dunes and their stabilization in Technologies for Wasteland Development, ICAR, New Delhi.

Gupta, N.L. (1989). Wastelands of Rajasthan : A Peep into Changes, 1960-61 to 1984-85, (Ed.) *Dimensions of Wasteland Development*, Concept Publishing Company, New Delhi.

Gupta, N.L. and Maroo, R.L., (1991). *Challenge of Wastelands Utilization Issues and Themes*, Academic Publishers, Jaipur.

Halgard, E.W. (1886). "Alkali Land, Irrigation and Drainage". University of California, College of Agriculture. Appendix No. 7 to the report of 1886.

Halgard, E.W. (1890). "Alkali Land, Irrigation and Drainage". California Agriculture Exp. Station, Annual Report.

Hammond, R. and McCullagh, P., (1978), *Quantitative Techniques in Geography*, An Introduction, Clarendon, Oxford.

Jain, Anita (1982). *Wasteland Utilisation in Udaipur District,* Ph.D. Thesis, M.L.Sukhadia University, Udaipur.

Jain, J.K., (1966), (Ed.) *Combating Desertification in Developing Countries*, Scientific, Jodhpur.

Johnston, J., (1972) *Economics Methods*, McGraw Hills, pp.8-16

Joshi, K.L. (1972). The Evolution and Problems of Landuse in Lahul, A Factoral Analysis. *NGJI*, XVII, No. 1, pp. 63-71.

Kalwar, S.C. (1971). "Crop Combination Regions of Jaipur District" *Proceedings of Fifth All Rajasthan Geographers Conference*, Udaipur, pp. 45-49.

Kalwar, S.C. (1973). "Methods of Determining Agricultural Efficiency – A Case Study of Jaipur District" *Studies in Geography*, University of Rajasthan, Jaipur, pp. 67-71.

Kalwar, S.C. (1976). "Rural Urban Fringe of Jaipur – A Case Study of Agricultural Land Use" Paper presented in Inter-disciplimary Seminar on Human Settlements held at Jaipur 25-29 April, 1976.

Kalwar, S.C. (1977). Agricultural Land use in Jaipur district, Unpublished Ph.D. Thesis, University of Rajasthan, Jaipur.

Kalwar, S.C. (1984). "Cropping Characteristics – A Case Study of Jaipur District" *Annals of the Association of Rajasthan Geographers*, Vol. IV, pp. 1-11.

Kalwar, S.C. (1987). "Forest Cover Monitoring and Management in Jaipur District" *Using Remote Sensing Data Annals of the Association of Rajasthan Geographers* Vol. VIII, pp. 59-65.

Kalwar, S.C. (1990). "Delineation the Crop Combination Regions of Jaipur District" Trends (Ed.) in *Ecological Geography*, Pointer Publications, Jaipur, pp. 126-138.

Kalwar, S.C. (1990). "Influence of Caste on Agriculture in Rajasthan – A Case Study of Gathwari Village" (Ed.) *Readings in Agricultural Geography*. Scientific Publishers, Jodhpur, pp. 209-227.

Kalwar, S.C. (1990). "Water Resources Management in Jaipur District" (Ed.) *Ecology of Land and Water Management – Dryland Experiences*, Kuldeep Publications, Jaipur, pp. 69-80.

Kalwar, S.C. (1990). "Irrigation and Cropping Characteristics in Saline and Alkali Soils" (Ed.) *Geographical Perspectives on Irrigation*, Rawat Publications, Jaipur, pp. 69-80.

Kalwar, S.C. (1990). "Morphometric Characteristics and Net Sown Area in the Khari River Basin" (Ed.) *Indian Geomorphology*, Concept Publications, New Delhi. pp. 339-352.

Kalwar, S.C. (1992). "Distribution Pattern of Crops in Rajasthan, (Ed) *Geographical Facts of Rajasthan*", Kuldeep Publications, Ajmer, pp. 159-165.

Kalwar, S.C. (1992). "Paryarniya Pradushan Samasya avam Unka Prabandhan" (Ed.) *Prayavaran Prabandhan Avam Vikas*, Pointer Publishers, Jaipur. pp. 52-63.

Kalwar, S.C. (1992). "Paryarniya Avakarman" (Ed.) *Paryavaran Prabandhan Avam Vikas*, Pointer Publishers, Jaipur. pp. 64-99.

Kalwar, S.C. (1995). "Rajasthan Men Parti Bhumi" *Rajasthan Patrika*, Jaipur 30th July, 1995 p. 3

Kalwar, S.C. (1996). Morphometric Characteristics and Productivity of Land : A Study of Inter-relationship in the Khari River Basin – *Proceedings of XVII Annual Conference of the Institute of Indian Geographers*, p. 85.

Kalwar, S.C. (1999). "Wastelands in Rajasthan" (Ed.) *Arid Ecology : Resources, Hazards and Rural Development Policies*, Pointer Publication, Jaipur, Vol. II, pp. 253-271.

Kalwar, S.C. (1992). "*Remote Sensing in Resource Geography*", Pointer Publishers, Jaipur.

Kalwar, S.C. (1994). (Ed.) "*Changing Contours in Arid Ecology*" Asian Environmental Council, Jaipur.

Kalwar, S.C. (1996). "*Prayavaran Avam Parti Bhumi*", Pointer Publishers, Jaipur.

Kalwar, S.C. (1998) Identification and Developments of Wastelands in Semi-Arid Areas of Rajasthan. Unpublished Research Project Report, ICSSR, New Delhi.

Kalwar, S.C. (1999). (Ed.) "*Arid Ecology : Resources, Hazards and Rural Development Policies*", Pointer Publishers, Jaipur, Volume I & II.

Kalwar, S.C. (2000). "*Prayavarn Sanrakshan*" Pointer Publishers, Jaipur.

Kalwar, S.C. (2001). "*Nirdhanta Unmulan Avam Gramin Vikas*", Pointer Publishers, Jaipur.

Kalwar, S.C. (2003). (Ed.) "*Environmental Issues and Sustainable Development*" Pointer Publishers, Jaipur.

Kalwar, S.C. (2005). *et al.* (Ed.) *Geomorphology and Environmental Sustainability.* Concept Publishing Company, New Delhi.

Kalwar, S.C. *et al.* (2005). Flood and Water Logging Problem in Hanumangarh District – Rajasthan (Ed.) *Geomorphology and Environmental Sustainability.* Concept Publishing Company, New Delhi.

Kanodia, K.C. and Patil, B.D. (1982). *Pasture Development in Desert Resources and Technology*, Vol I, Scientific Publishers, Jodhpur, pp. 263-305.

Kaul, O.N. (1962). Management of Chambal Ravines in Rajasthan. *Indian Foresters*, 88, pp. 725-30.

Kaul, R.N. (1985). Afforestation of Dune Areas in Sand Dune Stabilization, Shelterbelts and Afforestation in Dry Zones, FAO, Rome, pp. 75-85.

Khan, A.D. (1951). Diagnosis and Reclamation of Usar Soils. *Bureau of Agri. Infor. Tech. Bulletin No. 4.*

Khan, M.Z.A. (1986). Wasteland in Chhabra Tehsil, Kota district, Unpublished M.Phil. Dissertation, M.L. Sukhadia University, Udaipur.

Khandelwal, K.C. (1990). Wasteland in Bassi Tehsil, Unpublished M.Phil dissertation, University of Rajasthan, Jaipur.

King, K.F.S. and Chandler, M.T. (1978). *The Wasteland.* ICRAF, Nairobi.

Krishnan, A.; Bhatt, P.N. and Rokhecha, P. (1966). A Soil Moisture Regime and Micro – Climotological Study Over Sand Dunes in Western Rajasthan. *Ann. Arid Zone* 5(1):1-9.

Kumar, Anil and Pandey, R.N. (1989). *Wasteland Management in India*, Ashish Publishing House, New Delhi.

Madiman, S.G., 1957, (ed.), 1957, *Readings in Land Utilisation*, Vol. V, The Ind. Soc. Agrl. Eco., Bombay.

Mahmood, A., (1977), *Statistical Methods in Geographical Studies*, Rajesh, New Delhi.

Mandal, R.B., (1981). *Statistics for Geographers and Social Scientists*, Concept, New Delhi.

Mann, H.S. *et al.* (1976). A Study on the Moisture Availability and other condition of Unstabilised Dunes in the context of Present landuse and the Future Prospects of Diversification, *Ann. Arid Zone* 15(4):270-284.

Mann, H.S.; Ramana Rao, B.V. and Daulay, H.S. (1981). Maximization of Crop Production in Arid Regions, *Indian J.Soil Water Conservation.* 9 (2 & 3) : 141-53.

Menching, H.G. and Sharma, R.C., (1983). *Resource Management in Drylands : The Rajasthan Example*, Rajesh, New Delhi.

Mertia, R.S. (1984). *Studies on Improvement and Utilisation of Rangelands of Jaisalmer Region*, Manogr. N325, CAZRI, Jodhpur.

Ministry of Agriculture and Irrigation, Government of India –Report of the National Commission on Agriculture (1976) Volume V, p.178.

Ministry of Environment & Forests, Government of India (6.2.1986). National Landuse and Wastelands Development Council. Discussion, Papers, Minutes and Decisions.

Ministry of Environment & Forests, Government of India – National Wasteland Development Board (1985). Guidelines for Action.

Ministry of Environment & Forests, Government of India – National Wasteland Development Board (1986). Technical Task Group Report – Wastelands-Definition and Classification, pp. 1-12.

Ministry of Environment & Forests, Government of India – National Wasteland Development Board – National Land Use and Wastelands Development Council, First Meeting 6.2.1986, New Delhi – Discussion Papers, Minutes and Decisions.

Ministry of Environment & Forests, Government of India – National Wasteland Development Board – Challenge and Response, New Delhi, pp. 1-8.

Ministry of Environment & Forests, Government of India – National Wasteland Development Board (1987). Description and Classification of Wasteland, pp. 1-5.

Ministry of Food and Agriculture, Government of India (1961). Wasteland Survey and Reclamation Committee Report on the Locational and Utilisation of Wastelands in India, Part X, Uttar Pradesh, New Delhi.

Mohammad, N., (1981). *Perspective in Agricultural Geography*, Vol. III, IV, V, Concept Publishing Company, New Delhi.

Mukherjee, A.B. (1971). *Geographic Patterns of Changes in Agricultural Wastelands in Uttar Pradesh.* G.R. of India, XXXII, No. 2, pp. 120-32.

Muthana, K.D. and Shankarnarayan, K.A. (1978). The Scope of Silvipastural Management in Arid Region. *CAZRI, Souvenir*, ICAR, pp. 83-9.

N.R.S.A., Hyderabad (1985). Mapping of Wastelands in India from Satellite Imagery, 1980-82, Summary Report, Rajasthan.

National Commission of Agriculture, Ministry of Agriculture and Irrigation, Part V, Resource Development, 1976.

Narayana, V.V.; Dhruva and Ram Babu (1983). Estimation of Soil Erosion in India, *J. Irrig. Drain, Eng,* ASCE, 109 (4) : 419-34.

Padmini Pani *et al.* (2001). Delineation and Monitoring of Gullied and Ravinous Lands in a part of Lower Chambal Valley, India, using Remote Sensing and GIS, paper presented at the 22nd Asian Conference on Remote Sensing 5-9 November, 2001, Singapore.

Pandey, S.; Singh, S. *et al.* (1964). Orientation, Distribution and Origin of Sand Dunes in the Central Luni Basin. *Proc. Symp. Prob. Ind. Arid Zone*, Jodhpur, pp. 84-91.

Pandey, S. (1977). Changing Pattern of Cultivable Waste in Pharandra Tehsil, Uttar Pradesh. *Utt. Bh. Pat.* XIII, No. 1 and 2, pp. 35-44.

Pareek, B.L. and Singh, Richhpal (1976). Report on Soil Survey, Land Classification and Crop Investigation Survey of District Jaipur, State Soil Survey Organisation, Rajasthan, Jaipur.

Patra Punyatoya and Thakur Baleshwer (2005). Spatial Pattern of Land Degradation in the Northern Highlands of Orissa (Ed.) *Geomorphology and Environmental Sustainability.* Concept Publishing Company, New Delhi.

Planning Commission, Committee on Natural Resources, (1963), Study on Wastelands including Saline, Alkali and Waterlogged Lands and their Reclamation Measures, New Delhi.

Planning Commission, Committee on Natural Resources (1963). Study on Wasteland including Saline, Alkaline and Waterlogged Lands and their Reclamation Measures, Government of India, New Delhi.

Planning Commission, Committee on Natural Resources, (1965), Study of Survey and Reclamation of Ravines in India.

Planning Commission, New Delhi (1965). Study of Survey and Reclamation of Ravines in India.

Planning Commission (1986). Technical Task Group Report on Wasteland Submitted to National Wasteland Development Board, pp. 3-6.

Prajapati, M.C. (1979). Silvipastural System of Production in Ravines, *Proc. Summer Inst. Silvipasture Production for Marginal and Submarginal Land,* June 4-July 3, IGFRI, Jansi.

Prem Bhai (1985). Problems and Opportunities of Wasteland Development in National Seminar Opp. Prob. on Wastelands Dev. August 3, 1985, Society for Promotion of Wastelands Development, New Delhi.

Rachana (2002). Identification and Utilisation of Wasteland for Sustainable Development – A Case Study of Jhunjhunu district, Unpublished Ph.D. Thesis, University of Rajasthan, Jaipur.

Raheja, R.C. *et al.* (1962). "Study of suitable Trees, Grasses and Crops for Saline and Alkali Land". Prepared by the Working Group on Wasteland including Saline – Alkali and Waterlogged lands, Government of India.

Rai, R.K. *et al.* (1981). Hill slope, Land Use and Soil Erosion around Shillong, Meghalaya, *Geog. Rev.* Vol. 2, pp. 359-364.

Rajasthan Forestry and Bio-diversity Project, Forest Department, Government of Rajasthan, Jaipur.

Rao, V.L.S.P. and Bhat, L.S. (1959). The Role of Geographer in Landuse Planning. Bombay *Geol. Mag.*, Vol. 5 & 7(1).

Sankhikiya Rooprekha (2002). Jaipur District. Directorate of Economics and Statistics, Jaipur.

Saxena, S.K. and Singh, S. (1976). Some Observations of the Sand Dunes and Vegetation of Bikaner district in Western Rajasthan, *Ann. Arid Zone* 15(4) : 313-322.

Sehgal, K.K. (1977). Rajasthan District Gazetters, Jaipur, Directorate of District Gazetteers, Government of Rajasthan, Jaipur.

Sen, A.K., (1972) Land Utilization Mapping to Estimate the Wastelands of Arid Zone in Rajasthan by Photo interpretation Techniques, *Bulletin N.44, Ind. Nat. Sci, Aca,* pp.67-71.

Sen, A.K. (1989) 'Typology and Mapping Procedures of Wastelands in the Indian Arid Zone' in Yadav, H.R. (Gd)

Shafi, M. (1968). The Problems of Wastelands in India. *The Geographer*, Vol. XV, No. XXI (Special).

Shafi, M. (1969). Landuse Planning, Land Classification and Land Capability Methods and Techniques. *The Geographer*, XVI, pp. 1-8.

Shah, P. (1987). Economics of Wasteland Development Project undertaken by G.S.R.D.C. in Yadav, H.R. (ed.) *Wastelands-Diagnosis and Treatment*, Concept, New Delhi, pp. 175-211.

Shankarnarayan, K.A. (1977). Impact of Overgrazing on the Grasslands, *Ann. Arid Zone* 16:349-59.

Shankarnarayan, K.A. and Singh, K.C. (1990). Rehabilitation of Degraded Pasture land in the Arid Region of Rajasthan in Technologies for Wasteland Development, ICAR, New Delhi.

Sharma, A.K. and Singh, J. (1986). Deforestation in Uttar Pradesh : An Environmental Threat in Singh, H.H. *et al.* (ed.) *Geography and Environment*, Concept, New Delhi, pp. 61-76.

Sharma, H.S. (1976). The Problem of Ravine Erosion and its Effects on Land Use Pattern in the Lower Chambal Valley, *Essays in Applied Geography*, Ali Memorial Volume, University of Sagar, Sagar, pp. 155-82.

Sharma, H.S. (1980). *Ravine Erosion in India*, Concept Publishing Co., New Delhi.

Sharma, K.D. (1997). Recent Developments in the Reclamation of Surface Mined Lands, *Annals of Arid Zone*. 36 (4) : 311-326.

Sharma, K.D.; S.Kumar and Sharma, B.K. (1998). Rehabilitation of Gypsum Mined Wastelands in the Indian Desert, *Best Management Practice Bulletin*, N.1, CAZRI, Jodhpur, p. 24.

Singh, A.L., (1978), *Economics and Geography of Agricultural Land Reclamation*, B.R. Pub. Corporation, New Delhi.

Singh, A.L., (1985). *The Problem of Wastelands in India*, B.R.Pub., New Delhi.

Singh, Bharat (1985). An Approach to Wasteland Afforestation in Rajasthan, *National Seminar on the Wastelands of Rajasthan* (10-11 July, 1985), Foundation to Air Industrial Recovery, New Delhi.

Singh, Gurmel and Bali, Y.P. (1972). Survey and Categorization of Wastelands for their Reclamation and use in India. In *Proc. Symp. Reclamation and Use of Wastelands in India*, New Delhi.

Singh, H.H., *et al.* (1986). *Geography and Environment – Issues and Challenges*, Concept, New Delhi.

Singh, Jasbir (1971). Agricultural Colonisation of Cultivable Wasteland in India (1950-51 to 1965-66). *The Geographer*, IX, 2, pp. 135-49.

Singh, Jasbir. (1974). *An Agricultural Atlas of India : A Geographical Analysis*, Vishal Publications, Kurukshetra (Haryana).

Singh, Panjar (1990) 'Forage and Fuel Production from Degraded and Wastelands 'in Abrol L.P Narayana V.V.D (T.Ed) *Technology for Wasteland Development* ICAR, New Delhi.

Singh, R.P. (1980). Cropping System for Drylands of Indian Arid Zone. *Ann. Arid Zone* 19:437-43.

Singh, R.P.; Singh, H.P.; Daulay, H.S. and Singh, K.C. (1981). Fertilization of Rainfed Green Grass – Pearlmillet Sequence. *Indian J. Agric. Sci.* 51:498-508.

Singh, Rajvir, (2000). *Watershed Planning and Management*, Yash Publishing House, Bikaner.

Singh, S. (1982). Types of Formation of Sand Dunes in the Rajasthan Desert. (Ed.) *Perspectives in Geomorphology* 4:165-183, Concept Publishing Company, New Delhi.

Singh, S. and Shankarnarayan, K.A. (1993). Sand Dunes in the Great Indian Desert – Dynamics, Morphology and Management. (Ed.) *Changing Contours of Arid Ecology.* Vol. I, Asian Environmental Council, Jaipur.

Singh, S.N. (1969). Distribution and Changing Pattern of Cultivable Wastes in Kerkat Tehsil, Jaunpur Distt., Uttar Pradesh, *N.G.J.I.*, Vol. 15 No. 3 & 4, pp. 207-23.

Soni, R.C. (1972). Symp. Reclamation and Use of Wastelands in India. *Bull. Indian Nat. Sci. Acad.* 44 : 148-54.

Stamp, L.D. (1948). *The Land of Britain – Its Use and Misuse*, p. 433.

Stamp, L.D., (1962). *The Land of Britain – Its Use and Misuse*, Longmans, London.

Tejwani, K.G. and Ahuja (1956). Report on Ravine Reclamation in Madhya Pradesh, New Delhi : Central Water and Power Commission.

Tejwani, K.G. *et al.* (1960). Control of Gully Erosion in the Ravine Lands of Gujarat, *Journal of Soil and Water Conservation in India*, 8, 65-74.

Tejwani, K.C. (1979). Agroforestry in the Wasteland in Western Himalayan, *Proc. Seminar, Agroforestry*, ICAR, 1981, Imphal, pp. 220-33.

The Hindu (1986). How Fertile Lands Becomes Waste and Wastelands can be put to Effective use, *The Hindu* – Madras Issue 23.12.1986, p. 17.

Vashistha, B.B. (1997). Role of Arid Horticulture in Combating Desertification. (Ed.) *Desertification Control in Arid Eco-System of India for Sustainable Development* pp. 211-218. Agro Botanical Publishers (India), Bikaner.

Vats, P.C.; Singh, S. and Kaith, D.S. (1976). Types, Orientation and Distribution of Sand Dunes in Bikaner District, *Geog. Observ.* 12 : 69-75.

Verma B. and Chinnamani (1990). *Rehabilitation of Ravine Lands in Technologies for Wasteland Development,* ICAR, New Delhi, pp. 263-72.

Verma, B. and Patel, A.P. (1969). Erosion Studies on Soils of the Mahi Ravines in Gujarat, *Indian Journal of Agricultural Science*, 39, 512-22.

Vimal, O.P. and Tyagi, P.D. (1986). *Fuelwood from Wastelands,* Yatan Publications, New Delhi, pp. 26-37.

Wastelands (1986). *Challenge and Response*, A Document of N.W.D.B.

Wastelands Atlas of India – 2000, Ministry of Rural Development, Department of Land Resources, Government of India, New Delhi and NRSA, Department of Space, Government of India, Hyderabad.

Yadav, H.R.(1989)(Ed) *Dimensions of Wasteland Development,* Concept Publishing Company, New Delhi.

Yadav, J.S.P. and Agarwal, R.R. (1959). Dynamics of Soil Changes in the Reclamation of Saline Alkali Soils of the Indo-Gangetic Alluvium. *Journal Indian Society, Soil Science*, 7.

Yadav, H.R., (1986), *Genesis and Utilisation of Wastelands*, Concept, New Delhi.

Yadav, H.R. (1987), (Ed.) *Wastelands – Diagnosis and Treatment*, Concept, New Delhi.

Zila Sankhyaki Ruprekha (2002), District, Jaipur, Directorate, Economic and Statistics, Government of Rajasthan, Jaipur.

INDEX